Attention Authors

Manas Publications is fighting a war to tell the world that India can win the battle not only by the bullet but also by pen. There is no dearth of intellectuals in our country, but their knowledge is confined to them only. No sincere effort has been made by any other publisher to channelise their knowledge in national interest, which is why the talent of large number of intellectuals remain latent. An author always gives the raw material in the shape of a manuscript and it is the job of the publisher to convert it into a beautiful book. Manas always motivates the intellectuals by publishing their manuscripts since more than four decades and would like to publish your manuscript too. If you or your colleagues have any manuscript ready for publication or are working on it, kindly contact us with a detailed synopsis and list of contents for its best publication. If you wish, we can also suggest you a suitable title for writing related to your area of expertise. Manas is known for its publishing quality and commitments. We take utmost care in production and give wide publicity to the book as well as its author through our national and international distribution network.

Pakistan's Intelligence

Export House of Terror

Pakistan's Intelligence

Export House of Terror

Sudhakar Raje
Former Indian Diplomat

Manas Publications
(We Convert Fighters into Writers)
New Delhi-110002 (INDIA)

MANAS PUBLICATIONS
(Publishers, Library Suppliers, Importers & Exporters)
4402/5-A, Ansari Road (Opp. HDFC Bank)
Darya Ganj, New Delhi-110 002 (INDIA)
Off. ✆ 23260783, 23265523, Res. ✆ 23842660
Fax: 011-23272766
E-mail: manaspublications@gmail.com
manaspublications@yahoo.com

ISBN 978-81-7049-382-2
₹ 795/-.

Designed by
Manas Publications

Printed in India at
IYN Graphics, Delhi
and published by Mrs Suman Lata for
Manas Publications, 4402/5-A,
Ansari Road, (Opp. HDFC Bank),
Darya Ganj, New Delhi-110 002 (INDIA)

Contents

Preface

PAKISTAN is a terrorist state, and Inter-Services Intelligence (ISI) is its instrument of terror. Both were created virtually simultaneously. Consequently, for half a century and more Pakistan has been using ISI as the weapon with which to implement its doctrine of inflicting "a thousand cuts" on India, from which it was cut out.

This weapon has bled India for more than sixty years at will, because the pusillanimous pseudo-secularism to which the Indian dispensation is wedded and the phoney pluralism in which the Indian intellectual wallows have together conspired to kill both the political will and the national spirit of the Indian people.

Hence ISI poses a grave threat to India in general, and Hindus in particular. Aided and abetted by a number of terrorist outfits – either exported from Pakistan or made in India – this threat is growing graver by the day. But the particularly perilous part of the looming danger is the *Ummah* itself, sworn as it is to a global *Darul-Islam,* signalling that the very survival of Hindus as Hindus is at stake.

This multi-layered threat Hindus would ignore at their peril. They need to realise it, and to realise the reality they have to look at it without blinkers. Hence this attempt to look facts in the face.

SUDHAKAR RAJE

Dedicated to

The Memory of My Father

1

SMALL BEGINNING
Now Pakistan's Powerhouse

Immediately in the wake of India's partition and Pakistan's creation, the newly-formed Pakistani government set up two intelligence agencies, the Intelligence Bureau (IB) and Military Intelligence (MI). However, the ineffective performance of MI during Pakistan's first war on India, the Kashmir invasion of 1947-48, led to the formation of Inter-Services Intelligence (ISI).

Nascent Stage

Established in 1948, ISI was initially given a minor role in intelligence-gathering. Its specific, limited function was to keep track of foreign military attaches posted in Pakistan and Pakistani military attaches posted abroad. Its founder and first head was Maj. Gen. Cawthorne, a Bitish army officer who had opted to serve Pakistan after the partition of India and was at the time Deputy Chief of Army Staff.

Through the 1950s and 60s ISI worked unpretentiously as the third, juniormost, agency entrusted only with those areas of external intelligence that were not covered by the Intelligence Bureau and Military Intelligence. Initially, it had no role in the collection of internal intelligence, with the exception of the Northern Areas, i.e. Gilgit and Baltistan and Pakistan-occupied Kashmir (PoK). This was the nascent stage of ISI, when it was seldom in the limelight.

Today

Today, more than 60 years later, ISI is the largest and most powerful intelligence agency in the Third World, and one of the most sophisticated in the world. The power it possesses, the clout it wields, has been acknowledged and described in various ways in various quarters – Pakistan's private army, Pakistan's omnipresent but invisible government, supranational authority, a law unto itself, a state within a state. To quote a Pakistani columnist, "the roots of power in Pakistan lie not in the hallowed offices of the President or the Prime Minister, nor in the

Supreme Cout, but in the Army Headquarters in Rawalpindi and the ISI Headquarters in Islamabad."

ISI is also qualified to be called an international terrorist organization, as it is now the principal instrument of Pakistan's state-sponsored terrorism, which, while primarily directed against India, is also capable of causing devastation in any part of the world.

All in all, ISI is now at the pinnacle of power in Pakistan. With the political downfall of the military dictator, Gen. Musharraf, it seemed to be going through a rough patch in the form of civilian control and a non-political role, but, as a Pakistani journalist wrote, democracy notwithstanding, the Army will always loom large in the background, and where the Army is, there is ISI.

2

POWER PLAY

Dirty Domestic Politics

The modest and unassuming role with which ISI started proved just a short step towards its much larger functions of the following decades. For it was not long before this functional expansion began. When Pakistan's first military dictator Field Marshal Ayub Khan became President of Pakistan in the late 1950s, he enlarged ISI's role to include monitoring politicians for the purpose of sustaining military rule. Ayub Khan also suspected the loyalty of the officers of the Intelligence Bureau based in Dhaka, the then capital of East Pakistan, and so entrusted to ISI the responsibility of collecting internal political intelligence in that part of his fractured kingdom.

This was the thin end of ISI's political wedge. From then on, with the growing interference of the Pakistan Army in Pakistani politics, ISI's role in affairs of the state went on progressively expanding.

Before Ayub Khan's imposition of Martial Law in 1958, ISI used to report to the Commander-in-Chief (C-in-C) of the Army, but when Martial Law was promulgated that year all intelligence agencies passed under the direct control of the President-cum-Martial Law Administrator, and the three agencies—ISI, IB and MI—began competing to demonstrate their loyalty to the supremo and his absolute rule. ISI and MI became particularly active during the 1964 presidential election, keeping politicians, especially the East Pakistanis, under watch.

However, the 1965 Indo-Pak war came as a rude jolt for the whole intelligence apparatus and provoked a major crisis for it. When the war started, there was a complete collapse of the operations of all intelligence agencies of Pakistan, as they were bogged down in domestic chores like tapping telephone conversations and chasing political suspects.

Political Chaos

The chaotic situation resulting from ISI's consuming involvement in internal politics even in those early days was graphically described in a first-person account by Altaf Gauhar, who was then a high-level government official, published in the Pakistani newspaper *Nation* on August 17, 1997 under the title *How Intelligence Agencies Run Our Politics.* He wrote:

"I had an opportunity to watch quite closely the working of our intelligence agencies during the 1965 war with India. At that time ISI was headed by Brig. Riaz Hussain,who later became Governor of Baluchistan... I was in the Prime Minister's secretariat during the last days of parliamentary government in 1957–58, and Malik Feroz Khan Noon used to get reports of the contacts which military intelligence agencies were making with the leaders of different parties. There was little he could do about it since President Iskandar Mirza was drawing up his own plan to put an end to parliamentary rule in collusion with the C-in-C, Gen. Ayub Khan."

"Noon was resisting Mirza's pressure to grant a four-year extension of term to Ayub Khan. I remember Ayub Khan bursting into my office one afternoon in full uniform. I was relieved when he said : "Since the principal secretary has gone for lunch I thought I would ask you to request the Prime Minister to stay with me in Rawalpindi when he comes on a formal visit next week." He left the room before I could recover my breath. When I conveyed the message to the PM he said : "I know he wants me to give him an extension of term. His term does not end till 1959. Why is he in such a hurry?" Years later when I mentioned this incident to Auyb Khan he said: "The fellow was under the influence of his wife. He wanted to promote Gen. Sher Ali. My boys were keeping tabs on him."

"Once the Martial Law was promulgated in 1958 all intelligence agencies came under the direct control of the President and Chief Martial Law Administrator. The maintenance of national security, which was the principal function of these agencies, came to mean the consolidation of the Ayub regime, any criticism of the regime was seen as a threat to national security. The three intelligence agencies started competing with each other in demonstrating their loyalty to Ayub Khan and his system of government..."

"The President used to get regular reports on the political situation in the county from the ISI and the MI... On a few occasions the President gave me these reports, and it seemed to me that the agencies were keeping the politicians, particularly of the East Pakistan, under close surveillance. I rarely found anything insightful in their reports..." They were "based largely on gossip."

"The crisis of intelligence came during the 1965 war. Brig. Riaz was good enough to show me his set-up, an impressive affair judging by the sophisticated equipment and the operators at work. He told me he had contacts inside the Occupied Kashmir" (that is, "Indian-occupied") and in other major Indian cities, "I will flood you with news, don't worry." When the war started there was a complete blackout of news from the intelligence agencies. When there was nothing from the ISI for two days, I went to Brig. Riaz only to learn that all his contacts had gone underground..."

Intelligence Fiasco

A covert infiltration plan code-named "Operation Gibraltar" was put into action, which, says online encyclopaedia *Wikipedia*, "was essentially an intelligence fiasco, partly due to ISI having overestimated so-called "local support" to infiltrators in Kashmir and having underestimated the Indian response."

So, wrote Altaf Gauhar, "It did not take the Indians long to extract the whole operational plan out of the infiltrators who they captured when they entered the Indian- occupied territory in Kashmir. Four of them were put on All India Radio to make a public confession. I heard the details of the operation on the air in utter disbelief. I rushed to Muzaffarabad to acquaint Irshad with what I had heard. He fell back in his chair and moaned: 'The bastards have spilt the beans' ".

"After the ceasefire I brought these incidents to Ayub Khan's notice and urged him to review the working of these agencies. They have no idea of intelligence work", I submitted. "All they can do is investigative work like sub-inspectors of police, tapping telephone conversations and chasing suspects."

Because of its political obsession ISI was even reportedly unable to locate a whole Indian armoured division when the war broke out.

The dismal intelligence failure in the war led to Ayub Khan setting up a committee headed by Gen. Yahya Khan to examine the entire intelligence set-up of Pakistan. Altaf Gauhar was a member of this committee. Another member was one AB Awan. Gauhar wrote : "Yahya wanted the committee to recommend that officers of ISI and MI should be posted at district headquarters. Awan strongly opposed the idea, and I backed him. We could not understand the purpose of getting the military agencies involved in domestic administration. As we left the meeting Awan said to me, "They are planning to impose martial law." He proved right, though it took the Army quite some time to get rid of Ayub Khan after unleashing a popular campaign against him." Enter Gen. Yahya Khan, the next military ruler of Pakistan.

At this juncture ISI was reorganised (1966) and expanded (1969). Yahya Khan set up a National Security Council (NSC) to coordinate the functioning of Pakistan's spy-outfits. But the NSC was short-lived as a functioning mechanism, and ISI took over the coordinator's role, thereby assuming the leadership position.

Under Gen. Yahya Khan ISI became even more deeply involved in domestic politics, especially in East Pakistan, where covert operations were mounted by his second-in-command Maj. Gen. Ghulam Umar to ensure that no political party got an overall majority in the general elections. An amount of Rs. 24 lakh was spent for this purpose. Attempts were made by ISI to infiltrate the inner circle of the Awami League.

About the ISI role in this situation Altaf Gauhar wrote, "Gen. Akbar, who was the head of ISI and with who I had good relations when I was in service, requested me that I should introduce him to some Bengali academics and journalists. Had I given him any names they too would have been put on Rao Firman Ali's hit list of Bengali intellectuals. The operation proved a total disaster." Having delivered this blunt verdict Gauhar added a quote from *The Tragedy of East Pakistan* by Lawrence Zirling : "New efforts at a political solution might have been attempted later, but army intelligence failed time and again to correctly assess the situation, and the demeanour of the generals was hardly conducive to rational decision making."

Nevertheless the successive martial law regimes in Pakistan beginning right from the times of Ayub Khan went on strengthening ISI as against the other intelligence agencies, especially the Intelligence Bureau (IB), which came to be marginalised.

Bhutto Interregnum

In this series of military dictatorships there was apparently a civil interregnum when Zulfiqar Ali Bhutto became Prime Minister of Pakistan. ISI's status in this period seems unclear, and its analyses are even contradictory. For in his monograph *The Nefarious Activities of ISI* (online edition by VHP) Col. (retd.) Shyam Kumar writes that ISI lost its importance during Bhutto's regime who was very critical of its role in the 1970 general elections which triggered the chain of events leading to the partition of Pakistan and creation of Bangladesh.

On the other hand the fact remains that the ongoing politicization of ISI became increasingly blatant under ZA Bhutto, whose ambition to become the most powerful ruler of a dismembered Pakistan made him promote the agency as an instrument to serve his personal ends. For instance, when faced with a revolt by Baluchi nationalists in the wake of the liberation of Bangladesh in 1971, Bhutto suspected the loyalty of the Baluchi officers of the IB in Quetta and made ISI responsible for internal intelligence in Baluchistan.

Bhutto not only provided a thrust to ISI's external-intelligence-gathering role but envisaged an ISI that would "enhance the foreign policy options" at his command. Consequently, it grew at a never-before pace during his reign. When Pakistan embarked on its nuclear programme and Bhutto's fevered imagination came up with the "Islamic Bomb," he made more and more funds and freedom available to ISI.

The other reason why Bhutto promoted ISI was his desire to constantly keep tabs on the army top brass. The humiliation of the army in the 1971 war with India had temporarily put paid to the generals' political ambitions, but Bhutto wanted to ensure that the armed forces remained subordinate to his political authority. Here he was playing a double game. He promoted Gen. Zia-ul Haq partly because the then ISI chief Gen. Ghulam Jilani was actively lobbying for him. On the other hand he set up a Federal Security Force to counter the influence of ISI. Despite the move, ISI's political clout rapidly became such a dominating factor in the affairs of the state and the conseqent misuse of power so blatant that Pakistan's former finance minister Mushahir Hassan once described it as "the biggest source of corruption in the country", and held it responsible for several later political crises in Pakistan.

Villainous Zia

In July 1977, Gen. Zia-ul Haq seized power after ISI, working in tandem with the political opposition, brought about Bhutto's downfall. Later, during his trial, Bhutto said his first fatal mistake was appointing Zia-ul Haq as Chief of Army Staff. Actually, however, it would seem that the real fatal mistake he made was to place Lt. Gen. Ghulam Jilani at the head of ISI. For it was Jilani who later formed the "Gang of Four" with Gen. Zia, Gen. AkhtarAbdul Rehman (future ISI chief) and Gen. Faiz Ali Chisti, which ousted Bhutto in July 1977 and put Zia in power.

Thus yet another General became Pakistan's dictator, aided and abetted by ISI. About the sharply contrasting personalities of Zia and Zulfiqar, Kiran Doshi, a former Indian diplomat once posted in Islamabad, wrote in his book *Diplomatic Tales* (with his tongue-in-cheek) –"Zulfiqar Ali Bhutto had a ready smile. He was also a past master at lying. Zia-ul Haq was more grim and, unlike Bhutto, quite villainous." (Later Bhutto's daughter Benazir ridiculed Zia-ul Haq as "Zia-ul Muck.")

On assuming power Zia abolished the Federal Security Force set up by Bhutto. He also repaid the favour of Jilani's active backing by retaining him as the ISI chief even after his scheduled retirement. Later, Jilani became Governor of Punjab, where he handpicked Prime Minister Nawaz Sharif to play a political role scripted by martial law authorities.

Under Zia's dictatorship ISI regained its lost glory. It was expanded and entrusted with the responsibility of collecting intelligence about nationalist elements in Sindh, monitoring activities of Shia organizations all over the country that had erupted after the success of the Iranian revolution of 1979, as well as keeping tabs on various political parties, such as the Pakistan People's Party (PPP) of Benazir Bhutto and its allies, who, under the leadership of the Bhutto ladies Benazir and Nusrat, had launched the Movement for the Restoration of Democracy (MRD) in the early 1980s.

Indian columnist Muzaffar Husain, a keen Pakistan-watcher, gives only a slightly different analysis of the then prevailing situation and the roles played by ZA Bhutto and Zia. In October 2006 he wrote that in Bhutto's days ISI was very active in Baluchistan, and was mainly tasked with eliminating nationalist leaders in the region. For, in the opinion of the then ISI chief, it would be Baluchistan that would make the first attempt to break away from Pakistan.

When Zia became Pakistan's military dictator he made Hamid Gul the Army chief. Gul was Zia's confidante, as he was a supporter of the fundamentalist organization Jamaat-e-Islami (JeI). At that time Zia's uncle Gafoor was the head of the Jamaat, and both Zia and Gul were his disciples, so the uncle-nephew duo made Gul the chief of the Army, and later of ISI.

Gul proved his loyalty to them when, scenting the anti-Zia conspiracy hatched by Gen. Muzammil Khan, he arrested Muzammil, caught and killed all his co-conspirators. He also collaborated in the killing of Shahnawaz Bhutto in France. It was a time of Zia's Jihad on Bhutto's Pakistan People's Party (PPP).

Muzaffar Husain added that it was Zia who decided that Pakistan's nuclear weapons would be in the custody of the Army in general and ISI in particular. Added Husain that Pakistan was the world's only county where the atom bomb was under the Army's control.

In the chaotic period since ISI emerged as the sole spy set-up that ran the Pakistan show, progressing from interfering in domestic affairs to keeping opposition politicians at bay, it undertook hatchet jobs assigned to it by the martial law authorities. In his book *If I Am Assassinated,* ZA Bhutto wrote about how ISI spied on him. Soon ISI's indispensability to any clique ruling Pakistan became all too apparent. In less than five years after the successful coup against Bhutto, ISI became a symbol of the dreaded "midnight knock on the door" and, to quote Benazir Bhutto, "a state within a state."

Benazir versus ISI

By the time Benazir Bhutto came to power in November 1988 ISI had become so dominant that she sought to clip its wings by disbanding its political division and setting up a committee to review its functioning. This attempt contributed to her own downfall. In a bid to curtail ISI's powers Benazir discontinued the practice of appointing only a serving Lt. General recommended by the Army Chief as ISI's Director General, and instead appointed Maj. Gen. (retd.) Shamsur Rahman Kallue, who was close to her father, as Director General in place of Lt. Gen. Gul in 1989. She entrusted Kallue with the task of winding up ISI's internal intelligence collection role and of "civilianising" it.

This action of hers marked the beginning of Gul's feud with her, and he finally engineered her dismissal in August 1990. (It later became clear that ISI had surreptitiously revived its abolished political division without the knowledge of the political executive.)

During Benazir Bhutto's second tenure (1993–96) she avoided confrontation with two successive Army chiefs on the issue of appointment of ISI Director General. She did transfer part of the responsibility for the operations in Afghanistan, including the creation and handling of Taliban, from ISI to the interior ministry headed by Maj. Gen. (retd.) Nasrullah Babar, who had handled ISI operations during her father's prime ministership, but at the same time she also ordered that Lt. Gen. Parvez Musharraf, then Director General of Military Operations, be closely associated in Babar's Afghan operations.

However, elements within ISI that were close to Farooq Leghari, the then President of Pakistan, had Murtaza Bhutto, surviving brother of Benazir, assassinated outside his home in Karachi in September 1996. They also started a disinformation campaign in the media holding her and her husband Asif Zardari responsible for the murder. This campaign paved the way for her dismissal by Leghari in November 1996.

Muslim versus Muslim

In addition to the menace of the midnight knock another tactic ISI (and the Army) used to keep a stranglehold on Pakistan was the time-tested technique of "divide and rule" — in this case, divide the Pakistani Muslims into Shia and Sunni in order to rule them. As earlier mentioned, in the wake of the success of the Islamic Revolution in Iran in 1979 ISI began to use suppressive methods to keep the Shias of Pakistan under control. To this end it encouraged the formation of anti-Shia fundamentalist Sunni organisations like the Sipah-e-Sahaba. When the Shias of Gilgit rose in revolt in 1988 Gen. Musharraf used tribal hordes from the North West Frontier Province (NWFP) and the Federally Administered Tribal Areas (FATA) to suppress them brutally.

A footnote worth adding here is that the ISI-engineered poisonous rift betwen Pakistani Sunnis and Pakistani Shias literally led to poison. For according to Pakistani Urdu newspaper *Ausaf*, the Lashkar-e-Jhangvi militia had actually prepared in 2002 a new kind of poison to kill Shias *en masse*.

ISI's Muslim-splitting activities did not stop there. When the Mohajir Qaumi Movement (MQM, now called Muttahida Qaumi Movement) of Altaf Hussain rose in revolt in the late 1980s in Karachi, Hyderabad and

Sukkur in Sindh, ISI armed sections of the Sindhi nationalist elements to kill the Mohajirs. It then created a split between Mohajirs of UP origin (in Altaf Hussain's MQM) and those of Bihar origin in the splinter anti-Altaf Hussain group called MQM Haqiqi (meaning "real"). In Altaf Hussain's MQM itself ISI unsuccessfully tried to create a wedge between Sunni and Shia migrants from UP.

During these developments it could be clearly seen that the progressive rise in ISI's influence went hand in hand with the progressive weakening of the political leadership in Pakistan. Nawaz Sharif, for instance, was ISI's choice. When he became prime minister a veteran ISI-watcher commented : "In fact the ISI chief (along with the Army chief) is the shadow prime minister. Political instability and a weak prime minster give an edge to ISI. Therefore any attempt by Sharif to strengthen himself will be resisted by the agency. It puts its interest above everything else. It thinks it is Pakistan."

ISI became still more powerful under Lt. Gen. Hamid Gul. It was able to single-handedly cobble together the Islami Jamhoori Ittehad (IJI), a conglomerate of nine parties, to bring about the defeat of Bhutto's Pakistan People's Party (PPP) in the 1990 elections. That year ISI even carried out an "Operation Midnight Jackals" in a bid to coerce PPP members of the National Assembly into backing a vote of no-confidence against the Bhutto government.

ISI's internal political division had even been accused by many PPP members of assassinating Shah Nawaz Bhutto by poisoning him in France in 1985 in order to intimidate Benazir into not returning to Pakistan for directing the movement against Zia's military dictatorship. The truth of the matter remains unknown, but it is widely believed that the 1990 elections were rigged. Naturally Gul denied complicity, claiming that ISI's political cell, created by ZulfiqarAli Bhutto, only "monitored" the elections. All in all, by spreading its tentacles into every area of governance ISI became Pakistan's invisible government.

Mehrangate

Its nefarious political activities within Pakistan were exposed to public gaze with the arrest of a leading Pakistani banker by the name of Yunus Habib in March 1994. It came to light that ISI was involved in a massive corruption scandal dubbed "Mehrangate", in which top ISI and Army brass were paid large bribes by Habib, owner of Mehran Bank. Habib came out with the stunning charge that he had given 14 crore rupees to the then Pakistan Army chief Gen. Aslam Beg before the November 1990 elections for use in the elections. Gen. Beg admitted that he had indeed received the amount, but added that he handed over the entire money to ISI for election purposes. The General further revealed that

ISI had also been receiving funds from private sources within the country as well as abroad.

More disclosures followed. The ISI chief during the relevant period, Lt. Gen. Assad Durrani, confirmed in a sworn affidavit that he had received the money and had spent some of it for financing the election campaign of Nawaz Sharif and other opponents of Benazir Bhutto. The situation became still murkier when Pakistan's former Air Force chief Air Marshal (retd.) Asghar Khan, wrote to the then Chief Justice of Pakistan contending that by accepting money from private parties ISI had tarnished the image of the armed forces. Again Beg pleaded in a testimony before a full bench of Pakistan's Supreme Court on June 16, 1997 that ISI's political division was set up by the then Prime Minister Zulfiqar Ali Bhutto in 1975, and ISI worked directly under him. He claimed quite categorically that the Army had nothting to do with it. This defence was too dubious not to raise many an eyebrow, and was questioned by many Pakistani analysts of the prevailing situation. For ISI's political division had actually been functioning since the days of Field Marshal Ayub Khan's dictatorship, if not even before that, and despite nominally being under the prime minister used to take orders from the Army, ignoring the political authorities.

Commenting on the controversy generated by Gen. Beg's testimony, *Nation* wrote on 28.6.97: "The case has refocused public attention on what is widely percecived to be a government within a government — the intelligence agencies and their autonomous role in the political affairs of the country. The baneful influence of the intelligence agencies has spread its malign shadow over the political destiny of the county."

In the same vein Altaf Gauhar wrote in his earlier mentioned newspaper article *How Intelligence Agencies Run Our Politics* : "For Gen. (retd.) Aslam Beg to claim on solemn oath before the Supreme Court of Pakistan that ISI got involved in the internal politics of the country only after a special cell was created by Prime Minister Bhutto in 1975 is a culpable attempt at concealing the truth and distorting the record of the operations of the military intelligence agencies since independence. Sadly, the present government has only to report to the Supreme Court that the ISI deals with matters relating to Pakistan's national security, and that would be the end of Asghar Ali's writ petition against Aslam Beg. Who will provide a definition of national security to rule out the involvement of the ISI and the MI in domestic politics, which is seen as the biggest threat to the security and solidarity of Pakistan ?"

3

EGYPTIAN BEGINNING

Doublecross and Doubletalk

Gen. Zia-ul Haq became Pakistan's next military dictator when he seized power in July 1977, and in late 1979 the Soviet Union intruded into Afghanistan. This was when the Pakistan Army and its intelligence apparatus were smarting in the aftermath of the 1971 defeat at the hands of India, and Gen. Zia, having hanged ZA Bhutto, was *persona non grata* in the West. But with Soviet tanks rolling into Kabul at Christmas time in 1979 this situation reversed swiftly, and Zia the pariah suddenly became Zia the friend. As Vikram Sood, Secretary (retd.), Research and Analysis Wing (RAW), put it, "A tripartite relationship between the Americans, the Saudis, and the Pakistanis blossomed as the Afghan Jihad began to take shape." In the process it provided ISI a golden opportunity to spread its international wings for the first time. The Soviet invasion of Afghanistan made Pakistan, already a client state of the Americans, a country of paramount geostrategic importance for them, and in a matter of days the US declared Pakistan a "frontline state" against Soviet aggression. This in turn gave ISI a never-before boost, as it was given the pivotal role of functioning as the Pakistan Government's channel for supply of weapons and logistic support to the Afghan Mujahideen ("Warriors of Allah").

And as the weapons came from the US and their clandestine supply to the Mujahideen was a Central Intelligence Agency (CIA) operation (called "Operation Cyclone"), ISI worked as CIA's B team in carrying it out.

However, although the US-Pak nexus forged by the war in Afghanistan signalled ISI's entry into the international arena, its first brush with international Islamic terrorism happened on its home turf when it was not under military control as usual but on the side of the political dispensation.

Anathema to Washington

As stated earlier, despite Army Chief Gen. Aslam Beg's disclaimer in his deposition before the Supreme Court of Pakistan in the wake of the banker Habib case that the Pakistan Army had nothing to do with ISI, the fact was that ISI always took orders from the Army top brass, ignoring the chief political executive of the state. However, there was an exception to this rule when Lt. Gen. Javed Nasir became ISI chief during Nawaz Sharif's time. Nasir had a running feud with the then Army chief Gen. Asif Nawaz Janjua. A fundamentalist and a Punjabi of Kashmiri origin like Sharif, Nasir's loyalties were with Sharif rather than Janjua. In return, Sharif continued to extend his patronage to Nasir (during the period of ISI's liberal support to Taliban) despite the fact that the Pakistani press was full of reports of Nasir being anathema to Washington.

The Americans' unhappines with this particular ISI chief had quite a few reasons : The US was upset with Gen. Nasir, first because it was an open secret how actively Nasir was helping such fundamentalist bodies as Harkat-ul Ansar, which the US had branded a terrorist outfit, and Markaz Dawa al-Irshad (of which Lashkar-e-Toiba was the militant wing, both Markaz and LeT are ISI creations and work as its extended arms). Secondly, the Pentagon viewed Lt. Gen. Nasir as a major stumbling block in its efforts to buy back hundreds of shoulder-fired, surface-to-air Stinger missiles from the Afghan Mujahideen when the war was over. And thirdly the US was upset with Nasir's clear and close links with Egyptian terrorists operating from Pakistani territory.

Matters *apropos* ISI's Egyptian connection came to a head rather spectacularly with the bombing of the Egyptian embassy in the Pakistani capital of Islamabad on November 19, 1995. It was a suicide operation with a van carrying 400 to 500 kg of plastic explosives. Eighteen people, apart from the suicide bomber, were killed on the spot. The "Islamic Jihad" group of Egypt later claimed responsibility for the baffling terrorist attack in the heart of Pakistan.

Hidden Motive

In reality this incident was, to quote, "a classic case" of ISI "doublecross and doubletalk." This was explained at length by Youssef Bodansky, a reputed threat-analyst of the US and Director of the Congressional Task Force on Terrorism and Unconventional Warfare, who perceptively analysed the hidden motives behind the Egyptian embassy bombing in his book *Bin Laden, The Man Who Declared War on America*. He wrote: "But the Islamists were guests in Pakistan, hosted and sponsored by the local intelligence service. Initially, it did not make much sense that they struck out at the capital of a state that had been so hospitable to them and supportive of their cause. The facilities and camps of the Egyptians, just like those of all other international Islamist groups, were tightly controlled and supervised by Pakistani intelligence, the ISI. Very little could escape the notice of the ISI. The senior Egyptian commanders, many in Peshawar, Islamabad and Karachi for more than a decade now, had always had very close relations with the senior echelons of the ISI. It did seem unreasonable for the Egyptians to risk this relationship with a single bomb. And in fact they did not risk it. The relationship of the Egyptians with the ISI dictated the selection of Islamabad as the site for a spectacular act of terrorism".

"Because of the ISI's close relations with and tight control over the Islamists, it was virtually impossible for the Islamists to plan, much less carry out, such an operation without the ISI's knowledge. With Pakistan under international pressure to close down the Islamist infrastructure, the Egyptian Islamists would not have made the lives of their friends and benefactors in the ISI, who fought for their survival and sought permission for them to remain in Pakistan, more difficult by embarrassing them. The explosion in Islamabad served to confirm at least tacit support from individuals within ISI. So although the Egyptian Islamists had many good reasons to strike at Egypt, it was the interest of the ISI–based on the internal struggles in Pakistan that determined Pakistan and not a third country as the site for the bombing".

Phoney Coup

The roots of the explosion in Islamabad can be found in the "legend of the coup" against Benazir Bhutto. According to the official version, an Islamist group's military coup was narrowly averted in late September 1995. On September 26, a routine customs check of an official car in Kohat, on the Pak-Afghan border, caught Brig. Mustansir Billah and a colonel in civilian clothes trying to drive a car full of AK-type assault rifles and RPGs into Pakistan. When stopped, Billah tried to call another colonel in Lahore to confirm that the weapons shipment was authorized official business. The officers were arrested anyway. The investigation led to Maj. Gen. Zaheer-ul Islam Abbasi, a former senior ISI officer recently nominated commander of the Infantry Training Centre at Rawalpindi. According to the official version, these two generals, along with colonels Zahid and Amjad, were planning a coup for September 30. Using the weapons Billah was trying to smuggle, these senior officers would have tried to eliminate the high command and declare an Islamist state. More than thirty officers were arrested in connection with the alleged coup attempt.

In reality, the coup was a set-up, a purge of current or former ISI elements who had actively sponsored terrorism against the US. Both Billah and Abbasi had cooperated with and supervised Harkat-ul Ansar, Hizb-ul Mujahideen, and other Islamist terrorist organizations. They were deeply and directly involved in Kashmir operations. Had they wanted to, they would have acquired all the weapons they needed from stockpiles of Kashmiri terrorists on Pakistani soil rather than trying to smuggle them in from Afghanistan. Billah was arrested delivering weapons from the

Taliban to be used in deniable international operations. All the weapons and explosives in Billah's possession could be traced to US-financed supplies and not to the Pakistan government. If any of these items had been captured in the course of a terrorist operation, the Afghans would have been blamed, not Pakistan.

All in all, the end result of ISI's murky doings under Gen. Nasir was the worsening of the relationship between the US and Pakistan to such an extent that in Jannary 1993 the US placed Pakistan in the watch-list of countries suspected of sponsoring international terrorism. Apparently, however, the stand-off did not last long. For in just six months, in July 1993, the US removed Pakistan from this watch-list. The reason cited by the US was that Pakistan had taken certain remedial steps. It became known shortly afterwards what these steps were. In July 1994 the *Washington Post* reported that Pakistan had agreed to remove Lt. Gen. Nasir from the top post of ISI and undertake a total revamp of the spy set-up by removing Nasir's hand-picked men from it in exchange for taking Pakistan off the terror watch-list.

Central Facts

This whole affair highlighted two vital facts about Pakistan : The first, that it was the Army that was really in power, the second, that even within the Army ISI had grown into an extra-constitutional centre of authority. Both these were commented upon by the prominent Pakistani daily *The Nation*.

On August 23, 1995 the newspaper made an editorial comment as follows : "Theoretically, the Army has returned to the barracks, the GHQ has no role to play in the country's politics, and the Chief of Army Staff is a state functionary subordinate to the legally constituted civilian authority. Nevertheless, we still hear of a troika meeting off and on to discuss urgent and priority matters of state policy regardless of which party is in power, there is an undisguised endeavour by the elected representatives to stay on the right side of the generals. Unfortunately, the country's politicians look towards the army as the real power broker, whose support they think is necessary to acquire power or sustain it."

4

FIRST STEP ABROAD

CIA's B Team

The Afghan war was the first occasion when ISI actively entered the arena of armed international intrigue, hand in hand with the CIA. There was such close cooperation between the two that a number of officers from ISI's Covert Action Division received training in the US, and many covert action experts of the CIA were attached to ISI to guide it in its operations against Soviet troops. In the process ISI not only came into possession of large quantities of surplus terrorist arms and trained manpower, but also acquired hitherto denied intelligence and technology.

This was the time when ISI developed strategic operational linkages on two different levels : with fundamentalist Islamic groups the world over, from where recruits were drawn and material help acquired for the Afghan war, and secondly, with drug cartels, gun runners, the underworld, and assorted smugglers in several parts of the world. Thus ISI acquired membership of a worldwide crime syndicate.

ISI's Own War

The huge amount of CIA money handled by ISI as a result of the partnership between the two made it flush with funds. This led to its becoming more or less independent in planning covert operations, finally enabling it to conduct the Afghan war virtually on its own. In fact, the then ISI boss Akhtar Abdur Rahman has been called by the online encyclopaedia *Wikipedia* "the architect of the Afghan Jihad against the Soviet Union." Putting it bluntly Vikram Sood wrote : "CIA had abdicated its policy on Afghanistan to the ISI, and the Pakistani agenda in Afghanistan became the CIA's own... The relationship between the two agencies warmed up, and the CIA chief William Casey regularly briefed Gen. Zia about Indian military deployments. A grateful ISI chief, Gen. Akhtar Rahman, presented a 7000-dollar carpet to Casey." ISI took over Afghan warlord Gulbuddin Hekmatyar's fighting force called Hizb-i-Islami and made it the spearhead of its Jihad in Afghanistan. During this period CIA flooded Pakistan with arms, which were at the disposal of ISI.

ISI monitored the activities of the Mujahideen, provided them guidance and support, and, with the help of Army commando units, helped direct the operations inside Afghanistan. ISI, CIA and Mossad, the Israeli intelligence agency, jointly carried out a covert transfer of Soviet-made PLO and Lebanese weapons captured by the Israelis during their Lebanese operation in June 1982. These weapons were taken to Pakistan and then sent to Afghanistan. All this was kept a secret.

Trained 83,000 Mujahideen

For a full decade, from 1983 to 1993, ISI trained about 83,000 Mujahideen and sent them to Afghanistan. (Maj. Gen. (retd.) Rajendra Nath has put this figure at over two lakh in his review of the book *The Bear Trap : Afghanistan's Untold Story*, written by Pakistani Brig. Mohammad Yousef, Director of ISI's Afghan Bureau from 1983 to 1987, on the ISI role in the Afghan war.) While most of them were Afghans, they also included Pakistani Jihadists as well as Arab volunteers, called Afghan Arabs. ISI also worked as CIA's channel for promoting the smuggling of heroin into Afghanistan to make Soviet troops heroin addicts and thus reduce their fighting potential.

ISI's full involvement in the Afghan war provided it with a ready-made opportunity to hone its skill in covert action, as the US gave ISI agents extensive training in covert action techniqes. Additionally, ISI came into contact with intelligence agencies of other countries involved in the Afghan operation, establishing liaison with them. Selig Harrison of the Carnegie Foundation remarked that Gen. Zia had converted ISI into a Pakistani version of the CIA, FBI and Iran's spy agency Savak, all rolled into one.

All these developments in the field had a political origin—Zia's gameplan. Zia-ul-Haq positioned Pakistan as an indispensable ally of American interests against Soviet expansion in South Asia—and ISI as the indispensable clearing house through which funds and armaments would flow. Thus it was Zia, not CIA, who decided what insurgent groups got what. The arrangement was to have far-reaching consequences the US didn't foresee, making Zia and ISI the unlikely (and, in retrospect, disastrous) hinge of US policy in South Asia.

In the aftermath of this war, in which it had succeeded against a super power, ISI's clout grew phenomenally. It acquired a halo as the state's top security provider and its influence on Pakistan's foreign policy became an acknowledged fact.

According .o Brig. Yousef's book, such was the power of ISI in those days that at one time during the Afghan War against the Soviets it brought the world to the brink of the Third World War. This was when ISI launched military incursions deep into Soviet territory, provoking the local CIA chief to plead with Brig. Yousef not to "start the third world war by conducting these operations."

5

TALIBAN
ISI's Fanatic Creation

"After the Soviets were forced out of Afghanistan," Shamshad Ahmed, Pakistan's ambassador to UN, once said: "you left us in the lurch with all the problems stemming from the war: an influx of refugees, the drug and gun-running, a Kalashinkov culure."

The Pakistani solution to this multiple problem was Taliban.

ISI created Taliban as an extension of its Afghan involvement. In this it was helped by some major contributory factors prevailing during the Soviet occupation of Afghanistan. At the time the country had been reduced to a collection of territories ruled by despotic warlords, where corruption was rampant at the ruling level and great privation at the people's level. The common man yearned for peace and purity (on the promise of which Taliban later rode to power). Another factor that contributed to the initial goodwill for Taliban was that the transportation Mafia known as the Afghanistan Trade Transit and their allies in the Pakistan Government trained, armed and financed Taliban, which in turn cleared for Pakistan the previously unsafe route across Afghanistan to the Central Asian Republics of marauding bandit gangs.

Taliban's home-base is Kandahar, where the hijacked Indian Airlines plane was taken in December 1999. The hijackers were Pakistani members of the Harkat-ul Mujahideen (HuM), a terrorist outfit trained and supported by Taliban in Khost and some other places in Afghanistan. Taliban's leadership is mostly drawn from Pashtuns of Kandahar. The Kandaharis still offer prayers at the mausoleum of Ahmedshah Abdali, who put an end to 1500 years of Afghanistan's Hindu history and ushered in a medieval Muslim Afghanistan. They proudly recall how Abdali pillaged and looted Delhi and major cities of Punjab and established Afghan power in the eighteenth century. Pashtun leader Mullah Omar was actively helped by ISI in being accepted as the divinely ordained *Amir-ul Momineen* ("Leader of the Faithful") not only for the Pashtuns but for the whole of Afghanistan, in 1994. ISI was prominently present as Taliban moved into Kandahar to make it, and not Kabul, its centre of power.

Deobandi Products

Taliban, which means a student body, is made up of young Afghan products of Deobandi *madrasas* in the NWFP and Baluchistan regions of Pakistan run by a fundamentalist Islamic body called Jamiat Ulema-e-Islam (JUI). Consequently, Taliban ideology is simplistic to the point of being medieval. To quote their spokesman: "We want to live a life like the Prophet lived 1400 years ago, and Jihad is our right. We want to recreate the time of the Prophet."

With JUI alumni forming the vast majority of Taliban's rank and file as well as its leadership (though not Mullah Omar himself), the Jamiat was virtually its backbone. Ties between the two became so close that in response to a call for help from Mullah Omar in 1997 a Maulana by name Sami-ul Haq shut down his *madrasa* of 2500 plus students and sent his entire student body hundreds of miles away to fight alongside Taliban. The next year the Maulana persuaded 12 *madrasas* in Pakistan's NWFP to shut down for one month and send 8000 students to reinforce the Taliban army in Afghanistan.

What added substantially to this close equation was the fact that JUI leader Maulana Fazl-ur Rehman was a political ally of Benazir Bhutto. After Benazir became prime minister, Rehman gained access to the Government, Army, and ISI, whom he influenced in favour of Taliban. Around this time Taliban's influence in Pakistan was so pervasive that it had unprecedented access among Pakistan's lobbies and interest groups. As a result, at times Taliban could and did defy even the powerful ISI—a classic example of how a creation could go out of control of its creator.

Mullah Omar's lieutenants are a mixture of *madrasa* teachers and military commanders. Among Taliban cadres the overwhelming majority were Pashtuns from southern Afghanistan and western Pakistan, but there were also some volunteers from Eurasia to China (*Wikipedia*). They were (at least initially) trained and armed by the Frontier Constabulary, a quasi-military unit of Pakistan.

The basis of Taliban was laid when, in the early 1980s, CIA and ISI provided arms to any group fighting the Soviets, even gathering radical Muslims from around the world for the purpose. The US poured funds and arms into Afghanistan, and by 1987, 65,000 tons of US-made weapons and communication equipment were entering the war every year. Arms were also received from countries of the Middle East.

Pak Minister's Brainchild

Once Taliban was created, the entire strategy of nurturing it was the brainchild of Benazir Bhutto's interior (home) minister Maj. Gen. Nasrullah Babar. While ISI had used Afghan warlords like Gulbuddin Hekmatyar (to who, back in 1975, ZA Bhutto had also played host in a bid to destabilize the progressive government of President Daud, and who the US had supported during the Afghan war), primarily to see that a compliant regime was installed in Kabul that could aid and abet Pakistan's quest for "strategic depth" against India, Babar had more grandiose plans. He advocated the opening of a land route from Central Asia to the Baluchistan coast which would make Pakistan the strategic hub for the exploitation of the immense oil and gas reserves of the region. He thought Taliban could be fashioned into an instrument for this grand design.

What actually happened was that Taliban became an international menace in its own right because of its medieval Jihadi zeal. When it came to power, its regime—grandly called the Islamic Emirate of Afghanistan—was initially given diplomatic recognition by just three Muslim states, Saudi Arabia, the United Arab Emirates (UAE), and, of course, Pakistan. The regime was denied UN recognition because of its inhuman abuse of human rights.

Pakistan's support for Taliban was substantial — one year's aid (1997–98)—alone was worth an estimated 30 million dollars in wheat, petroleum fuel and other supplies.

Bamiyan Barbarity

Taliban controlled and ruled most of Afghanistan (including the capital city of Kabul) from 1995 until 2001, when it was driven out of power by US forces, aided by Britain and Afghanistan's Northern Alliance.

With its wanton destruction of the world famous, 1500-year old, gigantic Buddha statues of Bamiyan in March 2001 the regime had already invited isolation in the world community. Thousands of other statues in the Kabul Museum and elsewhere across Afghanistan were also reduced to rubble.

The act of Bamiyan destruction with mortar and artillery was condemned by UNESCO and many countries around the world. Saudi Arabia, home of Islam, and UAE denounced the act as savage. Japan offered to pay for the preservation of the statues. Sri Lanka asked Taliban to sell fragments of the statues so that they could be joined to recreate the originals, but Taliban pulverized even the fragments, so that no one could put them back together. Even the Government of Pakistan "implored Taliban to spare the statues." (*Wikipedia.*) Only India, home of the Buddha, accepted as one of *Dashâvatâra*, ("Ten Incarnations of God") did nothing beyond some meek hand-wringing.

About the destruction Belgian Indologist and historian Koenraad Elst said it is not the Muslims who are guilty, but Islam. Giving this quote from Elst well-known India-based French journalist and author Francois Gautier wrote in 2001: "Thus, the Taliban, who want to restore the early purity of Islam, really thought they were performing a righteous act by destroying the "heathen" Buddhist statues."

Apropos Bamiyan, Taliban's Islamic zeal as *but-shikan* ("idol-breaker") went to such lengths that, according to media reports that year, Taliban supremo Omar ordered 100 cows to be slaughtered to atone for delay in the destruction of the statues.

In the same month as the Bamiyan barbarity Taliban also issued a decree ordering infidels to wear distinctive yellow patches. Six months later, in September of that year, its isolation climaxed with the 9/11 bombing of the WTC and the 2001 war that drove it out of power.

Growing Menace

The menace of Islamic fundamentalism sponsored and supported by the ISI-Taliban nexus did by no means come to an end with the fall of Taliban from power in Afghanistan, where the present government's writ hardly runs outside the cities, while in Pakistan Taliban has so many friends and allies that Pakistan has been virtually "Talibanized", to quote Shourie's epithet.

A decade after it was forced out of power, Taliban is now actually better organised and more aggressive. This would obviously not have been possible without aiding and abetting by the powers that be in Pakistan. As columnist TVR Shenoy wrote in late 2001, "The Taliban is a creation of the Pakistani Army. A few years ago American intelligence estimated that "at least" one quarter of the Taliban's officer corps was actually Pakistani. Has anything happened since then to weaken those links between Pakistan and the Taliban?" It has not.

In fact, how strong Taliban's presence within Pakistan continues to be was indicated by press reports in June 2007. According to them a top Mullah of Islamabad claimed that more than one lakh suicide bombers, including 10,000 in the two *madrasas* under his control, were present in Pakistan and were ready to explode at the command of their superiors. "We favoured the Taliban not only in the past, we favour them even today," head Mullah Abdul Aziz declared.

The then interior (home) minister of Pakistan also said Taliban had enough arms to fight for the next 10 years – booty acquired during the Afghan war. Around the same time *Jane's*, the reputed London-based military intelligence journal, issued estimates of Taliban's armed strength that showed 45,000 men under arms, 650 tanks and other armoured vehicles, 250 aircraft, including fighter planes, and formidable artillery.

Medieval Mindset

And all this military might went hand in hand with a medieval mindset. For instance it was reported in April 2001 that the Taliban regime had decreed that it would not provide any services to men without beards. A decree issued by Taliban supremo Mullah Omar, copies of which were pasted at the gates of government buildings, said citizens without beard would not be considered for jobs or any other services, as "growing beard is the tradition of Islam's Prophet Mohammad that must be followed."

Around the same time it was also reported that the Taliban government had put some barbers of Kabul in jail for cutting the hair of young men in such a manner that they looked western. Barbers found guilty of popularising the "European cut" were sentenced to a week in jail. The Religious Police in Kabul caught young men with such hair styles and shaved their heads to bring them back to "normal", away from an "un-Islamic" haircut.

Still another instance in point was reported in September 2000: The Taliban regime had officially invited football players from Chaman, Baluchistan, to Kandahar to play friendly matches, but when the Pakistani team went to the playground wearing "un-Islamic" shorts they were taken into custody by the police in the presence of thousands of spectators and their heads shaved as punishment.

Oppressive Anti-Hindu Laws

The ridiculous nature of such incidents apart, how oppressively anti-Hindu the Taliban laws (popular in Pakistan) were, had been reported by *Nasheman*, the most widely-read Urdu journal of Bangalore, on September 19, 1999. Some of these shocking laws, made for Hindus and Sikhs living in Kandahar and Jalalabad, were as follows:

- No non-Muslim can build a place of worship.
- No non-Muslim can live in a home where a Muslim lives.
- No non-Muslim can file a complaint in a court of law against a Muslim.
- Non-Muslims cannot wear clothes traditionally worn by Maulanas.
- Every non-Muslim's home will have to display a banner of yellow cloth, so that people can know that it is a non-Muslim's home.
- No non-Muslim can take his wife out without her covering her head.
- Non-Muslim women can wear ornaments only made of iron.

In addition, it was reported earlier in December 1998 that the Taliban regime had made it compulsory for Hindus and Sikhs to wear yellow clothes in order to differentiate them from Muslims.

Indian Meekness

A fact of national shame for India was that this anti-Hindu edict of Taliban was condemned by various countries, but not the Government of India. The USA showed enough concern at Taliban's clamping a special dress code on Hindus and other non-Muslims at a meeting of the joint US-Russia Working Group on Afghanistan. The Russian Foreign Ministry issued a strongly-worded statement condemning Taliban, saying, "Russia deplores these acts violating common values, and demands unconditional respect of the rights of all religious minorities by the Taliban militia." The Russian media also condemned the Taliban act, saying it "harks of the darkest pages of the history of mankind when in Nazi Germany Jews driven into ghettos were bound to wear the yellow star of David." Holocaust survivors and lawmakers of Israel also condemned the Taliban edict against the Hindus, calling it a throwback to the Nazi era and "reminiscent of the most barbaric period in human history." A former judge of the Israeli supreme court and holocaust survivor said, "I have personally suffered it. We used to wear a yellow star with *Jude* (the German word for "Jew") to discriminate us from others." "It reminds us of a horrible past, of the dark period when human beings turned out to be more beastly than beasts themselvs," said another holocaust survivor. A member of the Knesset (Israeli Parliament) urged it to protest against the Taliban act. "The suffering of Hindus in Afghanistan is an issue for all Jews and the whole world," he declared in a statement. Even the Hindus in Afghanistan stood up to Taliban, and many of them expressed their anger at the yellow-badge decree. An elderly Hindu called it "disgusting". As against such widespread condemnation the only meek reaction of the Government of India to Taliban's harassment and humiliation of Hindus was a foreign ministry spokesman's statement "deeply deploring" the edict.

Israeli Courage

It would not be out of place to relate a very similar incident and the response to it. The *Canadian National Post* reported in 2006 that Iran had made a new law that compelled non-Muslims to wear distinct colour bands to identify them in public. The Jews would have to wear a yellow band and Christians a red one. According to the newspaper report the purpose of the law was to prevent Muslims becoming "unclean" by accidentally shaking hands with non-Muslims in public.

The Israeli reaction to the report was remarkable : "Whoever makes Jews anywhere wear the yellow star again will find themselves in a coffin draped in black," retorted a minister of the Israeli Government !

Plight of Sikhs

In point of harassment Taliban, while in power, did not differentiate between Hindus and Sikhs who have been living there for generations, and this has not changed even with its (nominally) going out of power.

For according to press reports in India in February 2007 the homesick Sikhs of Afghanistan, forced to wear yellow patches in the days of the Taliban regime, still hide in back alleys. In Kandahar, the Taliban home base, the Muslims stone or spit on them in the streets, and their children cannot go to school. In the late 1980s there were five lakh Sikhs acros Afghanistan. Now there are about 10 Sikh families in Kandahar, another 20 lonely men, their families in India, live as traders in the neighbouring Uruzgan, another Taliban stronghold, and similar small numbers are scattered across the country.

Muslim Women's Plight

The callous treatment of Muslim women under Taliban was graphically described in a long letter by Andre Habisch and 200 others published in the *Times of India* in 2000: "Since the Taliban took over Afghanistan in 1996, women have had to wear *burqa,* and have been beaten and stoned in public for not being "properly" dressed even if just the mesh covering in front of their eyes is absent. One woman was beaten to death by an angry mob of fundamentalists for accidentally exposing her arm while she was driving."

"Women are prohibited from going out in public without a male relative. Professional women, such as professors, translators, doctors, lawyers, writers, have been forced to leave their jobs."

"Depression is widespread. The suicide rate among women has risen significantly. Because they cannot work, those without male relatives are either starving to death or begging on the streets even if they hold Ph.Ds."

"Homes where a woman is present must have their windows painted so that they can never be seen by outsiders. She must wear "silent" shoes so that she is never heard."

"Women live in fear of their lives for the slightest misbehaviour. Medical facilities for women are negligible. At one of the rare hospitals for women a reporter found women patients—nearly lifeless bodies lying motionless on beds—wrapped in their *burqa,* unwilling to speak, eat, or do anything, slowly wasting away. Others have gone insane, and crouch in corners perpetually crying in fear."

"The term "human rights violations" has become an understatement. Men have the power of life and death over their women relatives, especially husbands over their wives, but an angry mob has just as much right to stone or beat a woman, often to death, for exposing an inch of flesh or offending them in the slightest way."

To this *Wikipedia* adds the following:

In February 1998 Taliban restrictions became so rigid after they took control of the city of Kabul that their religious police forced all women off the streets. "While in power the Taliban implemented the strictest interpretation of Sharia law ever seen in the Muslim world, and became notorious internationally for their treatment of women."

"Women were forced to wear the *burqa"* in public that covered them from head to toe, and prohibited from wearing clothes regarded as "stimulating and attractive" — even including the "Iranian *Burqa"*, which was considered insufficiently complete in its covering. They were prohibited from taking a taxi without a close male relative accompanying them, from washing clothes openly at a stream, or from having their measurements taken by tailors."

"Women were allowed neither to work nor to play (sports for women were banned), nor be educated after the age of eight, and till then were permitted only to study the Quran. Women seeking an education were forced to attend underground schools, where they and their teachers risked execution if caught. They were not allowed to be treated by male doctors unless accompanied by a female chaperon, which led to illnesses remaining untreated. They faced public flogging in the street and public execution for violation of the Taliban laws."

In fact, even now schoolgirls may even be poisoned for seeking education. On June 12, 2010, more than 40 schoolgirls in Ghazni were rushed to hospital after feeling sick from suspected poisoning. In the past Taliban fundamentalists have sprayed girls' schools with poison gas because Taliban do not permit women to be educated.

This extreme primitivism could become the ruling ideology because, suggests Muslim journalist Ahmed Rashid, the Taliban cadre were taught only the Quran, and that too by teachers who were themselves often barely literate. The students were brought up in a totally male society, in which absolute domination of women was a natural affirmation of manhood. As a result, Taliban leaders repeatedly told Rashid that if they gave women greater freedom or a chance to go to school, they would lose the support of their rank and file.

Brutalized Children

And if Taliban cared little for women, they cared less for children. According to press reports in April 2007 Taliban fighters had used children as human shields to flee to safety during the US offensive called 'Operation Kryptonite' launched to clear militants from the Kajaki dam area in the Helmand province of Afghanistan. A NATO spokesman stated, "During this action... Taliban extremists resorted to the use of human shields, specifically using local Afghan children, to cover as they escaped out of the area."

That Taliban could go even beyond using children as gun fodder was shown by two recent horrible instances. The first of these, reported in the press in July 2007, was its attempt to trick a six-year-old child into becoming a suicide bomber. The small boy, by the name of Juma Gul, who collected scrap metal for money, said Taliban terrorists had forced him to wear a vest which, they told him, would spray out flowers when he pressed a button. He said they told him that when he saw American soldiers "throw your body at them." The terrorists had cornered him in a Taliban-controlled district in southern Afghanistan's Ghazni province. "When they put the vest on my body I did not know what to think," said Gul, "but then I felt the bomb. After I figured out it was a bomb I went to the Afghan soldiers for help."

The other instance was, in a way, still more inhuman — a video showing a 12-year-old Taliban boy beheading a man before the camera. Reported around the same time as the Juma Gul story, the video circulating in Pakistan recorded the grisly death of a Pakistani militant accused of betraying a top Taliban leader killed in an airstrike in Afghanistan. In the video the boy, barely 12 and holding a knife in hand, denounced a blindfolded man before him as an American spy, then hacked off the captive's head and hoisted it in triumph by the hair. A man held the terrorist by his beard while the boy cut his throat. Shouts of *Allah-o-Akbar* rang out as blood spurted from it. The boy's photo had appeared in Indian newspapers along with the report.

In yet another example of inhuman fanaticism it was reported in July 2010 that Taliban militants executed a seven-year-old boy for being an American spy. The boy was publicly hanged in a village in Helmand province.

Even Donkeys Shot

How the fundamentalism instilled by Pakistani *madrasas* into the minds of its Taliban had made them mindless machines of destruction was also exemplified during their war with the Northern Alliance in the city of Mazar-i-Sharif.

Entering at 10 am on August 8, 1998, for the next two days the Taliban drove their trucks up and down the narrow streets of the city shooting to the left and right and killing everything that moved—shopkeepers, cart-pullers, women, children, and even goats and donkeys !

"Squeaky Shoes" Un-Islamic

Taliban interpreted the Sharia law even to ban a wide variety of social and recreational activities like movies, television, video, internet, music and dancing. Also ridiculously prohibited were kite-flying, hanging pictures in homes, clapping during sport events, and to wearing squeaky shoes.

The Religious Police of the Taliban regime's ministry for the protection of virtue and prevention of vice were empowered to mercilessly enforce these laws. Hundreds of them were out on the streets with long sticks, ready to beat offenders, - especially men who shaved and women not wearing their *burqa* properly. A woman caught wearing nail polish may have her fingers chopped off. Woman stepping out of home without the company of a male relative risked not only being beaten up but even being shot by the Religious Police.

US Ultimatum

In the wake of the horrendous 9/11 attack on World Trade Centre in the US, which killed 3000 people, the US gave the Taliban regime an ultimatum demanding that Osama bin Laden be handed over. Taliban refused, saying it had no evidence showing his complicity. On September 22, 2001 UAE and later Saudi Arabia withdrew their recognition of Taliban as the legal government of Afghanistan, leaving Pakistan as the only state with diplomatic ties. It is believed that on October 4, 2001 Taliban covertly offered to turn Osama bin Laden over to Pakistan for an international trial conducted as per Islamic Sharia law. Pakistan is believed to have rejected the offer, though they still recognized the Taliban regime. On October 7, 2001, before the onset of US Military action, the Taliban ambassador to Pakistan offered to detain bin Laden and try him under Islamic law if the US made a formal request and presented Taliban with evidence. The offer was summarily rejected.

The end of the Taliban rule began on October 7, 2001, when the US, backed by NATO and other allies, launched military action in Afghanistan, code-named Operation Enduring Freedom, and bombed Taliban and al-Qaeda camps. In November the Taliban retreated, from Kabul, and finally in December they gave up Kandahar.

Overwhelming Control

The end of the Taliban rule in Afghanistan by no means meant the end of the Taliban organization, the Taliban mindset, and the Taliban edition of Islam. Rather, Taliban have consolidated and spread. While many Taliban leaders and cadres were killed and captured during the regime's final days or fled the country, many others returned to their home countries and continued to work for the Taliban's goals. The Taliban supremo Mullah Omar continues to elude capture (and is now enjoying Pakistani hospitality in Quetta). Nine years after Taliban were driven out of power and Hamid Karzai installed as President, he still has limited control over large swathes of his country. According to an assessment of US National Intelligence only 30 per cent of Afghanistan is presently under government control while Taliban and assorted tribal groups (probably allied to Taliban) hold the rest of the country.

Actually Taliban are now so powerful in Afghanistan that recently Britain felt compelled to hold secret talks with them in an attempt to bring peace to the war-torn country. This was disclosed by the British newspaper *Daily Telegraph* in December 2007. According to the daily the British intelligence agency MI-6's meeting with Taliban took place half a dozen times in various Afghan villages. To maintain the appearance that Afghan President Hamid Karzai's government was leading the negotiations the secret meetings took place in the presence of Afghan officials. Up to a dozen Taliban leaders were present at these meetings, the newspaper reported.

On the other hand, according to a *New York Times* report from Kabul of June 12, 2010, Karzai doubts if US forces can defeat Taliban, "The President has lost his confidence in the capability of either the coalition or his own government to protect this country," former Afghan intelligence chief Amanullah Saleh said. In a further development, PTI reported in October that Karzai has launched direct, secret, high-level talks with Taliban to negotiate peace that would mean Taliban participation in power.

ISI Wants Taliban Restoration

As for Pakistan, Taliban has not only deeply penetrated it, but its running battle with Pakistani forces shows no sign of a Taliban retreat. Rather, it is the other way round, if a recent comment of the Pakistani newspaper *Daily Times* on the state's approach to insurgency in parts of NWFP, especially Swat, is to be believed. It says : "The frontier is all but lost, and it's a full-spectrum failure, ranging from military reverses to political and ideological loss. This is not a pessimistic view, it is a realistic assessment. What is happening in Swat is a replay of what we have seen in Waziristan, what we are witnessing in other tribal agencies, Bajaur for instance, and we shall witness in the settled lowlands of NWFP if this tide cannot be stemmed."

This realistic assessment stems from the ground reality that for a Taliban so powerful in Afghanistan, the border with Pakistan is easily crossed, especially when ISI is supporting a Taliban restoration along the Pak-Afghan border.

A detailed, on-the-spot *New York Times* report in January 2007 left no doubt about this situation. The *NYT* correspondent wrote: "Western diplomats in both countries (Pakistan and Afghanistan) ... say that Pakistani intelligence agencies, i.e., Inter-Services Intelligence (ISI) and Military Intelligence (MI) have been supporting a Taliban restoration... More than two weeks of reporting along this frontier... leaves no doubt that ... Pakistani authorities are encouraging the insurgents, if not supporting them".

"The Pakistanis are actively supporting the Taliban," declared a western diplomat in an interview in Kabul. He said, "He had seen an intelligence report of a recent meeting on the Afghan border between a senior Taliban commander and a retired colonel of the ISI."

"Pakistan has long seen Jihadi movements like the Taliban as a counter to Indian and Russian influence next door..."

"President Musharraf relies on the religious party Jamiat Ulema-i-Islam (JUI), which dominates this province, Baluchistan, as an important partner in the provincial and national parliaments."

"Hamid Gul, the former Director of Pakistani Intelligence, remains a public and unapologetic supporter of the Taliban, visiting *madrasas* and speaking in support of Jihad at graduation ceremonies."

A sidelight on this ISI-Taliban liaison is that both the *New York Times* report and an earlier *Associated Press* (AP) report in the same month said Taliban chief Mullah Omar was ISI guest in Quetta. A Taliban spokesman captured in Kabul said Omar lives in the Pakistani city of Quetta, protected by ISI. In September 2006 Gen. James Jones, then NATO's supreme commander, had told the US Senate Foreign Relations Committee that Quetta had become the headquarters of the Taliban movement.

However, according to Jan. 2010 reports, fearing Mullah Omar might be targeted by US, ISI helped him escape from Quetta to Karachi, where he established a new council. But now is Mullah dead or alive? On May 23, 2011 a major Afghan TV channel reported that he was killed while on way from Quetta to North Waziristan two days ago. A Pakistani security official confirmed the killing, but Pakistani Taliban promptly denied the report, saying, "Tehreeq-e-Taliban strongly denies that Mullah Omar was killed as claimed...."

Whatever the truth, Taliban's presence in Pakistan is now so formidable that in an article in the American journal *Newsweek* titled *Armed and Even more Dangerous,* Haider Ali Hussein Mullick described in September 2009 how the Pakistan Taliban have mutated into a new and virulent entity, and their ultimate goal is another 26/11. He wrote, *inter alia* :

"A new, more virulent faction is emerging in the volatile centre and south, which, if left unchallenged, has the potential to destabilise the nuclear-armed country. Pakistani military, intelligence, and law-enforcement officials say that within days of the Pakistani Taliban's apparent defeat, the new faction emerged, acutely aware of its weaknesses as well as the opportunities in the centre and south of the country. The new Taliban's strategy is to abandon the shadow governments in the north and execute precise attacks on the Army in the north. In the centre of Pakistan it plans to strengthen alliances, increase recruitment, and create shadow government in a part of the country where strong support for such alternative administrative bodies already exists. In the south, it will keep the money flowing by colluding with drug cartels and kidnapping syndicates. Their goal is to open multiple fronts in the centre and south to relieve pressure on the north, spreading the Pakistani military thin. The jackpot, Pakistani officials say, is another Mumbai-type attack in India.

There are signs the strategy is working. The new Taliban are making significant inroad in the country's central province of Punjab, in Baluchistan, and Karachi. And increased ties with groups like Lashkar-e-Taiba and Sipah-e-Sahaba, which are notorious for terrorist attacks in Islamabad, Kabul, and Delhi. Now the situation in Pakistan's centre and south is similar to what the north looked like two years ago, before the Taliban slowly out-administered the state. Amid multiplying radical *madrasas* and training camps run by Taliban allies, the Pakistani police, civilian intelligence, and judicial institutions are barely holding on. Thus, this new Taliban team is more dangerous than the old in its ability to give protection to terrorists."

And behind this terror conglomerate stands ISI, the source of its empowerment, aided and abetted by the USA. To date evidence of and admissions about the nefarious US-ISI-Taliban nexus keeps surfacing. For instance, US Senator John Kerry was on a short visit to India in April 2010 and was interviewed by the *Indian Express*. During the interview it was pointed out to him that Pakistan viewed terror groups operating on its soil as part of its strategic arsenal against India, and was asked for his comment on this: He replied: "Historically they have been. We all know how they were founded. We have partial responsiblity because we helped Pakistan in the development of the Taliban to take on the USSR in Afghanistan. We worked with the ISI, and the ISI worked with LeT and other Pakistani terrorist groups."

In a fresh revelation of this fact *New York Times* reported from Rawalpindi on March 14, 2010 that a US-trained ISI colonel is the key to Pak links with Taliban. Col. Imam (real name Brig. Sultan Amir) spent 20 years running terrorists in and out of Afghanistan, first to fight the Soviet Army, and later to help the Taliban as Pakistan's ally, to conquer Afghanistan in the 1990s. He still continues to train, recruit and finance the terrorists, and has helped the Taliban stage a remarkable comeback since 2006. According to the US and NATO officials, retired ISI officers like Col. Imam serve as a quasi-official bridge to Taliban and other terrorist outfits. Imam lived in Rawalpindi, just yards away from the Pakistan Army headquarters. He was so close to Taliban leader Mullah Omar that he visited him frequently.

Journalist and scholar Arun Shourie calls all this *Talibanisation* of the Pakistanis as a people. In his series of analytical articles on the Pakistani situation in the *Indian Express* in November 2007 Shourie wrote:

"Pakistan has lost control over half its territory... In the North-West the Maliks and Khans were already losing out to the Taliban. The latter had begun replacing them even in government committees – a better way to route outlays to itself... The sway of Taliban has now spread to FATA... But Talibanisation has started spreading from FATA to the adjacent districts of NWFP. In places like Tank, Dera Ismail Khan, Swat and so on the Taliban roam the streets freely and enforce their values. Barber shops and video parlours have been shut down. Men are required to grow beard. Music is banned. Girls have been prohibited from attending school. The card is a dread–a postcard is delivered at the house with the photograph of a severed head on one side, and, on the other, a simple note : 'Your daughter XYZ goes to school ABC, located at....' Parents have to take their child out of school, or risk her life or swiftly dispatch her to some other town".

"To compound matters, the Taliban are a very different force from what they used to be. They have metamorphosed. Their *modus operandi* are now very different from what they were... Taliban used to hit and run. Now they engage in extended, fixed battles. More important, the aim of the Taliban now is not that of a local militant group. Nor is their aim to undo Pakistan. Their aim is to take over Pakistan... to carry forward the Jihad to convert lands farther and farther away that are today the *Dar-ul Harab* into the *Dar-ul Islam*... And recent attacks and explosions show that they already have the capacity to reach into the very heart of Pakistan."

"Incidentally, this has been a major strategic mistake of the West, one of many, that is, to have shut its eyes to the fact that the Taliban getting revived and transformed, and instead, to have allowed itself to be diverted by the few al-Qaeda operatives that Pakistan has from time to time handed over."

"But Pakistan is not the only source from which the Taliban get aid... though they are fervent Sunnis, they are getting aid from Shia Iran... More than the aid they receive, the Taliban today have become self-financing... The Taliban are being much more nuanced about opium and heroin... the produce are an unfailing source of income."

"Pakistan having been proclaimed an Islamic state, Sharia courts having been set up since Zia's time, with what legitimacy can Islamabad move to crush the cleric who is enforcing the Shariah in FATA? As it moves to kill them in any case, Musharraf's army becomes an instrument of the Enemies of Islam".

"That problem goes beyond Musharraf and his army. It permeates every pore of Pakistan. Pakistan having declared itself to be an Islamic state the moderates on who the West rests its hopes, as do the wishful in India, just cannot stand up to the Mullahs... They have merely to ask, as they do at every turn, "If the object was to establish Pakistan as a secular state, as a state indifferant to India, as one in which not the Shariah but some alien law shall rule, what was the point of creating Pakistan, what was the point of partitioning India?"

"In a word the Taliban are not the cause of the Talibanisation of Pakistani society. They are the result. The *madrasas* are not the only ones that indoctrinate their wards in extremism... government schools indoctinate students no less..."

"Pakistan is today a dictatorship in the grip of the army and ISI... Pakistan is today a Talibanised society as the culmination of a choice it made 60 years ago–of being an Islamic state. Once the dust kicked up by Musharraf settles, whoever is in power in Islamabad will gravitate to the old, accustomed conclusion: There is only one way for Jihadis — deflect them to India."

An international footnote to this national Talibanisation of Pakistan was provided by the unambiguous alliance between Taliban and al-Qaeda. Top Pakistani Taliban leader Wali-ur-Rehman recently re-affirmed this alliance. In a video interview made available to Reuters in September 2010 he declared, "We totally agree with al-Qaeda ideology and agenda". He vowed to fight for imposition of Shariat all over the world, and added, "We will expand this Jihad during the next 10 years."

Taliban Abroad

Having thus mentally overwhelmed both Pakistan and Afghanistan, Taliban also threaten to destabilize other countries like Iran, Uzbekistan, even China. More violent fighters from these regions have come to bolster Taliban, the *New York Times* recently reported. Writing from Gurdez, Afghanistan, on October 30, 2007 its correspondent reported the arrest of a young man driving a truck laden with 1000 pounds of explosives. He had come all the way from Siberia and intended to be a suicide bomber for Taliban.

He was one of the several hundred foreigners who arrived to join Taliban during 2007, the largest influx since 2001. They are more violent, uncontrollable and extreme than even their locally-bred allies, said the report. They are coming from Uzbekistan, Chechnya, various Arab countries, and probably also Turkey and western China. In fact, this foreign Taliban has acquired so formidable a presence that Hanif Atmar, the Afghan foreign minister, said that their threats closed down 40 per cent of the schools in southern Afghanistan.

Opium Economy

The Taliban regime of the past had and the Taliban movement of the present has a robust economy, thanks to opium. Opium poppies have been traditionally grown in Afghanistan, and with the war shattering other sectors of the economy, it became No. I export of the country. Taliban provided an Islamic sanction for farmers to grow even more opium, although the Quran forbids Muslims from producing or imbibing intoxicants. Abdul Rashid, head of Taliban's anti-drug control force in Kandahar when Taliban was in power, explained away the contradiction by saying that he was authorized to impose a strict ban on the growing of hashish, because it is consumed by Afghans and Muslims, but opium is permissible because it is consumed by *Kafirs* in the West and not by Muslims or Afghans.

The sophistry apart, Taliban profited substantially from opium cultivation as also from assorted smuggling operations, especially of electronic goods. In 2000, when Taliban was in power, Afghanistan's opium production accounted for 75 per cent of the world's supply. In 2006 it was 90 per cent. According to a 2007 UN report Afghanistan now produces nearly 95 per cent of the world's opium. This marked the sixth straight year of growth since the Taliban regime was toppled in 2001, despite hundreds of millions of dollars pumped to halt cultivation, processing and trafficking of the drug. "The scale of the problem is huge," said the UN report. "Opium and heroin made from it are estimated to be worth some 3 billion dollars." It adds: "Afghanistan is locked in a vicious circle, in which drug money corrupts government and helps fund the Taliban insurgency."

Safe Haven

A major factor contributing to the continuing growth of Taliban (and al-Queda too) is that both have found a safe haven in Pakistan's No Man's Land, namely, the North Waziristan region. On September 4, 2007 *US News* reported from Miram Shah, capital of the region, that it has become a stronghold for Taliban as well as for al-Qaeda-allied Uzbeks, and provides locations for terrorist training camps. There is a regular flow of terrorists from Pakistan into Afghanistan, which is substantial enough to cause concern to Afghan President Hamid Karzai.

Official Pakistani denials notwithstanding, on the spot reporting of *US News* showed that Taliban move at large in the area. There is no policing in the entire North Waziristan region in the face of Taliban threats. Taliban turn up carrying weapons and strutting in the streets of Miram Shah. They appear all of a sudden in market places, issue orders, and disappear. Along with Taliban, about 3000 other militants are holed up in the area. The whole territory is so dominated by terrorists, that the US journal called it a tribal region officially outside central (Pakistan) government control. That control is exercised by Tehrik-e-Taliban Pakistan (Taliban Movement in Pakistan), generally known as Pakistani Taliban.

How overwhelming this control has become was strikingly demonstrated by a recent major event: The abduction of the Pak ambassador to Afghanistan, resulting in the Pakistan government's agreeing to the demand for official recognition of the role of Islamic law in the judicial process in NWFP.

The Pak ambassador, Azizuddin, who went missing on February 11, 2008 while on his way from Peshawar to Kabul, appeared on *Al Arabia* television, surrounded by armed militants, in mid-April, and said, "We were kidnapped by Mujahideen from the Taliban." His captors demanded the release of Mullah Obaidullah Akhund, military chief of Taliban, who once carried a reward of one million dollars on his head. Akhund, deputy to supremo Mullah Omar, was captured by Pakistan's security forces on March 1, 2007.

The Pakistani Taliban commander Baitullah Mehsud, accused by Musharraf of masterminding Benazir Bhutto's assassination, had also demanded Akhund's release in return for 256 Pakistani soldiers captured in south Waziristan in 2009.

Finally, Azizuddin was released in mid-May, after three months in captivity, in accordance with a deal between the Pakistan government and Taliban under which they agreed to swap 330 prisoners—250 Taliban militants in the government's jails, and 80 soldiers and officials in Taliban's custody.

This so-called accord alarmed the Americans, for while on the one hand the Bush administration was trying to cripple militants' safe haven in Pakistan before going out of office, on the other hand the new Pakistani government was trying to establish its credibility with the Pakistani public for whom al-Qaeda supremo Osama bin Laden was a hero – by distancing itself from the US-sponsored war on terror. Specifically, US counter-intelligence officials fear that the new Pak government may cut down the 120,000 Pakistani troops stationed in the border area or curtail flights by CIA's armed Predator aircraft. They also fear that any new agreement, like past accords brokered with the militants by Musharraf, would allow al-Qaeda and Taliban to regroup, rearm and plot new attacks in Pakistan, Afghanistan, Europe, and the US.

Apropos this compromise with terrorism by the new regime reputed Pak journalist Najam Sethi wrote in *Friday Times* on May 3, 2008, "The Pakistani/Afghan Taliban are hurting the Pakistani state by their provocative alliance with al-Qaeda foreigners. The Pakistani peace deals with the Taliban are doomed to fail if the Taliban/ al-Qaeda network refuses to heed the writ of the Pakistani state inside Pakistan. The demands for Shariatisation of Swat etc. are all red herrings. Conceding these will mean increasing loss of Pakistani sovereignty and territory to Taliban/ al-Qaeda."

This was precisely what happened. The government agreed to let judges in that province take into account advice from Islamic scholars in the judgemental process. Specifically, the relevant regulations in this regard relate to the Swat and Malakand areas, widely known as Taliban territory.

After establishing their sway in Pakistan's north-west, the Taliban also began making forays in the politically crucial Punjab province, calling for shutdown of internet cafes and cable TV networks and threatening to deface women who do not wear *burqas*. Owners of internet cafes, TV cable networks and music and CD shops in Muzaffargarh city in southern Punjab received threat letters and e-mails from the Taliban, who warned them to close down their un-Islamic and immoral businesses within 15 days or face the consequences. In the city of Kot Addu, Taliban warned women who do not wear *burqas* that their faces will be defaced with acid. Three dozen Internet cafes and music centres in Muzaffargarh were asked to shut down as they were making "society immoral." Similar threatening e-mails and letters were received by owners of all Internet cafes, cable networks and music shops in Kot Addu.

Some businessmen in Muzaffargarh contacted the police. But they were so frightened that they did not lodge complaints. Internet cafes and music centres in the region now shut down at sunset and a large number of women have stopped visiting local bazars. One shopkeeper told the *Dawn* newspaper: "No business is more precious than life."

Even Lahore appears to have become "Cultural capital to Taliban territory," as a newspaper headline put it. The bomb attacks on juice parlours-cum-dating joints and the mass burning of un-Islamic material by traders under threat from moral vigilante groups clearly indicated that the spectre of the Taliban has began to haunt Lahore, wrote a columnist under that heading.

To cap it all, the same month Mehsud held a meeting at a secret location in North Waziristan to discuss ways to carry out terrorist activities across Pakistan. Baitullah had even drawn up a hit list of as many as 300 top political leaders, including those of the ruling PPP.

Taliban ISI's "Client"

The American understanding of the ISI-Taliban link stops short of naming ISI as the creator of Taliban, but its overall view of this connection does dwell on its closeness. This was brought out in an interriew of Steve Coll, correspondent of the *New Yorker* journal. He is the Pulitzer Prize - winning author of *Ghost Wars : The Secret History of the CIA, Afghanistan, and Bin Laden, from the Soviet Invasion to September 11, 2001*. Coll did not call Taliban ISI's creation, but he did call Taliban ISI's client. He also stated about the triangular nexus between ISI, Taliban and al-Qaeda. The interview was on July 20, 2006. Some excerpts:

How do we understand the relationship between ISI and Taliban?

Taliban arose in the fall of 1994 and presented themselves as a sort of fact on the ground in southern Afghanistan, and rather quickly made contact with the Pakistan army and with the chief of its intelligence service (ISI). There was a meeting at ISI headquarters with some early leaders of Taliban and the ISI chief in the late autumn of 1994. It was an introductory meeting. From that beginning ISI became more and more involved with the Taliban. Throughout 1995 the collaboration between ISI and Taliban increased, and it became more and more a direct military alliance.

During a long period of the anti-Soviet war, ISI was proximate to Gulbuddin Hekmatyar, a Pashtun commander and an Islamist. But by the 1990's Hekmatyar was no longer effective as per judgement of ISI. The Taliban gradually proved themselves the better client.

You describe them as a client of ISI.

They received guns, they received money, they received fuel, they received infrastructure support. They also, we know, had on-the-ground support from undercover Pakistani officers in civilian clothes who would participate in particular battles.

Is it a fair characterization to say that Taliban were an asset of ISI?

They were an asset of ISI. It is impossible to understand Taliban's military triumph in Afghanistan, culminating in their takeover of Kabul in 1996, without understanding that they were a proxy force, a client of the Pakistan army, and benefited from all the material support that the Pakistan army could provide them.

Where does ISI stand vis-a-vis Taliban prior to 9/11?

Taliban remained an important client of ISI right up to 9/11. They were an ally of the Pakistan government, and ISI maintained contact with them to support their governance.

After 9/11 bombs started to fall on Afghanistan, there are a large number of Pakistanis, aren't there, that go across to fight?

Taliban drew, with ISI support, on a large number of volunteers who often came out of *madrasas* located (in Pakistan) near the Afghan frontier, sometimes out of Karachi. ISI had systematically built up an identification of interest between young Pakistanis and the Taliban cause.

Right up until 9/11 Taliban depended on an infrastucture that was rooted in Pakistani religious parties that were themselves managed in some important way as clients by ISI. If you were a volunteer to join the Taliban, whether you were a Pakistani or a foreign Arab, you arrived in Karachi and you passed through infrastructure that was quite striking in its size and robustness. Schools, bus companies, guest houses ... the whole system was a war-fighting system. On the Afghan border ISI's work is inseparable from the role of the religious parties.

In such a situation the post-Musharraf ban on Pakistani Taliban (Tehrik-e-Taliban Pakistan) was not likely to make any change. This ban was imposed in August 2008 in the wake of a spate of suicide bombings. The attacks were made in retaliation against military operations againat the militants in NWFP

In view of Steve Coll's rather disparaging description of Taliban as a "client" of ISI, it is remarkable that the attempted car-bombing of Times Square, the heart of New York, on May 1, 2010 stunned American officialdom into admitting that it was most likely an operation of Tehrik-e-Taliban, once considered incapable of an attack on the US.

Intense questioning revealed that Shahzad had received training by the Pakistan Taliban for some months before he parked an explosives-laden motor vehicle in the heart of New York. Besides, a Canadian weekly news-magazine *Macleans* reported that Shahzad was trained at a Lashkar base in PoK for three months in 2006. Pakistani officials had said that Shahzad was close to Jaish-e-Mohammad (JeM), who in turn had ties with Pakistani Taliban and al-Qaeda. According to some US administration officials, there were strong indications that Shahzad also knew some Pakistani Taliban members. In the meanwhile Taliban itself put out a statement saying that they have done it to avenge the killing of Baitullah Mehsud and two prominent Iraqi terrorists, Abu Hamza, leader of al-Qaeda in Iraq (AQ-I), and Abu Omar al-Baghdadi, purported head of its local affiliate, the Islamic State of Iraq. The statement appeared on a website commonly used by Islamists.

If the claim is genuine, it would be the first time the Pakistani Taliban have struck outside South Asia. Augmenting this view was another video, reported *Daily Times* on May 4 : "Tehrik-e-Taliban Pakistan (TTP) chief Hakimullah Mehsud appeared in a video... speaking in Pashto with English subtitles... 'Praise be to God, on the 4th day of April 2010, I give good news to the Muslim world about being alive and healthy... Taliban have penetrated terrorist America... and will give extremely painful blows to fanatic America'."

Pakistani Taliban later denied any role in the failed car-bombing, but praised Shahzad for a brave job done. In line with Pakistani statements, US investigators also traced his link with JeM in Pakistan, ABC reported. ABC also said he was in contact with former Tehrik-e-Taliban Pakistan chief Baitullah Mehsud, reported to have been killed in a US missile strike in 2009.

A JeM contact of Shahzad was linked with Karachi's Batha mosque. This mosque is run by JeM, where Pakistani terrorist Masood Azhar is a frequent visitor. The Batha mosque and a *Madrasa* in Karachi were provincial HQ of JeM. It was used as a base by JeM for recruiting young people. According to US sources, Shahzad had also been visiting south

Waziristan during his visits to Pakistan, and meeting Taliban leaders Hakimullah Mehsud and Qari Hussain.

On October 5, 2010 the Pakistani-American Shahzad was sentenced to life imprisonment. Reacting defiantly to the sentence, he warned the US that the war with the Muslims had just begun. When the judge asked him, "Didn't you swear allegiance to this country?" Shahzad replied, "I swore, but I didn't mean it," A video later released by the US Government showed him wearing the traditional Muslim dress, and carrying an automatic rifle in one hand and a Quran in the other.

An interesting development in the wake of the New York incident was how abruptly the Americans changed their goody-goody tone towards Pakistan. The US Secretary of State Hillary Clinton, who had loudly declared only the other day that Pakistan was fighting "my struggle" now sharply warned of serious consequences. On May 6 she declared in an interview to CBS : "We have made it clear that if — heaven forbid — an attack like this that we can trace back to Pakistan were to have been successful, there would be very serious consequences" for Pakistan.

A senior American official familiar with the situation in Pakistan said: "We are saying 'sorry' if there is a successful attack, we will have to act". Another said Pak Army chief Kayani has been essentially told, "You can't pretend any longer that this is not going on." And the US ambassador to Pakistan told President Zardari in forceful language that Pakistanis need to move more assertively against militants threaded through the (Pakistani) society, a Pakistani official admitted.

Incidentally, but not without relevance, the Americans know that the Pakistanis knew the whereabouts of both Taliban chief Mullah Omar and al-Qeada chief Osama bin Laden. In the wake of the disclosure by the US Attorney General Eric Holder that they had evidence to show Pakistani Taliban were behind the Times Square terror attempt, Hillary Clinton declared, "some Pakistani officials were more informed about al-Qeada and Taliban than they let on... I believe that somewhere in this (Pakistan) government are people who know where Osama bin Laden is, where Mullah Omar and the leadership of the Afghan Taliban is..."

All in all, Taliban is taking over Pakistan, if its own President is to be believed. Pak President Asif Ali Zardari made the startling admission that Taliban militants are present "in huge amounts of land in Pakistan and his Government is fighting for the survival of the country." The Taliban "do have a presence in huge amounts of land in our side. Yes, that is the fact," he said in an interview to CBS television network in February 2009. "Taliban... (are) trying to take over the state of Pakistan," he said. "So we're fighting for the survival of Pakistan." Pakistan has deployed about 120,000 soldiers to fight Taliban, who are suspected of harbouring al-

Qaeda members, CBS reported.

The realization of this dire scenario was reflected in the Indian media. MV Kamath bluntly says Taliban are winning in Pakistan. He wrote in *Organiser* of 11.1.09: "The Taliban and other extremist organizations have a real chance of winning in Pakistan. What they apparently want is power through bloodshed, not peace through economic progress. If our political parties do not understand that, they understand nothing. Constant appeasement is counterproductive. It betrays weakness."

What happens after Taliban win? Taliban say after Pakistan, it will be India. Pakistani Taliban chief Mehsud said in November 2009 he will turn to India once his mission in Pakistan is completed. "We want an Islamic State in Pakistan. If we get that, then we will go to the borders and help fight the Indians," Mehsud said in footage aired by Britain's *Sky News*.

Finally, the most disturbing aspect of the rise of Taliban is that the crux of President Obama's much-touted "Af-Pak policy" seems to be acceptance by the US of defeat in the war on terror — Hillary Clinton's sabre-rattling notwithstanding. Pointing out this emerging anti-climactic ending, *Indian Express* editor Shekhar Gupta wrote in March 2010: "The clearest indication that the US-led forces had thrown in the towel already came in the London conference when an idea so for whispered in off-record briefings was stated publicly : the need to find good Taliban to share power with. Even Hamid Karzai was made to endorse it. Nobody was talking of winning that war anymore, but only of bringing it to a stage where a large 'moderate' section of the Taliban can be persuaded to break rank and agree to a power-sharing arrangement."

This has recently been seen on both sides of the Af-Pak border. For instance on May 23, 2010 *Times Online* (London) reported that as a counter to Western efforts to force terrorists into laying down their arms, cadres of Afghan Taliban are earning reward money of two lakh Pakistani Rupees for each NATO soldier they kill.

And in Pakistan, on May 28, 2010 two Lahore mosques packed with Muslims of the Ahmadi sect (also called Qadianis) were atttacked and nearly 100 people killed. The police confirmed that the attacks were mounted by Pakistani Taliban. In the 1970s the Ahamadis were called "heretics" by Maulana Maududi, a leading Jamaat Mullah, and in 1984 Gen. Zia had issued an ordinance banning Ahmadis from calling themselves Muslims.

Here it is relevant to repeat that some years ago the Lashkar-e-Jhangvi militia had prepared a new kind of poison to kill their Shia victims *en masse* and its cadres had been given special training for its use.

In yet another horrible instance of murderous fanaticism, it was reported in November 2009 that Taliban terrorists in the Pashtun region of North-West Pakistan killed four boys on their way to school because they were Shia Muslims.

To conclude this account of Taliban— this ISI creation, client, whatever—on an ominous Indian note, Safdar Nagori, former chief of SIMI, the most active, made-in-India terrorist organization, who was arrested in March 2008, had openly declared that he regarded Taliban supremo Mullah Omar, not al-Qaeda's Osama bin Laden, the true Caliph of the Muslim world. The SIMI leader added that his aim was to wage Jihad in India under Mullah Omar's leadership.

In short, now Omar may or may not be dead, but the Jihad in India is to continue.

6

AL-QAEDA

ISI's Partner in Globalized Terror

Al-Qaeda, like Taliban, is the sequel of the Afghan war. After this war ended, the fighting force of thousands of Mujahideen that ISI had created, armed and trained for battle had weapons in hand but nothing to use them for, and became Taliban. As a parallel and contemporaneous development, al-Qaeda arrived in Afghanistan with its own Jihadist agenda. In 1996 Osama bin Laden moved to Afghanistan from Sudan. When Taliban came to power Osama forged an alliance between the two. al-Qaeda even trained a special brigade of fighters that was integrated into the Taliban army.

The Very Name

The very name al-Qaeda connotes violence. Explaining its origin in an interview with well-known Arab television channel *Al-Jazeera* in October 2001 Osama bin Laden said : "The name al-Qaeda was established a long time ago by mere chance. The late Abu Ebeida al-Banashiri established training camps for our Mujahideen against Russia's terrorism. We used to call the training camp al-Qaeda. The name stayed."

In the BBC documentary *The Power of Nightmare* writer and journalist Jason Burke pointed out that the name al-Qaeda was first brought to public notice in the 2001 trial of Osama bin Laden *in absentia* and four associates accused of the 1998 US embassy bombings in Kenya and Tanzania in East Africa. An order issued by President Clinton in connection with these attacks also listed half a dozen other organisations with which Osama bin Laden was associated. According to the testimony of one Jamal-al Fadl, a self-proclaimed founding member of al-Qaeda who was tried and convicted for terrorism against the US, initially the organisation was also called the Islamic Army.

Jamal claimed that during the war with the Soviets, bin Laden was initially funding a group called Maktab al-Khadamat, based in Pakistan, which was engaged in training Muslims willing to go to Afghanistan to fight. After the Soviet withdrawal Osama still wanted to continue the Jehad, so he set up a new group that initially went by two different names, al-Qaeda and Islamic Army, before eventually settling on the former. Thus, al-Qaeda was established in either late 1989 or early 1990. However, according to *Cable News Network* (CNN) sources there are documents showing that the organisation was set up in August 1988. They even specifically refer to it as al-Qaeda al-askariya, meaning a military base.

According to these sources, al-Qaeda was formed at an August 11, 1988 meeting between several senior leaders of Egyptian Islamic Jihad, Abdullah Azam, and Osama bin Laden, where it was agreed to join bin Laden's money with the expertise of the Islamic Jihad organization, and take up the Jihadist cause elsewhere after the Soviets withdrew from Afghanistan. Notes of another meeting of bin Laden and others on August 20, 1988 state: "al-Qaeda was basically an organized Islamic faction, its goal is to uplift the word of God, to make His religion victorious." In 1996 bin Laden Issued a *fatwa* which amounted to public declaration of war against the United States of America and any of its allies. Again on February 23, 1998, Osama bin Laden and Ayman al-Zawahiri, leader of Egyptian Islamic Jihad, along with three other Islamist leaders, issued a *fatwa* calling on Muslims to kill the Americans and their allies where they can, when they can. They declared: "The ruling to kill the Americans and their allies — civilians and military — is an individual duty for every Muslim who can do it in any country in which it is possible to do it. This is in accordance with the words of Almighty Allah."

Again, in an al-Qaeda video released on May 23, 2010, Anwar al-Aulaki, an American-Yemeni Mullah, whose internet sermons are believed to have helped terrorist strikes on the US, called for killing American citizens. (Reportedly, he has now been added by CIA to its list of assassination targets despite his American citizenship.)

Monumental Western Miscalculation

In a perceptive analysis of the factors responsible for the emergence of bin Laden and al-Qaeda, former British Foreign Secretary and Leader of the House of Commons Robin Cook wrote in the *Guardian* : "Bin Laden was a product of a monumental miscalculation by Western security agencies. Throughout the eighties he was armed by the CIA and funded by the Saudis to wage Jihad against the Russian occupation of Afghanistan. Al- Qaeda, literally the database, was originally the complete file of the thousands of Mujahideen who were recruited and trained with the help from the CIA to defeat the Russians. Inexplicably, and with disastrous consequences, it never appears to have occurred to Washington that once Russia was out of the way, bin Laden's organisation would turn attention to the West."

Actually it spread to other directions as well. A researcher named Richard Engel wrote in his study titled *Inside al-Qaeda : A Window into the World of Militant Islam and the Afghani Alumni* : "After the beleaguered Soviet troops pulled out of Afghanistan following a decade of fighting, many Mujahideen became convinced that a force of devoted Muslim believers could defeat any army, even one belonging to a superpower like the Soviet Union. Some Mujahideen made it their goal to bring their holy war from the mountains of Afghanistan to their home countries."

Global Reach

This heralded the spread of Islamic terrorism in the form of al-Qaeda.

According to a *Jane's Security News* report of July 26, 2001, al-Qaeda has become a conglomerate of groups spread throughout the world operating as a network. It has a global reach, with a presence in Algeria, Egypt, Morocco, Turkey, Jordan, Tajikstan, Uzbekistan, Syria, Xinjiang in China, Pakistan, Bangladesh, Malaysia, Myanmar, Indonesia, Mindanao in the Philippines, Lebanon, Iraq, Saudi Arabia, Kuwait, Bahrain, Yemen, Libya, Tunisia, Bosnia, Kosovo, Chechnya, Dagestan, Kashmir, Sudan, Somalia, Kenya,Tanzania, Azerbaijan, Eritria, Uganda, Ethiopia, and in the West Bank and Gaza."

Impressive as this list is, it is now outdated. Deserving new additions would be the USA, major countries of Europe like Britain, Germany, Spain and the Netherlands, and even Australia in the Far East.

Kashmir is already there, but increasing areas, even distant ones, of India have now to be added.

Despite this globe-girdling presence, the location of al-Qaeda's international headquarters is a matter of conjecture. Osama bin Laden had arrived in Afghanistan from Sudan, and since the founding of al-Qaeda till about 1991 he was in Afghanistan and in Peshawar in Pakistan. In 1991 he returned to Sudan, where the headquarters were relocated till about 1996, when Osama returned to Afghanistan. The present base of al-Qaeda is unknown, but a senior Pakistani journalist has recently written that al-Qaeda is headquartered in Pakistan's tribal areas. More specifically, a correspondent of the American news service *Los Angeles Times*-World Press (LAT WP), writing from Peshawar in September 2007, stated that the dusty frontier city of Peshawar is the organisation's birthplace.

Structured Set-up

Although a far-flung multinational conglomerate, an *Ummah* (Brotherhood) of Islamic terrorist bodies, in itself too al-Qaeda is a well-structured set-up. Headed by Osama bin Laden,with Ayman al-Zawahiri as No. 2, it had a *Shura* (Governing Council) that regulates all activities from planning and funding to executing operations. It even pays regular salaries to around 200 members of the core group.

Golden Chain

This makes it clear that al-Qaeda's financial resources are equally well-structured. In March 2002, authorities in Bosnia, Sarajevo, raided the offices of the Benevolence International Foundation (BIF) due to suspected funding of al-Qaeda. The raid uncovered a handwritten list containing the names of twenty wealthy donors sympathetic to al-Qaeda. The list, referred to as The Golden Chain, contains both the names of the donors and the names of the recipients. Seven of the payments were made to Osama bin Laden. Most accounts are vague on what year the Golden Chain document was written, some say 1988, counterterrorism "tsar" Richard Clarke says it dates from 1989. A number of the Saudis on it have been under scrutiny by US officials as to whether they have supported terrorism in recent years. The donors named include:

1. The bin Laden brothers. Their first names are not mentioned. Osama bin Laden was said to have scores of wealthy brothers.
2. Adel Batterjee, wealthy Saudi businessman and founder of BIF. Mentioned as a recipient three times. The US declared him a terrorist financier in 2004. Batterjee is also mentioned in a 1992 *New York Times* article as the chairman of the World Assembly of Muslim Youth (WAMY), flying out wounded Saudis fighting in the Bosnian war and giving them free medical treatment. BIF stopped operating in Saudi Arabia but expanded its operations in the US.
3. Wael Hamza Julaidan, Saudi millionaire and one of the founders of al-Qaeda, listed as recipient. The US declared him a terrorist financier in 2002.
4. Saleh Kamel, Saudi billionaire, and majority shareholder of Saudi conglomerate Dallah Albaraka. In 2003 *Forbes* called him one of the richest persons in the world.
5. Sulaiman Abdul Aziz al-Rajhi, another Saudi billionaire. The SAAR network is named after him.
6. Khalid bin Mahfouz, another Saudi billionaire. A lawyer for bin Mahfouz later argued that he did contribute a small amount of fund to the Mujahideen in the late 1980s, but only at the behest of the US and Saudi Arabia.

Surrogates

Osama bin Laden had also privately identified three charity fronts most used to finance al-Qaeda. Among them he named the Benevolence International Foundation (BIF) even after it had been shut down in Saudi Arabia and shifted its base to Chicago in the US. The two others were the Muslim World League (MWL), a Saudi charity close to the Saudi government, and the Qatar Charitable Society (QCS). This organization was publicly linked to an assassination attempt on Egyptian President Hosni Mubarak in 1995. The charities would receive funds that could be withdrawn in cash and a portion of the money used for legitimate relief purposes and another portion diverted for al-Qaeda operations. The money for al-Qaeda operations would be listed in the charities' books as expenses for building mosques or schools or feeding the poor.

At the same time al-Qaeda's character as a conglomerate plays a significant role in its expansion. Commenting on its technique of growth through affiliation, former CIA Director George Tenet said Osama bin Laden's organization is placing increased emphasis on developing surrogates to carry out attacks. There are as many as 24 such surrogates, led by Lashkar-e-Toiba, Jaish-e-Mohammad, Al-Badr, and Jamiat Ulema-e-Pakistan. Even Taliban have been co-opted by al-Qaeda during the last few years.

Consequently it is growing into a more and more formidable international threat and has been designated a terrorist organization by a number of organizations, including :

- United Nations Security Council.
- North Atlantic Treaty Organization.
- Commission of the European Communities of the European Union.
- United States Department of State.
- Australian Government.
- Government of India.
- Public Safety Authorities, Canada.
- Israel Ministry of Foreign Affairs.
- Japan's Diplomatic Bluebook.
- South Korean Foreign Ministry.
- French General Secretary for National Defence.
- Dutch Military Intelligence and Security Service.
- United Kingdom Home Office.
- Russia.
- Swedish Ministry for Foreign Affairs.
- Turkish Police Forces.
- Swiss Government.

Bruce Riedel, reputed American expert on the Muslim Middle East, wrote in the prestigious *Foreign Affairs* journal (May/June 2007), "al-Qaeda is a more dangerous enemy today than it has ever been before. The organisation now has a solid base of operation in the badlands of Pakistan. It's reach has spread throughout the Muslim world."

Actually, it would be truer to say this reach has spread throughout the whole world, Muslim as well as non-Muslim. This is borne out by a

PTI news report of June 6, 2010, according to which US President Barack Obama secretly sanctioned deployment of US special forces to as many as 75 countries of the world as part of a largely secret war against al-Qaeda and its fellow-terrorists.

A broad regionwise survey of the presence and power of al-Qeada would give an alarming idea of the calamitous capacity of this global terror machine:

Pakistan

Al-Qaeda has spread throughout Pakistan. In fact, it rules the North-West region of Pakistan. This is the result of the long-standing and close nexus between it and ISI. It now has strongholds all over the state, not just in the tribal areas along the border with Afghanistan. It has recruiting and training centres in many major Pakistan cities like Karachi and Quetta.

The Pakistani newspaper *Daily Times* has described South Waziristan as a territory separated from Pakistan and annexed to al-Qaeda. Americans even fear that al-Qaeda may in time threaten the survival" of Pakistan.

In the meanwhile it is an open secret that Pakistan has become a safe haven for an assortment of terrorists including not only cadres of al-Qaeda but also its top-rankers, and although the Pakistan Government kept claiming that it does not shelter Osama bin Laden—a claim that many Pakistan-watchers took with a bushel of salt—it did harbour Abu Obaidah al-Misri, the mastermind behind many an al-Qaeda plot, who reportedly died of an infectious disease in 2008 in Pakistan. This powerful chief of the al-Qaeda network's external operations trained recruits in hideouts in Pakistan and sent them out on terrorist assignments. He was an explosives expert and a veteran of terrorist activity in Afghanistan, Bosnia and Chechanya. Reportedly, he has been replaced by Khaled Habib, who—according to terrorism expert Rohan Gunaratna, author of *Inside al-Qaeda*—supervised al-Qaeda's "internal" operations in Pakistan and Afghanistan, or possibly Midnat Mursi, a chemist who headed al-Qaeda's efforts to develop unconventional weapons.

USA

In a video broadcast on the *Al-Jazeera* television channel Osama bin Laden had publicly claimed responsibility for the horrendous 9/11 attack on the World Trade Centre. Even the White House is an al-Qaeda target, Russian newspaper *Komsomolskaya Pravda* reported.

Far more ominous, according to captured al-Qaeda leaders and documents a far bigger assault than 9/11, called American Hiroshima, is planned, in which nuclear bombs that have already been smuggled into the US will be exploded in a number of major American cities, including

New York, Washington, Boston, Las Vegas, Miami, Chicago and Los Angeles. The expected resultant carnage has been bluntly put in a manifesto in June 2002, in which al-Qaeda spokesman Abu Gheith openly wrote : "We have the right to kill 4 million Americans—2 million of them children —and to exile twice as many, and wound and cripple hundreds of thousands".

The capacity and willingness to issue such an awesome threat has a long history. For it was in 1986, even before al-Qaeda was set up around 1988-89, that Maktab al-Khidamat, the precursor organisation to al-Qaeda, opened its first branch in the US at the Islamic Centre in the city of Tucson in the State of Arizona. Counterterrorism expert Rita Katz later called this Centre basically the first cell of al-Qaeda in the US, where it all started. A number of leading future al-Qaeda figures were connected to the Tucson branch in the 1980s and nineties. They included Mohammad Bayazid, one of the founders of al-Qaeda two years later, Hamza Julaidan, another founder of al-Qaeda, Saudi multimillionaire and president of the Islamic Centre for some years, Widh el-Hage, bin Laden's future personal secretary, and Mubark al-Duri, al-Qaeda's chief agent for the purchase of weapons of mass destruction. Throughout the 1980s the Tucson mosque provided money, logistic support and fighters to the Mujahideen fighting in Afghanistan.

Al-Qaeda operative Khalil Deek ran military training camps in Southern California in the early 1990s. Deek was a member of an al-Qaeda sleeper cell based in Orange County and was reportedly under investigation by US intelligence since late 1980s. Rita Katz learnt of these camps when speaking to an FBI agent in early 2002. She was told the FBI had known about the camps for years but had not acted because of the wall between criminal and intelligence investigations. FBI said the information about the camps was Intel information, Unusable.

While FBI just watched al-Qaeda, CIA actually helped it. CIA contractor Billy Waugh trained al-Qaeda operatives around the globe, possibly for more than a decade. In his 2004 autobiography he wrote, "I worked right there with these al-Qaeda operatives." This training took place between 1989, when he was hired by CIA, and 2001, when he began his last assignment for the agency in Afghanistan.

And now fast forward to the present: The two attacks on World Trade Centre : In 1993, Ramzi Yousef used a truck bomb to attack the World Trade Centre in New York City. The attack was intended to break the foundation of Tower One, knocking it into Tower Two, bringing the entire complex down. Yousef hoped this would kill 250,000 people. The towers shook and swayed out but the foundation held, and he succeeded in killing only six people (although he injured 1,042 others and caused nearly $300 million in property damage.) After the attack, Yousef fled to Pakistan and later moved to Manila. There he began developing plans to blow up a dozen American airliners simultaneously, to assassinate Pope John Paul II and President Bill Clinton, and to crash a private plane into CIA headquarters. He was later captured in Pakistan.

In 1996 bin Laden personally engineered a plot to assassinate Clinton while the president was in Manila for the Asia Pacific Economic Cooperation Conference. However, Intelligence agents intercepted a message just minutes before his motorcade was to leave.

The September 11, 2001 attacks were the most devastating terrorist acts in American history, killing approximately 3,000 people. Two commercial airliners were deliberately flown into the World Trade Center towers, a third into the Pentagon, and a fourth, originally intended to target the United States Capitol, crashed in Pennsylvania. The attacks were conducted by al-Qaeda, acting in accord with the 1998 *fatwa* issued against the United States and its allies. Messages issued by bin Laden after September 11, 2001, praised the attacks while denying any involvement. He asserted that America was massacring Muslims in Palestine, Chechnya, Kashmir and Iraq and that Muslims should retain the right to attack in reprisal. Evidence has since come to light that the original targets for the attack may have been nuclear power stations on the east coast of the US.

And then Osama threatened the US : If you execute the 9/11 plotter, we'll kill captured Americans. He said in a message released on March 24, 2010 that al-Qaeda will kill any captured American if the US executes the mastermind of the Sept. 11 attacks or other al-Qaeda suspects. In the audiotape aired on *Al-Jazeera* television, the al-Qaeda leader explicitly mentioned Khalid Sheikh Mohammad, who was captured in Pakistan in 2003. In 2008, the US charged Mohammad with murder and war crimes in connection with the Sept. 11, 2001 attacks on the US. Pentagon officials have said they will seek the death penalty for him. Four of his fellow-plotters are also in custody. "The White House has expressed its desire to execute them. The day America makes that decision will be the day it has issued a death sentence for anyone of you that is taken captive," Osama said, addressing Americans.

Europe

In Europe law enforcement agencies have dicoversed al-Qaeda cells in Britain, Italy, France, Spain, Germany and Albania. In many parts of Europe al-Qaeda operatives are an invisible part of large North African communities. According to a *LAT-WP* despatch from Madrid, Spain, in October 2007, increasing numbers of militants from mainland Europe are currently travelling to Pakistan to train and plot attacks. These aspiring Mujahideen include not only militants with Arab, Turkish and North

African backgrounds but even European converts. In Britain senior members of the House of Lords say, Britain "has been deeply infiltrated by radical Islam". Thousands of young British Muslims have sworn allegiance to Jihadism. Some of their terror attacks have failed because, says *Israel News*, the perpetrators are in the kindergarten stage of complex Jihadist capabilities.

Apparently, however, that stage is past. For the *Daily Telegraph* reported on June 13, 2010 that young British Muslims are being groomed by al-Qaeda for a Mumbai-style attack on targets in Britain. Britain's internal intelligence agency MI-5 has warned that they could unleash a wave of easily-planned guerrilla-style terrorist attacks similar to the massacre in Mumbai, the report said.

On the other hand, in a bizarre show of fundamentalism, radical Muslims seeking to introduce Sharia laws in Britain have said the British Queen would be forced to wear a *burqa* in public, according to a media report in November 2009. Abu Rumaysah, spokesman for pro-Sharia campaigners "Islam 4 UK", said the Queen would be forced to cover up in public from head to foot, with only her eyes visible. "If the Queen decides to go outside, she is to cover herself like every other woman," Amjed Choudary, an Islamist leader, was quoted as saying by the *Daily Express*. Choudary is the right-hand man of exiled Mullah Sheikh Omar Bakri Mohammad.

Elsewhere in Europe an al-Qaeda cell's planned attack was recently discovered in Denmark. The police in Belgium have also admitted that there were militant Islamists in the country who had international contacts with al-Qaeda leaders, and possessed the ability, desire and opportunity to commit terror attacks. In Germany the *Stern* magazine reported in late 2001 that the state's intelligence agency BND believed that nearly 30 terrorist cells were operating in the country, and they were capable of launching 20–30 attacks like 9/11. Another source even suspected that Osama bin Laden was using Germany as a base.

Middle East

In the Muslim Middle East, al-Qaeda is vigorouly active. In Iraq "al-Qaeda in Iraq" (AQI) is a dreaded organisation, with an extensive network throughout the Middle East, North Africa, and Europe. The bungled terrorist attacks in London and Glasgow in the UK are believed to be "AQI-related" if not AQI-directed.

India

Finally India. Al-Qaeda supremo Osama bin Laden's deputy Ayman al-Zawahiri lashed out against India, a couple of years ago, accusing its "Hindu rulers" of killing more than 100,000 Muslims in Kashmir. He not only made an explicit threat against Hindus in Kashmir, but added that attacking the US and its allies, including Delhi, was their 'legitimate' right. Although this is generally considered al-Qaeda's first threat against India, it is in fact not so, for in April 2006 Osama bin Laden had himself spoken of a 'Crusader-Zionist-Hindu war against Muslims', indicating clearly that for him Hindus were as much an enemy as Jews and Christians.

The later threat does not mean al-Qaeda has newly arrived in India. Years ago *Jane's Security News* had compiled a list of the world's countries and regions where it was actively operating, and that list included Kashmir.

Since then, aided and abetted by Pakistan's ISI and its terrorist outfits within this country, al-Qaeda seems to be spreading across India. This has been clearly indicated by a group of al-Qaeda operatives arrested in the North-East not long ago, as well as the complicity of terrorists trained by or connected with al-Qaeda in Mumbai and Hyderabad bombings. And last year, in 2010, India has been twice warned about al-Qaeda's deadly designs on the country.

India is in great danger of being the target of the next attack from al-Qaeda or one of its several splinter groups, particularly those operating from Pakistan, according to Steve Coll, head of a prominent US think-tank. Testifying before the House Armed Services Committee, Coll said India-focused terrorist organizations operating from Pakistan had been successful in recruiting talented operatives from educated classes and urban centres and were much more powerful than their allied organizations fighting on the Pakistan-Afghanistan border.

"India-focused groups such as Lashkar, having enjoyed collaborative support from the Pakistani state for so many years, are larger, its ranks include scores of volunteer doctors and other postgraduate professionals," Coll said.

Coll is a former managing editor of *The Washington Post*. He expressed similar fears about India in a recent interview with the *Indian Express* editor Shekhar Gupta: "The potential of these India-focused groups, with or without clandestine collaboration by Pakistani security forces or al-Qaeda central, to repeat or exceed the scale of the provocative attack carried out in Mumbai on November 26, 2008, presents, one of the most serious current threats."

In another warning, CIA has warned India and Brazil that they face emerging threats from al-Qaeda and Taliban. Saying that US was at war with al-Qaeda and its affiliated terrorist organizations, CIA Director Panetta warned that fighting spread of deadly weapons is a core issue, especially in light of Osama bin Laden describing the acquisition of nuclear weapons as a religious duty. Panetta said the US was lagging behind in the cyber war and added that he feared the next Pearl Harbor might be a cyber attack.

On the other hand, in a damning indictment of the American responsibility in these developments on-line encyclopedia *Wikipedia* observes : Bin Laden has been called one of CIA's best weapon customers, and the US support for the Afghan Mujahideen "the model for state-sponsored terrorism." It adds : The US was actively recruiting internationally for Muslim radicals. The perpetrators of the first World Trade Centre bombing in 1991 allegedly used a manual written by the CIA for the Mujahideen fighters in Afghanistan on how to make explosives.

Terrorism Bible

Al-Qaeda even has what Westerners call bin Laden's Terrorism Bible. According to internet sources, in the period since 9/11 few more chilling documents have surfaced than *Military Studies in the Jihad against the Tyrants*, a how-to terrorism guide book prepared for the use of Osama bin Laden's cadres. The 180-page volume, seized from the Manchester, England, home of a bin Laden follower, offers the Jihadists guidance on subjects like assassination, forging documents, and preparing poisons in its 18 chapters which are actually called lessons in this textbook on terror. Apart from the introduction and the opening, they are as follows:

- Necessary qualifications and characteristics for the organization's member.
- Counterfeit currency and forged documents.
- Organizing military bases, apartments, hiding places.
- Means of communication and transportation.
- Training.
- Weapons : Measures related to buying and transporting them.
- Member safety.
- Security plan.
- Special tactical operations.
- Espionage (1) : Information-gathering using open methods.
- Espionage (2) : Information-gathering using covert methods.
- Secret writing and ciphers and codes.
- Kidnapping and assassinations using rifles and pistols.
- Explosives.
- Assassinations using poisons and cold steel.
- Interrogation and investigation.
- Prisons and detention centres.

Car-bomb Guide book

There is also an on-line guide on how to explode car-bombs. According to an *Israel News* report in early 2007 al-Qaeda in Iraq (AQI) has put its experience in mass murder on the internet for the benefit of its cadres around the world in the form of an on-line training course on bomb attacks.

The bombing manual, available in Arabic on a Jihadi website, contains a number of key pieces of advice for car-bombers. It instructs terrorists not to park their vehicles illegally (lest they are towed away from the intended target), and advises the car-bomber to leave the scene quietly if he plans to blow up the vehicle from a distance in what a1-Qaeda calls non-martyrdom operations.

The manual points out the precise spots inside a vehicle where explosives should be placed and recommends various targets, like cinema theatres and sports stadiums. It also instructs the terrorist to monitor the route of the enemy, and note how they leave the cinema or the stadium at the end of a show or a game. It also gives instructions on how to carry out suicide bombings, explaining in detail how suicide bombers can fool security guards. The manual even suggests the correct speed to drive a vehicle packed with explosives into a target. Besides cinemas and stadiums it also mentions festivals, celebrations and demonstrations as possible targets.

Whether or not car bombers learn this text book, it is a fact that a car or truck loaded with explosives has for years been a terrorist's weapon of choice across the globe, from Iraq to America. The 1995 bombing of a building in Oklahoma City, USA killed 168 people. Hundreds were injured. Since 9/11, car bombs have wreaked varying degrees of havoc in Baghdad and Kabul, Peshawar and Glasgow.

"One of the things that's striking is they're incredibly effective," said Gary Lafree, director of the National Consortium for the Study of Terrorism and Responses to Terrorism at the University of Maryland. "They're lethal."

From 1970 to 2007, terrorists used car bombs at least 1,495 times, according to research by the terrorism response centre in Maryland, USA. The centre tracked 876 in the Middle East and North Africa, 212 in Western Europe and 163 in South Asia. Among the biggest culprits were the Taliban and al-Qaeda, the centre found.

Al-Qaeda's Atom Bombs

The most frightening feature of al-Qaeda for the whole world is that it is nuclear-armed.

Al-Qaeda has acquired at least 40 nuclear weapons including suitcase nukes and even missile warheads. In addition, it had plans to assemble its own nuclear weapons with material purchased on the black market. Osama bin Laden also paid Pakistani and Russian nuclear scientists to maintain and expand his nuclear arsenal built up with hundreds of millions of dollars over a period of a decade.

The US government's indictment of bin Laden had charged that he had made efforts to obtain components of nuclear weapons as far back as 1992. And in November 2001, he had openly boasted in an interview with a Pakistani journalist that he had hidden such components as a deterrent.

Later, a report in March 2004 said the al-Qaeda network claimed to have bought ready-made nuclear weapons on the black market in Central Asia, the biographer of al-Qaeda's No. 2 leader was quoted as telling an Australian television channel. In an interview with the channel, Pakistani journalist Hamid Mir said Ayman al-Zawahiri claimed that smart suitcase bombs were available on the black market. It was not clear when the interview between Mir and al-Zawahiri took place.

In the interview Mir recalled saying to al-Zawahiri that it was difficult to believe that al-Qaeda had nuclear weapons when the terror network didn't have the equipment to maintain or use them. Dr. Ayman al-Zawahiri laughed and said, "Mr. Mir, if you have 30 million dollars, go to the black market in Central Asia, contact any disgruntled Soviet scientist and a lot of smart briefcase bombs are available," Mir said in the interview. "They have contacted us, our people went to Moscow, to Tashkent, to other Central Asian states, and they negotiated, and we purchased some suitcase bombs, "Mir quoted al-Zawahiri as saying. Mir described al-Zawahiri as the real brain behind Osama bin Laden. "He is the real strategist, Osama bin Laden is only a front man," Mir said: "I think he is more dangerous than bin Laden."

On the other hand, in *Islam & Terrorism* (2004) Anwar Shaikh called Osama bin Laden a true *Mujahid* (one who kills or gets killed in the name of Allah) and adds, "He believes himself to be the apostle of Jehad, because he is determined to make it a worldwide revolutionary movement..."

American Hiroshima

Al-Qaeda's earlier-mentioned 'American Hiroshima' nuclear bombing project has also been recorded in an American book-*The al-Qaeda Connection: International Terrorism, Organized Crime, and the Coming Apocalypse* by Paul Williams, a former FBI consultant. According to Williams, former CIA Director George Tenet told President Bush after 9/11 that at least two suitcase nukes had reached al-Qaeda operatives in the US. The news sent Bush through the roof, writes Williams. He adds, bin Laden had virtually unlimited funds to spend on his nuclear terrorism, because he was in control of the heroin industry of Afghanistan.

According to Williams' sources, thousands of al-Qaeda's sleeper agents have been deployed into the US to carry out their individual roles in the coming American Hiroshima. Bin Laden's goal, confirmed the book, was to kill at least 4 million Americans, 2 million of whom must be children.

The number of fully assembled nuclear weapons in al-Qaeda's possession is estimated to range between a dozen and 70. "Terrorists have *carte blanche* to carry practically anything they want across our national line (with Mexico) at this time", said Chris Simcox, founder of a citizen action group called the Minutemen Civil Defence Group.

ISI-al-Qaeda Partnership

ISI's close relationship with al-Qaeda has long been an open secret that the US acknowledged only in late 2001. Curiously enough, there had been an apathetic reaction earlier within US officialdom to a secret memo prepared by the State Department's Chief of Counterterrorism Michael Sheehan in 1999 in the wake of the bombing of two US embassies in East Africa the previous year, which made new suggestions on how to contain bin Laden. The suggestions called for efforts to cut off his funds by curbing terrorist money-laundering and end the sanctuary and support to al-Qaeda, for which the document called Pakistan the key. Additionally, it called for persuading the Muslim Middle Eastern states of Saudi Arabia, UAE and Yemen to help isolate al-Qaeda. Sheehan's plan landed with a resounding thud, a former official remarked. "He couldn't get anyone interested."

As the al-Qaeda grew more and more powerful, the US began to pressurise Pakistan to bring it under control. The Pakistanis pretended to cooperate, but did little. When they offered to establish a special unit to capture bin Laden, the CIA willingly financed and equipped it. "But this was going nowhere," a CIA official said. "The ISI never intended to go after bin Laden. We got completely snookered."

Alarmed Americans

Their disillusionment with the Pakistanis apart, the Americans are increasingly aware of the heightening al-Qaeda threat to them. Even as late as February 2008, US Director of National Intelligence Mike McConnell told a Senate panel that al-Qaeda is steadily improving its ability to recruit, train and put in place operatives capable of carrying out attacks inside the US. He said the top duo of al-Qaeda has promoted a new generation of lieutenants. He warned that al-Qaeda was improving the last key of its ability to attack the US—recruiting Western militants capable of blending into the American society. This testimony was based on new evidence that al-Qaeda operatives in Pakistan were training westerners, most likely including American citizens, to carry out attacks.

This warning was repeated in a PTI report a few months later. Datelined New York, June 21, the report said: Dozens of white Europeans, trained in terrorist camps in Pakistan's tribal belt, have been dispatched to plan attacks against Europe and possibly the US, in what the American intelligence fears may be the beginning of a new breed of al-Qaeda-affiliated terror. The terrorists, *ABC News* said quoting intelligence sources, hail from the Netherlands, Denmark, Germany, Romania and Estonia.

There is growing evidence that some European recruits may have already gone operational, the television network said, adding that two of the suspects arrested in a September 2007 plot to kill American soldiers in Germany were native Germans. An April 2008 report from Europe also noted that an increasing number of European nationals attended training in Pakistan and were later involved in, or suspected of, terrorist offences in the EU.

Intelligence officials told *ABC News* that the remote tribal areas along the border between Pakistan and Afghanistan have in the last several years become a haven for terrorist recruiting and training. Hundreds of radicals from across the region have flocked to al-Qaeda training camps in the area. Intelligence officials believe al-Qaeda has successfully completed a major goal: recruiting and training Western would-be terrorists.

The American description of Pakistan as al-Qaeda's refuge is not a mere flourish. For according to media reports in mid-2007 a Terrorism Index jointly prepared by the US Centre for American Progress and the prestigious *Foreign Affairs* magazine rated Pakistan as the country most likely to become the next al-Qaeda stronghold after Somalia. Over 100 foreign policy experts were surveyed for the study.

Global Jehad

Actually, things have come to such a pass that this refuge has become more dominant than those sheltering him. Reputed Pakistani journalist Najam Sethi recently expressed grave concern over the al-Qaeda networks proliferating all over Pakistan. In his view al-Qaeda wants to entrench itself in Pakistan to make it a base for a global Islamic revolution. Hitherto, ISI and other Pakistani intelligence agencies always sought the help of al-Qaeda networks for their covert operations against other countries, but now the same networks kill ISI officials. They even made attempts on the lives of President Musharraf and his ministers, which would not have been possible without the support of al-Qaeda sympathisers within the Pakistan Army. Media reports from Pakistan in September 2007 said three prominent ISI terror groups, Jaish-e-Mohammad, Lashkar-e-Toiba, and Sipah-e-Sahaba, have also joined hands with al-Qaeda to step up terrorist activities, particularly targeting the Pakistan Army. This was borne out by two recent terror strikes in Rawalpindi, the garrisnon town, in which 25 people were killed and 70 injured. Those killed were ISI people. "The near simultaneous blasts bore the al-Qaeda signature," wrote *Times of India*.

Commenting on this situation US-based researcher Haider Ali Hussein Mullick wrote: "For the first time in more than 30 years Pakistan is consumed by an internal threat—a predominantly Pashtun ethnic separatist movement, which has joined forces with the Taliban and al-Qaeda against the Pakistani military on the enemy-of-my-enemy-is-my-friend logic." Writing in the same vein and referring to the late Benazir Bhutto Indian columnist-MP Rajiv Shukla said she vociferously advocated freedom, democracy, modernisation and rights of women, but "these words do not figure in the dictionary of religious extremists, and anyone speaking this language is their enemy, therefore, everyone who pledges to fight the war on terrorism would obviously be al-Qaeda target."

Interestingly enough, Najam Sethi notes that the al-Qaeda network in Pakistan also includes Pakistanis who are Pathans, Punjabis, and possibly Urdu-speakers. Therefore, he concludes, al-Qaeda is now as much a Pakistani phenomenon as it is an Arab or Afghan phenomenon.

Unique Public Relations

Ayman al-Zawahiri recently participated in a unique exercise in public relations. He was heard in a lengthy audiotape posted on an Islamic website answering more than 900 questions put to him on extremist Internet sites by al-Qaeda supporters, critics and journalists in December 2007. He reiterated that al-Qaeda does not kill innocent people despite the fact that it has not only killed thousands of them but has publicly expressed its plan to atom-bomb the American people.

Asked if there are any women in al-Qaeda, the terrorist leader simply answered "No". But a *New York Times* report on May 23, 2008 gave a long and interesting account under the heading "al-Qaeda woman warrior uses internet to rally others." Writing in French under the name Oum Obeyda (real name Mallika al-Aroud), this Brussels-based female has become one of the most prominent Jihadists in Europe. She calls herself a female holy warrior for al-Qaeda. In a rare interviev she said, "I have a weapon. It's to write. It's to speak out. That's my Jihad."

"Women are coming of age in Jihad and are entering a world once reserved for men," said Claude Moniquet, president of the Brussels-based European Strategie Intelligence and Security Centre. Mallika is a role model, an icon who is bold enough to identify herself. For her the Taliban was a model Islamic government.

Despite such mild PR gestures, al-Qaeda continues its training in terror techniques. A captured American-turned-Islamic terrorist by the name Bryant Neal Vinas alias Bashir al-Amriki, who had agreed to become a suicide bomber in attack on a US railway system, revealed in a court hearing the al-Qaeda training in terror that he was given in Waziristan between March and July 2008.

Vinas said there were three Basic Courses:

- The first offered an introduction to AK-47, machine gun and pistol.
- Then came a class in explosives. This 15-day course taught students to manufacture suicide belts, how to tuck the belts around their waists, and how to test the battery and voltmeters.
- The third offered an introduction to rocket-propelled grenades.
- Besides, there were other classes which offered instruction in forgery, poison and advanced bombs.

Aviation Network

Al-Qaeda even has its own fleet of planes. It is believed to be operating a clandestine aviation network including several Boeing 727 aircraft, turboprops and executive jets, according to a *Reuters* story. Based on a US Department of Homeland Security report, the story said al-Qaeda is possibly using aircraft to transport drugs and weapons from South America to various unstable countries in West Africa. A Boeing 727 can carry up to 10 tons of cargo. The drugs eventually are smuggled to Europe for distribution and sale, and the weapons are used in conflicts in Africa and possibly elsewhere. Gunmen with links to al-Qaeda have been increasingly kidnapping some Europeans for ransom. The profits from the drug and weapon sales, and kidnappings can, in turn, fund more terrorism activities.

Thus armed, trained and equipped, al-Qaeda does not stop at just threatening the Government of Pakistan, it even threatens the people of Pakistan. Warning the people of Pakistan that they would face painful punishment from Allah if they failed to back the militants to check the grave threat to their country from the US, al-Qaeda's second-in-command Ayman al-Zawahiri said in December 2009 that "sincere" Muslims have a duty to join Jehad. Zawahiri said in the message released on radical Islamist websites, "If we stand by passively without offering due support to the Mujahideen, we shall not only contribute to the destruction of Pakistan and Afghanistan, but also deserve the painful punishment of Almighty Allah."

An abrupt twist in this threatening scenario happened when, on May 2, 2011 Osama bin Laden was found and killed by a US commando team in Pakistan, which the American media is now calling "Terroristan." He was living for six long years in Abbotabad, a garrison town only 40 miles from Pakistan's Capital and 60/65 miles from India (-and two years before that in another Pakistani town). It was obviously inconceivable that the Pakistani powers-that-be did not know about his hideout, which was a stone's throw from a military establishment.

In carrying out the commando assault and gunning down Osama bin Laden the US did **not**: 1. Take the Pakistan government into confidence,

2. Care about attacking a place in a foreign , 'Sovereign' State, 3. Care for what the Pakistanis – even the world – will say.

And when Gen. Kayani tried to cover up his mortification with some sabrerattling, saying there would be a strong response to a repetition of something like this, the American response was swift and two-fold-in word and deed. The US mounted still bigger Drone attacks on terrorist positions within Pakistan, and both President Obama and Secretary of State Hillary Clinton bluntly said: We're telling you to find out terrorist leaders hiding in your country, and take them down, – if you don't, we will.

And what was the Indian response? The Prime Minister declared the American way is not our way, and we shall continue to "engage" Pakistan – that is, we shall keep talking and talking and talking with the rulers of 'Terroristan'. And the Home Minister, in his wisdom, stated that this – Osama's removal from the scene – did not mean the end of terrorism, and India must be "very vigilant" *until* Pakistan dismantles its terrorism-infrastructure. That means the Congress-led UPA Government is going to wait for something that will never happen.

On the contrary, according to post-Osama *Wikileaks,* interrogations of nearly 70 Pak prisoners at Guantanamo have revealed that al-Qaeda is now likely to turn its focus on India. Many of them belong to terrorist groups that have been active in Kashmir for several years to "fight Hindus".

7

OPERATION INDIA

Instrument of Execution

A systematic and sustained 'Operation India' was launched when Gen. Zia-ul-Haq came to power in 1977. He drew up a plan, codenamed "Operation Topac"for the subversion of India.

According to the documents prepared by the Government of India's Home Ministry, the broad objectives of this plan were :

1. To undermine India's national will and security structure by pursuing the doctrine of a "thousand cuts".
2. To exploit India's porous borders to make its border states vulnerable to subversion.
3. To prevent India from emerging as a strategically important power in the region.

Multiple Benefits

For the execution of this plan the designated instrument was ISI – a role for which it was now well-equipped. For, as seen earlier, its full involvement in the Afghan war had brought it multiple benefits. First and foremost, it had given ISI a tailor-made opportunity to hone its skills in covert action. Second, it had gained access to huge quantities of weapons made available by the Americans to this frontline friend free of cost with the crucial advantage of deniability. Along with the arms came the manpower trained in their use. And third, it had developed links not only with fundamentalist Islamist terror groups of the world but also with the underworld of drug smugglers and gun-runners. To cap is all, it had succeeded against a superpower like Soviet Russia.

And of course ISI was not alone when it entered India. It began with, and has always had, unstinted support from the Pakistan Army, other espionage outfits, and Government departments. These have all the more enhanced ISI's already formidable capacity to cause havoc in India.

Open Invitation

On the other hand India's dangerous porous borders were an open invitation to ISI to cross over, which it did, to inflict a thousand cuts on this country by conducting a well-orchestrated countrywide terror campaign.

The calamitous consequence has been that India continues to fight a no-win and no-end battle against Islamic terror spearheaded by Pakistan's ISI. As of today, things have come to such a catastrophic pass that one wonders, has not Operation Topac succeeded ?

7(a)

PUNJAB

The Khalistani Extension

ISI's Covert Action Division had designs on India as long back as the 1950s, that is, more or less since its establishment, but in the 1960s its role was expanded to promote what was initially called the Sikh Home Rule Movement, headed by London-based Charan Singh Panchi, subsequently transformed into the Khalistan movement, headed by Jagjit Singh Chauhan. Thus, ISI's anti-India agenda had gone international from the very beginning. It worked in tandem with CIA during the Nixon administration in helping this secessionist movement, in which many Sikhs residing in the USA, Europe and Canada got involved.

Khalistani Handle

ISI took up in a big way the task of arming, training and guiding Punjab terrorists, using the Khalistani handle. Since then a number of them, including members of the first and second Panthic Committees are permanently based in Pakistan, where ISI coordinated their activities.

ISI's active involvement with Punjab terrorists was revealed from time to time by arrested or surrendered Punjab militant leaders and by recovery of huge arms dumps at their instance. For instance, Gurdip Singh Sivia, leader of the dreaded terrorist outfit Babbar Khalsa, UK, who surrendered in August 1992, admitted that during 1989, aided and abetted by ISI, he had arranged as many as five successful infiltrations of terrorists from Pakistan into India.

Later, the media reported in April 1994 that a US House of Representatives Committee's Task Force on Terrorism report said: "ISI began to take direct control of the Sikh movement when ISI made the city of Derra, in Pakistan, the primary source of weapons for the Sikh, Tamil and Kashmiri liberation movements ... The Pashtun population of Karachi rapidly became the store-front for the tribal arms front, taking care of transportation throughout Pakistan as well as smuggling overseas."

ISI's Secrecy

How secretly ISI did all this was also described by Sivia. He related how, despite regular contacts with the Punjab terrorist leaders, ISI officials took great care to hide their own identity. They called themselves Chaudhary. The seniormost among them was referred to as "Bada Chaudhary" and the juniormost as Munshi.

ISI's role in smuggling arms to the militants in Punjab was also confirmed by the interrogation of a key arms smuggler by the name of Karimbhai Hasanbhai. Arrested in November 1992, Karimbhai admitted smuggling as many as 22 consignments of weapons from Pakistan into India.

Plan K-2

Then there was the plot involving top terrorist Lal Singh alias Manjit Singh, who was the coordinator of Khalistani militants and was based in Pakistan. He and a top ISI spy by the name of Mohammad Sharif were smuggled into India to carry out a grand plan called Kashmir-Khalistan Front, codenamed K-2. Its aim was to balkanise India by forging a strategic alliance among Punjabi and Kashmiri militants and Muslim fundamentalists in order to spread terror in other parts of India. The tasks assigned to this front by ISI included coordination of smuggling arms from Pakistan, building up a network of hideouts, and training of Muslim fundamentalist youths in association with Indian Muslim terrorist outfits like SIMI.

At the same time ISI also exploited the differences within the Punjab terrorists. Commenting on the split in the second Panthic Committee, Dr. Sohan Singh, who was himself a protege of ISI, said after his arrest in November 1993 that ISI played an important role in creating it. With the departure of leaders of this committee from Pakistan and adoption of a low profile by Pakistan-based Babbar Khalsa leaders, the First Panthic Committee of Wassan Singh Zaffarwal again came into prominence and Zaffarwal became ISI's most trusted tool.

Even then ISI took great precaution while dealing with Punjab terrorists on Pakistani soil. It isolated them, confining them to separate locations. Their handlers observed such strict security that ISI's telephone numbers were not disclosed even to top Khalistani terrorists like Paramjit Singh Panjwar. Militancy in Punjab was brought to an end by early 1990s by supercop KPS Gill and his men.

In this they were helped by two factors : First, most of the Sikh terrorist groups found little popular support in (Indian) Punjab, Second, the Indo-Pak border could be effectively fenced and policed on the plains of Punjab unlike in the mountainous regions of Kashmir and the North-East. Still Khalistani terrorism claimed an estimated 25,000 people dead during a decade ending in 1993.

Punjab Militancy Revived

However, this did not mean ISI lost its interest or its role in Punjab was over. Rather, the Indian media reported in 1999 that it was tying to revive militancy there. It was employing new strategies for the purpose, and also pressurising the remaining militants to undertake some sensational terrorist action, according to official sources. "Pakistan-based Punjabi militant groups, particularly Khalistan Commando Force (Panjwar), Babbar Khalsa International, and International Sikh Youth Federation are under pressure from ISI to undertake some sensational terrorist actions here," according to these sources.

About 30 leaders of various Khalistani groups are believed to be living in Pakistan with the active support of ISI. The emergence of new militant groups has also been discovered. These comprise splinter groups like Dal Khalsa, Babbar Khalsa (Parmar), and Tigers of Sikh Land. A terrorist by name Keval Singh belonging to an outfit called Khalistan Zindabad was arrested in March 1999. He was carrying more than 30 kg of RDX for explosions at public places in Punjab.

Many Other Indicators

There were also various other indicators of ISI efforts at reviving terrorism in Punjab. For instance prior to Keval Singh's arrest one Mandeep Singh was also arrested and letterpads of KCF-P containing threatening letters demanding ransom recovered from him. Later, in June 1999, three Babbar Khalsa International (BKI) terrorists and a local contact in Vadodara, Gujarat, were arrested by the city's police. They confessed that a consignment of weapons was being smuggled from Pakistan. The same month yet another militant Balwinder Singh was arrested in Hoshiarpur in Punjab and RDX and detonators seized from him. His interrogation revealed that he and a Pakistani had entered India through Kashmir in January that year and had brought AK-47 rifles with them. Balwinder had received three weeks' training in handling arms and explosives in Pakistan.

That the active collusion between ISI and Khalistani terrorists is continuing to date has been confirmed by the statement of the Punjab Director General of Police in a press conference in January 2008 that currently ISI is helping Babbar Khalsa to regroup in Punjab. He said this terrorist group had engineered the Ludhiana bomb blasts in October 2007 and had planned elimination of Dera Sacha Sauda chief Gurmitram Rahim Singh and some other heads of religious sects in Punjab. It is known that cadres of this group function out of the Dera Sahib Gurdwara in Lahore. In India its armed cadres have been reactivated in Punjab, Haryana and Delhi.

The police had also identified a new Khalistani terrorist group operating in the Malwa region called the International Liberation

Revolutionary Force. Besides this, militants released from jails are being re-used for terrorist activities in Punjab and elsewhere in India.

Indian intelligence agencies have also discovered the emergence of narco-terrorism with a growing nexus between Pakistani drug smugglers and Khalistani militants.

While all this was going on, Sikh Jathas visiting Pakistan on pilgrimage were being subjected to shrill anti-India and pro-Khalistan propaganda. To cap it all, a former ISI chief, Lt. Gen. Javed Nasir, a Muslim, was appointed President of the Pakistan Gurudwara Prabandhak Committee. Nasir has packed this committee with Sikhs involved in Khalistani activities.

Joint Punjab-Kashmir Strategy

ISI's joint Punjab-Kashmir strategy has been in operation for more than a decade. For instance, violent incidents in Punjab in June 1994 involved a Punjab terrorist, two militants from Kashmir, and a Muslim from Pakistan. Actually, the Americans say this strategy goes back 30 years. A report by the Task Force on Terrorism and Unconventional Warfare of the US House of Representatives and released in February 1993 had clearly stated that Pakistan had been training Sikhs and other Indian separatist movements... since the 70s... as part of ZA Bhutto's strategy and also of his effort to take revenge for India's support for an independent Bangladesh.

The report said initially Pakistan supported Sikh militancy to make it difficult for India to defend Kashmir, and recruited Sikhs for training in Afghanistan's Mujahideen camps for the purpose. This came to light (unambiguouly and independent of India's assertions) when one such camp in a place called Paktia was raided. Among those killed during the attack were some Sikh trainees.

Terrorist Elite

On November 14, 2005 *Pioneer* published a list of 20 top terrorists and criminals of India enjoying Pak hospitality for long years despite several international treaties and conventions, including Interpol Red Corner Notices (RCN) against 14 of them. They included the following Khalistanis:

1. *Wadhawan Singh Babbar*, Chief of Babbar Khalsa International, which was involved in insurgency in East Punjab during the 1980s. He is wanted in over a dozen cases of murder and sedition, as well as in connection with the assassination of East Punjab's the then Chief Minister Beant Singh.

2. *Ranjit Singh Neeta*, Chief of Khalistan Zindabad Force. He is wanted in cases of murder, bomb blasts, and smuggling of arms into India.

3. *Paramjit Singh Panjawar*, leader of Khalistan Commando Force. He is

wanted in more than a dozen cases of murder, treason, conspiracy and arms smuggling. It was this self-styled Lt. General of the Force who openly admitted to Channel 4 BBC TV that his cadres were trained in Pakistan.

4. *Lakhbir Singh Rode*, leader of the International Sikh Youth Federation, is wanted in cases of arms smuggling, conspiracy to attack government leaders in Delhi, and inciting religious hatred.

5. *Gajinder Singh*, leader of Dal Khalsa, is accused of hijacking an Indian Airlines plane from Srinagar to Delhi in 1981. He later hijacked it to Lahore.

All five live in and operate from Lahore. They had committed terrorist acts during the 80s. After staying dormant for some years they became active again and organized the 2005 twin bomb blasts in Delhi's cinema theatres. Interpol RCNs are pending against all five.

ISI Common Link

Even as late as 2007 attempts continued in Pakistan to whip up radical Sikh separatism, said National Security Advisor M K Narayanan. In the wake of bomb blasts in October 2007 in Ludhiana, Ajmer and Hyderabad's Mecca Masjid, Narayanan said they did not seem to be interlinked other than the fact that ISI involvement is suspected, that is the common link.

Referring to the Ludhiana blasts Narayanan said : "There has been a manifest attempt in Pakistan to build up a radical Sikh environment... We had intelligence about four to six months back that a lot of effort was going into attempts to foment militancy... We have also seen signs of resuscitation of militant groups in Canada, US and Germany. Another similar report said in the absence of enough ground support in India attempts to revive Khalistani terrorism are being made in the US, Canada, Germany, Britain, France, Norway and Belgium, besides, of course, Pakistan.

Specifically, ISI's demand that militants of Babbar Khalsa International (BKI) come above ground is driving the group to desperation. "Despite their (the militants') shrinking base, limited resources and the near absence of public support for militancy, terror coordinators within the country and abroad are trying to rope in their old associates and those released from jails, as well as family members of dead militants," said a highly placed source.

Islamists and Criminals

Along with their continuing ISI links the Khalistanis also seem to have joined hands with Islamist terrorists and criminals. "There are reports that the Punjab militants have kept close contact with Hizb-ul Mujahideen, Al-Barq, and the Jammu-Kashmir Islamic Front," said a senior intelligence official. It was further reported that representatives of Babbar Khalsa International (BKI) and other Khalistani terrorist outfits and those of Lashkar-e-Toiba (LeT) had a meeting recently in Berlin in which it was decided that on the one hand the Khalistanis would extend financial support to LeT, while on the other LeT would provide logistical support to BKI to carry out terror strikes in India.

Intelligence sources have even said that the National Socialist Council of Nagaland (Isaac Muivah) (NSCN-IM) had got in touch with a Britain-based Sikh body called Parliamentarians for National Self-determination for modelling their "Position Paper" on the pattern of the Khalistani position paper it had drawn up.

Some reports also suggest that leaders of the Khalistan Liberation Front (KLF) and BKI tied up three years ago with crime gangs based in Uttar Pradesh to carry out kidnappings in order to raise funds for the now-defunct Khalistan movement. Jagtar Singh Hawara, a BKI leader who reportedly masterminded the twin bomb blasts in cinema theatres in New Delhi in May 2005 and was arrested, maintained contacts with members of the organization in Germany.

"There are certainly some diehard elements from Punjab groups who are very much around. Not all elements have been eliminated. There are certain people left around," admitted former Intelligence Burean (IB) chief Arun Bhagat. "They have the expertise, and it requires just two or perhaps three people to organize an operation like the Ludhiana blast," he added. KPS Gill held BKI responsible for it and said, "They are trying to reactivate themselves in Punjab. They still have their links in Pakistan, and also with other terrorist outfits."

Chinese Pistols

That these links are in place and also active came to light when the Amritsar police disclosed in May 1996 that they had foiled yet another ISI plot to smuggle arms and ammunition from across the border into Punjab. These included Chinese pistols. A similar plot was foiled earlier in March the same year when a Pakistani was caught with nearly 40 kg of RDX in his possession. The arms seized in May were sent by ISI for BKI operatives.

Foreign Funds

Khalistani terrorists have been receiving foreign funds since long. Reports in the Indian media in September 1996 said a confidential report prepared by the Government of India's Joint Intelligence Committee the previous year (1995) stated that extremist groups of Punjab continued to maintain their links with their foreign financial sources. The report listed 23 such groups, some of which operated from India, others from various foreign countries like the US, the UK, Canada, Malaysia and Hong Kong.

Apart from diversion of *golak* collections from Gurudwaras whose control had been seized by Khalistani organizations, the JIC said large sums continued to be collected by their leaders during visits abroad or through direct appeals made at congregations and conventions abroad. The committee estimated that Rs. 600 crore had come from Pakistan and other countries into Punjab during the decade 1981 to 1991. Even legal channels like the Foreign Contribution Regulation Act were reportedly used for the inflow of funds during this period, when terrorism was at its peak.

Some prominent cases of such funding were mentioned in the JIC report:

1. The International Sikh Youth Federation (ISYF) had been routinely sending money through 'hawala' channels to various fundamentalist groups.
2. Details were available of payments made to the Panthic Committee of Dr Sohan Singh and Lakhbir Singh Brar and Baba Thakur Singh of the Damdami Taksal, totalling Rs. 70 lakh.
3. In May 1992 the UK-based Council of Khalistan held a Sikh convention and gave £86,000 (Rs. 47 lakh) to the second Panthic Committee.
4. The following year (1993) the Babbar Khalsa unit in France sent Rs. 10 lakh to Punjab.
5. The branch in Germany sent DM 300,000 (Rs. 7 lakh). Later, in 1995, it sent Rs. 2.7 crore for various groups.

These disclosures were made by a militant by the name of Gurwinder Singh who was caught with a consignment of 24 kg of heroin. An ISI agent settled in the US, by the name of John Singh, reportedly corroborated that drug money was being used to finance hardcore Sikh extremists.

JIC said these instances were only illustrative, but they showed that the influx of money and drugs into Punjab was very much on. Large-scale funding of the Khalistani movement had been going on since the early eighties, and the flow still continues. It is only the quantum that may have come down.

Congress Leaders' Complicity

And now a new twist to terrorism in Punjab has been lately added by a book that spills the Congress beans. It is an autobiographical account titled *Bikhra Peinda* ("Lost Path") written in Gurmukhi by an unknown Sikh writer, Sandeep Kaur, widow of slain Babbar Khalsa International terrorist Dharam Singh Kashtiwal. The 500-page book, illustrated with scores of photographs of former terrorists and Khalistan ideologue Bhindranwale, reveals that BKI terrorist Madha Singh used to take refuge in the home of Punjab Congress Committee chief and former Punjab Deputy Chief Minister Rajinder Kaur Bhattal in Sangrur district.

Bhattal naturally rubbished the allegation, but the writer said she stood by every word she wrote. "It is unadulterated truth, " she asserted. In fact it was not only Bhattal, she also referred to the terrorist links of Lakhbir Singh Randhawa, a senior Punjab Congress leader and former Minister. "It is quite well known that he used to give shelter to militants during his election campaign," she says.

The firebrand writer said she was not frightened. She says, "Now I want to tell the world how even the so-called respected leaders across the political spectrum also pander to militants." In fact, unmoved by the controversy generated by her book, she said she is all set to write a sequel revealing the names of all politicians and leaders of Shiromani Gurudwara Prabandhak Committee who not only harboured terrorists but also used their clout to get them released.

7(b)

HIMACHAL PRADESH

New ISI Strategy

ISI-promoted insurgency in Punjab also targeted adjoining Himachal Pradesh. Here the proxy war has been used for instigating communal violence in Himachal as well as contiguous northern states. As early as in 1994 ISI was believed to have planned to push a sizeable number of trained, armed Afghan mercenaries and others belonging to several international fundamentalist groups into Himachal Pradesh with the objective of unleashing widespread communal violence.

According to Indian intelligence this was a strategic move to ease some of the pressure mounted on insurgents in the Kashmir Valley by India's security forces. There was evidence to indicate that Chamba in Himachal Pradesh was one of the strategic sites ISI has decided to infiltrate armed mercenaries into the state so that they could link up with Pak-trained Punjab ultras in a bid to organize large-scale terrorist operations in the region. The arrest of some Kashmir militants in Chamba showed that the new ISI strategy was in operation.

8

KASHMIR
ISI's Killing Field

ISI's role in Kashmir began with the opening of this second anti-India insurgency front in the late 1980s, but the ground for it had been laid long back. The basic plan was already outlined in "Operation Topac", the grand design against India drawn up more than three decades ago, and it was already in action in Punjab.

For Kashmir, however, the objective was much larger, and consequently the subversion plan was substantially extended and made operational on a number of levels. These were: covert action, paramilitary forays, political manipulation, brainwashing campaign, and perverse international action. The plan was pursued on the following lines:

Covert Action

1. Forge ideological and operational alliance of Kashmiri militants and fundamentalist Indian Muslim groups with covert networks in India's interior.
2. Establish intelligence networks in major cities like Udhampur, Jammu etc.
3. Set up high-tech intelligence communication facilities in the region.
4. Cause demoralising among India's security forces through casualties inflicted on them, pressure of human rights groups, and strains and stresses of hazardous antiterrorist duties.

Paramilitary Action

1. Control and direct activities of militant groups with an elaborate communication system mainly controlled from points in PoK, like Muzaffarabad, Kotli, Sialkot etc.
2. Bring hitherto unaffected areas like Jammu into the vortex of militancy.
3. Identify hostile elements like turned spies and former militants, and eliminate them.

Political Action

1. Project a "freedom movement" in Kashmir by orchestrating activities of the terrorists and Pakistan-sponsored politico-religious organisations.
2. Bolster pro-Pakistan support groups, human rights lobbyists and similar elements to promote secession.
3. Float and sustain a conglomerate of political parties subservient to Pakistan and project it as the third party to the Kashmir dispute representing wishes and aspirations of the Kashmiri people.
4. Spread disaffection and cause alienation among Kashmiris using the religious card, alleged atrocities of the security forces, and similar tactics.
5. Create and exploit pro-Pakistan front organisations among religious bodies, students, youths, government servants etc.
6. Organise agitations, Bandhs and similar programmes in Jammu and Kashmir for gaining publicity mileage for secessionism.

Propaganda Action

1. Manipulate the media by building up assets in the local media and bribing them to follow a pro-Pakistan agenda.
2. Use the media for sustained propaganda against India and its security forces, eulogising action of terrorists as freedom fighters, and highlighting activities of overground secessionist bodies.
3. Use terrorists to force unwilling journalists into submission.

International Action

1. Put India in the dock by internationalising the Kashmir issue, project India as violator of UN resolutions, and charge it with a dismal human rights record.
2. Emphasize strategic parity of Pakistan with India as a guarantor of stability in the region.
3. Build and support anti-India lobbies among opinion-makers, think tanks, and leaders of Islamic countries.
4. Emphasize commonality of strategic interests of powers like China and the US with those of Pakistan.
5. Cultivate and exploit foreign political personalities, academics etc. for the international promotion of the secessionist agenda.
6. Organise protests, seminars and similar activities abroad to provide legitimacy to the secessionist policy in the eyes of the world and derive publicity mileage.
7. Use the Pakistani electronic media like Television, Radio, and special broadcasting stations like Sada-e-Hurriyat for influencing the international media to support the Pakistani position on Kashmir.

8. Recruit large numbers of foreign mercenaries as terrorists, and also forge links with international terrorist outfits.
9. Intelligence encirclement of India by establishing covert networks in its neighbouring countries.
10. Use infiltrators from Bangladesh to destabilize the North-East and cause disruption in other areas.

Taliban Model

In the execution of this strategy ISI's own creation Taliban was of immense help. The US report on terrorism prepared during the Nawaz Sharif regime by Youssef Bodansky, known for his research on transborder Islamist terrorism, stated: "The terrorist training system in Afghanistan is fully integrated with the system of *madrasa* in Pakistan," and graduates from here are sent into Kashmir, Central Asian states, and to Xinjiang in China, as Taliban considered the *Ummah* (Islamic community) one united, organic whole. "The importance of Islamist subversion for Islamabad is reflected in the growing numbers of Afghan and Pakistani expert terrorists being infiltrated into Kashmir and Tajikstan," the report said.

The report also anticipated escalation of terrorism, and quoted Brig. (retd.) AR Siddiqi, who wrote in an article about the possibility of the Taliban Jehad becoming a model for extremists in Kashmir sooner or later. It also referred to the statement of the then Afghan envoy at a seminar in Karachi that "Taliban will extend support to Kashmir in Jehad..." Siddiqi wrote that Taliban would not leave their Kashmiri brethren alone, something ex-Pak Army chief Gen. Aslam Beg had also written.

Four Stages

According to a US report of 1993, two factors made Pakistan turn its attention to Kashmir directly. The first was the fairly sudden emergence of Islamic fundamentalism in Kashmir, fomented assiduously by the Jamaat-i-Islami of Pakistan and by its Kashmiri affiliate Jamaat-i-Islami-e-Kashmir. It received an added boost from Iran because the paternal branch of Ayatollah Khomeini lived (and was still living as of 1993) in Kashmir. The second was the completion by ISI, by 1985, of a vast training infrastructure for the Afghan Mujahideen that could just as well be used for training other groups. Therefore, the report went on to say, it was not long before Afghan terrorists trained... by CIA instructors had been smuggled into India with the purpose of organising acts of terror.

The direct recruitment of militants from Kashmir began in 1986, and was controlled from the very start by ISI. The strategy for this involvement was refined in four stages.

The first stage was of low-intensity conflict with the state government between 1987 and 1989. The purpose during this phase was to agitate the local population and build up support for the Islamist militant cause. "By 1990 there were no less than 30 militant organizations in Kashmir, of whom 29 were receiving assistance and shelter in Pakistan," said the US report.

The second phase began in 1989–90. During this period the terrorists sent into Kashmir were much better trained, and had much better arms, such as AK-47s and AK-56s.

The third phase, according to the report, began in autumn 1991, when ISI brokered an alliance between Hizb-ul Mujahideen, Allah Tigers, and Ikhwan-ul-Muslimeen (formerly student wing of Jammu-Kashmir Liberation Front). The weaponry provided to the terrorists improved in this period, and rockets and mines were added. Many of the militant outfits that proliferated in this period had been created by ISI for specialised terrorist operations in Kashmir. These included Allah Tigers and Al-Umar Mujahideen. Hizb-ul Mujahideen also set up clandestine subgroups like Nasir-ul-Islam and Jamiat-ul Mujahideen for "specialised terrorist operations" (in other words, assassinations). It was Jamiat that openly shot dead a well-known Hindu human rights activist in December 1992.

The fourth phase was launched by ISI in the spring of 1992 by infiltrating 500 Afghan Mujahideen into Kashmir. According to a US report journalists visiting the headquarters of the Hizb-ul-Mujahideen in Kashmir saw Afghans, Sudanese and Libyans who were not individual soldiers of fortune but part of an international terrorist network, a wholly new and dangerous force in world politics.

The report also mentioned the role of Jamaat-i-Islami in the escalation of terrorism and quoted its chief Qazi Hussain Ahmed as saying : "Kashmir shall go on bleeding until Kashmiris are given the right to decide their future" – namely, to establish an Islamic state.

Foreign Mercenaries

Thanks to ISI, the role of foreign mercenaries in Pakistan's war in Kashmir has been substantial. Faced with a depletion in the number of local recruits, ISI intensified recruitment of Afghan nationals for continued militancy in Kashmir. About 2000 trained Afghans were reportedly readied for penetration into the Valley. When the UN stopped assistance to Afghan refugees in camps scattered all over Pakistan, ISI tried to tackle the problem of the large number of unemployed Afghan refugees crowding the job market in Pakistan with a two-pronged strategy. One part of it was to arm several thousands of them and send them back to Afghanistan, dubbing them Taliban. The other was to train them for terrorism in Jammu and Kashmir, particularly in the Doda district, to force a Hindu exodus on the lines of the Pandits in the Valley. The strength of this force was estimated at around 10,000.

Earlier in 1992 also ISI had inducted Afghan and Arab guerrillas as well as nationals of other Muslim countries like Bahrein, Egypt and Sudan. ISI equipped them with AK-74 rifles, considered a much deadlier weapon than AK-47 and AK-56. These rifles are manufactured in Pak ordnance factories.

Training Infrastructure

Terrorists assembled from various countries were given training by ISI in a large number of camps. Initially, during the Afghan war and later under the Taliban regime these camps were mostly located in Afghanistan. Since the fall of Taliban from power they have moved largely to PoK, with a fair number on Pakistani soil. As a whole, the size of Pakistan's terrorist training programme was impressive. By late 1990 an estimated 5,000 Kashmiris were trained in Pakistan. The next year the number was around 10,000. That year ISI got so openly involved that it put Brig. Mohammad Salim, an ISI officer, in charg of Kashmir operations. According to a US task force report, there were so many candidates by 1992 that it was decided that these elite recruits had to be trained in new camps that ISI set up for them at Larkana, Sargodha, Murree, Sialkot, Lahore and some other places.

Made in Pakistan

The weapons and explosives used in Kashmir are increasingly identical with those provided to the Afghan Mujahideen by ISI. Pakistan says they are available in the open market in Peshawar, Derra etc. Nevertheless, a US report of 1994 said arms used in Kashmir are more and more of unique types available only from official sources, and in the case of Kashmiri Islamists could not have come from any other source but ISI.

Actually, Indian intelligence had learnt more than a decade ago, in mid-1996, that ISI itself was procuring arms by buying them in NWFP's tribal areas. It had received reports indicating that Pakistan was openly encouraging large-scale illegal manufacture of light weapons in these areas. Their main bulk buyer was ISI. These illegal factories had mushroomed in a big way in half a dozen areas, and specific orders were placed by ISI with the tribal leaders with the intention of pushing these consignments into India.

The scale of this clandestine enterprise can be gauged from the report in July 1996 that in September the previous year (1995) certain Army officers had bought arms worth nearly four million Pakistani Rupees, which they allegedly wanted to use to force an Islamic revolution in Pakistan by assassinating political leaders and army brass.

While the coup was busted, intelligence reports confirmed that most of the weapons bought by the coup leaders finally found their way into Kashmir and Punjab.

The idea behind the large-scale shopping for arms in the tribal areas was that they could be easily smuggled out through Afghan couriers. Moreover, since the manufacturing units had been directed not to emboss identification marks on the weapons their origin could not be traced. These arms were bought with money from smuggling drugs into Europe and the Middle East. This was confirmed by revelations made by scores of captured Pak-trained terrorists.

Actually, there were those in the Pakistan army who looked beyond conventional arms for Kashmir. For instance Brig. Bashir wrote in the Pakistani paper *Nation* in October 1991, "Supporters of the (militant) movement should supply to the terrorists surface-to-air missiles, because such weapons will inevitably raise the cost of war for India."

Government Admission

The end-result was the Government of India's recent admission that cross-border terrorism is spreading and infiltration rampant. The agenda paper for the chief ministers' conclave held in 2006-end confessed that infiltration had trebled in comparison to the same period in the previous year.

That ISI has been arming, training, funding, and logistically supporting militants fighting the Indian security forces in Kashmir has been acknowledged in the West. The British Government had stated that there is a clear link between ISI and three major terrorist outfits. The British newspaper *Guardian* also reported that it had uncovered evidence proving that ISI's Kashmir cell was funding and controlling new terrorist outfits that were being openly raised in Pakistan.

The Americans too have been finding the same situation. A US report during the Nawaz Sharif regime by Youssef Bodansky, known for his studies on transborder Islamic terrorism, said ISI activities in Afghanistan are of growing importance to Pakistan for confronting India with escalation of terrorism and subversion. Another objective was to acquire flow of oil and gas from Central Asia in pursuit of its trans-Asian axis strategy.

The report stressed the crucial importance of Pakistan's long-term plan to build up a highly professional and tightly controlled core of terrorist operatives. To this end ISI allotted specific areas of operation to the Valley's local terrorist factions. The Janbaz Mujahideen was to give training in subversion to Kashmiri militants in PoK and carry out bloody hits. This wing was commanded by Afghans and Sudanese. At the time of the report it was headed by an ISI-trained functionary by the name of Parvez Haider. Then there was the Harkat-ul-Jihad, led by a Pakistan-born Kashmiri named

Shahid Masood. It was made up of former soldiers of Afghan and Libyan armies. The hits they carried out were deadly, effective and incisive. The mercenaries attached to the Harkat-ul-Jihad were experts in weapons and explosives mainly used in the Muslim Middle East terrorism zone.

For all these groups the Kashmir desk of ISI provided the training, supplied the arms, decided the deployment, and organised the logistic support. It was then headed by Brig. Mohammad Salim. Most of the armed terrorist factions operating in the Valley were his creation.

According to a Government of India report of 1992 ISI had also made efforts to float a united front through the JKLF-Tehrik-e-Hurriyat— a conglomerate of militant groups. In addition it tried to set up a United Jehad Council, combining various militant organizations.

ISI even set up a special force disguised in Indian Army uniforms to assist the major operations. Its commander, Col. Farooq, had sent the first such detachment into Kashmir in July 1991. This was disclosd in 1994 by a US House Committee report on Pakistan's export of terrorism.

8(a)

JAMMU
Forcing Hindu Exodus

ISI took Pakistan's proxy war on India from the Kashmir Valley to Jammu more than a decade ago, when, in 1994, it decided to push a sizeable number of trained and armed Afghan mercenaries and others belonging to several international fundamentalist groups into the Doda region of Jammu. As stated earlier, according to Indian intelligence this was a part of the ISI strategy to ease some of the pressure mounted on insurgents in the Valley by India's security forces. There is evidence to show that ISI intended the infiltrators in Jammu to link up with Pak-trained Punjab ultras in a bid to organise communal tensions and terrorist strikes in the whole region. This newly-adopted ISI strategy led to terror acts in Doda, Kishtwar and Bhadervah that spread fear in the Hindu population in these districts.

Hindu Exodus

This was as per plan. For the ISI policy in Jammu was different from its policy in the Kashmir Valley in the sense that while in the Valley the militant groups were prompted to openly demand Kashmir's merger with Pakistan or its independence, in Jammu the aim was to engineer a mass exodus of Hindus so that the demographic balance could tilt against them. The killing of prominent BJP leaders in mid-1994 also created a fear psychosis among Hindus and made them leave their hearths and homes. During the prime ministership of IK Gujral, ISI had even planned mass killings and public hangings of pro-India people at public places to scare Hindus into a forced mass exodus.

Another aspect of ISI's Jammu plan was directing armed secessionist groups to position themselves on the Pir Panjal mountain ranges and conduct operations on the lines of army strategy advance striking group, supply reinforcement core group, and support group to reach the Jammu region. From these locations the militants could pose a serious threat to the highway connecting Jammu and Srinagar.

Political Manipulation

The current situation in the state of Jammu and Kashmir as a whole shows that ISI has taken its Jihad into a broader action plan. This involves supplementing terrorism with activities related to stoking of public dissension against India through demonstrations and protests, infiltration of the police and security forces, and even electoral politics, as well as exploiting surrendered terrorists to foment secession. In order to manipulate the political process various separatist leaders of Jammu and Kashmir have been making the rounds of New Delhi, Islamabad, and even Washington, where they were invited in July 2007.

India, the "Enemy"

However, such politicking has not changed Pakistan's commitment to violence and terror in the state. A few months ago Pakistan's minister for Jammu and Kashmir Affairs Tahir Iqbal said if there was no total pullout of Indian troops from the state, Jehadi groups would get active again (as if they were not already there). Then again, very recently the terrorist organization HuM declared it was not prepared to give up violence till a settlement on Jammu and Kashmir was in sight.

In an interview with Lt. Gen. (retd.) Hamid Gul, former Director General of ISI, the Pakistani journal *Herald* asked him: "Would the army revert to its old position if Musharraf was not present ?" His answer was "Most likely yes. When a soldier joins the army he is taught that India is an enemy and Kashmir is to be liberated. If you have abandoned Kashmir, you might as well abandon the Army". And finally, despite the Kargil fiasco former prime minister Nawaz Sharif had threatened, before he was overthrown by a military coup, that there will be many more Kargils, unless the Kashmir problem is solved.

Hindu Holocaust

To sum up this gory account of Islamist murder and mayhem, leaders of Kashmiri Pandit Sangharsh Samiti stated in April 2008 that the Pandit community had faced as many as six massacres from 1997 to 2003. Media reports in 2007 summarised the atrocities on the Kashmiri Pandits in the following stunning statistics:

- Hindus killed by terrorists : More than 93,000.
- Hindus tortured and murdered : More than 1,100.
- Hindu families whose homes were looted : 95 per cent.
- Hindu families whose homes were set on fire : More than 20,000.
- Hindu families that lost their farms which were their only means of livelihood : 20,000.
- Hindu families that lost their orchards : 12,500.
- Forcibly occupied, looted and torched shops and factories belonging to Hindus : 14,430.
- Forcibly occupied or torched Hindu educational institutions : More than 100.
- Hindu religious and cultural institutions burnt down : More than 100.

This Hindu holocaust is by no means at an end. Rather, a conglomeration of terrorists has openly declared that Jihad will continue. Pakistan-based terrorist groups and secessionist leaders in Pakistan-occupied Kashmir recently came together in a conference in Muzaffarabad in PoK to reaffirm their commitment to the revival of Jihad in Kashmir. The conference was attended by United Jihad Council chief Syed Salahuddin, Lashkar-e-Toiba chief Zaki-ur Rehman, and leaders of terrorist factions based in PoK. The conference, titled Azam-i-Jihad (Resolve for Jihad) was attended by about 1,000 militants. It called upon the PoK Government to set aside 75 per cent of its budget for Jihad in Kashmir and train its youth on a war footing for the purpose. Terrorist leaders attending the conference included Sheikh Jamil-ur Rehman of Tehrik-ul Mujahideen, Abdullah of Jamiat-ul Mujahideen, Attiq-ur Rehman of Harkat-ul Mujahideen, Farooq Qureshi of Al-Badr, Mastoid Surfraz of Hizb-e-Islami, Uzair Ghizali of Pasban-i-Hurriyat, and Ghulam Mohammad Safi, convenor of Tehreek Kashmir.

Even now Salahuddin has threatened Jihad in Islamabad and Lahore in case the new Pakistan government dragged its feet on Kashmir. "Pakistan government has become pro-India. And this has relegated the struggle for Azadi in Kashmir to the background", he charged at a press conference at Sialkot in Pakistan. "If this policy continues, we would be forced to wage war in Lahore and Islamabad," he warned. He asserted that militants would ensure that the armed campaign in Kashmir continues.

Actually, it is going to be continued even by the Pakistan army itself. For although Army spokesman and the new Army chief's trusted aide Maj. Gen. Athar Abbas declared in May 2008 that the "Army was an apolitical force and Gen. Kayani had decided that it would remain within the constitutional boundaries," he also made it clear that "the Army would live up to the expectations of the nation ... after all, the nation has an aspiration on Kashmir, and the military would play a role to fulfil it ..." The meaning of these words should be clear to all those who were aware of the fact that Kayani had directed terrorist violence in Kashmir for more than a decade.

What the generals are saying, the politicians are repeating. To quote columnist Raja Mohan, "The new dispensation in Islamabad has returned to the bad old habit of projecting to its domestic audiences that Kashmir is at the centre of Pakistan's diplomatic engagement with the rest of the world." The new Kashmir Affairs minister has said Kashmir was a basic issue which cannot be set aside. In his first speech as Prime Minister, Gillani also declared, "I want to assure our Kashmiri brothers and sisters that their sacrifices will not go waste." And President Zardari had to promptly eat his words when he said those active in Kashmir were terrorists instead of freedom fighters. The grim truth behind all such talk was summed up by *Organiser* columnist Nalapat in one sentence : "Kashmir today is where it was in 1988 – on the cusp of a Jihad." Around that time the then Prime Minister Nawaz Sharif had said let Kashmir become part of Pakistan and thanksgiving prayer will be offered in the mosque of Srinagar. This ambition has not changed.

Against this bleak background it is apparently time to recall that pithy phrase of Atal Behari Vajpayee — "the human rights of inhuman terrorists". For the UPA dispensation is reported to have decided to provide a relief package to the dependents of terrorists killed by security forces in encounters in Jammu and Kashmir.

The extent of the murder and mayhem caused by these terrorists, whose families are now sought to be rewarded, can be gauged from the souvenir published by the J-K police in 2003. It says there were 56,041 incidents of violence, including 10,093 explosions, 29,931 firing incidents, 5,561 cases of arson, 763 rocket attacks, 4,597 abductions, 229 cases of hanging to death, 275 arms snatching cases, and 4,592 other acts of violence from January 1990 till December 2002.

And this unending proxy war on India has been in a way aided by the successive governments of India. For "Kashmir was given Rs. 125000 crore in the last 60 years, but much of it fell into the hands of extremists who hold most of the key government positions," says VHP leader Anandshankar Pandya.

9

NORTH-EAST
Towards Another Kashmir

The tentacles of ISI reached North-East India around 1990. After the encouraging results of its proxy war in K-1 (Punjab) and K-2 (Kashmir), K-3 (North-East) appeared a suitable region for opening a third front of the war theatre. Its choice in this respect was also helped by the fact that there were already militant groups in the area which could together launch a full-scale anti-India insurgency if adequately aided and abetted. The major ones among them are :

United Liberation Front of Assam (ULFA)

ISI established initial contacts with ULFA through the Punjab secessionists who were already under its management. During December 1990 and January 1991 an important ULFA activist by the name of Munim Nabish (later appointed resident agent in Bangladesh) went to Islamabad, the capital of Pakistan, and Karachi, and met an ISI officer just called Chaudhary (the same secret name ISI officials had adopted while keeping in touch with Pakistan-based Punjab terrorists, as noted earlier). At this meeting arrangements were finalized for senior ULFA leaders to visit Pakistan. When arrested and interrogated by the Assam police Nabish admitted his visits to Pakistan. The ULFA top brass — chairman Arbindo Rajkhowa, vice-chairman Pradeep Gogoi, general secretary Golap Barua and C-in-C Paresh Barua, also went to Islamabad with Nabish and visited the Afghan border during March–April 1991. Here they met Afghan warlord Gulbuddin Hekmatyar, who promised to supply arms to ULFA. Rajkhowa's diary and other seized documents confirmed this visit.

The most notorious among the ULFA terrorists is Paresh Barua, who has a host of crimes in his name, including multiple murders and dacoities. Currently holed up in Bangladesh, he has close links with ISI, which gives him all help. (In fact senior Indian Army officer Lt. Gen. RK Chhabra says ULFA terrorists sheltered in Bangladesh work under ISI.)

The first batch of ULFA militants went to Pakistan in June 1991 to attend a two-week course in the use of mortars. Since then a number of batches have received arms training in Pakistan. This was revealed in the interrogation reports of captured/surrendered cadres like Sujit Das, Binod Das, Pranab Barua, and Abdul Hamid. A certain Col. Farooq of the Freedom Party, an anti-India group, acted as the conduit between ULFA and ISI. The Bangladesh authorities colluded with providing fake passports to ULFA cadres.

In August 1991 ULFA paid four lakh US dollars to Col. Farooq for procuring sophisticated arms from Pakistan. This was revealed in the interrogation report of Kamakhya Prasad Rana alias Abdul Karim, who was arrested on the Indo-Bangla border in September 1992.

In 1992, in the face of a strong Indian offensive, ISI put pressure on Paresh Barua, Arbindo Rajkhowa and others not to surrender to the Indian authorities. In February of the same year Robin Handiqe, a senior ULFA leader, went to Nepal and met Pervez Afzal, a counsellor in the Pakistan embassy in Kathmandu. Afzal told Handiqe that ISI would provide arms to ULFA through Punjab terrorists.

Again the same month, February 1992, a meeting of ULFA's General Council was informed that as a condition for help ISI had instructed the outfit to sabotage oil refineries, railways, and other vital Indian installations. In October 1993 Col. Sajjid of ISI met ULFA vice-chairman Pradeep Gogoi at a hotel in Chittagong. Later, the two visited a new ISI training camp in the Chakma area. At these and many other meetings with different ULFA leaders ISI promised to supply arms and communication equipment to the outfit on condition that ULFA promised to protect and side with Muslims in the event of communal riots, attacked Indian security forces, and agreed to hijack a plane to gain publicity.

ULFA shifted its training centre from Myanmar to Bangladesh in 1989–90, as the terrain and trekking routes to Bangladesh were comapratively easier. ULFA set up camps at a number of locations in Bangladesh like Adampur, Anamtilla, Chotadamari etc. where hundreds of cadres were trained. Soon after setting up these camps its leaders came into contact with fundamentalist Islamic groups in Bangladesh and began collaboration with them. The currently close connection between ULFA and Bangladesh is also indicated in the report that ULFA is said to have kept Rs. 200 crore in banks in Bangladesh.

An ominous update on the ULFA threat in the North-East was the arrest in Guwahati in February 2007 of a cadre trained in how to hijack a plane. In his interrogation the hard core militant told the police that an Afghan-trained ULFA leader had recently trained a team of 16 cadres near the Indo-Bhutan border on the basics of hijacking an aircraft. The plan was to hijack a plane from one of the several airports in the North-East and take it to Bangladesh or Nepal and then onwards to Afghanistan or Pakistan to pressurise the Government of India to release some senior ULFA leaders currently in jail.

Clearly, ULFA's involvement with fundamentalist Islamic terrorism is getting deeper by the day. While its collaboration with Pakistan's LeT and Bangladesh's HUJI in Assam's serial bombing in October 2008 was pointed out by an intercept, earlier intercepts have confirmed the presence of ULFA cadres in training camps near Muzaffarabad in PoK. A batch of ULFA cadres was also given advanced training in HUJI camps in Bangladesh in April 2008. ULFA funds come largely from drug-trafficking, smuggling heroin grown in Myanmar. It also owns a number of businesses in Bangladesh. In particular, it has come to light that ULFA has a substantial financial stake in the Bangladeshi media in the form of the *Daily Star* newspaper owned by Transcom Media, a leading media group of Dhaka. *Assam Tribune* reported on July 30, 2008 that ULFA's business interest in Bangladesh was no secret, but what had come as a surprise is the revelation about its stakes in a leading media house in the neighbouring country.

"Even as Indian security agencies kept up pressure on Dhaka to shut down enterprises run by ULFA, the militant outfit has quietly expanded its business portfolio in the country. New Delhi had, a couple of years ago, furnished a list of businesses suspected to be owned by ULFA, along with a series of account numbers. Dhaka told India that none of the business entities could be traced. ULFA's business interests were diverse, ranging from driving schools, nursing homes, hotels to garment export houses to deepsea trawlers," the Assam daily reported.

National Socialist Council of Nagaland (NSCN)

NSCN grew out of a secessionist body called Naga National Council (NNC) set up by London-based separatist AZ Phizo. When, during repeated rounds of talks in 1965, Prime Minister Indira Gandhi offered the Nagas everything except sovereignty, the NNC leaders refused the offer and formed a separate guerrilla organization, National Socialist Council of Nagaland, in 1980. As the epithet `Socialist' shows, the outfit was formed under deep Chinese communist influence. Since then the Communist agenda has been marginalised and replaced by the Islamic agenda promoted in the ISI-Bangladesh nexus.

NSCN was given help by ISI through official Bangladesh agencies like Directorate General of Forces Intelligence (DGFI) as well as anti-India groups like JeT and Freedom Party. In April 1990 its chairman Isaac Swu visited Pakistan to procure arms for his organization. He was contacted by ISI through the Freedom Party and travelled on a Bangladesh passport. In January 1991, NSCN's finance secretary Khayao Hurey was arrested by the Indian security forces. He revealed during his interrogation that his organization had received one million Takas (Bangladeshi Rupees) from the High Commission of Pakistan in

Bangladesh. Documents seized from Kamakhya Prasad Rana alias Abdul Karim, mentioned earlier, also revealed that both NSCN and ULFA were getting guns from ISI, which were smuggled across the Thai-Cambodian border. According to Indian intelligence, Pakistani embassy officials in Thailand are helping NSCN and other North-Eastern insurgent groups to procure arms.

Another intelligence report said Swu and Muivah, chairman and general secretary of NSCN, met ISI official Sajjad Ali at the liaison office of the insurgent outfit in Bangkok in February 1994. In this meeting NSCN agreed to impart training to activists of Islamic Sevak Sangh (ISS) at NSCN camps in North Cachar Hills of Assam and Garo Hills of Meghalaya.

People's Liberation Army (PLA)

ISI's nexus with PLA, yet another North-East terrorist outfit, came to light when a document seized in January 1991 from one Biren Singh alias German, finance secretory of PLA's armed wing Revolutionary People's Front (RPF), exposed the link. Later, two ISI operatives Nasiruddin alias Mahiruddin alias Dilip and Yusuf Khan alias Pradeep, came to Imphal from Bangladesh with a group of PLA activists in February 1994. Both ISI men were of the rank of Junior Commissioned Officer.

According to a US Congressional report of February 1993, the seized documents of the Manipur-based PLA stated that Pakistan was willing to extend all help to it, which would be channelled via Myanmar. Although PLA had also established contacts with the governments of Bangladesh and Myanmar, the Pak response was the most important for them, said the report. Bhorot Singh, leader of RPF, had developed contacts with Pakistani officials in Bangladesh in the late 1990s and asked for help for a full-scale war against the Indian Government, in response to which PLA was given various types of arms, the report added.

United Islamic Liberation Army (UILA)

According to the US report the telling impact of ISI-aided terrorism in North-East India was the emergence in 1992 of this Islamic Army as the dominant subversive organisation in the region, especially in Manipur. By the time the report was released, a year later ISI had not only initiated but extended its operations in this state.

Tripura's Terrorist-friendly Minister

Tripua has a terroist outfit called All Tripura Tribal Force, which is aided by ISI and HUJI. How deeply Islamic terrorism has penetrated here came to light when Tripura state government's food minister and Marxist leader Shahid Choudhary had to resign following an inquiry into his link with HUJI terrorist Mamun. Several ministers in the North-East have been accused in the past of helping insurgent groups with funds and vehicles as well as providing them shelter in official quarters, but Chaudhary is the first to have an inquiry instituted against him.

The charges against the Marxist minister are : He had liaison with Mamun, he rented a home for him in Agartala, he helped him get a Permanent Resident Certificate and passport, and he visited Mamun's rented shelter place several times with his wife. Chaudhary is the only Muslim minister.

Mamun was arrested on March 27, 2008 at Agartala by the West Bengal CID following the arrest of two Bangladeshis carrying arms, explosives as well as documents giving details of Army bases in North Bengal. He is suspected of involvement in a fake currency racket across the North-East. "He is believed to have circulated fake currency worth Rs. 200 crore in the past few years," an official source said.

Within three months of Mamun's arrest another Bangladeshi ISI agent by the name of Sagam Ali was arrested after long surveillance. His belongings included SIM cards of Gramin Phone Company of Bangladesh, Airtel, Aircel and Reliance, all active, a passport and an identity card containing differing biodata, and a document sent from Karachi. The identity card was issued by a fundamentalist Islamic body of Bangladesh called Hazrat Shah Sultan Giasuddin Aulia, widely known as HAJO.

Seven Sisters

The secessionist-terrorist groups operating all over the North-East came to be collectively known as the United Liberation Front of Seven Sisters (ULFOSS)—the Seven Sisters being the North-East states of Assam, Arunachal Pradesh, Meghalaya, Manipur, Mizoram, Nagaland and Tripura.

ISI Coordination

For all these underground outfits the coordinator was ISI, and its instrument of coordination was ULFOSS. In December 1993 Lt. Gen. Malik, the then GoC-in-C, 3 Corps, admitted to newsmen visiting Kohima that this terror union, although not yet very strong, was expanding all over the Seven Sisters region with the help of ISI and patronage of Bangladesh.

A US administration report of early 1994 also dwelt at length on how ISI had spread its tentacles in the North-East. In a severe indictment of Pakistan for exporting Islamic terrorism, the report of the US House of Representatives, prepared after years of research and analysis, said seized documents of PLA revealed the close liaison between it and ISI, whose help had enabled the terrorist outfit to acquire advanced weapons like AK-47 automatic assault rifles and rocket-propelled grenades (RPGs).

Real Agenda

ISI even went to the extent of actively recruiting potential terrorists in the region and taking them to its training camps. Actually this enthusiasm reflected not ISI's willingness to train North-East terrorists to further their cause, but to serve its own Islamic agenda. The Americans realised this, because the US report added that ISI's covert action fostered the growth of Islamic militancy among the general population of the whole region. This was confirmed by the case of Assam. In February 1994 the Assam police unearthed the existence of a Pakistan-sponsored fundamentalist Islamic rebel group called the Social Reform Army ofAssam with its base at a place called Mankachar on the Indo-Bangla border. It was then found that at that time there were as many as 15 Muslim bodies in the state engaged in spreading fundamentalism among immigrants.

The defence ministry reported that ULFA had started recruiting Muslims in their ranks. It even circulated in 1993 a document describing East Bengal settlers in Assam as an integral part of the Assamese society. In January 1994, the home minister also expressed concern at ISI's growing involvement with North-East extremists by helping them with arms and funds and running training camps for them in Bangladesh. Clearly ISI had infiltrated into all militant groups in the region, especially ULFA, in a big way. This took place when these groups shifted base from Myanmar to Bangladesh. ULFA was the first to do so.

Detailed evidence of these nefarious activities of ISI is also recorded in a 1994 book titled *Insurgency Movement in North-East India* by Phanjoubam Tarapot, a journalist in Manipur. It lists a number of instances of the nexus between ISI and extremists. The book said Irenghan Bhorot, chief of RPF, PLA's armed wing, was in direct contact with the Pakistan Army.

Outside the North-East but just across the border in Bangladesh ISI had found another instrument for its Islamic agenda in the form of the Jamiat-e-Islami organisation. Its training camps for fresh recruits from Assam and elsewhere in the region were in the guise of Jamiat-e-Islami Chhatra Shibir, said a top Border Security Force (BSF) official in August 1994. He also revealed that an outfit called Muslim Volunteer Force had cropped up in Muslim-dominated areas to collect recruits for ISI. BSF had intercepted some correspondence of this Force asking fundamentalist organisations in the state to send at least 10 boys each to these camps.

Disintegration Plan

All in all, for more than a decade ISI has been actively exploiting the ethnic and regional susceptibilities of Indians of the North-East for promoting sedition. And clearly there is an Islamic agenda driving this exploitation, for Muslim organisations have mushroomed like barber shops in the North-East, thanks to ISI.

The Bangladesh government agency DGFI is working in tandem with ISI on the North-Eastern front of its proxy war on India. In 2006 Col. Farooq Rehman of the Freedom Party, an insurgent outfit, openly claimed that his party, in association with J-e-I, had been working with DGFI Maj. Gen. Mohammad Nasim to chalk out and implement a plan, with ISI's help, to disintegrate North-East India.

The anti-India collaboration between the governments of Pakistan and Bangladesh is underlined by the fact that nearly three-fourths of the staff in the Pakistan High Commission in Bangladesh consists of intelligence officers. There are also reports of Pakistan army officers supervising the training of North-East issurgents based in Bangladesh.

Bad to Worse

This whole terror-situation in the North-East is currently going from bad to worse, with more and more ISI-sponsored outfits coming up. Media reports from Silchar in March 2006 said the Subsidiary Intelligence Bureau (SIB) and the intelligence wings of the army and paramilitary forces had all alerted the border states about the ever-expanding ISI network, now aided and abetted by al-Qaeda. The same year the Assam police arrested a hard-core Jehadi by the name of Alam from a hideout in the State capital of Guwahati itself, and identified him as a kingpin of ISI activities in the North-East. Around the same time came the startling revelation in the book *Fulcrum of Evil* by MK Dhar, former Joint Director of Intelligence Bureau, about the close proximity of the chief minister of a Northern state with ISI.

Security Board Alarm

To add to the seriousness of the situation, the latest report of the Social Security Board to the home ministry sounded an alarm over the rise of various groups like Muslim Youth Organization, Muslim Ittehad Sangh, and Islamic Sangh, which are working as ISI stooges in East and North-East India along the West Bengal-Bihar-Nepal border.

The Board report said financial assistance for these bodies came from the Habib Bank of Pakistan and the Islamic Development Bank of Jeddah in Saudi Arabia. It also pointed out the mushrooming of mosques and *Madrasas* in the border areas, and identified more than 70 of them as having links with anti-India elements.

Migrant Target

A new addition to the dangerous developments in the region, especially in parts of Assam, was made in November 2006 when Lt. Gen. RK Chhabra, GOC of the Tezpur-based 4 Corps, revealed that ISI and DGFI of Bangladesh had both targetted the migrant population of Assam's 'char' (riverine) areas. He said they had been carrying out large-scale recruitment of youths in these areas — that are difficult to administer — and have given them training in arms.

"Their number was increasing day by day. They were into all kinds of things—drug trafficking, fake currency, gun-running and so on. They were going to Bangladesh, taking training there, and coming back to Assam again. They were there as sleeper agents, and would carry out violent and subversive activities whenever ISI wanted them to do so," the GOC said.

Inner Line Permits

No less serious is the situation in Meghalaya. The North-East Students' Organization (NESO) has expressed deep concern at ISI-al-Qaeda - sponsored fundamentalist bodies becoming stronger by the day, while its constituent Khasi Students' Union (KSU) demanded introduction of Inner Line Permits to curb massive influx of anti-national elements into the state. More specifically, Intelligence inputs warned of possible terror-strikes by Jamaat-ul Mujahideen and Harkat-ul-Jehadi Islami terrorists of Bangladesh.

To add an ominous footnote to the terror situation in the region, a recent report in *Jane's Intelligence Review* says China is emerging as the main source of arms to terrorists in North-East India. In fact most arms supplies for them are from China, says the report. The United Wa State Army (UWSA), a rebel outfit in Myanmar, acts as the middleman between Chinese arms manufacturers and North-East terrorist groups.

In 2001, Myanmar intercepted a consignment of several hundred Chinese assault rifles that UWSA was transporting to Manipur for Indian terror outfits. While the trend had been growing over the past some years, it was in 2004, when a massive arms consignment was seized in Chittagong, Bangladesh, that the black market was exposed for the first time. Over 1700 assault rifles, 400 Uzi submachine guns, 150 rocket-propelled grenades and a large quantity of ammunition originating in Hong Kong were seized. It came to light that these weapons were meant for North-East insurgent groups.

Bleak Future

Finally, ISI's active help in coordinating insurgent groups in the North-East of India and providing sophisticated weapons as well as training for their cadres has now progressed beyond just coordination and apparently aims at their integration, according to recent information. Media reports, from Shillong in November 2007, quoted BSF IG Jai Prakash Sinha as saying that ISI is integrating all North-East-based terrorist organisations under one umbrella, assuring them of logistics and other support. "At a meeting held in a Bangladesh border town three months ago, the ISI put into action its plan to destabilise the region," the IG said, adding that the meeting was attended by key personalities of the banned ULFA as well as militants from Nagaland and Manipur.

The meeting was hosted by Bangladesh's intelligence agency Directorate General of Forces Intelligence (DGFI), members from al-Qaeda and the Islamic fundamentalist organisation Jamaat-e-Islami. ISI promised all support, but stressed that North-East-based militant organisations must come under one umbrella to facilitate coordination and action, the IG said.

Sinha said it has also been learnt that ULFA was trying to forge a link with the Nepal Maoists to use Nepal as a buffer zone. "Over the years, the DGFI has been very active in the region, trying to recruit Muslim youths who can be trained in subversive activities in Bangladesh and pumped back to the region to carry out violence."

Sinha revealed that 44 youths belonging to the Muslim United Liberation Tigers of Assam (MULTA) recently went to Bangladesh for training in arms and explosives. These youths had re-entered the region to carry out subversive activities. MULTA was one of the 14 Islamic terrorist outfits operating in Assam.

Obviously the ISI plan will be tremendously facilitated by India's highly porous border with Bangladesh and the unprecedented infiltration of Bangladeshis all over this region. All in all the situation is serious enough for Col. Shyam Kumar (retd.) to observe in his book *The Nefarious Activities of Pakistan's ISI*: "These factors have made available to the ISI a situation on the platter that has the biggest potential of serving the nefarious Pakistani plans of disintegrating India. Unfortunately, the Indian decision-makers, including the politicians, have so far failed to see the writing on the wall. If the North-Eastern situations were to be allowed to deteriorate like this, by the next six or seven years Pakistan would find itself on the verge of achieving in the North-East what it failed to achieve in Punjab and Kashmir."

That this could happen sooner than later was shown by the latest carnage in Assam, when, on October 30, 2008, nine synchronised bomb blasts took place within seven minutes in four cities of the state, including Guwahati, leaving 77 dead and 300 wounded. An intercept by security agencies of a conversation between Muzaffarabad in PoK and operatives in Bangladesh clearly suggested that this was a joint operation by LeT and HUJI in which ULFA was also actively involved.

Every well-informed observer of the situation in Assam knows that the principal cause of the violence that has traumatised this state is the massive influx of illegal migrants from Bangladesh. The prolonged agitation of the Assamese people against this threat culminated in the Assam Accord of 1985. The Rajiv Gandhi Government enacted the Illegal Migrants (Determination through Tribunal) Act. But the IMDT Act was a cure worse than the disease. Far from checking the infiltration of Bangladeshis, it further gave a boost to it. This happened bacause the Rajiv Gandhi Government had deliberately introduced certain flaws into the Act, which neither the Congress nor any of the political parties were subsequently willing to remove. After another prolonged legal battle by anti-foreigner forces in Assam, the Supreme Court, in its July 2005 verdict, struck down IMDT Act as unconstitutional and urged the Central Government to take effective steps to stop the influx of Bangladeshis. Indeed, the Supreme Court warned that large-scale infiltration from Bangladesh constituted external aggression against Assam. The Guwahati High Court's warning was no less dire. It observed once that "illegal Bangladeshi immigrants are slowly becoming the kingmakers in Assam and will reduce indigenous Assamese to a minority..."

There are numerous other instances of warnings sounded by people in authority. For example, in 1996, TV Rajeshwar, a former Director of IB and the then Governor of Uttar Pradesh, had warned, through a series of newspaper articles, that unchecked illegal immigration from Bangladesh into Assam and other border states in the North-East "could some day lead to a third division of India." When he was Governor of Assam, Gen. (retd) SK Sinha had also cautioned about grave consequences for India if the problem of Bangladeshi infiltration is not tackled firmly.

How has the UPA Government reacted to these warnings? By doing nothing. Prime Minister Manmohan Singh has been a Rajya Sabha member from Assam for the past 18 years. Has he ever spoken, either as PM or as MP, about the threat posed by infiltrators from Bangladesh who have changed the demography of several districts of Assam completely?

In fact, he did something to the contrary. On July 15, 2004, Sriprakash Jaiswal, minister of state for home affairs in the UPA Government, said in the Rajya Sabha that 1,20,53,950 illegal Bangladeshi migrants were residing in 17 states and Union territories as on 31 December 2001. He also said that 50 lakh Bangladeshis were living in Assam. Dr. Singh happened to visit Guwahati the following day. He was confronted by the state's Congress Chief Minister Tarun Gogoi and his other party colleagues who were concerned that Jaiswal's reply in Parliament could affect the Congress party's prospects in the 2006 Vidhan Sabha elections in Assam. They put pressure on the Prime Minister that the official statement be retracted. Dr. Singh succumbed to pressure and publicly stated that he doubted the authenticity of the information provided by his own junior minister. A week later, Jaiswal told Parliament that the information that he had provided about Bangladeshi infiltrators was unreliable and based on hearsay !

VHP Vice-President Anandshankar Pandya has put the figure of Bangladeshi immigrants at three crore, and according to former BJP President Rajnath Singh, these infiltrators form the backbone of sleeper terrorist cells in India.

9(a)

WEST BENGAL

ISI's Transit Point

When Assam and the North-East of India are so highly infested with ISI agents it is no wonder West Bengal has not escaped its pernicious presence. In fact, Kolkata, the state capital, has become the epicentre of ISI network in North-East, said a report in March 2006. It said the city has become a shelter for North-East terrorists.

Records of the West Bengal and Kolkata city police show the arrest that year of Maulana Ghulam Yahya Allah Baksh, an Imam of Mumbai's Haj House and linkman of al-Qaeda, who hailed from the 24 Parganas district. The Imam provided cover to Kashmiri terrorists and their arms and ammunition. Then there was Mohammad Mohsin Husain Sayeed, arrested in Kolkata. He was found passing on to ISI information on the movements of the Indian Army in the North-East. He had made several trips to the North-East states and briefed ISI through e-mail. An ATM card of a bank in Lahore was also recovered from his possession. Further, a Pakistani by the name of Walker and another Muslim named Inamul Haque, who were arrested in Howrah, turned out to be ISI agents. Inamul was caught while on his way to Bangladesh to hand over documents and maps of Indian defence interest to a contact there. Walker, who was from Multan, passed on similar information to a Pakistani army officer by e-mail and on the phone. Besides these, two terrorists linked to Jaish-e-Mohammad (JeM), Baqi and Abu, were hunted down and captured at Bashirhat in north Bengal.

Much earlier, the arrest of two Muslims from Kashmir had revealed that Muslim youths from Kolkata, Bhagalpur and Hyderabad were sent by ISI to Pakistan for arms training through an agent based in Kolkata. This agent, Shafaqat Ali Siddiqi, used to smuggle them *via* Bangladesh and was paid by Pakistan for the job. These instances show that Kolkata had become a safe haven and transit point for terrorists and ISI operatives.

To show how really safe, a funny footnote : Wanted on charges of terrorism, murder and extortion Bangladeshi gangster Fateh Ali *alias* Subrata Bayen lived comfortably as Chief Minister Buddhadeb Bhattacharjee's neighbour in a posh area of the state's capital for more than a year until he was arrested in October 2008.

9(b)

BIHAR

ISI's Recruiting Area

Adjacent to West Bengal, Bihar has also been an area of growing activity for ISI for a long time. This came to light when two Muslims arrested in May 1994 in Bhagalpur confessed that they belonged to the ISI-sponsored Pakistani terrorist outfit Ikhwan-ul-Muslamin. They also confessed that they had received training in Pakistan the previous year (1993).

Another captured terrorist by the name of Salauddin described how an ISI agent in Kashmir had brainwashed him and some others, all from Bhagalpur, to form a group. They were taken to Bangladesh, from where they were sent to Karachi. From there they were taken to an unknown hilly destination where they were trained in handling AK-47s, rocket-launchers and hand-grenades as well as explosive-making by a Pakistan Army man. After the training they were taken to Islamabad, where, on filling some form, they were told that they had become members of Ikhwan-ul-Muslamin.

10

UTTAR PRADESH

Ten Thousand ISI Agents

A development in the ISI-guided Khalistani movement in Punjab was that when things became too hot in Punjab ISI engaged in 1994 in regrouping Punjab terrorists in Uttar Pradesh in the Terai region. A news-story in *Organiser* in March 1994, titled *ISI Network in Uttar Pradesh*, said that terrorist Jarnail Singh of Punjab and a mysterious, Rishikesh-based woman, so-called sister of an area commander of Khalistan Liberation Force (KLF), were organising operations for ISI in Terai.

According to reliable sources Ghulam Rasool, Abdul Karim and Dr. Jalis Ansari, all ISI operatives in India for five years during the 1990s and major accused in more than 200 bomb blast and murder cases all over the country, were close to this woman. Abdul Karim was a resident of Pilkhua, UP, and the state police had declared an award of Rs. 50,000 for information leading to his capture. He had escaped from jail four times, reportedly with the help of a Janata Dal legislator whose patronage he enjoyed. The police had also declared an award of Rs. 2 lakh for Ghulam Rasool.

The dense Terai forest offers a safe haven to terrorists in UP. After the flushing-out operations in Punjab a number of the terrorists there shifted to Terai, where they quietly resumed their activities. Since then the major thrust of ISI has been in Terai, where, according to Intelligence sources, there are currently 400 active and 10,000 sleeping agents of ISI.

At the same time ISI tentacles are spreading all over UP, mainly in the districts of Kanpur, Aligarh, Varanasi, Allahabad, Mau, Moradabad, Meerut, Pithaurgarh, Pilibhit, Lakimpur Khiri, Gorakhpur, Basti, Haridwar, Dehradun and Saharanpur. As many as 40 out of 65 districts in UP had become ISI-sensitive more than a decade ago, while ISI had built up a solid base in 8-9 of them.

Some Kashmiri Muslims living in different parts of Saharanpur district were also reportedly involved in ISI activities, for which ISI paid them generously. With the help of some Muslim leaders in the district, ISI activists helped the Kashmiri Muslims obtain ration cards and get their names registered in voters' lists. Bangladeshi infiltrators were also involved in some major clandestine activities in the state.

Further, a students' organization having a base in almost 80 per cent of colleges in the state was also used by ISI. According to intelligence reports some educational institutions near the Nepal border were used in a big way for training terrorists. Former chief minister Kalyan Singh had asserted as far back as in 1994 that even the state capital of Lucknow had an established ISI centre.

The same year substantial activity in the hilly Uttarakhand region of UP was also indicated by the presence of heavily armed men in the jungles of Kumaon. In fact, Kumaon had become an ISI centre, according to an extensive report in the Hindi journal *Panchjanya*. ISI infiltration into Uttarakhand was also confirmed by central intelligence agencies.

Currently too ISI has been found to have active and expanding plans in UP. For instance, in September 2007 the Jammu and Kashmir police had alerted their UP counterparts about ISI affiliate Lashkar-e-Toiba's recruitment drive in the state for escalating violence in the Valley.

An LeT cadre by the name of Mohammad Sadiq, arrested in the Udhampur area, confessed he had gone to join the Deoband institution in 2004 after passing his higher secondary school exams, where he stayed for two years and was persuaded by a duo of the Deobandi inmates to join LeT.

Then in December the UP Task Force arrested two suspects in Barabanki in connection with the serial bomb blasts at Varanasi in March 2006. They were found carrying RDX and SIM cards. According to the STF the bomb blasts were the work of the Bangladeshi terrorist organization HUJI.

Two terrorists hailing from eastern UP were involved in the serial blasts in Gorakhpur in May 2007, but Saba, the HUJI mastermind behind them, was absconding. The two arrested in Barabanki were Kashmiri and Mujahid, of whom Mujahid was a *Madrasa* teacher from Jaunpur district and Kashmiri a Unani doctor in Azamgarh district. It was Kashmiri who had directed HUJI's UP unit to carry out the Gorakhpur blasts. The explosives were brought from Bangladesh and local links were used to procure bicycles to carry them to the blast sites. Six more terrorists were involved in the whole plot, but their identity is not known. Later, Saba was tracked down in Jammu and gunned down in an encounter with security forces in the Kishtwar district. He was also believed to have been involved in the train blasts in Hyderabad.

Meanwhile the Jammu and Kashmir police arrested one Sajjad, suspected of involvement in the bomb-blasts in UP. He was a Maulavi and owed allegiance to HUJI. Security agencies were also investigating the role of Tuffail Hussaini, considered the mastemind of the train blasts in Mumbai, in connection with the UP blasts as well. He is believed to be the head of a HUJI front called Mujahideen Islam ul-Hind. Tuffail was also suspected to be connected with the serial bomb blasts in Delhi in 2005 and the Gorakhpur blasts in 2007.

The UP Special Task Force also gunned down two suspected LeT members in an encounter in December 2009. Apart from bombs and other weapons they had a map in Urdu showing the area around the chief minister's residence. During the encounter they raised the slogan "Lashkar-e-Toiba Zindabad!"

That there are definite linkages between various Pakistani terror groups active in different parts of India was underlined by the fact that Sabauddin, terrorist-suspect arrested in connection with the Bangalore Institute of Science attack, was also involved with terrorists operating in UP. In fact, he was arrested in Lucknow on his associate Nasir revealing to the police in Bangalore that one of the persons who had helped kingpin Hamza to carry out the Institute attack was holed up in UP.

Actually it was in connection with the attack on the Rampur CRPF camp that Sabauddin was arrested by the STF. For this attack Sabauddin was asked to handle one Mohammad Sharif, who had already been sent money by LeT. Sharif hailed from Rampur district. He had earlier been contacted by LeT commander Abdul Aziz in Dhaka, in 2006. The commander asked him to report to Sabauddin, and together they planned to target a military convoy on the Moradabad-Bareilly road. However, as the spot of the attack was too far from their hideout in Rampur town Sabauddin got approval for the plan to attack the CRPF camp.

During his interrogation by the police, Sabauddin said he was inspired by a Dr. Salar to join LeT. This Salar was killed in an encounter with the STF the morning after the blasts in Varanasi in March 2006. Sabauddin described him as the Pakistani doctor. Sabauddin was a student in Aligarh, where LeT contacted him and arranged his meeting with Salar. Salar motivated him and sent him to Pakistan.

The Varanasi blasts investigation highlighted the failure of the government to tackle HUJI, the prime suspect, said *Indian Express*. The Varanasi attack is perhaps the only one in the past few years where the alleged bombers were identified. New Delhi even sent the names of the Bangladeshis with their native towns and mobile phone numbers to Dhaka, but to no avail. The bombers had earlier studied in Deoband. The police arrested Waliullah, a Mullah from Phoolpur in Allahabad district, on April 5, 2006, for harbouring the three bombers. Waliullah's interrogation report mentions Bangladesh-based HUJI operation commander Assadullah Munirul-Islam, who is one of the mentors of Hyderabad twin blast accused Shahid Bilal.

The Varanasi devices were placed in pressure cookers—the same technique and device used in 2005 Delhi serial blasts and in Mumbai train serial blasts later in 2006. But no one knows how to join these dots.

Waliullah, who is in a Ghaziabad jail, mentioned the name of a sitting UP MP for his political patronage.

It was the *modus operandi* of HUJI operatives in Varanasi that came as an eye-opener for security agencies. Waliullah claimed that the bombers Mustafeez, Zakaria and Bashiruddin crossed over from Bangladesh to India in March and reached his *madrassa* with explosives. The next day Bashiruddin went on a recce mission with Waliullah from Allahabad to Varanasi while the other two prepared the IEDs. They identified the targets—Gowdhulia ghat, the railway station and the Sankatmochan temple and returned to Allahabad the same day after picking up three pressure cookers. Waliullah said he left his mobile phone in Phoolpur so that his location could not be traced.

On the fateful day the bombers left with IEDs in the bags and with instructions not to be in touch with each other. That was the last Waliullah saw of them, and in the evening the bombs exploded. The bombers escaped back to Bangladesh. "The addresses are being verified", was the one line written in the official record of the Varanasi blast case regarding police efforts to nab the bombers.

11

DELHI

ISI Terror in India's Capital

Secular India's capital has been Islamic terror's target for long years. Initially, it was in the mid-eighties that Khalistani terrorists had caused explosions all over Delhi. At that time they used low-tech transistor bombs that were based on TNT and did relatively little damage. In the decade that followed ISI formed an active partnership with the Khalistanis to continue terror strikes in Delhi. This came to light when the Delhi Police nabbed some Punjab militants at the Delhi railway station in February 1993. They confessed they had been trained by ISI to bomb civilian targets throughout the capital.

Triple Terror

It was a long-term plan that culminated in a spectacular act of terrorism in New Delhi in 2005—a triple bomb blast on Dewali eve, October 29, which claimed 63 lives and left 227 injured. Almost two years after the first chargesheet in the case was filed by the Delhi Police, a special court ruled in 2008 that there was enough evidence against the perpetrators, LeT terrorist Tariq Ahmed Dar and his four associates. Dar had briefed his co-conspirator Abu Ozefa in Srinagar that bombs could be planted on crowded buses at peak hours. Currently in Tihar jail, he also admitted his involvement in transfer of Hawala money on commission. An amount of Rs. 4.86 lakh had been deposited in his HDFC Bank account in Srinagar just before the blasts. The transaction was traced to a country in the Middle East.

HUJI Sleeper Cell

By this time a terrorist cell was clearly in place in the capital. For a week after the Jaipur blasts a HUJI terrorist, Abdul Rehman, was arrested in Delhi with RDX in his possession. While central intelligence agencies interrogated him to find out if he was involved in the Jaipur blasts, they also tried to ascertain if he was a member of a HUJI sleeper cell operating in the capital.

Supershock

In the meanwhile came the super-shock— the terrorist attack on Parliament. On December 13, 2001 a gang of five terrorists attacked Parliament House resulting in a 45-minute gun battle, in which 9 policemen and a Parliament staffer were killed. All the five terrorists were also killed by the security forces and were identified as Pakistani nationals. The attack took place around 11:40 a.m., minutes after both Houses of Parliament had adjourned for the day. The terrorists entered Parliament in a car through the VIP gate of the building. Displaying Parliament and Home Ministry security stickers, the vehicle entered the Parliament premises. The terrorists set off massive blasts and used AK-47 rifles, explosives and grenades for the attack. Senior Ministers and over 200 Members of Parliament were inside the Central Hall of Parliament when the attack took place.

A statement made by the then Home Minister L K Advani on December 18 said, *inter alia*:

"It is evident that the terrorist assault on Parliament House was executed jointly by Pak-based and supported terrorist outfits, namely, Lashkar-e-Toiba and Jaish-e-Mohammad. These two organizations are known to derive their support and patronage from Pak ISI. The investigation so far carried out by the police shows that all the five terrorists who formed the suicide squad were Pakistani nationals. All of them were killed on the spot and their Indian associates have since been nabbed and arrested."

The breakthrough in the investigation of the case was achieved with the arrest of Syed Abdul Rehman Gilani, a lecturer in a local college, whose interrogation led to the identification of two other accomplices, Afzal and Shaukat Hussain Guru. The wife of the latter disclosed that her husband and Afzal had in the afternoon of 13 December 2001 left for Srinagar. This information was immediately conveyed to the JK Police who apprehended both of them. A laptop computer and Rs. 1 million in cash were recovered from them. They were later brought to Delhi.

Interrogation of the accused has revealed that Afzal was the main coordinator who was assigned this task by a Pakistani national, Gazi Baba of Jaish-e-Mohammad. Afzal had earlier been trained in a camp run by Pak ISI at Muzaffarabad in Pak Occupied Kashmir. The hideouts for the five Pak terrorists were arranged by Shaukat Hussain Guru. During the subsequent raids, the police recovered from two of these hideouts a lot of incriminating material including a large quantity of ammonium nitrate and other ingredients used in preparing improvised explosive devices, a map of Delhi and three police uniforms.

"The incident once again establishes that terrorism in India is the handiwork of Pakistan-based terrorist outfits known to derive support and sustenance from Pak ISI. The hijacking of IC-814 Flight to Kandahar, the terrorist intrusion into the Red Fort and attack on J & K Legislative Assembly complex at Srinagar were masteminded and executed by militant outfits at the behest of the ISI. Lashkar-e-Taiba and Jaish-e-Mohammad in particular have been in the forefront in organizing terrorist violence in our country".

"Last week's attack on Parliament is undoubtedly the most audacious, and also the most alarming act of terrorism in the nearly two decades-long history of Pakistan-sponsored terrorism in India. This time the terrorists and their mentors across the border had the temerity to try to wipe out the entire political leadership of India, as represented in our multiparty Parliament".

The spectacular terror attack stunned India and was condemned by world leaders. *Wikipedia,* the American online encyclopedia, called it a "high profile attack by Pakistan-based Kashmiri militants" and the US media reported it extensively. Articles on the shocking event appeared in leading American newspapers like *New York Times, Washington Post, Wall Street Journal,* and *National Review.* According to *New York Times,* citing the attack the US Administration aimed at the assets of the terrorist group in Pakistan, while *Wall Street Journal* argued that "9/11 rules should apply to India too".

At home Prime Minister Vajpayee declared in his address to the nation, "We shall triumph over terrorism," at the same time admitting, "We are fighting terrorism for the last two decade." Home Minister Advani was more strident and told a press conference, "We will liquidate them (the terrorists) whoever they are, and wherever they are." For India, reported *Wikipedia,* the attack showed that "Pakistan, an ally in the war on terror, was (itself) a terrorist nation." In a bizarre rebuttal Pakistan's military spokesman Maj. Gen. Rashid Qureshi claimed that the Parliament House attack was a drama staged by Indian intelligence agencies to defame the freedom struggle in occupied Kashmir.

In 2003 the Government of India stated that security forces had killed the mastermind of the attack in Kashmir. Earlier, in December 2002, four Jaish-e-Mohammad members were convicted for their roles in the attack. Afzal Guru, convicted of being the main cospirator, was sentenced to death, but the sentence was stayed when his family made a mercy petition to the then President.

As of today, the farcical situation is that this convicted killer has not only not been hanged for long years after his terrorism, but going by the specious arguments of the ruling Congress, a decision on his mercy petition could take even longer. It saidAfzal's petition was 27th in a list of 28, and the government could take a decision only in the order in which they were filed. "That's what the law says," AICC spokesperson Manish Tiwari blandly told reporters.

12

RAJASTHAN

Teaching "Hindu" India

In the busiest market places, at the busiest hour in the evening, Islamic terror struck Rajasthan's capital city off Jaipur on May 13, 2008. With chilling precision as many as 9 bombs went off within 12 minutes in various localities of the pink city, killing 80 people and injuring over 150. It was a horrendous serial bombing reminiscent of Mumbai's local trains carnage.

Well-choreographed Attack

Rajasthan's Direcfor General of Police AS Gill said the attacks were designed to cause maximum havoc and the spots had been selected with care. The bombs had been efficiently assembled and the bikes to which they were strapped were bought just hours before the strike. "It was a well-choreographed attack carried out with considerable local support," the DGP asserted.

Top intelligence sources were more or less sure that the decision to target Jaipur was taken more than a month ago in Pakistan, with Bangladesh-based terror group HUJI used as the instrument for carrying it out. At the same time other sources believe the whole operation was planned about four months ago. Advance reconnaissance was done at that time, and even a dry run had been carried out in the final phase 3-4 days before the actual bombing.

Giving more, similar details a *Mumbai Mirror* report of May 15 said, according to analysts of the blasts they were planned and executed with military precision by local elements with full support from explosives experts of terrorist groups like HUJI. Sleeper cells trained in planting bombs were esconced in the city, experts from security agencies said.

Evident Local Support

At least 7– 8 modules were put into service to carry out the bombings planned well in advance. In all 30 to 40 persons were involved in the conspiracy. Local support in planting the bombs was evident. The actual bomb-makers appeared on the scene just hours before the blasts. The executors were seasoned terrorists, and they must have had several meetings with the locals. Such detailed planning could not have taken place without sympathisers.

The *Times of India* said the strike was the work of terrorists displaying tell-tale tactics of LeT and SIMI. SIMI has significant presence in Jaipur. Still, with the needle of suspicion mainly pointing to HUJI, the Jaipur police rounded up 45 Bangladeshis for questioning. They were found to be staying illegally in Jaipur district. In fact two local organizations, Nagrik Morcha and Rajput Karni Sena, charged in a press conference that about 50,000 such migrants were currently staying in Rajasthan.

Indian Mujahideen

The probe took a new turn when within a couple of days of the bombing an e-mail sent by one Guru Al-Hindi surfaced, claiming the responsibility for it on behalf of a previously unknown outfit calling itself Indian Mujahideen. Investigations revealed that its text was first drafted about a month ago, but was repeatedly edited until the final version was prepared two weeks before the bombing. The editing was meant for making the contents of the 5-page note more rabid. As proof of its authenticity the note correctly quoted the frame number of one of the bikes laden with a bomb.

Warning in the e-mail of more such attacks, Indian Mujahideen even claimed to have divided itself into three wings : a Shahabuddin Ghori Brigade for attacks in South India, a Mehmud Ghazanvi Brigade for targetting North India, and a Shaheed Al-Zarqawi Brigade for suicide attacks on various Indian cities.

Indian Mujahideen also declared in the e-mail that it wanted to teach Hindu India a lesson. Spewing venom on Hindu religious beliefs and Hindu deities, it threatened open war against India. Along with the e-mail the terror group also sent a video clip to a TV channel.

The IM put out a manifesto to explain its ideology, according to which it is "raising the illustrious banner of Jihad against the Hindus and all those who fight and resist us, and have begun our revenge with the help and permission of Allah—a terrifying revenge of our blood, our lives and our honour that will, *Insha Allah*, terminate your (Hindu) survival on this land. The IM manifesto calls on Hindus to realise that "the falsehood of your 33 crore dirty idols and the blasphemy of your deaf, dumb, mute and naked idols of Ram, Krishna and Hanuman are not at all going to save your necks from being slaughtered by our hands". Additionally, the manifesto demanded that Hindus change their attitudes lest another Ghauri shakes your foundations and Ghaznavi massacre you, proving your blood to be the cheapest of all mankind. And there was more of this kind.

Real Mastermind

Despite the Indian Mujahideen e-mail, however, Intelligence sources continued with their initial assessment that HUJI was the real mastermind behind the serial bombing. Sections in the media expressed the belief that Indian Mujahideen could be a camouflage tag for HUJI.

The Jaipur bombings had remarkable similarities with two major acts of terror – Malegaon in Maharashtra and Hyderabad. The bombs in Jaipur had been strapped to bikes in Malegaon, as Maharashtra DGP Roy pointed out. As for Hyderabad, the Rajasthan Police noticed the remarkable similarities the Jaipur bombing bore with the explosion at the Gokul Chat Bhandar. The shapes of the devices were the same, as was the way in which the ball bearings and pellets were used to make them more lethal. The IEDs used in Hyderabad and Jaipur bombs had similar C-shaped cores, IGP Pankaj Kumar said. In addition, bombs in both attacks had directional charges, which made them still more deadly, as the explosions could be directed, he said.

Thanks to teamwork of state police forces the case was solved within a few months and conspiracy uncovered with the arrest of key plotter Shahbaz Hussain. His interrogation revealed plans to trigger explosions in Delhi around Diwali. Next in line was the Mahakaleshwar temple in Ujjain to be targetted.

A curious, final footnote : Investigations revealed that the bags used for carrying the bombs were of Chinese make not available in the local market but available in Delhi and Mumbai. The police also found that ingredients used to make an unexploded bomb they found could be easily bought in shops in the Chandni Chowk market in Delhi. This indicates that although the bombs may have been made in Jaipur there could be a trail leading to Delhi.

Deobandi Madrasas

The *Times of India* report that expressed the posibility of Indian Mujahideen being a camouflage for HUJI, described HUJI as a Deobandi outfit which has grown beyond its base in Bangladesh. This significant observation has a history in Rajasthan, where ISI has been using the method of proliferation and control of *madrasas* for almost a decade and a half.

The process started with the northern (Indo-Pak) border districts of Barmer and Jaisalmer, according to a *Hindustan Times* report in April 1994, where *madrasas* were run and controlled by members of Muslim fundamentalist organizations like Tablighi Jamaat, who were trained by ISI and other Pakistani spy outfits. They were funded with substantial foreign money from Pakistan as well as from countries in the Middle East.

The idea of capturing Muslim schools was initiated with a group of young Muslims from Mumbai being sent to a bordering village in Barmer district, who started preaching Islam. Encouraged by the local response the group members then fanned out in other villages and started controlling *Madrasas*. The State Intelligence found that these were trained ISI agents who had been sent to get jobs in the *Madrasas* and then spot suitable talents for further training. A helpful factor here was the fact that most Muslims living in Rajasthan's border districts had relatives living in Pakistani villages across the border.

ISI-Smugglers Alliance

Along with these undercover agents ISI also used smugglers operating on the border for successfully sending huge consignments of arms and ammunition for terror strikes in Punjab, Jammu and Kashmir and UP's Terai region. Similar large consignments were also smuggled into Gujarat and Maharashtra through the state's southern border.

In order to facilitate this clandestine operation a senior ISI official actually convened a meeting of the smugglers during the initial phase in 1994 and threatened them that if they did not help in smuggling consignments from Pakistan into Rajasthan's border districts ISI would see to it that their business of smuggling drugs, gold and other valuable items become difficult.

12(a)

MADHYA PRADESH

ISI's Roving Spy

Barely a week before Republic Day, 2008, the Madhya Pradesh police busted an ISI module and arrested a Pakistani national from Karachi and his two associates from the city of Sagar, a major Army base. The trio had been supplying information on Indian Army movements to ISI for the past some months. Incriminating documents were seized from the house of Imran Varsi, a Pakistani. Of the other two, Iqbal and Akhtar, Iqbal used to get money from Dubai, which he passed on to the Pakistani.

With Iqbal's help Varsi had managed to procure a ration card and a PAN card, and was even about to apply for a passport, showing himself to be a domicile of Sagar. ISI had sent Varsi to Delhi from Karachi in 2003. Later, he went to Kolkata, and from there to Bangladesh, where he got married. The MP police recovered his marriage certificate issued by the Bangladesh authorities. The couple returned to Kolkata and since then had been living in various parts of India, including Srinagar and Mumbai, all the while supplying information to ISI through e-mails and by telephone.

13

GUJARAT

Terror's Sea Route

The brazen terror attack on the famous Akshardham temple in Gandhinagar, Gujarat, on September 25, 2002, was unusual on two counts, first because it was an international event, as the temple is a shrine of an internationally reputed spiritual organization attracting over two million visitors annually, and secondly because the event lasted for a whole night.

That evening two terrorists came to one of the temple's gates in a car with bags full of automatic weapons and grenades, jumped the fence, rushed to the main walkway of the temple, and opened fire at devotees. From there they charged towards the main shrine, but the volunteers quickly locked it from inside, preventing the terrorists' entry by mere seconds. The terrorists then rushed into the adjoining exhibition hall, where they went on a shooting spree killing men, women and children.

All this happened in 5–10 minutes, by which time the police and commando units arrived at the temple and launched a search for the terrorists, who had gone into hiding on the 23-acre temple complex. In the meantime the then Deputy Prime Minister LK Advani ordered the famed Black Cat commandos to be airlifted from Delhi to join the hunt for the terrorists. They arrived and took positions by midnight. The hunt and shoot-out continued sporadically through the night. Finally, in the morning the Black Cats found the terrorists hiding in the bushes on the grounds of the temple and ended the 14-hour-long confrontation by gunning down both of them. The total casualty count was 33 dead and 70 wounded.

ISI terrorism in Gujarat, although strikingly exemplified by the Akshardham strike, is actually more than a decade and a half old. For the 330 km-long Gujarat-Rajasthan border is highly vulnerable, across which ISI has been sending terrorists for years. Several Bangladeshis and even Iranians arrested on the Kutch border in 1992 were ISI couriers, and the weapons they were carrying were of Pakistani, Chinese and Russian origin. A large, secret cache of such weapons was discovered in the state in July that year.

Since then terrorists have consistently targeted Gujarat. In May 2002, five bombs went off on buses in Ahmedabad injuring 26 people. It was the first act of violence by Gujarat-based Jihadists. In June 2004 the Lashkar-e-Toiba dispatched two Pakistani nationals from Jammu and Kashmir to execute a Fidayeen attack on Gujarat. In February 2006 the Maharashtra-based Students Islamic Movement of India (SIMI) planted a sophisticated suitcase bomb, built by an expert, Zulfikar Fayyaz Kagzi, on the Mumbai-Ahmedabad Express train. What mindless hatred was behind this all? The answer was given by Parveen Swami, a correspondent of *The Hindu* (August 1, 2008) in a damning article. Identified was a man called Maulana Sufiyan Patangia, who is running Lal Masjid, a Muslim seminary in Ahmedabad.

On the pretext of defending his community, Patangi is known to have raised Rs. 3,75,000 from one Abdul Bari, a top financier of the Lashkar and Rs. 5 lakh from two Saudi-based Jaish-e-Mohammad financiers, Farhatullah Ghauri and Abdul Rehman. According to Swami, Patangia has also been in close touch with a top Gujarat mafioso, Abdul Latif Sheikh, as well as Pakistan-based Indian don Dawood.

ISI's plans for a network of agents in Gujarat go back more than a decade. This came to light when a London-based Muslim trader Ismail was arrested by the Anti-Terrorist Squad (ATS) of Gujarat Police on suspicion of planning terrorist acts. He was looking to recruit locals in the state. The move was said to be the brainchild of one Col. Farooq of ISI, who had deputed Bilal Ahmed Beg, chief of an outfit called Jammu and Kashmir Front, to prepare a list of potential recruits in Gujarat. Ismail used to visit Ahmedabad often for this purpose. During this talent hunt he had come into contact with one Gyasuddin, who was later arrested along with Ismail. He had been asked by Ismail to buy two homes in Ahmedabad for the ISI base where its terrorists could come together to organise their strikes.

Ahmedabad Link with 7/11

Incidentally, Ahmedabad's link with 7/11 was discovered when a document relating to the serial bombing of Mumbai local trains was found hidden in a mosque in Ahmedabad. Commenting on the discovery Jt Commissioner of Police Ashish Bhatia said, "It was originally prepared by one of the accused of Mumbai 7/11 serial blasts and a SIMI leader of Maharashtra, Ehtesham Siddiqi, during his stay in Arthur Road Jail after his arrest in the 7/11 terror strike. He had provided the same to SIMI hardline leader Safdar Nagori."

Bhatia added that it was not clear how Siddiqi conveyed the details of the document to Nagori, who in turn circulated it among SIMI cadres in Ahmedabad. SIMI terrorist Usman Agarbattiwala had done the Gujarati translation. Acting on a tip-off the Ahmedabad police found a plastic bag hidden in a well inside the mosque. The bag contained a register giving details of police investigation in the 7/11 Mumbai blasts in Gujarati, information on police interrogation techniques including details of narco-analysis test, and most importantly, a training manual for terror camps across the country.

A relevant development in the terror scene that needs to be noted here is that while infiltration of Pakistan-sponsored terrorists into India has traditionally been through the mountainous terrain on both sides of the country – Kashmir and North-East— terror strikes in Gujarat marked the begining of sea routes. In particular, the state's coast is used for smuggling large quantities of explosives into the state, as also for transit.

For instance, intelligence agencies investigating the serial bomb blasts in Mumbai in 1993 found that only one-third of the RDX smuggled into the country for the operation was used in Mumbai. The rest was taken to Gujarat and Karnataka, with Ahmedabad, Surat, Bangalore and Hubli as intended targets. Before that, when a Khalistani terrorist was caught in July 1992 while trying to steal into Mumbai at ISI's behest, he led the police to a cache of arms hidden in Ahmedabad. Again in 1996 a huge consignment of arms and communication equipment was seized in the Mehsana town of Gujarat that included RDX and more than a hundred pistols with Pakistani markings.

According to intelligence sources the idea of the large-scale smuggling operation was conceived a month before at a meeting of ISI top brass and a fundamentalist Islamist organization called Markaz-ul-Vallah-dar-Irshad. The task of pushing in the arms and explosives was assigned to Markaz's militant outfit named Panj Sipah Sahiban. The quantity of the RDX was big enough to wreck important business centres of Ahmedabad and Mumbai with a series of bomb blasts.

The use of Gujarat's sea coast for terrorist traffic signifies not only a growing danger for India but also a global danger that the Americans acknowledge they share with this country. After a meeting with top Indian defence and strategic brass in 2007 US Admiral Timothy Keating said, "Possibilities of their (terrorists') using maritime domain are alive... such attacks are already happening, with attempts on some US Navy ships and on commercial shipping lines."

That these routes are being increasingly used by terrorists in different parts of the world was clearly accepted by the American Admiral when he said the US was in dialogue with a number of countries, including India, on counterterrorism measures like the Container Security Initiative.

14

MAHARASHTRA

ISI-Underworld Gang-up

The deadly presence of ISI in Maharashtra first burst into public attention with the horrendous serial bombing of Mumbai on March 12, 1993, when its agents exploded as many as 13 bombs within three hours, killing over 200 people and wounding over 1000.

Agencies investigating the blasts that rocked this commercial capital of the country found tangible evidence of a link with ISI. Additionally, they also found connection with Sikh extremists and the Mumbai underworld. The investigation of some local suspects led to the discovery of a list of telephone numbers of ISI operatives, based both in Pakistan and India, showing that ISI had masterminded the bombings. One of the accused, Farooq Pawle, later confessed that ISI had trained him.

Also uncovered was the contact between ISI and its Lahore-based liaison man by the name of Bittu, a Sikh terrorist who provided intelligence for the explosions. Bittu was a former activist of the All-India Sikh Students Federation, and was a conduit between ISI and Mumbai's notorious don Yakub Memon in plotting the terrorist act.

Once the blueprint for the strike was ready, Yakub Memon was asked by ISI to select his own team to execute the plot. Accordingly, he organized the group, fixed the spots for the explosions, and purchased the new cars and scooters required to carry the bombs. After the RDX was made available to him he arranged the assembling of the bombs. Finally, in order to ensure that the whole operation went off without a hitch, its ISI sponsors conducted a secret, fortnight–long training camp for Memon's men in Dubai, for which they were flown there from Mumbai in early February.

The cover story of the *Sunday* magazine's issue of March 21-27, 1993 provided the following information on the ISI plot :

On January 20, 1993 the Intelligence Bureau (IB) passed on a message from RAW, the external secret service, to police forces in the country warning that ISI had targetted Indian cities, particularly Mumbai. This intelligence had come from moles inside Pakistan. The RAW report was discussed at a meeting of the Government's Joint Intelligence Committee

(JIC). Initially, it was thought that ISI's intention was to blow up a nuclear power plant, which could be passed off as an accident caused by shoddy maintenance. Tight security at all nuclear installations had forced ISI to give up the plan.

Earlier, as stated, in July 1992 one Manjit Singh, a cadre of the terrorist organization Khalistan Commando Force (KCF) was arrested at the Dadar railway station in Mumbai while trying to sneak into the city. He confessed he was there at ISI's behest, which was planning an attack on the city. His interrogation led to the arrest of two ISI agents in Mumbai.

ISI's personnel policy for clandestine operations was to operate through locals and to restrict its own involvement to planning and supplies. So it had initially used Sikh militants in India. But after Manjit Singh's arrest ISI realised that it was too risky to use Sikhs in Mumbai, and so turned to local gangsters. As a result, almost every person arrested by the Mumbai Police in connection with the serial bombing turned out to have links to the `D' Company of Dawood Ibrahim, the godfather of Mumbai's underworld. Incidentally, there is evidence indicating that Yakub Memon was smuggled out of Dubai into Pakistan on board a Pakistan International Airlines flight.

The serial explosions were structured like a classic intelligence operation on a need-to-know basis. For instance, the men who drove the cars told the police that they did not even know the vehicles were loaded with explosives. Likewise, the suitcase bombers did not know what was in the suitcases.

The choice of the explosive used for the bombs was in itself significant. It was a plastique called Semtex, and its use strongly suggested a foreign hand in the carnage. No plastique is manufactured in India. As pointed out earlier, in the mid-eighties, when Sikh militants caused explosions all over Delhi, they used low-tech transistor bombs that were based on TNT and did relatively little damage. Semtex is used only when a large number of people are meant to be killed.

Moreover, while most advanced countries manufacture their own Semtex, one of its constituents, a high-density explosive called PETN, was made only in Czechoslovakia in the 1980s. In 1990, under US pressure, Czechoslovakia halted its manufacture, and since then there are no fresh soures of Semtex. But by then the Czechs had already exported 1000 tonnes of PETN to Col. Gadaffi's regime in Libya, who offered to terrorist organizations and friendly states like Pakistan, which in turn supplied large quantity of PETN to the Afghan Mujahideen. So there are very reasonable grounds for believing that ISI was the source of the Semtex used in the Mumbai bombing. Incidentally, even after this serial bombing the state government was taken by surprise at the huge quantities of explosives that landed on the Konkan coast.

Immediately in the wake of the horrifying havoc, the then Prime Minister of Pakistan Nawaz Sharif issued an official denial of responsibility or complicity. But Ghulam Ishaq Khan, before stepping down as President of Pakistan in July 1993, had furiously rebuked Sharif for ISI's involvement in the event, according to a book in Urdu, titled *Will Pakistan Break Up*? by one Muneer Ahmed, that was published in 2006. When Sharif tried to deny it Ishaq Khan retorted, "Mr. Prime Minister, don't try to convince me. The ISI is behind these blasts, and I have got the proof of it."

The author says Ishaq Khan told Sharif that the green signal for these blasts was given by ISI chief Lt. Gen. Javed Nasir himself. Nasir belonged to a fundamentalist Islamic body called Tablighi Jamaat, which was patronized by the Sharif family.

The author also said that he had proof to show how the Indian gangsters Memon brothers were kept in Karachi as goverment guests and later taken to Dubai.

Muneer Ahmed, who in 1994 had faced a sedition case for writing a book on the political role of intelligence agencies in Pakistan, had in this book also highlighted the role of the ISI and the Army in the country's political instability. He wrote that Sharif had assigned ISI chief Nasir and Intelligence Bureau chief Brig. Imtiaz to prepare a report on who was responsible for the Mumbai blasts. The duo cooked up a report blaming the Government of India itself for what happened. Ishaq Khan rejected it and insisted that it was the handiwork of ISI. And so did the US when the Minister of State for Foreign Affairs Sadiq Kanju showed it to American diplomats, the writer added.

This holocaust history of Mumbai repeated itself when the serial blasts in the city's crowded local trains killed 200 people and wounded 700 on Juy 11, 2006. Again, ISI masterminded the plot, and its affiliate Lashkar-e-Toiba (LeT) executed it. The conspiracy was hatched in Pakistan in March 2006, and again the terrorists who were assigned its execution were given training by an LeT commander in Bahawalpur in Pakistan's Punjab. The next month some Indian facilitators of the plot were contacted.

While LeT was in charge of the whole operation and had its own team, it also co-opted activists of the outlawed SIMI and JeM. When all was ready, 11 Pakistanis arrived in Mumbai from Bangladesh, Nepal and across the Gujarat border. Their Indian aides arranged four safe houses in the city for them. One of the Pakistanis had brought 20 kg of RDX explosive with him, for which ammonium nitrate was procured locally. The bombs were assembled, put inside 5-litre pressure cookers and planted in seven crowded local trains originating from Churchgate terminal station. Each bomb was planted by a two-man team comprising one Pakistani and one Indian.

Revealing these details Mumbai Police Commissioner AN Roy told reporters that 15 persons were arrested, most of whom were LeT cadres, some of them had been to Pakistan twice or thrice and were trained by LeT commander Azam Cheema. All 14 bomb planters got off their respective trains at different stations, except one, Salim. He was killed by the bomb he himself planted. His body remained unclaimed, but Salim was identified as a Pakistani living in Lahore.

Describing the attack as professional and well-planned, Roy said one of the terrorists, Faizal, used to receive money through Hawala channels from one Rizwan Dawre, a key LeT operative believed to be based in Saudi Arabia. "We recovered 26,000 Riyals from Faizal. Dawre used to get the money from Pakistan, which he sent to Faizal in Mumbai. During the past five years Faizal received Rs. 60 lakh *via* Hawala from Dawre," Roy revealed.

On October 23, 2006 National Security Advisor MK Narayanan told the CNN-IBN TV channel that the Government had pretty good evidence of ISI's involvement in the Mumbai blasts. However, he said, "Certain legal issues" have to be "clarified" before Pakistan could be given details of this involvement through a bilateral anti-terrorism mechanism. "In a particular instance of major terrorist attack where we have definite proof of Pakistani involvement, or the involvement of terrorist outfits in Pakistan, and since we are not prepared for hot pursuit and that kind of stuff, let us see what Pakistan does with the evidence we give them," he said. He claimed that as evidence India could even give Pakistan specific locations, names etc. What all this verbiage amounted to was that the Government of India was waiting for Godot —something that never happens.

Meanwhile Mumbai continues to be on the active hit list of terrorists. After seven LeT operatives plotting to bomb more than a dozen sensitive sites in the city were caught in UP, the Maharashtra Anti-Terrorism Squad (ATS) started hunting for three or four sleeper cells that are suspected to be active. One of those arrested in UP was one Fahim Ahmed of Mumbai who had rented a room in the city's red-light district for sheltering the Fidayeen coming for the attack. Fahim had received training in an LeT camp in PoK. He had carried out a survey of possible bombing sites and was going to use the room for storing arms and explosives.

Then PTI reported that about two weeks ago a team of three Bangladeshi (HUJI) terorists had entered India and their probable targets were Mumbai's share market and atomic centre. This intelligence led to an encounter between two terrorists carrying RDX and the police in Thane district near Mumbai, in which the terrorists were gunned down.

A day after this incident the State ATS confirmed the intended targets. The RDX recovered from the terrorists "can easily be used to carry out six blasts," said ATS chief Karkare.

Apart from such miscellaneous marauders, a startling discovery of how terrorists of assorted outfits are running loose all over Mumbai is the presence in the city of the nefarious Pakistani fundamentalist terrorist organization Al-Badr. This came to light when ATS of Mumbai Police, in collaboration with the Kutch police, busted in July 2007 a sleeper cell of the outfit operating from Bhendi Bazar area of the metropolis. A Pakistani Mohammad Salim Memon and two local operatives were arrested. Unbelievably enough, it came to light that the Pakistani was living there for more than 30 years! Even a couple of months earlier, in May, Memon had been arrested for trying to sell 30 fake credit cards in his possession.

Memon was recruited in June 2006 by ISI operative Khalid Turqi, who travelled to Mumbai on a valid passport and was tasked with setting up the Mumbai cell of Al-Badr's Indian module. He had smuggled into Mumbai a consignment of Rs. 24 lakh in fake currency, which had been brought into India by the organization's Kutch cell. Half of this amount was sent to the Hyderabad cell.

One of their Indian associates, Sultan Ansari, had even acquired a fake driving licence for another key Pakistani operative, Abdul Khaliq Taiyyab to help him acquire a local identity.

How Memon managed to live in the city for so long without getting identified as an illegal migrant is a question to which the police have no answer.

After the fake currency consignment of Rs. 24 lakh, Al-Badr had planned to smuggle a crore of Rupees into the country via the sea route. The other Indian associate, Irfan Lakhani, was given Rs. 1 lakh in fake money for circulation. He found it easy to do so through the small shop he ran.

The Indian module of Al-Badr put together by ISI was given the task of establishing a safe sea route from Karachi to a border district of Kutch in Gujarat and from there to Mumbai and Hyderabad for bringing in arms, explosives, drugs and fake currency. Even a Global Positioning System (GPS) handset was recovered from the module. After the sea route was established, the initial consignment of Rs. 24 lakh was just a dry run, said the Kutch police.

Mumbai Techniques

The manner in which the Jaipur bombings were carried out made it clear that the terrorists used the same techniques and tactics that they perfected in the course of numerous attacks on Mumbai over the past several years. Mumbai had been bombed as many as eight times since the serial blasts of 1993. These blasts have become a blueprint for terrorists on how bombings are to be engineered across the country with the least likelihood of being arrested or even identified.

Commenting in the wake of the Jaipur horror on how serious the situation is, Intelligence expert B. Raman said Indian cities are bearing the brunt of terror tactics like high-intensity blasts at crowded places that have been first used in conflict zones like Afghanistan and the Gulf region since the eighties. In fact, Mumbai was the first Indian city to face deadly serial bombings on a massive scale in March 1993.

Malegaon

Outside Mumbai, Islamic terrorist activities have been in evidence in quite a few cities and towns of Maharashtra. The most noticeable among them is the town of Malegaon. Its links to ISI came to light when four powerful bomb blasts took place there within five minutes on September 6, 2006, killing more than 30 people and injuring more than 300. Just two months before 7/11, on May 10, the police seized more than 40 kg of RDX explosive, 16 AK-47s, and 4000 rounds of ammunition in Malegaon.

Another major terror target in Maharashtra was the RSS headquarters in Nagpur. On June 1, 2006 terrorists made an attempt to storm it, but the attack was foiled and the terrorists shot dead. In his statement thanking the Government and the police, the then RSS Sarsanghchalak revealed that the RSS HQ had been on the hit list of terrorists for the last four years.

That it continued to be there was reiterated by Nagpur Police Commissioner Dr. Satyapal Singh in an interaction with the media in March 2008. He stated that the power plant and the Reserve Bank office in the city were also in terrorist crosshairs.

Just a couple of days earlier, investigations revealed that an ISI agent SayeedAhmed alias Mohammad Desai had made calls to Pakistan and London from Satara in Maharashtra. He was hiding in the Satara district after escaping from custody in Pune on January 23. He had provided vital information to ISI officers in Pakistan. He was planning to leave for Bangladesh, and from there to Pakistan.

Mohammad Desai was the third case of an ISI agent being arrested in Pune. In April 2007 an engineering college student in the city Vishal Upadhyaya was arrested in April 2007 in a spying case. He had fallen in love with a Pakistani girl while chatting on the internet. She happened to be an ISI agent. Under her influence he visited Pakistan twice and underwent arms training by ISI. And in February the same year Shailesh Jadhav, a former Havildar in the Army was caught with classified documents in his possession. Desai had stayed at Jadhav's house in Satara, and was in regular touch with an ISI officer in Pakistan named Tayyab.

Jalgaon

Around this time, on March 7, there was also a report from the town of Jalgaon that a regular selection programme had recently been held probably for identifying young Muslims fit for training as terrorists in Pakistan. Educated youths from Jalgaon, Malegaon and Sambhajinagar had been called to attend.

Some cadres of the banned SIMI had been found in Jalgaon not long before this suspicious programme. When, in the wake of the Jaipur serial bombing, Maharashtra ATS chief Jt. Commissioner of Police Hemant Karkare was asked about SIMI activities in the state, he replied, "There are apprehensions that some front organizations of SIMI have been floated. However, there is no evidence or intelligence yet to suggest the formation of SIMI's women's wing, Shaheen Force, in the state."

Against this background the state police and ATS combed suspected terrorist hideouts. In the beginning of June a bomb was found in a theatre in Navi Mumbai, which the police defused.

14(a)

GOA

Bali-type Threat

That Goa would be targetted by Islamic terrorists had been predicted by the Israelis about six years ago when the Government of Israel warned Israeli citizens against going there for Christmas in view of a possible al-Qaeda strike. That time the strike did not take place, but in February 2008 the media reported that yet another strike might happen sooner than later. For a Red Alert was declared in Goa after two terrorists arrested in Karnataka confessed planning bomb attacks in Goa. Fortunately, their plan could not be implemented as they did not receive the promised consignment of RDX from Pakistan. According to intelligence sources the terrorists had planned to carry out Bali-type bombing in Goa, and had visited the state thrice to survey coastal and crowded places. Highly placed police officials said the Jehadis had the famous Calangute beach of north Goa on their hit list, as well as a popular disco on the beach.

A favourite tourist destination for foreigners, Goa has been on the terror radar for some time, with alerts being sounded in 2005 as well as 2006 ahead of the tourist season. In 2005, the then tourism minister of the state went public with an international intelligence agency warning of a terrorist outfit's plan to hit foreign tourists in the state. According to another media report, for the past many years there have been reports about terrorists planning a Bali-type attack in the state.

Goa IG Kishan Kumar said, "The suspected terrorists stayed in guest-houses here and went unnoticed because the tourism industry did not cooperate with the police". There was a high alert even during the International Film Festival here in 2009. Despite these repeated warnings security in Goa is as poor as elsewhere in the country. The coastal police department was set up in 2006, but "till date we don't have even a motorcycle", said an officer of the department. Of the three police stations under it, one has just 10 policemen who patrol nearby beaches, while the strategic Harbour Police station doesn't even have an officer.

15

SOUTH INDIA

ISI Terror's New Target

Islamic terrorism initially arrived in the South when two Pakistanis were captured in August 1992 while trying to blow up a train near Chennai. Since that small beginning bomb attacks during the past decade and a half show that South India is emerging as ISI terror's new target, aided by a growing number of local outfits. A consolidated look at some major strikes that have taken place :

February 14,1998

In the first big terrorist attack on a South Indian city, a series of explosions ripped through the rich textile town of Coimbatore in western Tamil Nadu, killing 59 and wounding more than 250. It was with this event that the presence of indigenous terrorist cells in the South first came to light. For nearly 170 persons, mostly cadres of Al Ummah as well as some from All India al-Jihad Committee were rounded up. Also arrested was Abdul Nasser Madani, leader of the Kerala-based People's Democratic Party.

October 12, 2005

A suicide bomber walked into the office of the Hyderabad police task force and exploded a bomb carried in a backpack.

December 28, 2006

Terrorists barged into the prestigious Indian Institute of Science (IISc) campus in Bangalore and opened fire indiscriminately, killing a professor. The attackers were believed to be a part of an LeT module.

May 18, 2007

A powerful bomb blast killed nine people and wounded more than 50 at the Mecca Masjid in Hyderabad during a Friday congregation.

August 20, 2007

Twin blasts in Hyderabad killed more than 40 people. The Andhra Government held terrorist outfits of Pakistan and Bangladesh responsible.

The December 2006 attack on the Bangalore IISc was Karnataka's first ever brush with terrorism. In Tamil Nadu, with the rounding up of almost all cadres of Al-Ummah in the Coimbatore blasts case, the state believed it had wound up its only terrorist outfit. That it was not so became clear when an e-mail bomb threat in December 2005 was traced to a cyber cafe in a place near Tirunelveli, where Al-Ummah had reportedly become active again. In July 2006 the Coimbatore police claimed to have busted a conspiracy to unleash terror in the city, rounding up some members of another little known outfit called Manitha Neethi Pasarai (MNP) receiving foreign funds.

In Kerala, the acquittal of Madani cannot erase the communal past of Islamic Sevak Sangh (ISS), by which name PDP was originally known. Though Kerala itself has not witnessed any major terror attacks, there are indications that many Pakistan-based terror-groups have active modules or linkages with some fundamentalist groups in the State, pointed out an August 2006 study by the Delhi-based Institute for Defence Studies and Analysis. The report also mentioned incriminating evidence of cooperation between Kerala-based groups and major pan-Islamic terrorist organizations that enjoy political patronage in Kerala.

16

KARNATAKA

Terror Camps on Indian Soil

The terrorist network in South India is wider than had been thought, as recent events have started showing. That it is ISI-sponsored was proved by the arrest of two terrorists, Mohammad Ali Hussain and Mohammad Fahad, in Mysore on October 27, 2006 after a shootout. They belonged to Al-Badr, and were found to carry quite an assortment—sketches of the Karnataka state secretariat Vidhan Soudha, and its newly-built annexe Vikas Soudha, a satellite phone with numbers linked to Kashmir and Pakistan, a laptop computer, an AK-47 rifle, a foreign-made pistol, chemicals useful for making Improvised Explosive Devices (IEDs), a digital camera, and, finally, passports.

Here it is relevant to recall that only one-third of the RDX explosive smuggled into India for the serial bombing of Mumbai in 1993 was actually used for the operation and the rest sent to Karnataka and Gujarat. This reveals the links among the various terror strikes across the country, including the sensational strike in December 2005 at the Indian Institute of Science in Bangalore. Two suspects were arrested in this connection, Raziuddin Nasir in Davengere in Karnataka on January 11, 2006 and Sabauddin in Lucknow on February 9. Their account revealed that the notorious Abu Hamza was the kingpin of the plot.

A *Times of India* despatch from Kalghatgi, Dharwad, on February 2, 2008 reported under the heading "Terror camps, Pak flags in Karnataka" as follows:

Chilling evidence of terrorist training camps inside the country, on Indian soil, came to light when three Islamic radicals were recently interrogated by Karnataka police. Their grilling unearthed the fact that a dense forest area bordering the Dharwad and Uttar Kannada districts of Karnataka was being used to train terrorists in the use of arms.

Sources said this could well be the first time that a terrorist training camp of Islamic fundamentalists had been detected in South India, where a spate of terror attacks has taken place in the last few years.

A police raid on the camp site showed Pakistani flags flying in the area. The discovery of the camp proved a much deeper terrorist penetration in South India than had been suspected. The terrorists revealed to the police that they had established a base in Kalghatgi and were preparing for a Jihadi strike. There were about 20 young men at the camp.

One of those visiting it was Ghouse alias Nasir, who had undergone extensive arms training in Pakistan in 2004-05, including how to make IEDs. It later came to light that he is the son of Hyderabad-based Maulana Naseeruddin, who is facing trial for the November 2004 killing of former Gujarat minister and BJP leader Haren Pandya. Ghouse/Nasir received training with LeT in Pak and had travelled to Bangalore before returning to Hyderabad. Shahid Bilal, who had planned bomb blasts at key places in Hyderabad and was believed to be the key figure in recent terrorism plots in many parts of the country, was a follower of Naseeruddin. This Maulana is the founder-president of an outfit called Tahreek Tahfooz Sharia-e-Islam, and in his trial he has been charged with facilitating the travel and training of terrorists involved in Haren Pandya's murder.

Ghouse/Nasir wanted to go to the USA to spread terror there, but since it was difficult to get entry into that country he had twice pleaded with terrorist leaders to at least send him to Iraq as a Fidayeen, but they made him drop the idea as they thought that there is so much to do in India. Ghouse went to Mecca thrice. During his second trip in 2005 he met Bilal's brother Abdul Samad. In 2006 Samad got him a fake passport and sent him to Pakistan for arms training. After finishing the training in the period from May 2006 to January 2007 he was sent to India for terror and subversion.

The report on the terrorist training camp in the jungles of Dharwad district had a small but significant bit of information — one of the visitors to this camp was an MBBS student. The significance of this news lies in the fact that the tentacles of Islamic terrorism are spreading in the Muslim student community of the state. The recent arrests of students of top professional colleges in Karnataka for their links with terror groups have made the state police ask educational institutions to tighten screening during the admission process. This warning about the need for stricter screening came in the wake of the arrest of some medical students linked to the banned SIMI, while such terrorist outfits recruit both unemployed persons as well as intellectuals.

17

ANDHRA PRADESH

Crawling with Terrorists

Andhra's capital Hyderabad has many ISI sympathizers. This became evident during investigation that followed the powerful twin bomb blasts that killed more than 40 people. Actually, a clear hint of spreading terrorism in the state was given by a Pakistani of LeT when he confessed his role in the 2005 bombing of the Hyderabad police headquarters.

Evidence gathered at the bombing sites by the police indicated a military stamp. For the box in which the explosives were packed had a unique boat design that is associated only with military use. The shape ensures that the explosive inside does not get scattered but explodes at the very spot, causing maximum impact, said a police officer. The box appeared to be locally made, so the police questioned arrested terrorists with ISI links to find out where the training to make such specially-designed boxes was given. They also questioned local carpenters. This type of box had not been used before by the terrorists. The explosive used for the blasts, an ammonium nitrate emulsion called Neogel-90, also known as ANFO (Ammonium Nitrate Fuel Oil) was so powerful that it could generate heat up to 5000°C.

Apparently Pakistan's ISI and Bangladesh's HUJI (called al-Qaeda affiliate) had joined hands for this terror act. One of the four suspects involved in the blasts, Shadab Khan, was said to have close links with ISI, besides being in constant touch on the phone with Mohammad Shahid alias Bilal, the HUJI commander suspected to be the mastermind behind the plot. The other three were picked up in the Muslim-dominated 'old city' area of Hyderabad. They were all members of a fundamentalist Islamic organization called Dargah-Jehad-o-Shahadat. This reveals that the extent of penetration of international terror groups in the state is staggering. When and where these ISI stooges would strike nobody knows. "They are there and can be put to use whenever the handlers want. The operatives and their handlers are as of now faceless. It becomes extremely difficult to identify them, as many operate in a close group, especially in modules, with each module having about three to four operatives," the source said.

It is estimated that around 2000 Pakistanis have infiltrated Hyderabad in the guise of university students. The proportion of foreign (especially

Pakistani, Bangladeshi and Iranian) students at Osmania University has shown a marked increase in recent years. Added to this, a student of Aligarh Muslim University, Fasi, arrested as a suspect, revealed that a number of young Muslims from Hyderabad had been sent to Pakistan for training in terrorism and sabotage. There is also an organization in Hyderabad called Ikhwan-ul-Muslimeen that is behind the arming and training of local Muslim youths.

Many mosques in the city are used by ISI as propaganda centres. More than a decade ago, it was reported that *Khateebs* (who deliver *Khutba*, the Friday sermons) in mosques in Hyderabad were used by ISI to build up support among Indian Muslims for Pakistan on Kashmir. Some of these *Khateebs* even equated Kashmir with Palestine and prayed for Allah's support to Kashmiri Muslims in their struggle for "independence". Some Islamic scholars admit that reference to Kashmir, Bosnia, Palestine and Afghanistan in Friday *Khutba* is a common feature in Gulf countries.

The Andhra BJP charge that Hyderabad had become the nerve-centre for ISI activities is not without substance. For more than half a dozen mosques in the city were reportedly equipped with fax machines in Arabic for communication with ISI agents. ISI chose the *Khutbas* to spread its message because they are delivered only in Arabic!

There are 4000 mosques in Hyderabad, and ISI was not leaving any stone unturned to spread its tentacles among them, the media had reported a decade and a half ago. Even at that time some student organizations in Andhra Pradesh, particularly an outfit called State Islamic Organization (SIO) had come under ISI influence.

All in all, ISI presence in Andhra has become so noticeable that the state government has set up several teams to track its activities and weed out sleeper cells. Such cells have reportedly been activated not only in Hyderabad but in the neighbouring districts of Nalgonda, Warangal, and Mehbubnagar as well.

18

KERALA

"Seamless Terror Network"

Islamic terror has been evident in Kerala for a decade and a half. It was in 1994 that ISI was reportedly building bases along the Kerala coast and had identified about 40 villages as possible locations for landing arms. Some persons and groups were even provided with funds to buy up real estate in certain pockets of the state. The Kerala government had admitted at the time that unidentified boats had been sighted off the Malabar coast. And now, in the beginning of this year, a Muslim shopkeeper Altaf Ahmad was arrested in Kerala's hill district of Idukki. He confessed to have been a cadre of Hizb-ul Mujahideen (HuM) for the last 15 years. He was trained in Pakistan in the latter half of the 1990s in handling arms and explosives, and then came down to Kumily, a border town frequented by tourists, where he worked in a local Kashmiri handicrafts shop for the past seven years. There are hundreds of Kashmiri traders selling handicraft articles in Kerala's tourist spots. The police say the border town of Idukki, with its harsh terrain and sparse population, is fast becoming a haven for terrorists. Presently, a terror network exists in Kerala. *The Pioneer* wrote in its editorial on January 10, 2008:

"Kerala's Home Minister Kodiyeri Balakrishnan appears to be unfazed by the real extent of the threat posed by Hizb-ul Mujahideen operatives in the State. Or else he would not have suggested that extremists are travelling to God's Own Country for rest and recreation. The minister would do well to reconsider his views and accept the ground reality in Kerala, with its Islamist organizations like NDF and PDP, that affords ISI-trained terror operatives from Jammu and Kashmir to park themselves without being detected for seven long years, posing as traders. Mr Balakrishnan, a leading light of the CPI(M) in Kerala, might not be able to publicly admit the actual threat posed by the likes of Altaf Ahmed Khan, the Hizb-ul operative arrested in scenic Kumili town, because of his party's close association with Islamist outfits with an extremist agenda. But intelligence inputs make it abundantly clear that there is a clear ideological link and operational bridge between Kashmiri Islamists and those who share their hate agenda in Kerala."

"That Altaf Ahmed Khan had been living in Kumili for the last seven years, untouched by the police despite several tip-offs from competent sources, raises serious questions about the commitment of both the Congress and the CPI(M) in combating Islamist extremism. It is obvious that what is lacking is political will, for intelligence agencies in the state as well as at the Centre have been untiring in their effort to draw attention to this festering problem. Islamists in Kerala are well entrenched in the political system of the state, and this ensures safety and patronage, both for themselves as well as their compatriots from other states. In the clamour of competitive communalism to pander to the Islamists in the hope of garnering Muslim votes — witness the manner in which the Congress and the CPI(M) have gone out of their way to secure the support ofAbdul Nasser Mahdani, who never got his just desserts for the Coimbatore bombing. There seems to be a consensus across the political spectrum to turn a blind eye to the alarming spread of radical Islam. Its implications are lost on those whose responsibility is to protect Kerala's and India's interests. The recent arrest of Altaf Ahmed Khan shows that Islamists have established a network of sleeper cells and hideouts far away from the prying eyes of security agencies. Who would have thought that Kashmiri terrorists on the run would seek and find refuge in Kerala? More alarmingly, who knows how many terrorists have been provided with refuge?"

A helpful factor for ISI growth in South India is the far-from-cordial relationship between the administrations of Kerala and neighbouring Tamil Nadu. When ISI-trained extremists escaped to Kerala after committing crimes in Tamil Nadu, the Kerala authorities gave no cooperation to the Tamil Nadu police in apprehending them. On the other hand, extremist set-ups in Tamil Nadu receive all help in Kerala, ranging from weapons to funds and from shelter to training. The deadly terrorist organization of Tamil Nadu, Al-Ummah, had recently held a three-month arms training camp in a village in the Trichur district of Kerala. It was attended by the notorious Keralite Madani and a leading Tamil terrorist Badshah for the whole period.

Apart from the political and ideological rivalry between Kerala and Tamil Nadu administrations proving a facilitating factor for terrorism, Kerala's soft attitude towards terrorists in general and SIMI in particular is clearly costing the country dear.

The Kerala link to the Ahmedabad blasts confirms that Gujarat has only paid for the failure or reluctance of the Leftist government to act against fundamentalist elements thriving in the state.

At least two training camps were reported from the forests of Kerala, cocking a snook at the ban on SIMI. The first camp for physical and mental conditioning of SIMI cadres was held in 2006 in Binanipuram in Ernakulam district, followed by another training workshop in December 2007 at Vagamon in Idukki district. After each of these camps, police cases were filed. Following the Binanipuram camp, the Kerala police even managed to round up 18 SIMI activists on August 15, 2006. But the investigations never went beyond the arrests. Sometime later they were released after the police failed to bring charges. Two of the released even attended the second SIMI camp at Vagamon, Idukki, in December 2006 and January 2007. Going by the statement of Kerala Home Minister Kodiyeri Balakrishnan, the state government was under pressure to set the SIMI men free. "When we took police action against some of them, there was a hue and cry from human rights activists saying that minorities were being targeted," he told reporters.

The LDF government's casual attitude and its failure to bring charges against the organizers of the Binanipuram camp emboldened SIMI to hold another training session for around 40 cadres from UP, MP, Delhi, Gujarat, Karnataka and Jharkhand in December-January 2007. Activists were given commando training covering aspects like jungle warfare including the medicinal herbs and plants that must be consumed for survival, rock climbing and scaling and sliding using a rope. The trainees were also taught how to avoid giving away too much information during police interrogation. Shockingly enough, even the 2007 training camp was reported to the Kerala police, but no investigation was undertaken.

The reluctance of the various governments in Kerala to act against fundamentalist elements in the state is not a new phenomenon. The Kerala Assembly had in 2006 passed a unanimous resolution demanding the release of Coimbatore blasts accused and PDP leader Abdul Nasser Mahdani on humanitarian and medical grounds. Not only this, CPM leader TK Hamza even called on the PDP leader in jail in March, 2006, after which Mahdani announced his support for the LDF in the 2006 Assembly elections.

The probe into Kerala's terror links with the Valley, which began after four suspected militants from the state were killed in Kupwara in October 2008, revealed that many key players in the network had been followers of Mahdani, and were acquitted in the 1998 Coimbatore serial blast case in 2007. Mahdani, a Maulavi, had previously converted his outfit, Islamic Sevak Sangh, into the People's Democratic Party after the demolition of the Babri structure. The Kerala police found Mahdani's one-time associates among the dead, the absconding and the arrested. These loyalists had torched a bus, plotted to finish off CPI(M) leaders, and planned to blow up bridges and buildings to exert pressure on the Government to get Mahdani released from a Tamil Nadu jail. Though Kerala's links with Lashkar-e-Toiba were exposed only a couple of years ago there had been indications about attempts to send youths from the state to Pakistan for ISI training as far back as the late nineties. AV George — who had been a police circle inspector from March 96 to May 98 in Kozhikode — had deposed before the Judicial Commission probing the communal flare-up at Marad in 2002 that the police had arrested two persons who tried to move to Pakistan for ISI training. According to the Marad Judicial Commission report, AT Muhammed Ashraf and MV Subair were arrested in March, 1998 while they were trying to escape from Kozhikode after the arrest of Ooma Babu, an accused in the Coimbatore blast case. Ashraf had revealed that he was sent to Pakistan by Mahdani for obtaining training under the ISI. Subair was also instructed by Mahdani to go to Pakistan for ISI training.

In February 2009, in a serious warning to the Kerala Government, the GOC of Southern State, Major General Shivshankar, told Chief Minister Achutnandan bluntly that ISI was lending financial and ideological support to various terrorist outfits and that the state should view it seriously, but unmindful of such warnings both CPM and UDF are backing Islamic militants.

A few months later *Malayala Manorama* in its August 31 issue revealed startling police investigations of Jehadis using money, flashy cars, dresses, etc. to lure Hindu girls into love, marriage, conversion and eventual disappearance or transportation to Kashmir for Jehad. The police report said almost 500 Kerala girls have gone missing during the previous two years. Even in 2009, 30 'girl missing' cases were registered in police stations across Kerala every month. National media reports say that almost 4000 girls go missing every year.

Finally, acknowledging this serious state of affairs Kerala Chief Minister Achutnandan declared in August 2010 that the fundamentalist Popular Front of India (PFI) wanted to make Kerala a Muslim-majority state in the coming 20 years.

19

TAMIL NADU

Fortresses of Terror

The RDX attack on LK Advani's life in Coimbatore during an election campaign drew attention of the country to extensive network ISI has set up in Tamil Nadu. It showed that Pakistani terrorists and ISI affiliates have a formidable presence in the state. The Coimbatore blast, which missed Advani but killed 60 people, was the tip of the iceberg.

The Coimbatore-based Islamic fundamentalist organization Al-Ummah is the most notorious Muslim body of Tamil Nadu. When two of its activists were caught in Chennai with explosive devices it was found that one of them was its leader Kovai Batcha, a Keralite. Batcha, his brother Mohammad Khan and half a dozen of his associates were all trained by ISI in Pakistan and later infiltrated into Tamil Nadu via Kerala.

Al-Ummah was set up in 1992, and since then has been involved in several bomb blast cases. In 1993, when Hindu Munnani president Rajagopalan was murdered in Madurai, 16 top men of Al-Ummah, including Batcha, were rounded up in a storming operation organized by police commissioner Ganeshan in the Kottaimedu area. This area had become such a stronghold of the group that even the police feared to venture there. Batcha was released from jail in Chennai, but even while in jail he continued planning operations by passing information through his visitors. As a free man in Chennai he moved about with his own security escort of 30 armed guards. Besides Al-Ummah, there are several other terrorist outfits in Tamil Nadu.

Tamil Nadu has an 1150-km-long coast, and there was no policing of it to speak of (there still isn't). This situation is exploited by ISI. It functions in the state on three levels. In the coastal regions of Chennai, Nagapattinam, Thanjavur, Thiruvayur and Ramnathpuram in the border district of Coimbatore, terrorists have built up virtual fortresses. They are so secure that not even the police can penetrate there. The districts of Vellore, Chenglepet, Thiruchirapalli and Namakkal have become shelters for the terrorists. And in districts like Dindigal, Madurai, Thirunelveli, and Tutikorin terrorism is currently in the initial stage, so individual killings are resorted to.

Even among the terrorist fortresses in the state the small town of Kilakarai in Ramnathpuram district stands out. Apparently it is an ISI base and an arms training centre. In the same district Rameshvaram is just 18 km from Sri Lanka and Dhanushkodi is Land's End of India. The 18-km long desolate stretch of land between Rameshvaram and Dhanushkodi is under terrorist control and the zone for their arms training camps.

The factor that helps ISI terrorism in Kerala and Tamil Nadu is political rivalry. When Tamil terrorists escape to Kerala, the Kerala police are not at all keen on catching them. On the other hand, as stated earlier, extremist set-ups in Tamil Nadu receive all help in Kerala, from weapons and funds to shelter and training.

A relevant aspect of the situation in Tamil Nadu is that for ISI purposes Tamil Nadu has a convenient geography. Its extensive coast is a mere 18 km from Sri Lanka, and there was substantial support for Tamil Tigers in Tamil Nadu. According to an old US report ISI was actively wooing LTTE to promote turmoil in the state. Around the same time *Jane's Defence Weekly* had reported that US and Britain had tried to dissuade Pakistan from linking up with LTTE – apparently at the request of New Delhi and Colombo.

20

ALL-INDIA AGENDA

India "Sinking Ship"

Subverting India is the be all and end all of ISI. Underlining this fact way back in June 1994 Prakash Singh, former Director General, Border Security Force, wrote "We seem to be in the octopus grip stretching from Kashmir to Kerala and Maharashtra to Manipur." Parthasarathy had also once stated in an article that a senior ISI official had proudly proclaimed that it was the aim of ISI to weaken India from within and had added that he had no doubt it would succeed in achieving this objective.

Facilitating Factor

An important material factor facilitating this programme was the easy availability of arms and manpower. While conducting the war in Afghanistan virtually on its own, ISI had trained more than 80,000 Mujahideen and sent them into battle. These men had been contributed by various Muslim countries, but when the war ended the donors refused to take them back, with the result that a huge mass of trained fighters with nothing to fight for was at ISI's disposal.

Secondly, after the US success in Afghanistan, the Americans saw to it that the weaponry and technology used in that war were made available to the frontline state of Pakistan free of cost, and with the added advantage of deniability. Covert armed action had been successful in Afghanistan, and there was no reason why it would not succeed in India as well.

It did, with disastrous results for suicidally soft India. Kashmir has been burning for 50 years. In Punjab, Khalistan has again reared its head. In the North-East ISI has been successfully aiding and abetting any number of terrorist-separatist outfits. Mumbai had to witness 26/11. And in South India terror training camps are being held in Karnataka and Kerala, while metropolitan cities like Hyderabad in Andhra are literally crawling with terrorists. What the reader of the book needs to understand is that this situation was scripted by ISI.

On August 6, 1993, just a few days before India's Independence Day, a meeting took place in Pakistan's capital Islamabad, in which the then ISI chief Lt. Gen. Hamid Gul boasted: "Pakistan is situated between two sinking ships, the former Soviet Union and India. I played my role in destroying the Soviet Union. Now I want to sink the other ship."

Gul's Boast

This was the clearest possible expression of ISI's all-India agenda. And it was no empty boast. After setting up the Kabul cell of ISI, which worked as the channel for American arms to the Afghan Mujahideen, Gul had run the Kashmir cell in the late 1980's. Even after his retirement Gul had remained an active consultant to the agency. Embarrassed by his boastful talk the Benazir Bhutto government told him to be discreet, as Pakistan had narrowly escaped being branded a terrorist state by the US. But this did not mean ISI men turned boy scouts. Rather, ISI involved nationals of various foreign countries like Afghanistan, Bangladesh, Libya, Sudan and the LTTE of Sri Lanka in its Jehad on India. This extension of manpower indicated that ISI's 'Operation Destabilization' project was adopted virtually as Pakistan's strategic objective vis-a-vis India.

Planned Proxy War

Thus was launched a planned proxy war on India. For it to be comprehensively effective, different fronts were opened, like relentless infiltration, urban terrorism, pumping in fake money, a nefarious nexus with the underworld, and fomenting socio-religious alienation. But of course the main weapon of the war remained terrorist violence.

The systematic deployment of ISI's expert terrorists into India began in mid-1990, according to a US task force report in April 1994. These highly-trained operatives were sent to build up a countrywide support system. Actually, Indian intelligence found that such groups had been active much earlier. Since then ISI's war on India is going on all over the country. ISI terrorists strike virtually at will, whenever and wherever they choose to do so, and ISI has a frightening array of terrorist outfits at its disposal to carry out the strikes.

Even as long back as in 1994 Prakash Singh, ex-Director General of BSF, had expressed the apprehension that "ISI operations in India have indeed assumed frightening proportions." To date this situation continues, as shown by the centre's admission that terror is spreading across the country. Towards the end of 2006 the Central Government admitted that cross-border terrorism has spread to the country's interior. The agenda paper prepared for a chief ministers' conclave at that time said there was a manifold rise in grenade attacks in Kashmir and there was no respite in insurgency in the North-East.

21

PAKISTANI TERRORIST ORGANISATIONS

Indian Surrender at Kandahar

The initial ISI probe into India was carried out with cadres of an outfit called Jamiat-i-Tulba. Since then it has built up a multitude of terrorist organizations, some set up in Pakistan, others sponsored in India. According to an official document released in mid-1993, a decade and a half ago, there were over a hundred of them, out of which about two dozen were active at that time. As of 1996, six major organizations and several smaller ones were operating in Kashmir. Their strength was estimated at between 5,000 and 10,000 armed men. Actually ISI's very first terrorist outfit was a borrowed one. For it had taken over Afghan warlord Hekmatyar's fighting force Hizb-i-Islami to spearhead the Afghan Jehad, which was later transformed into a Kashmiri organization and renamed Hizb-i-Islami-e-Kashmir.

Jammu-Kashmir Liberation Front (JKLF)

However, the oldest and most widely known indigenous ISI creation was the Jammu-Kashmir Liberation Front (JKLF). It was meant to lead the brigade of terror outfits either created or sponsored by ISI. But it demanded independence for the whole of Kashmir, including PoK. Consequently it fell foul of ISI, which was providing assistance to it with the objective of incorporating Kashmir into Pakistan. As a result JKLF fell out of favour, and ISI plotted to weaken it by transforming its student wing into a separate and pro-Pak body called Ikhwan-ul-Muslimeen. However JKLF is now again rearing its head, thanks to the strident Muslim separatism that the Hurriyat conglomerate is championing. Ikhwan proved itself by kidnapping Indian Oil Corporation executive director Doraiswamy. This pro-Pak group was very active a decade and a half ago. Its leader Hilal Ahmed Beg was in the forefront of the campaign for Islamization of Kashmir. After the divorce with JKLF, ISI's choice for carrying on its Kashmir agenda was Hizb-ul Mujahideen (HuM), one of the most active terrorist groups in the Valley which espoused Kashmir's merger with Pakistan. It thus became the most powerful. Even in 1994, it was estimated to have a force of 4500 cadres and possessed an arsenal of

9000 weapons. Actually, an Indian national, Mohammad Yusuf Shah alias Salahuddin, has been the face of HuM since 1991. Though this outfit has lately not been as active as it was during the 1990s, it is believed to still provide logistical support to Lashkar-e-Toiba (LeT) and Jaish-e-Mohammad (JeM) in the Kashmir Valley through its network in the local population.

Salahuddin had even contested the 1987 assembly elections in Jammu and Kashmir as a Muslim United Front candidate. Before becoming chief of PoK-based Hizb he was district commander of the Valley-based Jamaat-i-Islami Kashmir till 1989. An Interpol Red Corner Notice (RCN) has been pending against him since 1998. A Hizb-ul-Mujahideen commander Abdul Rashid travelled to Bangladesh from Pakistan on a valid passport. From there he sneaked into Kolkata. He had been appointed district commander for Doda and was on his way to Jammu when arrested. Another terrorist Mushtaq Hussain actually had an Indian visa on which he had visited Pakistan.

Kashmiri Jamaat-i-Islami

Hizb-ul-Mujahideen is closely affiliated with another Pakistani body, Jamaat-i-Islami, from which it received funds, weapons and training assistance apart from ISI's contribution. However following the organizational principles recommended by Tehran and Khartoum it changed into the Kashmiri Jamaat-i-Islami, with a quasi-legal character as a socio-educational body, with HuM as its clandestine terrorist arm. In 1991 it set up several clandestine subgroups like Nasir-ul-Islam and Jamaat-ul-Mujahideen to carry out specialized terrorist operations.

According to a government document this body indulged in large-scale intimidation, torture and exploitation of the people in the Valley in 1993. It even printed posters and distributed leaflets ordering women not to leave the valley without its permission. The document said medical establishments and health centres in Jammu and Udhampur confirmed large-scale abortions by unmarried Kashmiri women. They had been raped by the militants and ordered not to leave the valley in order to cover up the atrocity.

Al-Badr

Another major and quite old terrorist organization was Al-Badr Mujahideen, generally known Al-Badr. It is reportedly as thick as thieves with ISI. It is also the richest of Pakistani Jihadi outfits, and is extremist Wahabi in orientation. Its special feature was that it was formed in the then East Pakistan.

Actually, Al-Badr was an offshoot of Jamaat-e-Islami (JeI), then an East Pakistani organization. JeI formed Al-Badr in 1971 at the instance of

ISI to counter the independence movement for the creation of Bangladesh. It became notorious for carrying out, in December 1971, a massacre of hundreds of Bengali intellectuals who supported the liberation movement. Before the fall of Dhaka ISI shifted all cadres of Al-Badr to West Pakistan to prevent their falling into the hands of the liberation force and the Indian Army.

In the face of worldwide condemnation of the carnage ISI had to disband Al-Badr, and it was dormant during the 1970s. Under President Zia-ul-Haq it was reactivated in the 1980s and used in the Afghan war. It worked in tandem with Jamaat-e-Islami of Pakistan on the one side and Hizb-e-Islami (HeI) of Gulbuddin Hekmatyar on the other. ISI's deep involvement in this war was underlined by the fact that nearly 6000 Arabs from Middle East countries flocked to Peshawar in Pakistan to join the Jehad. ISI entrusted to Al-Badr the task of training and motivating them. Abdullah Azam, the Palestinism Mullah considered the mentor of Osama bin Laden, and bin Laden himself were put through their Jihadi paces by Al-Badr when they reached Peshawar.

After the withdrawal of Soviet troops from Afghanistan Al-Badr played an active role in helping the Afghan Mujahideen overthrow the Najibullah government and capture power in April 1992. It was closely associated with the Mujahideen government till it was overthrown by Taliban in September 1996. Al-Badr's close association with Hel of Hekmatyar, who was at that time at daggers drawn with Taliban, which was born in 1994, created tension in the relationship between Al-Badr and Taliban. It lasted till 9/11, but thereafter Al-Badr, Taliban and Hel came together for a joint Jehad against the US and NATO forces in Afghanistan. Al-Badr has its headquarters in the North West Frontier Province (NWFP) of Pakistan and was the first to introduce suicide terrorism. It is believed to have the largest number of cadres from outside the Indian subcontinent.

Al-Badr is named after the site of the historic battle near Medina, fought by followers of Prophet Mohammad on March 17, 624 against the army of Mecca, in which they were victorious. This battle finds special mention in the Quran, and Muslims look upon Prophet Mohammad's victory as heralding the beginning of the conquest of the world by Islam. Apropos this battle the late Anwar Shaikh wrote in his book *Islam: Sex and Violence* in a chapter titled *Jehad and Civilization: The Battle of Badr*. "The battle of Badr is a tiny event by any stretch of the imagination, yet it has significantly influenced the course of human history... because it served as the first practical exposition of the Islamic doctrine known as `Jehad' ."

"*Jehad* is an Arabic word which literally means endeavour, but as an Islamic doctrine it implies fighting in the way of Allah (the Arabic God) to establish his supremacy over unbelievers until they relinquish their faith to become Muslims or acknowledge their subordination by paying a humiliation tax called `Jazia'." "The doctrine of Jehad... incorporates the Arab custom of *razzia* (raiding for booty) ... It was sheer looting ... This institution of brigandage known as *ghazwa* (*razzia*) had existed long before the advent of the Prophet Mohammad. The Umayyad poet al-Qutami has alluded to this custom in two of his verses: "Our business is to make raids on the enemy, on our neighbour, and our own brother in case we find none to raid but a brother." "The Prophet made sure that brigandage no longer remains a low and haphazard affair, but a highly respected and disciplined organization, stamped with divine approval: "Know that paradise is under the shades of swords." (*Sahih al-Bukhari*: 4. 37). Thus, Sword became the connecting link between pillage and paradise.

Al-Umar

Later ISI shifted its support from Hizb-ul-Mujahideen to another outfit called Al-Umar for intensifying its activities. Then a major chunk of ISI's arms supply and other help went to this body.

Al-Umar came into the limelight with the kidnapping in 1993 of the brother-in-law of Ghulam Nabi Azad, then Civil Aviation Minister of the Government of India.

Janbaz Mujahideen

Yet another major terror group that ISI formed was Janbaz Mujahideen. For Pakistan's long-term plans it was necessary to have at its disposal a highly professional and tightly controlled core of terror cadres. This was just such a force. There was a regular ISI task force assigned to run the Janbaz Mujahidden, and it operated from ISI safe houses.

Jaish-e-Mohammad (JeM)

Jaish-e-Mohammad (JeM) was set up in 2000 by the notorious terrorist Masood Azhar released by the Government of India on December 31, 1999 along with two other terrorists in exchange for the passengers of an Indian Airlines plane hijacked from Kathmandu to Kandahar, the Taliban base in Afghanistan. This hostages-for-prisoners swap cost India dearly, for it was immediately after being set free that Azhar founded JeM, one of the most dreaded outfits, whose terror record includes attacks on Parliament (2001) and Ayodhya (2005). A Pakistani of Bahawalpur, Azhar was a product of the ultra-fundamentalist Binori *madrasa* in Karachi. He joined Harkat-ul-Mujahideen (HuM) and was sent to India to supervise the merger of the two Harkats — Harkat-ul-Mujahideen and Harkat-ul-Ansar. He stayed on in Kashmir Valley and supervised a number of terror attacks before being captured.

JeM is banned in India, was declared a terrorist organization by the US, and also banned there in 2001. In 2003 Pakistan banned two JeM splinters, Khuddam-ul-Islam underAzhar and Jamaat-ul-Furqan under one Jabbar, a suspect in an attempt to assassinate Musharraf. JeM is also officially banned in Pakistan since 9/11 but it continues to be active. There is an Interpol Red Corner Notice (RCN) on Azhar for a number of crimes. His saviours — hijackers Mohammad Ibrahim Athar Alvi, Zahoor Ibrahim Mistry, Shahid Akhtar — are also on the wanted list. Incidentally, the Indian suspicion that the hijackers and terrorists freed at Kandahar continue to move freely in Pakistan was confirmed by arrested Hyderabad terrorist Riazuddin Nasir, who told the police that he regularly spotted Masood Azhar and his brother Ibrahim Athar at the Binori mosque in Karachi during 2006-07. It was reported in October 2009 that Jaish-e-Mohammad was setting up a large new base just outside Bahawalpur town in Pakistan's Punjab province with anti-Hindu inscriptions on its walls. Pakistani authorities have turned a blind eye to the base. Jaish's new site may contain underground bunkers or tunnels. On the inside walls there are painted inscriptions, including a warning to Hindus and Jews, with a picture of Delhi's historic Red Fort. The bases of JeM and a string of other terror groups in Punjab have gone largely unnoticed by the Pak authorities.

Harkat-ul-Ansar

Harkat-ul-Ansar was formed in 1993 by Saadatullah Khan by merging two Pakistani terror groups, Harkat-ul-Jihad-i-Islami and Harkat-ul-Mujahideen. According to another source Masood Azhar was initially the HuA leader who later set up JeM. It was an offshoot of Harkat-ul-Ansar which had kidnapped five foreign tourists in Kashmir in 1995. In 2003 it split into two factions, Khuddam-ul-Islam (KuI) and Jamaat-ul-Furqan (JuF), both of which Pakistan had to ban the same year. In turn JeM had two offshoots, Lashkar-e-Jhangvi and Sipah-e-Sahaba, both of which are mainly involved in targeting Shia Muslims in Pakistan. Based in Pak-occupied Kashmir (PoK), HuA has operated not only in Kashmir but also in Myanmar, Tajikstan and Bosnia. It was banned by the US in 1997. For sometime it functioned through a body called Al-Faran. HuA has a large number of non-Kashmiris in it, including those from Pakistan, Afghanistan and the Middle East. Many of these terrorists were trained in Afghanistan by ISI agents. HuA also received generous financial aid from ISI.

Other Outfits

To this array of major Pakistani terrorist bodies ISI keeps adding many other outfits with varying degrees of potential and effectiveness. To list a few:

Al-Jehad: Once a formidable outfit with a strength of about 4000. Now broken up into a number of small factions.

Al-Barq: Set up in 1993. Was paid a million Rupees per month for infiltration into India.

Tehrik-ul-Mujahideen: A radical group supported by Middle-East countries.

Muslim Mujahideen: Formed in 1992 as parallel to Hizb-ul-Mujahideen as a result of violent factionalism.

Harkat-ul-Jihad: A highly professional terrorist group made up of veterans from Afghanistan.

Hizb-ul-Momineen: A small and not very effective Shia body.

Sipah-e-Sahaba: Linked with those engaged in Jehad not only in Kashmir but also in Chechnya, Central Asia and elsewhere. Its unusual feature: this extremely sectarian Sunni organisation routinely killed Shia Muslims.

Jamiat-ul Mujahideen: A small group.

Islami Inqilab Mahaz: A group working in collusion with Jago Mujahideen, an outfit based in Dhaka, capital of Bangladesh.

Hezbullah: Not a major player now.

Dukhtaran-e-Millat: The only women's extremist body. Its members are usually used as couriers of terrorists. Was recently in the news in connection with an "Islamisation" drive in Kashmir.

To this plethora of terrorist bodies set up or sponsored by Pakistan can also be added the Pakistan Army itself. To quote Col. Shyam Kumar in *The Nefarious Activities of ISI*: "The fundamentalists, the Mujahideens, have a stranglehold on the Pakistan Army and the civil administration. A sizeable portion of the Pakistan Army is highly indoctrinated in Islamic teachings. There is no distinction between Pakistan's regular armymen and Mujahideens." The fundamentalists claim a right to fight anywhere in the world where Islam is in danger. According to their ideology war must be total, and terror must be used as an essential weapon of war.

A strange but related case was a Pakistan Army officer himself turning a militant. A report in June 2007 said Shahzad Khan, a militant commander arrested by the J & K police was a Captain in the Pakistan Army during the Kargil War in 1999 and joined a militant group in 2001. He was considered the most wanted militant commander in the Valley since LeT commander Salahuddhin *alias* Bilal moved to Pakistan the previous year.

22

LASHKAR-E-TOIBA (LeT)

Three Islamistans in India

Lashkar-e-Toiba (LeT) is at the top of the Pakistani terror teams wreaking havoc on India. Among the many terrorist groups that ISI uses in India LeT has certainly played the most dangerous role. Besides several terrorist attacks in Jammu and Kashmir, including that on the State Assembly in Srinagar, it was also involved in the attacks on the temples ofAkshardham and Ayodhya, as well as on the Red Fort of Delhi in December 2001, its terror reaching a spectacular climax in Mumbai on 26 November 2008 (26/11).

300 Sleeper Cells

This unending series of tremendous strikes reveal how deeply this Pakistani terrorist organization, aided and abetted by ISI, has infiltrated this country. In a newspaper article in June 2005, titled *ISI-LeT Nexus Exposed* G Parthasarthy wrote: "Barely a year ago the former Director General of ISI, Lt. Gen. Hamid Gul, told a friend of mine that the LeT had succeeded in establishing "300 sleeper cells to mount terror strikes in towns and cities across India." Earlier, in April 1999, LeT's chief of military operations Lakhvi had told the Pakistani paper *Nation*, "We are extending our networks across India ... To set up Mujahideen networks across India is our one target." He added: "We are preparing the Muslims of India, and when they are ready, it will be the start of the disintegration of India."

The relentless terror campaign directed at major Indian cities shows that Lakhvi's words were not an empty threat. Mumbai Police have asserted that Lakhvi's subordinates planned the July 11 serial bombings, financed their architects, and trained their perpetrators." Police Commissioner Roy named the city (Bahawalpur) and even identified the road and house where the terrorists were trained by LeT commander Muhammed Azam Cheema.

LeT's Origin

LeT was initially formed in 1990 in Afghanistan to fight Soviet forces, and was largely made up of cadres from Afghanistan and Pakistan. Later it became the armed wing of Markaz-ud-Dawa-wal-Irshad, a fundamentalist Islamic organization in Pakistan. Markaz itself was set up in 1987, inspired by the role of Osama bin Laden in Afghanistan. Its leader was Hafiz Mohammad Saeed, a professor at the University of Engineering and Technology, Lahore. With patronage from ISI and Osama, Saeed set up a complex at Muridke, near Lahore. It has now grown into the venue of annual congregations of terrorists and their sympathisers, including senior Pakistani civil and military officials. Under Saeed's leadership Muridke has also become a cesspool of rabidly anti-India, especially anti-Hindu, Jihadism. Here Saeed preached hatred of all *kafirs*, especially Hindus, Jews, and Christians, who he declared enemies of Islam. In an interview to the Urdu newspaper *Khabrain* in Pakistan he said the Quran supported the concept of Jihad, and they would support it, and they would also extend support to organizations active in Jihad anywhere in the world.

Saeed also vowed that the objective of LeT was not just a Jihad in Kashmir but also to create three Muslim homelands, with Pakistan and Jammu and Kashmir constituting one, the Muslims of North India constituting the second, and the Muslims of South India forming the third. In February 1996 he again declared, "Jihad in Kashmir would soon spread to entire India. Our Mujahideen would create three Pakistans in India."

Two years later, in February 1998, al-Qaeda supremo Osama bin Laden formed the International Islamic Front for Jihad against Jews and Crusaders, aimed at mounting terrorist attacks against American and Israeli interests, and LeT promptly became its founding member, proclaiming that its aim was to unfurl the green flag of Islam in Washington, Tel Aviv, and Delhi. When LeT attacked the Red Fort of Delhi, Saeed boasted that he had succeeded in unfurling that flag in Delhi. He is considered a prime example of Pakistani patronage of terrorism. In fact, in the considered opinion of Pakistan-watchers Saeed set up LeT in order to facilitate a direct role for ISI in Jammu and Kashmir operations.

The prominence LeT came to acquire in Pakistan can be gauged from the fact that even Prime Minister Nawaz Sharif, while in power, deferred to it. His information minister Mushahid Hussain was a regular visitor to its headquarters in Muridke. It appears that LeT even had advance knowledge of the Pakistani establishment's anti-India designs. For instance, a month before Pakistan launched the Kargil attack on India LeT's chief of military operations Zaki-ur-Rehman Lakhvi had announced that a war was imminent.

Markaz to Jamaat

Although the moving spirit behind everything LeT did was Saeed, for the record he was the head of the charitable organisation Markaz-ud-

Dawa wal-Irshad, which changed its name to Jamaat-ud-Dawa (JuD) when LeT was banned.

The exact relationship between LeT and Markaz/Jamaat has some slightly differing versions, which is also the case with the account of how Markaz came into being. According to one story, during his tenure as a college teacher of Islamic Studies Azam Cheema came into contact with a group of extremist professors at the department of Islamiyat (Islamic Religion and Culture) in the engineering college in Lahore, who were connected with the fundamentalist Jamaat Ahl-e-Hadis sect, and were engaged in setting up Markaz as a platform to draw recruits for the Jihad in Afghanistan. It was sited on a 160-acre campus near Lahore donated by Pakistan President Gen. Zia-ul Haq. By 1986, aided by generous contributions from ISI, CIA and Osama bin Laden's close associate Abdullah Azam, Markaz laid the foundation for an armed wing. This was Lashkar-e-Toiba. Initially LeT cadres were trained at camps in the Afghan provinces of Kunnar and Paktia.

Saudi Connection

According to another version, in 1986 Saeed and two other professors at the Lahore University of Engineering and Technology, Hafiz Abdur Rehman Makki, who is also a close relative of Saeed, and Jaffar Iqbal (who took Abu Hamza as his *alias*) together set up Markaz-e-Dawa-wal-Irshad (Centre for Preaching and Guidance). Saeed and the others had been to Saudi Arabia for higher education in Islamic Studies, where they got together with Saudi scholars at the Medina University. The connecting link and a major influence was Shaikh Abdullah Azam, a Palestinian who had links with Ikhwan-ul Muslimoon of Egypt and was a well-known ideologue of the Afghan Jihad. A year later LeT was launched to participate in the Afghan Jehad where it fought alongside the Afghan Mujahideen outfit Itihad-e-Islami.

According to yet another version of the LeT–Jamaat-ud-Dawa connection, when the US declared LeT a terrorist body in the wake of the attack on Parliament House in New Delhi and banned it— with Pakistan following suit reluctantly, LeT got around the ban in Pakistan by renaming itself Jamaat-ud-Dawa and began to bill itself a charitable organisation. It even arranged aid for victims of the 2005 earthquake in Kashmir. Actually, this is an LeT show, and despite the ban both LeT and its charitable cover have flourished in Pakistan. LeT has expanded its membership, its operational reach, and its influence. It still operates training camps for terrorists, and the Muridke campus is actually a huge training complex, complete with a conference centre, a *Madrasa*, and even fish farms.

As for LeT's charitable side, Jamaat-ud-Dawa (JuD), it has also become so big that it runs an educational network of *Madrasas*, schools and even a couple of colleges. It also runs a network of mosques, nearly a dozen dispensaries, and two hospitals. It has an elaborate organizational structure, with separate departments for preaching, *Ulema*, martyrs, teachers, students, even a peasants and labour wing. Then there is a press and publications department, and even a spokesman to attend to inquiries from the media.

JuD is in the very good books of Pakistani officials, but the US classified it as a terrorist outfit in April 2006, calling it an *alias* of LeT. Pakistan, however, allowed it to conduct social service programmes, raise funds, and run *Madrasas*.

Quranic Companions

By 1993 LeT had put in place the infrastructure it needed for terrorism in India, and since that year it has been active in the Kashmir Valley, its operational reach steadily extending across India over the years. Even as it carried out the first major strikes in Kashmir it had demonstrated its desire and capacity to operate on a larger scale. On the first anniversary of Babri demolition, an LeT team of three carried out a series of bombings across North and West India. While one of them was caught, two escaped and went on to set up elaborate LeT networks in alliance with SIMI. One such functioning network was uncovered in the capital itself during investigation into the 2005 serial bombings in Delhi. A noticeable feature of this strike was the method of secrecy used. It was that the identifies of the Pakistani perpetrators of the bombings were not known to their Indian counterparts except by their Arabic *Kuniyat*, that is, *aliases* drawn from the names of the companions of Prophet Mohammed.

From 1998 onward a growing number of Pakistanis participated directly in LeT's pan-India operations. Then from 2003 onwards it exploited the Gujarat events to build up a pool of local supporters for more and more terrorist projects across the country. In LeT's vision there can be no peace with India. The only means of engagement with India, a predatory Hindu entity, can be through a Jehad-without-end, wrote the *Frontline* journal in an extensive survey of terrorism in India titled *War on Many Fronts* in December 2005.

Top Guns

Leading the LeT war on these fronts are veterans of the terror business. The more prominent among them are: Azam Cheema, Muzammil, Abu-al-Qama, Abu Hamza, Rasool Khan `Party', Abu Qahafa, and Ibrahim.

Azam Cheema: During investigations into the July 11, 2006 Mumbai serial train bomb blasts, Azam Cheema's name emerged as the key LeT coordinator of the conspiracy. Faisal Ataur Rehman Sheikh, a central Mumbai-based figure in the train blasts case, was given Rs 1.80 lakh by Azam Cheema to recruit and send youth from Mumbai to Pakistan for training. Among people who went were Dr. Tanvir Ahmed Ansari, Suhail Ahmed Shaikh and Zameer Shaikh, all arrested in the July 2006 blasts, and Feroze Ghaswala, arrested on May 9, 2006 in connection with a huge arms and explosives haul in Aurangabad. Ansari, who got training at a Lashkar camp between May–July 2004, named Azam Cheema as a key figure for operations in India. Cheema organized training camps in Pakistan for Indian Muslim youths in the handling and use of arms and explosives. He also pushed the youth to avenge atrocities on Muslims in India. As overall military commander of LeT Cheema's main role is to launch Jihadis into India. He is a shadowy figure, but intercepted conversations between him and LeT's operational commander for Kashmir Abu-al Qama showed that Cheema controlled every LeT commander operating in India. An Interpol Red Corner Notice (RCN) is pending against him.

Muzammil *alias* Abu Huraira: Muzammil has been identified by Lashkar-linked terrorists arrested in India as operations commander for the India region, reporting directly to overall LeT operations commander Zaki-ur-Rehman Lakhvi. Sabahuddin Ahmed, an LeT-trained Bihari youth accused in the December 2005 Indian Institute of Science (IISc) attack case in Bangalore, worked directly under Muzammil, who had tasked him with providing suicide attackers and weapons for assault on targets in Mumbai. Muzammil suffered two major operational disappointments in March 2005 and later in May 2006 when the Delhi police killed a group of militants planning an attack on the Indian Military Academy and when the Maharashtra police seized a huge cache of arms and explosives at Aurangabad, said Sabahuddin.

According to Raziuddin Nasir who met Muzammil frequently during his stay in Pakistan, networks that were once reporting to Azam Cheema were handed over to Muzammil around 2006. After the Mumbai blasts of 2006, according to Nasir's statement, during dinner Muzammil proudly claimed that the train blasts were carried out by the LeT with explosives arranged from J&K.

Abu-al-Qama: This LeT commander, based in Muzaffarabad in Pakistan, emerged as the key figure behind the execution of a series of blasts in New Delhi around Diwali in October 2005. He is one of the commanders of the three Lashkar operational sectors in Jammu and Kashmir. Abu-al-Qama had tasked an operative code-named Abu Huzaifa and his associate Abdul Rehman "Mota" to set up the 2005 serial bombings in Delhi, and then Tariq Ahmed Dar, a Srinagar-based pharmaceutical salesman, was charged with its actual execution. Abu-al-Qama is also believed to have had charge of an aborted bombing operation in January 2006.

Abu Hamza: Hamza is believed to be the man who fired the weapons in the IISc attack in Bangalore in December 2005. He panicked and aborted the attack after his gun jammed. He was trained for the attack for nearly one month by the ISI by using photos of IISc and location data from internet maps.

Rasool Khan 'Party': An Indian gangster from Gujarat linked to Dawood Ibrahim in the early 1990s, "Party" was involved in the killing of former Gujarat minister Haren Pandya. He is believed to be a key link between ISI and LeT in Pakistan.

Abu Qahafa: Till early 2006 Abu was amongst the highly regarded teachers of advanced commando techniques in a four-month module of specialized training given to select candidates under the Lashkar set-up. He was subsequently re-allocated to the India operations set-up of Muzammil. Under the commando training set-up he provided detailed training in handling of weapons, field tactics of guerrilla warfare—ambushing, raiding, hiding out, camouflaging, map reading, reconnaissance, caching weapons and communications.

Ibrahim *alias* Ali: Considered second in command in Muzammil's pan-India operations for the LeT, Ibrahim replaced a man called Abdul Azeez as Muzammil's deputy after Azeez, who directly supervised the December 2005 IISc attack, was criticized by operations commander Lakhvi at an annual LeT operations review meeting in early 2006 for spending more than Rs 50 lakh in one year and achieving only partial success with the llSc attack. Ibrahim is a close relative of LeT chief Hafiz Mohammad Saeed. An expert in computers, he is said to be constantly connected to the Internet via a laptop or a cell phone. Like Azeez before him, he travels frequently to Nepal to personally take care of logistics and arrange the movement of trained militants in and out of India. He also sends money through various routes for sleeper-cell members requiring finance in India.

The interrogation of Kasab, the sole surviving perpetrator of the latest Mumbai carnage, has also thrown up the names of some LeT top guns. They are Muzammil, Abdur Rehman Makki, and Zia-ur Rehman Lakhvi. According to the latest available information Muzammil has apparently replaced Al-Qama as LeT's India chief, while Makki is second in command of Jamaat-ud-Dawa and head of its political affairs division. In his booklet *Tareekh-e-Islam ke Fidayee Dastay* ("Fidayeen Squads in Islamic History"), published in Lahore in 2004, he claimed that LeT Fidayeen Hafeez Mohammad Akmal, who attacked the Bandipur BSF HQ in Kashmir in 1999, was the first suicide-bomber. Lakhvi has been a top commander with LeT since 1992, and an instructor at its terrorist training camps.

According to other sources of information on LeT's top echelons, at a meeting in February 2003 at the Muridke base of LeT one Abdullah Mujahid, currently held in Guantanamo, was appointed chief of operations in India, and it was him that Muzammil succeeded. But the dating here seems to be uncertain, because in September 2002 Muzammil reportedly supervised the storming of the temple in Gandhinagar, Gujarat, with LeT cadres in Ahmedabad working under his command to facilitate the strike.

Among Muzammil's most ambitious projects was a June 2004 plot to assassinate former home minister LK Advani. A Pune resident by name Javed Shaikh was tasked with conducting two Pakistanis to Ahmedabad for the strike. The plot was uncovered and could not be carried out. Shaikh was also involved in a separate plot to bomb the Bombay Stock Exchange. A Kashmiri medical student in Pune by name ManzoorAhmed Chilloo was tasked by his LeT controllers in Srinagar with liaising between Shaikh and the operatives who would have eventually carried out the attack.

Yet another top terrorist of LeT is its ace recruiter Abdul Karim "Tunda". He was the top field operative of LeT in India until he disappeared, probably fleeing to Bangladesh after the Jalandhar blast in 1997. He had recruited a number of young cadres during the period 1996 to 1998.

LeT's Female Terrorists

A new development in the terror war on the Kashmir front is that the existence of women of Kashmiri origin in the ranks of Lashkar-e-Toiba has been discovered. Many such women travelled to Pakistan on valid visas along with male accomplices and returned to the Valley after receiving arms training. The presence of women in LeT ranks came to light after the arrest, reported by the media in late 2004, of a 20-year old woman Khalida Akhtar in Srinagar. Her interrogation revealed that LeT has been raising a group of women terrorists of Kashmiri origin and providing them ideological and arms training in camps situated in Pakistan-occupied Kashmir.

Khalida's interrogation also revealed that apart from subversive activities, these women, most of whom are young and attractive, were being used to trap army officers and jawans and get an insider's view into troop movements and operations, so that LeT could gain vantage positions during encounters. Khalida herself was arrested when she had come to meet an army officer in a park in Srinagar. She was acquainted with him, had been meeting him for sometime, and had actually plotted his killing by LeT's area commander in Srinagar.

This 'refinement' of LeT tactics of training attractive young women for espionage through seduction of Indian armymen for obtaining sensitive information on security arrangements had a remarkable exception, the first in two decades of militancy in Jammu and Kashmir, when an active female cadre of LeT was shot dead by security forces along with her terrorist husband, who had earlier organized the massacre of more than

30 Hindus. In 2005 there had been a *burqa*-clad female suicide bomber who blew herself up.

Al-Qaeda Outsourcing

On August 8, 2007 al-Qaeda issued a threat saying attacking the US and its allies including Tel Aviv, Moscow, and Delhi was their legitimate right. This threat came barely a week after National Security Advisor MK Narayanan said during an interview: "Terror groups like LeT are a part of al-Qaeda, so in a way al-Qaeda cells are already here."

Indian Army sources have also confirmed that al-Qaeda is outsourcing its terrorism in Kashmir through various outfits including Paskistan-based Jaish-e-Mohammad and Lashkar-e-Toiba. This was stated by Lt. Gen. Panag, GOC, Northern Command, in a press conference in Udhampur on September 15, 2007. "Al-Qaeda is a pan-Islamic terrorist outfit which has its sleeper cells across the world to carry out terror activities. It has outsourced much of its work to various terrorist outfits in many parts of the world, and these include LeT and JeM," he said.

ISI Relationship

Needless to say, LeT and ISI have a close relationship, and it actually had eyewitnesses. Giving one such instance in the US journal *Time*, journalist Ghulam Hasnain described how he watched LeT operatives monitoring wireless transmissions from their field units on a Fidayeen suicide-squad attack on Srinagar airport. During the strike, he wrote, a colonel-rank ISI officer called to ask for details of the operation.

International Presence

Although LeT terrorism is mostly India-specific it is also acquiring a steadily widening international presence. LeT cadres have fought in Iraq and operated in East Africa. It has also built up influential presence among the growing group of radical Islamic networks in South Asia. In fact, "The Lashkar under Saeed has made it clear that it sees the war in Kashmir as just a stepping stone to establishing Islamic rule throughout South Asia," wrote *Times of India* on September 2, 2007.

LeT also has operational cells in Britain, USA and Australia, and they are active enough for America and Australia to now view LeT as a global threat. British investigators found that the terrorists involved in the 2005 bombings of the London underground local train system had visited LeT facilities in Pakistan.

That even the international presence of LeT can be India-specific was indicated by press reports in September 2010, according to which US intelligence agencies have informed India that LeT has some 200 cadres present in Sri Lanka who intend to use it as an entry point to enter India.

What is more significant, Lashkar has apparently built up a regular web of Western recruits. For years it has actively recruited westerners, especially Britons and Americans, serving as a farm for Islamic militants. For their training there are al-Qaeda camps accessible to English-speakers. "These camps are ideal for people who speak English," said US investigator Evan Kohlmann. "Newbie militants... perceive that Lashkar-e-Toiba are below the radar. They are less likely to attract negative attention. It is an easier ladder rung to reach. Lashkar is seen as a rung to get to al-Qaeda."

LeT's western-oriented propaganda attracts converts like David Hicks, an Australian whom it trained and provided a letter of introduction to al-Qaeda. He translated terrorist material into English for Osama bin Laden, who he met at a camp in Afghanistan, before his capture in late 2001. Another such convert was a Muslim Briton, Aabid Khan. When the British police arrested him at Manchester airport on his return from Pakistan in June 2006, they found a trove of terrorist propaganda and manuals on his laptop that the trial judge later described as amongst the largest and most extensive ever discovered. The haul included maps and videos of potential targets in New York and Washington. This Briton had organized training expeditions to Pakistan for his confederates.

LeT's fund-collection activities also show its international reach. Although during the 1990s it received funding from ISI for carrying out terrorist attacks in Kashmir, it now has multiple sources. LeT has opened fund-raising arms in Saudi Arabia, UAE and Kuwait. It also collects donations from the Pakistani expatriate community in the Persian Gulf and Britain, as well as from Islamic NGOs and Pakistani and Kashmiri businessmen. And it continues receiving funds from ISI.

All in all, to quote former CIA analyst Michael Scheuer, "LeT are a much more international organisation than they were in 2002. They are better trained, and operate all over."

Focus on India

Despite its internationalism, LeT's focus on India remains, and Musharraf's political exit has not made a difference to it. In fact, LeT's India-specific violence continues with the same old violence, as is evident from the 26/11 attack. Top LeT leaders Sajia Mir, Abu Hamza and Abu Qahafa had actually escorted the attackers when they set sail for Mumbai on board the Pakistani ship *Al Hussaini*.

LeT top gun Zarar has admitted plotting the carnage. According to January 2009 reports in the *Wall Street Journal* and *The Times*, UK, Zarar Shah has confessed to the LeT having planned the 26/11 strikes : "Pakistan's own investigation of the terror attacks in Mumbai has begun to show substantive links between the 10 gunmen and the terrorist group (Lashkar) which its powerful spy agency spent years supporting." The report commented on the big fear in the West and India that Pakistan would ultimately release all militant leaders, as it did after taking them into custody for a few months after the 2001 Parliament attack.

LeT's agenda, outlined in a pamphlet titled *Why We Are Waging Jihad*, clearly states that it is restoration of Islamic rule over all parts of India. LeT founder Saeed had said exactly the same thing years ago – "Jihad is not about Kashmir only. It encompasses all of India." Saeed has constantly targetted India and the US in his Friday sermons in Lahore, and called them enemies of Islam. The LeT-affiliated journal *Ghazwa* also asked in its issue of September 23, 2005: "Remember what happened to USSR, and then think about India — how can it resist Jihad?"

Worldwide Caliphate

For LeT the Jihad in Kashmir is not just a battle over territory, but a part of an irreducible conflict between Islam and infidel. It is committed to the eventual creation of a Caliphate to rule over all the world's Muslims, and asserts that Jihad must continue until Islam dominates the whole world and Allah's law is enforced everywhere in the world. For LeT the Quran itself is a manifesto for Jehad, so infidel/Hindu Indian rule in Kashmir is necessarily evil, and, as Saeed had declared some years ago, "The Hindu is a mean enemy, and so the proper way to deal with him is the one adopted by our forefathers, who crushed them by force." India is a part of a global system of oppression that must be overthrown by force. The LeT spokesman Nazir Ahmed bluntly stated, "Through the Jihad that the Mujahideen have launched in Kashmir, Islam will become dominant all over the world."

As of today, the aftermath of the latest attack on Mumbai is proving a period of reverses for the LeT/Jamaat duo. LeT was already banned in the US in Musharraf's days, and the General had followed suit, while Jamaat-ud-Dawa has invited not only a ban but also condemnation from the UN. But once the dust settles, things may well go back to normal. Within Pakistan an official ban on a terrorist body never meant much, and it would be idle to expect it to stop a huge terror machine like LeT in its tracks. By now LeT in Pakistan has grown into a state within a state, while its parent or offspring or whatever, Markaz-turned Jamaat, has more than a thousand organizational units across Pakistan. This danger cannot be simply wished away.

Rather, the danger is doubly growing. For the LeT chief on January 2010 moved an application to launch yet another social welfare trust in Lahore. The now-banned Jamaat-ud-Dawa (JuD), which has served as a front for the LeT, has initiated measures to register a society called Al Noor University (Trust). The memorandum of the trust states that Hafiz Mohammad Saeed will be the founder-member and first chairman. Many among the 14 members of the Board of Governors are known JuD or LeT functionaries. Consider them: Hafiz Abdul Rauf: director of JuD's public welfare wing, has been named the trust's general secretary. Zafar Iqbal: he was director of JuD's education wing, and is going to be the trust's joint secretary. Hafiz Abdul Rehman: he was director of JuD's justice and fatwa wing and has been given the task of being the information secretary of the trust. Ameer Hamza: a former editor of JuD publication *Ghazwa*, is also a member of the trust.

During a recent interview to *Indian Express* reputed American journalist Steve Coll said: "To me, the Lashkar's style is worrying in terms of the kind of spectacular game-changing attack that it might be able to produce. I am more worried about India, frankly, than I am about Europe or the US, because there is a lot of talent in these Lashkar groups. Some of those proselytising networks have been able to recruit and radicalise scientists, doctors and other talented people. So, if they can get from here to there and from there to here, then as we saw on 26/11, they can wreck a lot of havoc. And that was not a representation of the highest level of talent that those groups can put together. That was a sort of medium-talented group, I would say."

Thus empowered, LeT targets India even outside India. For instance, on May 20, 2010 an Indo-Tibetan Border Police security convoy in Jalalabad carrying Indian officials was attacked by it with a remote-controlled IED. Within the country LeT has even diversified its terror. During a visit to Delhi in the same month Chhattisgarh Chief Minister Raman Singh stated that "Maoists may have some links with LeT." This has been borne out by the evidence available with the internal security establishment showing that Lashkar is offering weapons and explosives technology to Maoist terrorists.

In such circumstances it is no wonder even JuD is not above finding excuses to threaten India. Now it is river water. On May 30, 2010 JuD leader Hafiz Saifullah declared that Pakistan was ready to wage a war with India over the issue of water-sharing. Incidentally just a week before this threat, on May 25, Jamaat-ud-Dawa chief Hafiz Saeed's release from house-arrest by the Pakistan Government was confirmed by the Pakistani Supreme Court for lack of evidence. The government had not furnished enough evidence including dossiers handed over by India. Saeed is one of the masterminds of 26/11.

A grave update on the LeT–JuD gameplan: It has been recently reported that LeT is planning to acquire biological weapons with the help of al-Qaeda. According to a *Times of India* report of May 11, 2011, a Pakistani prisoner at Gunatanamo has revealed that LeT was in touch with a US-based "al-Qaeda anthrax operative" in its efforts to acquire weapons of mass destruction.

A day earlier, May 10, the paper also carried an article pithily titled *No LeT Up*, in which the author wondered in the subtitle – "Could Lashkar-e-Toiba replace al-Qaeda as the foremost Jihadi group?"

All in all, now LeT has become as big a threat as al-Qaeda, US Secretary for Homeland Security Janet Napotano acknowledged during a visit to India in the last week of May 2011.

23

HUJI

Bangla Hobé Afghanistan

The Pakistan terrorist set-up that is currently hogging still more limelight than LeT is Harkat-ul-Jihad-e-Islami-Bangladesh (HUJI-B). Actually the `B' for Bangladesh was a later addition to its Pakistani origin. For Harkat-ul-Jihad-e-Islami (HUJI) was originally set up in Pakistan in 1980 as a militia for the Afghan war. After the Soviet pullout many cadres of this militia shifted to Bangladesh. After 9/11 more terrorists left Pakistan and moved to Bangladesh. Consequently, the original HUJI receded into the background. Then the year 1992 saw the birth of HUJI (Bangladesh), reportedly on instructions from Osama bin Laden. When the Pakistani terrorist body Harkat-ul-Ansar was outlawed, its Bangladeshi remnants returned home and joined the new HUJI. With its slogan A*mra Sobai Hobo Taliban, Bangla hobé Afghanistan,* the new outfit's primary aim was to establish Islamic rule in Bangladesh. Later, HUJI-B became part of the International Islamic Front (IIF) set up by bin Laden in 1998.

Although now a Bangladeshi organisation, with the appendix "B" more or less out of use, HUJI still operates out of both Bangladesh and Pakistan. In Bangladesh, however, it is much more prominent and has bases and camps in areas around Chittagong and Cox's Bazar, stretching all the way to Myanmar in a region known for smuggling and arms-running.

A startling aspect of the interrogation into the Hyderabad twin blasts was the confession of Jalaluddin Mullah alias Babu Bhai, who worked closely with prime accused Shahid Bilal. Mullah confessed to being a key piece in a jigsaw of terror that stretched from Bangladesh to Pakistan, goes via terror camps in PoK, touches New Delhi, Mumbai, Varanasi, Bijnore and Unnao in UP, and finally Hyderabad. He admitted to making several deliveries of explosives, including RDX, across the country since 2004. Mullah's 17-page statement reveals that both he and Bilal were working for Assadullah, a HUJI commander who runs a *madrasa* in Dhaka. Said Ajit Doval, former Director, Intelligence Bureau, "What is lesser known and more serious is HUJI's intimate and old linkages with al-Qaeda. Now that al-Qaeda the world over is in the business of outsourcing terror through franchise, this organisation should figure high on the security ladder."

Network across India

As recent terror strikes have shown, HUJI has developed a network across India. Many HUJI members and sympathisers have been arrested from West Bengal and Uttar Pradesh in the past so many years. In India the outfit has three dreaded faces. The most prominent among them is Abdul Sahil Mohammed *alias* Shahid Bilal, who built the network in the South and most probably masterminded the three terror attacks in Hyderabad. He is now reportedly in Pakistan. The second is Jalaluddin Mullah *alias* Babu Bhai, known to be the commander for north India, who was arrested by the Special Task Force of Uttar Pradesh in June 2008. He not only confessed to have delivered explosives, including RDX, across India since 2004, but is also an accused in the abduction of Khadim Shoe Company chief Partha Roy Burman from Kolkata in 2001. The third, the previously mentioned Rasool Khan "Party" from Gujarat, is believed to be the head of the outfit's Maharashtra operations. He had recruited Bilal into HUJI.

The transcript of a narco test on a HUJI cadre by the name Muthakhil, arrested for attack on STF camp in Hyderabad in 2005, revealed the following information: He received explosives training in Bangladesh, and he and some others were indoctrinated to carry out attacks against India. In Pakistan there is training in shooting, commando, mortars, rocket launchers and other items used in war. These assets of ISI find their way through Rajshahi district on the Indo-Bangla border. A man called Tajuddin sends all Pakistani explosives and ammunition to India. HUM trains children for Jehad in *madrasas*.

ISI's Cat's Paw

Commenting on HUJI's links with other terrorist bodies, terrorism-expert Ajai Sahni says, "HUJI is the cat's paw of ISI and DGFI" (Directorate General of Forces Intelligence) of the Bangladeshi military establishment. LeT and JeM get help from Pakistan, and SIMI cadres provide local support. Consequently, the recent strikes in India, especially in the south, are not pure HUJI operations but multi-group affairs. At the same time HUJI's own track record in terror is substantial. Security agencies believe it was involved in the Sankat Mochan temple attack in Varanasi, the Mumbai blasts, the Malegaon blasts in September 2006, the Hyderabad blasts, as well as the attack on the US consulate in Kolkata in January 2002. In Bangladesh it was believed to be involved in two unsuccessful attempts to assassinate Sheikh Hasina in 2000 and a plot to finish off progressive intellectuals.

Described also as al-Qaeda's Bangladesh affiliate, HUM is believed to receive direct funding from al-Qaeda. It also receives money from charities mainly from Saudi Arabia and Pakistan. In India, the organisation has enough funds (*Indian Express*), its operations funded through smuggling in fake currency, drugs, and even cattle. The cattle are smuggled from Rajasthan, Punjab, Haryana, Delhi and Madhya Pradesh to Bangladesh *via* Bihar, West Bengal and Assam. The magnitude of this operation ranges from 15-20 lakh animals per year to as high as 50-60 lakh. The trucks transporting them return with arms and ammunition.

ISI's Launch Pad

Calling HUJI in India ISI's New Front the *Pioneer* wrote in its editorial on December 28, 2005: "Interrogation by Delhi Police's Special Cell of three members of HUJI-B for their role in a terror attack in Hyderabad reconfirms what has been known for a long time that ISI has been using Bangladesh both as a recruiting ground for terrorists and a launching pad for terrorist outrages against India. As early as January 1999, Delhi Police arrested Syed Abu Nasir, a Bangladeshi who had come as the leader of a team of 10 to blow up the United States embassy in Delhi and consulate-generals in Kolkata and Chennai on Republic Day that year. As Youssef Bodansky pointed out in his book, *Bin Laden: The Man who Declared War on America*, the entire operation was decided upon at a conference of terrorist organizations and Saudi charitable bodies in Dhaka on September 17 and 18, 1998. Bodansky has further stated that in the spring of 1998 ISI had entered into an agreement with al-Qaeda under which the latter was to carry out terrorist strikes in India in the name of fighting Americans and Zionists in lieu of sanctuary and support. The HUJI-B became its striking arm. Bodansky, and Rohan Gunaratna in *Inside Al Qaeda: Global Network of Terror* have stated that bin Laden had a major hand in its establishment in 1992 by a group of Bangladeshis who had returned from fighting Soviet troops in Afghanistan. HUJI-B has been responsible for a number of violent crimes in Bangladesh. Though put on its list of terrorist organizations by the US State Department in May 2002, it continued to function with impunity in Bangladesh until it was finally banned in October following bomb blasts in 63 of the 64 districts of the country on August 17, 2005.

HUJI-B has had close links with Bangladesh's fundamentalist Islamist parties like Jamaat-e-Islami and Islami Oikya Jote. In fact, several important leaders of the former have been its important functionaries. The HUJI-B has also had close ties with the Jel's student organisation, Islami Chhatra Shibir. It has been running training camps in the Chittagong Hill Tracts in Bangladesh. The widely-circulated Bangladeshi daily *Prothom Alok* had provided detailed information about these camps and terrorist activities in the area in a series of five articles in August 2004. The ISI has been supporting secessionist ethnic rebel groups of north-eastern India since the 1950s when Bangladesh was East Pakistan. Expelled after Bangladesh's liberation in 1971, it staged a comeback after Sheikh Mujibur Rahman's assassination on August 15, 1975. It has close ties with Bangladesh's Directorate General of Forces Intelligence and National Security Intelligence and helps both to run 195 camps in Bangladesh for India's north-eastern rebels. It is the author of the plan to set up an Islamic republic comprising parts of north-eastern India and Myanmar. The only thing not known is whether India has a plan to foil its diabolical designs. Judging by its action, it has none that is effective which, to say the least, is a shame.

Islamic Federation

How far or near in the future the ISI-HUJI plan for yet another Islamic state carved out of secular India, indicated by the *Pioneer* editorial, is, only our pseudo-secular dispensation can say, but at least a federation of Pakistan and Bangladesh is reportedly on the ISI agenda.

Commenting once on the creation of Bangladesh and defeat of Pakistan Gen. Hamid Gul said, "As a matter of military strategy, it was not very necessary to repent the establishment of Bangladesh, because we will one day make it capable enough to carry out anti-India acts." This has proved true, so true that for India Bangladesh has now become *The Other Pakistan*, —the telling title of a perceptive piece published in *Tehelka* on August 12, 2006. The article, written by Ajai Sahni, Executive Director of the Institute for Conflict Management, makes two pertinent points: First, "Now the ISI has arrived at a strategic consensus with the Bangladeshi forces to export terror into India", and secondly, "Bangladesh has become a safer haven for the terrorists".

Opening with the observation that there is now relentless animosity and campaigns of terrorism against India from Bangladeshi soil the writer notes the curious fact that "the Pakistani military junta, the architects of the genocide of 1971 in which over three million were slaughtered, had so quickly regained influence through ISI to arrive at a strategic consensus with the Bangladeshi forces in their war of a thousand cuts against India."

From then on the article describes in detail how, with the arrival of ISI on the scene, Bangladesh deteriorated into a fundamentalist, terrorist-friendly, and finally terrorist state. It bears extensive quoting:

"Hardline Islamist parties, principally the Jamaat-e-Islami and its offshoots the chief collaborators (with Pakistan) in the genocide of 1975 (have) once again secured a position of centrality turning Bangladesh into a region... colonized by Deobandi-Wahabi radical Islamism.

Military-Mullah Nexus

The unholy Military-Mullah nexus, the hallmark of Pakistani power politics, was back in play in Bangladesh within five years of its creation: Abbas Ali Khan, the Jamaat's *amir* at the time (of lifting the ban on it in

May 1979) declared, "Whenever any kind of aggression comes, it shall come from India alone. Consequently, the psychology of the defence forces of Bangladesh must be anti-Indian".

Anti-Indianism and Islamist extremism have since then become systematically entrenched in mass psychology in Bangladesh. Even Mujib's daughter Hasina had to significantly alter policies, changing them in favour of support to terrorist organizations operating from Bangladesh soil against India, illegal migration... and Islamisation of the country.

This radicalisation found its most dangerous manifestation in the large numbers of Bangladeshis who were mobilized for the Jehad in Afghanistan, where they found cause with ISI, Taliban and al-Qaeda. While the mindset was being forged by thousands of private and state-run *madrasas* across the country, the tools and techniques of Jehad were being evolved in training camps in Pakistan and Afghanistan...

Bangla Taliban

Radicalisation accelerated sharply after the fall of Taliban in 2001 with thousands of Taliban and al-Qaeda fighters fleeing Afghanistan... In the early stages several hundred Taliban and al-Qaeda cadres are believed to have been transported by ship from Karachi to Chittagong and were then believed to have been trucked down by Bangladesh's Directorate General of Forces Intelligence (DGFI) to hidden camps... . Since then there have been periodic reports of shadowy movements of al-Qaeda cadres and activities of al-Qaeda linked operations, including funding agencies, across or through Bangladesh.

By mid-2002... Bangladesh emerged as an important staging post for Pakistan-based Jehadi groups operating against India... One of the most troubling aspects of these developments is the emergence of joint operations, using Bangladeshi, Pakistani and Indian Islamist groups and cadres for terrorist strikes on Indian soil.

Subsequent to the Hyderabad police office attack on October 12, 2005 it was discovered that as many as 500 Hyderabadi youth had undergone arms training in Bangladesh and Baluchistan through the HUJI network.

It is clear that Pakistan is increasingly outsourcing many of its terrorist operations to groups in Bangladesh in order to disguise its direct involvement ... It is equally clear that the Bangladeshi establishment, including the DGFI, the Army and certain elements within the country's political leadership, are willing partners in this enterprise of terrorism.

Ajay Raj Sharma, the then Director General of BSF, disclosed in September 2004 that ISI had shifted its training camps and launching pads of Kashmiri terrorists to Bangladesh.

The same year Indian intelligence noted that

- ISI had been developing a nexus between Indian insurgent groups from the North-East, Islamic fundamentalists, and criminal elements in Bangladesh,
- ISI was appointing Pakistani nationals trained as Maulavis in *madrasas* and mosques in Bangladesh,
- The top leadership of North-East Indian insurgent groups was being jointly handled by ISI and DGFI, and
- Bangladesh was being progressively consolidated as a prime staging post for terrorist and espionage operations against India.

Open Secret

In view of the whole situation so comprehensively described in Sahni's article the mere acknowledgement of it by the Government of India looks pointless. National SecurityAdvisor MK Narayanan told the media in October 2006 that Bangladesh has become a launch-pad for terrorism into India, while the home minister recently said there was conclusive proof of Dhaka's hand in Pakistani terror operations in India. For BSF IG JP Sinha recently gave the information that ISI and DGFI are jointly recruiting Muslim youths from Assam for training them in Bangladesh for Jihad, and this recruitment drive has reached alarming proportions. The recruited agents work in groups of 15 to 20 and are involved in sabotage and in aiding and abetting terrorist outfits like Muslim United Liberation Tigers of Assam and HUM.

Further, underlining the official nexus between Pakistan and Bangladesh Col. Farooq Rehman of the insurgent outfit Freedom Party openly claimed in 2006 that his party, in association with the terrorist group Jel, had been working with DGFI's Maj. Gen. Mohammad Nasim on a plan, in collaboration with ISI, to disintegrate North-East India.

A recent refinement of the Bangladeshi complicity in ISI's proxy war on India was that terror networks along the Bangladesh-West Bengal border are pushing in cadres in the guise of students. Once in India with 'student' stamped on their papers, they don't have to worry about law enforcement agencies for the duration of their visa. When the visa expires, they disappear into the so-called Islamic study centres spread all over India from Lucknow to Hyderabad. "We know of networks that take care of everything for their transit, transport, and other requirements," said BSF IG Somesh Goyal.

In March 2008 the US banned HUJI, describing it as a global terrorist organization. It said HUJI was behind most recent terror strikes in India. It was already on the US list of terrorist organizations since 2003.

24

ISI-FRIENDLY NEPAL

Terror's Regional HQ

Next to Bangladesh, Nepal has been so convenient a base for ISI's anti-India operations since long that nearly a decade and a half ago it made Nepalese capital Kathmandu its regional HQ, as reported by Hindi journal *Panchjanya* in December 1994. Initially set up in a hotel in the capital city, it was later shifted to a location near Birganj, where it was equipped with high-powered transmitters.

Permanent ISI Base

However, even two years later Kathmandu continued to be an ISI base, according to a report in August 1996. Another report a year later even said it had become a permanent base from where ISI was aiding and sheltering Kathmandu-based Kashmiri militants. An arrested Kashmiri militant by the name of Fayaz confessed that he was offered a bait of Rs. 2 lakh per blast to disrupt Republic Day celebrations in India that year and a safe passage to Nepal. Fayaz said more than 6000 Kashmiri traders were living in Nepal at that time, and many of them were hand in glove with ISI. He also said arms and ammunition were supplied from there to terrorist groups operating in the Terai belt on both sides of the border, in UP and Nepal.

Diplomatic Cover

Intelligence sources suspect that ISI may even be using diplomatic bags to smuggle RDX into Nepal, as they are immune from scrutiny by authorities as per the Geneva Convention governing international diplomatic relations. Obviously this was possible only because the Pakistan embassy in Nepal was in league with ISI in the nefarious business. The involvement of the embassy was reported by *Observer* in July 1996 on the basis of a confidential note of the home ministry of the Government of India. Highly placed sources in the ministry told the newspaper that Nepal-based ISI men were at the time planning a series of explosions in India in several key areas like defence and petroleum installations, busy market places and bridges and important persons.

Open Border

A major facilitating factor for ISI in Nepal in its designs against India has been while its agents initially used to cross over into India by the Burma-Bangla route, they now cross over the porous Indo-Nepal border, as Nepali and Indian citizens. Another facility, admitted even by Nepali authorities, was the large influx of foreign funds in the name of construction of *madrasas* and mosques in the border region.

ISI's Recruiting Ground

Many foreign newspapers had also reported at that time that ISI was conducting secret training camps in the hilly districts of Nepal. It was even sending young Nepali and Indian Muslims to Pakistan, Bangladesh, Afghanistan and several Arab countries for terror training in the name of higher education in Medicine and Engineering. On the surface this was being done by a Nepali body called the Islamic Development Association, aided by another set-up called Nepal Islamic Yuva Sangh.

A Nepali citizen, arrested by Delhi police in June 2009 as a terror suspect, Mohammad Umar Madani was reportedly given the task of recruiting youths for the Lashkar-e-Toiba. "He was specifically asked by his handler to recruit youths from the metros who are graduates and have expertise in computer technology," said Joint Commissioner of Police PN Aggarwal. "Madani was working on talent-spotting for terrorist activities, sending them for training to Lashkar camps in Pakistan, and then getting them to India. He sent about 30 men for training to Pakistan, including one Kamal Ansari, who was arrested in connection with the Mumbai train blasts," said a senior police officer.

Madani is reported to have been in touch with key LeT functionaries like Zaki-ur Rehman Lakhvi and Mohd Yakub, who told him to recruit two youths each from the four main metros, i.e., Delhi, Mumbai, Kolkata, Chennai for terror training. "Madani was also told to pick youths from coastal areas who were good sailors, as well as those who had worked in fireworks factories," said Aggarwal. Although born in Bihar's Madhubani district, Madani is now a Nepali citizen, having shifted to Saptari district in Nepal about 25 years ago.

Madani is the son of a *madrasa* teacher and shifted from Bihar to Nepal in 1983. In 1995, he started a *madrasa* in Saptari, Nepal, followed by another one in Kathmandu the next year. Madani was initiated into Jehadi activities in 1996. He was given the task of building a strong base in Nepal for easy infiltration into India. His brother, Hafiz Mohammad Zubair, is also a Lashkar operative based in Qatar.

In 2000, when Madani visited Pakistan, he was told to pump terror funds into India through Nepal. Madani then came in contact with one

Saifullah, who opened several bank accounts across Nepal to facilitate easy flow of money from Pakistan.

ISI had also joined hands with the international underworld engaged in the drug and cattle smuggling trade in Nepal. Drugs worth 9.5 crore Rupees and more than 5000 cattle were once confiscated on the Bihar border.

A final footnote of modern times: Nepal's Maoist supremo and once secular Nepal's Prime Minister Prachand had disclosed during a visit to India that ISI had offered to help his outfit through direct or indirect means. He did not indicate the nature of the help that ISI was willing to offer, but said he had declined it.

400 Madrasas

However, Nepal's Hindus are now stuck between Jehadis and Maoists. "Nepal as a Hindu nation is slowly losing its identity. The Hindus in Nepal are in a difficult state with Jehadis and Muslims targeting them from one side and Maoists from the other," VHP chief Ashok Singhal said recently at a gathering of journalists in Mumbai. Over 400 *madrasas* in Nepal are engaged in teaching their students anti-India and anti-Hindu lessons.

25

SIMI

"You Are Secessionist !"

Among ISI's Indian extensions, at the top of the heap is the Students' Islamic Movement of India (SIMI). SIMI is also a chilling example of how, despite a continuing ban and the Supreme Court's harsh strictures on its secessionism, such fundamentalist Islamic terrorist outfits are allowed to grow unchecked in secular India.

SIMI was founded at Aligarh in UP on April 25, 1977 by Mohammad Ahmedullah Siddiqi, now Professor of Journalism and Public Relations at a university in the USA. It was originally an offshoot of the Jamaat-e-Islami Hind, a fundamentalist Islamic body. SIMI is a follower of Deobandi brand of Islam, and its mission is to liberate India and create Islamic society.

In a full-page Sunday Story on March 2, 2008 *Indian Express* described "SIMI's Second Coming", in dispatches from correspondents Johnson and Rajeev. The latter pointed out that unlike in the past SIMI is attracting the educated in Kerala, while the former said the recent arrest of the Bangalore techie-terrorist Yahya Kammakutty, charged with links with SIMI, shows how the banned outfit has become active in south India.

An erstwhile SIMI leader, who now edits a newspaper run by one of Kerala's barely-concealed Islamic fundamentalist outfits, piously claims, SIMI was never really militant and cannot be held responsible for what some of its members may do once they leave the organization. This was exactly what former UP CM and secularist Mulayam Singh had said when he gave it a clean chit, declaring SIMI was not a terrorist organisation. Facts, however, are very much otherwise.

Kozhikode was Kerala's biggest SIMI base since the days of its mid-1980s campaign for liberation of India through Islam until the ban in the wake of 9/11. Since then many SIMI men got into other Islamic outfits and political parties in Kerala and now stand charged with terrorist acts.

For instance, Basheer, an aeronautical engineering student of Ernakulam, is a suspect in the Mumbai serial bombing and is now said to be based in the Gulf. A high-profile SIMI leader in Kerala, he has been one of the key men in its revival after the ban. He was also connected to an LeT commander, Abu Sultan, whom Mumbai cops later killed in an encounter. Another electronics engineer and a teacher were also caught in 2007 with seditious SIMI literature. This had shown that, unlike in the past, SIMI was now drawing the educated Muslims in Kerala. This phenomenon is not limited to Kerala. When, on April 9, 2008, the Mumbai police arrested two SIMI operatives Irshad and Asrar, it was found that Irshad, Maharashtra SIMI president in 2001, is a civil engineer, while Asrar is a computer expert.

The Kerala intelligence department is also tracking a well-developed girls' wing that SIMI has reportedly set up in the state. This again is not a solitary activity. For in Madhya Pradesh too, SIMI had started enrolling women, probably under a separate wing called Shahin Force. In Dhar the city police had seized some letters from SIMI activists indicating that there are also female cadres of the organisation.

In the recent past Kerala saw a rash of unprecedented extremist activities, especially in the State's north, that reveals a strident growth of Islamic fundamentalism. These include the kidnapping and disappearance of a free-thinking Maulavi, as well as deadly pipe bombs. SIMI is a key suspect in these incidents.

Many SIMI leaders are now high profile leaders of other Islamic outfits, some they founded, others they penetrated. These include Koya and Abubaqar, Supreme Council members of the innocuously named National Development Front (NDF). The outfit, according to state Intelligence, is the most dangerous body in Kerala. Further, current state *Amir* of the JeI and other prominent Muslim community leaders were top SIMI men, several others in a slew of lesser Muslim organizations.

Jaleel, the CPM's poster boy for Muslims in north Kerala in a previous Assembly poll, was an important SIMI leader. More alarming was the fact that SIMI men had dispersed into at least a dozen front outfits in the state and had developed links with LeT. These fronts operated under such labels as counselling and guidance centres working for behavioural change, but were in reality being used for spreading extremist Islamism among the youth. One of these bodies was founded by a SIMI leader who is the brother-in-law of a top NDF leader. He is in the business of printing Islamic publications— including incendiary leaflets on the sly for both SIMI and NDF. Others, like the recently floated Islamic Student's Association (ISA) that aim to tap the campuses for the energy to grow, have large numbers of SIMI men.

The seven-year-old ban on SIMI has not prevented SIMI men from getting together, and these gatherings largely go unnoticed. Some 25 top SIMI leaders had met in Kozhikode in 2005. Regular get-togethers of SIMI men still take place in places like Thrissur, Malappuram, Kozhikode and elsewhere under cover of nominated outfits.

The SIMI revival story is repeating itself elsewhere in south India, as is shown by the case of Yahya Kammukutty, an engineer who was in 2007 drawing a monthly salary of more than one lakh Rupees. According to Karnataka detectives Yahya could be at the top of the banned SIMI's discreet controlling hierarchy in southern India. He was found to be in touch with more than 30 young men, all active SIMI men who attended three secret meetings in north Karnataka in the second half of 2007 to plot terror attacks.

Nominal Fronts

Since the ban SIMI has also been organizing students under various nominal fronts to get around it, especially in the coastal and northern parts of Karnataka. Organisations with innocuous names like Karnataka Forum for Dignity as well as various forums for young professionals are in reality screening grounds for recruitment of cadres. The Forum for Dignity is closely connected with SIMI in its new incarnations in Kerala and Tamil Nadu like NDF and Manitha Neethi Dasarai.

There are also several fringe outfits through which SIMI operates. Most of these outfits are abundantly funded by countries of the Middle East.

The chance arrest of two terror suspects in Karnataka's Davangere region on January 11, 2010 led police investigators to believe that they were trying to strengthen SIMI in order to carry out or logistically support terrorist activists – planned and funded by LeT and other terror outfits – in Karnataka, Goa and Andhra. One of the two was Raziuddin Nasir, son of Hyderabad's Maulana Naseeruddin, who, as noted earlier, is himself facing trial for criminal conspiracy in Gujarat. Nasir is part of a group put together by a senior SIMI leader called Adnan *alias* Hafeez, an engineering graduate of Bijapur in north Karnataka. He also provided the funds. The others are mostly medical students of north Karnataka.

Several sleeper cells of full-time SIMI cadres are also present in Maharashtra. Arrested SIMI leader Peedical's phone records revealed that several persons from the interior of the state had contacted him.

SIMI was tapping into various resources already available with front organizations newly set up by it in coastal Karnataka and north Kerala. Advisor to the Karnataka Governor on home affairs PKH Thakaran, former chief of RAW, described the arrest of a SIMI group as the tip of an iceburg.

Despite the ban SIMI clearly continues to be active in Maharashtra. The two major terror strikes with which SIMI is linked are both in Maharashtra– the July 11, 2006 ("7/11") Mumbai train blasts, and the September 2006 bomb blasts in Malegaon, a Muslim-dominated town. Reports in March 2007 from another town in the state also told about efforts SIMI is making to send batches of young Muslims to Pakistan for training in terrorism. Apparently indoctrination for this purpose is also being attempted. According to police sources some women-teachers in some schools in Nagpur are encouraging students to take Jehadi training. They give Jehadi literature to them to read, and also show them films and pictures of violence in order to incite them. The police said schools in half a dozen localities of Nagpur have been targeted for identifying suitable candidates.

A still bigger event *vis-a-vis* SIMI which took place very recently was that Safdar Nagori and Shibli Peedical Abdul, SIMI's all-India and south India chiefs respectively, were arrested by Madhya Pradesh police in Indore along with a dozen state leaders of the organization on March 27, 2008. The top two were wanted in Maharashtra for printing and distributing Jehadi literature in 2006. They are also wanted in Karnataka in connection with a plot to bomb Hubli airport. Nagori and Siddiqi, said to be secretary of Maharashtra SIMI, are closely connected. During Nagori's arrest the MP police seized a letter by Siddiqi, arrested and in jail after 7/11, to Nagori, which indicated this link. `Basically, this letter is a confession that Siddiqi and Nagori were in league with the perpetrators of the 7/11 blasts, it is asserted. Siddiqi's narco-analysis test reportedly also revealed his links with LeT commander Azam Cheema as also with the Jaish network.

New SIMI recruits are tech-savvy — all children of the Internet age. They hold religious discussions on networking sites and Islamic forums, and know the intricacies of e-mail usage, even how to avoid being caught through digital evidence.

SIMI may be banned but its funding sources are alive. When the Kerala police raided SIMI's state HQ in Kozhikode soon after the ban in 2001, the seizures they made included account books that showed a massive inflow of money from the Gulf countries through the Hawala route. "We have estimated that the state had at least Rs. 10,000 crore coming in every year from the Gulf by the Hawala route," says Kerala's Intelligence Chief Punnoose. That SIMI was a willing Indian extension of ISI was proved decades ago during an interface that ISI arranged between top Khalistani and Kashmiri terrorists with Pakistani terrorist outfit Jel in Lahore in the late 1980s. In this meeting it was decided that SIMI would extend all cooperation to Khalistani terrorist Lal Singh in his operation from Aligarh under an assumed Muslim identity.

The police interrogation of Tahir Jamal, ex-president of the Maharashtra unit of SIMI, and his associate Saqib Nachan also confirmed that prominent SIMI leaders had been directed to provide all possible help to Khalistani terrorists and also form trained groups of Muslim youths in their areas. According to police and intelligence sources Bashir, a former president of SIMI, had visited Lahore in January 1992 and finalized a plan to send young Indian Muslims to Pakistan for an arms training course that included anti-aircraft guns. Records showed that SIMI was given substantial funds through Hawala transactions to finance this operation.

An ideological twist was recently added by Nagori in his statement to the police, saying he regarded Taliban supremo Mullah Omar the true Caliph of the Muslim world, and was working to establish links with him through friendly NRI contacts in the Gulf region, in which he had made considerable progress. Nagori said his aim was to wage Jehad in India under Omar's leadership. He had great respect for Osama bin Laden, but could not consider him a Caliph as he had been uprooted from his own soil. So he considered Mullah Omar more capable of heading a new Islamic Caliphate. Admiration for Omar appeared a common thread among key SIMI leaders arrested with Nagori, such as his brother Kamaruddin, and Shibly and Adnan, key organisers for SIMI in south India. Even the rank and file of SIMI cadres are veering towards such Talibanization.

That the SIMI chief was drawn to Mullah Omar also emerged in the interrogation of Raziuddin Nasir, arrested from Hubli. Nasir is a well-trained terrorist and has reportedly undergone all five levels of training imparted in LeT camps in Pakistan. He had first got in touch with Adnan, who in turn set up a meeting with Nagori in Bhopal last year. In this meeting the two agreed to work together for attacks on Israeli and American tourists in Goa. According to Nasir, Nagori even claimed he was raising an army for Mullah Omar. For this he first made his brother Kamaruddin SIMI's training-in-charge (also described by the media as the organization's "chief of operations in Andhra Pradesh"). Kamaruddin took this responsibility with great dedication. A tempo driver by profession, he drove his tempo until 1.00 p.m. and then spent half the day in organizational activities. He said he wanted to earn just enough to feed himself.

The systematic nature of the training in SIMI camps was proved by computers seized by the police, which revealed training plans, motivational Jehadi music and even speeches made by Maulana Masood Azhar. Kamaruddin also disclosed that with help from Shibly and Adnan he was able to organize a series of training camps in 2007 in Karnataka between April and September, in Kerala in October-November, in Madhya Pradesh in December, and in January 2008 somewhere in Gujarat.

There is even a regular syllabus for the trainees. A well-documented course in terrorism was recovered from the arrested SIMI leaders. Outside of Jammu and Kashmir SIMI is the only outfit in India to have in place literature-based military training. The syllabus is backed with a strong ideological content, and the training, which is on many levels, goes into details of military support required as backup for the ideological literature. SIMI leadership was holding subversive training camps in Kerala, MP, UP and West Bengal.

Actually the virulent nature of SIMI's Islamic indoctrination is not a new phenomenon. It has been there for years, as admitted by Javed Anand, general secretary of a body called Muslims for Secular Democracy and editor of its publication titled *Communalism Combat*. In a recent newspaper article Javed wrote, *inter alia*:

"... Muslim leaders and the Urdu media are wilfully blind to the malevolence sheltering in their own backyard... The nefarious nature of SIMI has been evident from the moment it emerged from the womb of the Jamaat-e-Islami (JeI) in 1977 ... In less than a decade it inherited the legacy of the founder of JeI, Maulana Abul Ala Maududi, who argued that all Muslims must strive for an Islamic state".

"True to its ideological mooring, in the '80s SIMI produced eye-catching stickers proclaiming: Secularism, NO, Democracy, NO, Nationalism, NO, Polytheism, NO, Only Islam. These stickers adorned many Muslim homes and shops throughout India."

"Saeed Ahmed Khan, former SIMI Mumbai chief, confessed that he visited Pakistan in 1991 after learning that the ISI was training Indian youths to cultivate the culture of jihad. At a SIMI conference in Kanpur in 1999, a seven-year-old boy Gulrez Siddiqui told an audience of 20,000: "The warrior of Islam, the destroyer of idols/My lion, Osama bin Laden". Those who addressed the gathering, long-distance telephonically, were Hamas founder, Sheikh Yaseen, head of the Jamaat-e-Islami, Pakistan, Qazi Hussain Ahmed, and the Imam of al-Aqsa mosque, Israel/ Palestine. Two years later, at a gathering of 25,000 Muslim youths in Mumbai, SIMI reiterated that the time has come for Indian Muslims to launch an armed Jehad in India with the establishment of an Islamic Caliphate as the ultimate aim".

SIMI's posters pasted in the by-lanes of Muslim mohallas across the country following the demolition of the Babri mosque had the invocation: "*Ya Ilahi, bhej de Mahmood koi* (Oh Allah, send us a Mahmud)". The reference was to Mahmud Ghaznavi, revered as a *But-Shikan* (Destroyer of Idols). Urdu papers received press releases from SIMI on their official letterhead with a logo depicting a Quran and an AK-47 perched on top of a globe.

Apropos the recent legal imbroglio related to the lifting of the ban on SIMI, the Central Government's 42-page affidavit in the Supreme Court was a clear refutation of the 'no fresh evidence' argument. It gave a list of 349 cases that were filed against SIMI prior to February 2006 as well another 60 odd others which were slapped later. That is not all. Investigations have provided strong evidence that SIMI and its hardline version Indian Mujahideen were also involved in blasts across the country, serial explosions in Mumbai suburban trains, Jaipur, courts in Lucknow, Varanasi and Faizabad, in Bangalore and Hyderabad. Central and state intelligence agencies see the growing arc of SIMI's bombings as marking its transformation into a full-scale terror outfit.

Finally, in a stinging stricture the Supreme Court described the banned SIMI as a secessionist movement. "You are a secessionist movement, you have not stopped your activities," a Bench of Justices SB Sinha and Markandeya Katju observed while rejecting a petition by SIMI challenging the ban on it. SIMI was represented by Salman Khurshid.

As if to thumb its secessionist nose at the court the banned SIMI will now fight elections! It was reported in August 2009 that some members of the organisation who attended a secret meeting to form an outfit under a new banner were arrested by Akola police. As many as 35 SIMI members, 14 of them having cases registered against them, attended the meeting in Mana village in Akola district. The police had received information that an *Ijtima* (religious gathering) going on in a mosque at the village was in fact an indoctrination programme to float a new outfit. Akola, Amravati, Khamgaon and Yavatmal in Maharashtra have been SIMI hotspots, with many arrests in the past in Akola.

Investigations further revealed that SIMI was also hatching a bigger plan to float some frontal organizations, and one of the pivotal ones is now vaguely known as Wahadat-e-Islam (Unity of Islam). The aim of these frontal organizations was to covertly perpetuate the SIMI ideology. There were even plans to tie up with political parties to fight assembly elections.

There have also been reports that China was working on a Maoist - SIMI nexus in South India. Indian intelligence agencies were reportedly on the trail of a sinister plan of the Chinese for integrating the operations of Maoist groups with SIMI. A top officials of the Intelligence Bureau said a meeting between some middle level leaders of the two organizations was held in Bengaluru for the purpose. Chinese intelligence, it is learnt, is bent on creating an Islamist-Maoist nexus in South India. Chinese interpreters in the Indian intelligence establishment have evidence that makes it clear that the Chinese have already prepared a blueprint for the operation in South India and would in the near future create several human interest think-tanks in South India for garnering support from the intellectual community and to use the state's inteliigentsia as a major propaganda machinery for its sinister designs.

To cap it all, with an international network of its own now in place, SIMI has even decided to omit India from its name and assume a global Islamic identity as Students' Islamic Movement (SIM).

26

MADE-IN-INDIA TERRORISTS

ISI's Indian Proliferation

Proliferation of Islamic terrorist bodies across India has gone on unchecked for years. ISI has been setting up Indian terrorist outfits in different parts of the country since long.

Prominent among them was Kafla-e-Sakht Jan set up a decade and a half ago at ISI's instance. Its units were formed in Gujarat, Uttar Pradesh, Madhya Pradesh, Delhi, Maharashtra and Rajasthan, with the mandate to fight anti-Islamic forces.

Other terrorist bodies set up during this period were Students' Islamic Organisation, Jamaat-e-Islami Hind, and Inqilab-i-Islam Ayatollah. While Inqilab was set up in Gujarat, another organisation set up in Gujarat and Punjab was Harkat-ul-Jihad-e-Islam. This body was tasked with uniting anti-national elements in the two states. The return of normalcy in Punjab had been a big setback for ISI, so this organization was launched to recover lost ground through a regrouping of residual Khalistani terrorists.

Yet another ISI-supported Indian terrorist body of this period was an underground outfit in the North-East called Assam Muslim Tigers, which was to look after Muslim interests in the entire North-East. Through this set-up ISI wanted to spread its tentacles in West Bengal as well. Around this time ISI also started sending foreign mercenaries into Gujarat. All in all, the number of Indian Muslim terrorist organizations has grown substantially. The major ones among them:

HuM

A strident indigenous terrorist body functioning in Kashmir since long is Hizb-ul-Mujahideen (HuM), armed wing of the pro-Pak Jamaat-e-Islami and currently Jammu and Kashmir's largest terrorist organization. The wide spread of its network can be realised from the fact that HuM supremo Salahuddin is also chairman of the United Jihad Council (UJC), Kashmir's largest militant conglomerate, and he has been operating in the Valley for years in tandem with a bunch of militant outfits like Save Kashmir Movement, Farzandan-i-Millat, Al-Istiglal, Al-Nasreen, and Al-Haq Mujahideen.

Even way back in 1991 the HuM chief had said a stage in the struggle for self-determination had come where Kalashnikovs alone were insufficient, so remote-controlled explosive devices, rocket launchers, and light machine guns were being brought into use. And this has not changed.

In July 2007 Hizbul had reportedly ruled out any dialogue with the Central Government on Kashmir and was determined to continue with armed terror. "Hizb-ul Mujahideen will neither drop the gun nor be part of any dialogue process," Hizbul commander Gazi Misbah-ud-Din told a news agency. "The gun is our potent weapon..." Ghazi said, adding it is the gun that would force India to vacate Kashmir.

In the meanwhile Hizb terror continues. For in February 2008 its financial chief Farooq Ahmed Dar was killed in a gun-battle with the police. He had been active in the Valley for 7–8 years.

Any other means, however outlandish, are also good enough for HuM if they can be used to promote the Islamist agenda. For instance, Shah Rukh Khan's movie *My Name is Khan* found endorsement from Hizbul Mujahideen. This is what the Gujarat Anti-Terror Squad (ATS) stumbled upon while interrogating *mujahid* Bashir Ahmed Baba, suspected to have been scouting in Gujarat for impressionable recruits for terror training in Hizbul Mujahideen facilities in Pakistan-occupied Kashmir. Bashir, known in Kashmir as the Pepsi Bomber (for his expertise in turning empty cans of soft drinks into explosive devices), had been asked by his handler in PoK, Bilal Shera, to use the movie as an indoctrination tool. ATS sources said Bashir was specifically told to use the movie to propagate the idea that Muslim youth across the world were facing humiliation and derision, and they need to come together for Jihad. When nabbed on March 13 from Anand, ATS recovered from Bashir a ticket for the Shah Rukh Khan movie at a theatre in Ahmedabad. Bashir confessed he had gone to see the movie as instructed by his boss in PoK, Bilal Shera.

JuM

The same stridency as Hizbul was earlier shown by another terrorist outfit in Kashmir, namely, Jamiat-ul-Mujahideen (JuM). In a statement faxed to the local news agency Kashmir News Service (KNS) JuM declared that Kashmiri separatists had turned down a proposal for a round-table conference in Srinagar after consultation with the terrorist leadership in the state. Its spokesman had termed an Indo-Pak dialogue on Kashmir as futile in solving the Kashmir issue, and said the Jihadis were strongly against the process.

Rejecting talks, the JuM spokesman declared that the resolution of the Kashmir issue lies only in "bullets and bombs": *Masla-e-Kashmir ka hal goli our bomb ke zariye se hi mumkin hai* ("it's only bombs and bullets that can solve the Kashmir issue"), the spokesman was quoted by KNS as asserting.

Ahle Hadis

The recent RDX haul case in Aurangabad showed a SIMI operation, but of the dozen men arrested in that connection there were some who were not members of SIMI but followers of an Islamic sect called Ahle Hadis, known as Salafists. Flourishing on funds received from the Middle East, especially Saudi Arabia, the Salafists claim that their religious beliefs constitute pure Islam as practised by the first three generations since Prophet Mohammad. "We firmly believe that one should bend only before Allah," says Shaikh Nazir Sheikh, Imam of the Ahle Hadis mosque in Aurangabad. There are as many as 11 Ahle Hadis mosques in Malegaon. Elsewhere, Ahle Hadis have spread from Mumbai to Delhi to Benaras.

Maharashtra minister Chhagan Bhujbal had given a clean chit to this clearly suspect sect when its name figured in the Ghatkopar (Mumbai) blast case in 2002.

This is only a brief glimpse of a few major terrorist organizations that ISI either set up or sponsored in India. Their total number is a matter of conjecture based on available intelligence. According to BSF sources, in the beginning there were as many as about 140 terrorist outfits operating in Kashmir, with a total strength of around 12,000. Out of them the following were active at the time:

1. **Al-Jehadia Police Commandos.** A small group that allied itself with HuM.
2. **Allah Tigers.** Became well-known for enforcing fundamentalist Islamic laws.
3. **Al-Umar Mujahideen.** A blood thirsty group known for wrapping bombs around the bodies of its victims and blowing them up to pieces.
4. **Al-Burq.**
5. **Dukhtaran-e-Millat.** The only known women's body. (*Dukhtaran* means "daughters", derived from Sanskrit *duhitr*.)
6. **Hezbullah.** A fundamentalist, pro-Pak group.
7. **Hizb-ul-Mujahideen.**
8. **Hizb-ul-Momineen.**
9. **Jammu-Kashmir Liberation Front (JKLF).** Now again active.
10. **Ikhwan-ul-Muslimeen.** A formidable militant group favoured by Pakistan that kidnapped IOC executive director Doraiswamy.
11. **Jamiat-ul-Mujahideen.** A breakaway group of Jamaat-i-Islami. Notorious for committing brutal crimes.
12. **Muslim Janbaz Force.** Came into the news when it kidnapped two Swedish tourists in Kashmir.
13. **Pasdaran-i-Islami.** Came into the news when it attempted to kidnap 7

Israelis and a Dutch woman from a houseboat in the Dal Lake in Srinagar. (Attempt aborted.)

14. **Muslim Mujahideen.**
15. **Harqat-ul-Ansar.**

Finally, one more terrorist body, **Jamaat Islami**, of that period merits special mention:

Alluding to an emerging alliance between the Sikh and Kashmir terrorists, aided and coordinated by the Jamaat Islami, Pakistan's *Daily News* (August 1, 1991) quoted a Panthic Committee Service report which said: "The pact between the Sikhs and the Kashmiris, according to a Pakistani Sikh source, is part of an effort to bring together the separatist elements throughout India... Plans are afoot to approach groups in Tamil Nadu, Nagaland and Mizoram to join hands. The Jamaat Islami's role in coordinating the agreement between the Kashmiris and the Sikhs has been a vital one... It is the Jamaat which is egging on the Sikhs and the Kashmiris to cooperate with other separatists and they have established a link with a Hong Kong black market arms dealer for providing arms and ammunition".

Later, in 1996, at least six major militant organizations and several smaller ones were operating in Kashmir. Their strength was variably estimated at between 8,000 and 10,000 armed cadres.

The current terror scene is the same. Rather, the terrorist plethora flourishes. LeT, HUJI and SIMI (with its offshoot IM) are wreaking coordinated havoc across India, with a number of peripheral outfits centred on SIMI and HUJI in the South, some with fancy names in Sanskrit.

Indian Mujahideen

The latest addition to this terror team is Indian Mujahideen (IM), which initially came into the limelight with the bomb blasts in Jaipur. It also claimed responsibility for the recent attacks in Ahmedabad and Bangalore. Not much is known about its organizational structure and cadre. Some official sources call it a hardline version of SIMI, while others said it could be a loose grouping of cadres from SIMI and HUJI—a sort of international alliance for terrorism in India. Yet another theory was that a breakaway trio of SIMI leaders had adopted the name "Indian Mujahideen" just before the Jaipur strike for the sake of more limelight.

Whatever the real position, the probe into Indian Mujahideen's recent attacks on major cities has thrown up its links across India. In particular it has shown the terror link between Maharashtra and Gujarat with the contents of the e-mail it sent out just ahead of the Ahmedabad explosions. It specifically warned of attacks on former Chief Minister Vilasrao Deshmukh and Home Minister RR Patil to avenge "state reserve police force attacks on our *masjids* and our homes, the insult of our Quran and your enmity with the Muslims in Digras and the nearby areas of Yavatmal and the burning alive of three Muslims in Jalna with the backing of police." A reference was also made to the troubles faced by *madrasa* students and Muslim women.

For the fundamentalists in Maharashtra, the Gujarat attacks are a clear revenge against the 2002 post-Godhra riots. They had earlier tasted failure in attacking Gujarat when intelligence inputs helped the Maharashtra police seize around two dozen assault rifles and RDX ammunition in a raid in 2006. The module was busted but its head, SIMI operative Zabiuddin Ansari, managed to give the police a slip. In yet another unsuccessful operation, a bomb planted on the Mumbai-Ahmedabad express in February 2006 failed to go off during its running time.

But now IM has struck again. Investigators probing Pune's German Bakery blast in February 2010 got compelling information that the attack was the handiwork of the Indian Mujahideen. The breakthrough was based on a telephone call IM co-founder Riyaz Bhatkal made to an operative in Nepal on the day of the blast on February 13, claiming credit and exchanging congratulations for the attack. The operative, Salman *alias* Chotu, was arrested weeks after the blast and is in custody in Delhi. During interrogation he told that on February 13, shortly after the Pune blast, he received a call from Riyaz Bhatkal on the Thuraya phone he was using there, a source said. Riyaz immediately congratulated him. When Salman asked him what the congratulations were for, Riyaz told him to switch on the TV to see the outfit's latest work.

So far, Indian Mujahideen have struck as many as seven times during November 2007 to February 2010. For every attack there was an e-mail dwelling on the so-called reason, ranging from torture of Muslims to Kashmir. Basically it is the same – the Islamic agenda. The first, the Varanasi court blasts of 21 Nov 2007, were described as Islamic raids. The Jaipur attack was linked to a broader global jihad. The Delhi serial blasts of Sept. 19, 2010 were followed by an e-mail titled 'eye for an eye' and said 'Delhi was chosen because it is your most strategic Hindutva hub. And the Delhi Jama Masjid shootout e-mail said: For the first time in 63 years we bring the screams and cries of our Kashmiri Muslims to your cities'.

In general the emergence of strong local terror outfits behind the recent serial bombings have so alarmed the government that just hours before the multiple explosions that rocked the Gujarat capital home ministry officials had spoken to police chiefs of states where homegrown networks are well-entrenched and asked them to mount vigil. In almost all recent terror attacks it was seen that these local terrorist bodies, who till recently were only offering logistical help to outside outfits like LeT and HUJI, now have the cadre and the expertise needed to plan and execute their own terror attacks in a highly professional manner.

And local terrorists have local explosives. The use of locally and easily available explosives like ammonium nitrate, fuel oil, Neogel-90 and sulphur, as well as attachment of cheap local brands of clocks as timer devices is evidence that the bombs are assembled locally by terror modules in place.

It is also evident that the explosives available for terror strikes across India cover a large variety. The ones so far discovered are:

- Neogel-90, an ammonium nitrate emulsion, also known as ANFO, Ammonium Nitrate Fuel Oil (Hyderabad twin blasts).
- RDX-ammonium nitrate (Mumbai and Malegaon).
- RDX and TNT (Mecca Masjid).
- RDX (Delhi).
- Pure ammonium nitrate (Varanasi).

Home-grown Terror

A sad epilogue to the current terror scene across the country was provided by a presentation made before the central cabinet by National Security Advisor Narayanan on September 18, 2008 in which he admitted that home-grown terrorism is emerging as the new threat to the nation's secular fabric. He also conceded that India's intelligence agencies have come to realise the domestic character of terror networks only last year.

Referring to recent terror strikes Narayanan said the terrorists involved were not only ideologically determined but also educated, well-trained and tech-savvy. "They are well-versed in cyber, mobile technology, and are trained in making bombs from substances like ammonium nitrate," he stated.

Much of this assessment is based on interrogation of arrested SIMI leader Nagori and his associates. However, Narayanan was not able to shed much light on the new terror outfit Indian Mujahideen which claimed responsibility for Ahmedabad, Jaipur and New Delhi.

In the meanwhile half a dozen top Indian terrorist leaders featuring in a published list of 20 most wanted criminals enjoying Pakistani hospitality for years are as follows:

Maulana Masood Azhar, leader of Jaish-e-Mohammad, man behind the attack on India's Parliament on December 13, 2001. He is also wanted for an attack on the J&K Assembly on Oct 1, 2001, in which 38 people were killed. He currently lives in and operates from Bahawalpur, Pakistan.

Hafiz Mohammad Saeed, co-founder of Lashkar-e-Toiba, also held responsible for the attack on Indian Parliament. He operates from Muridke town, near Lahore in Pakistan.

Syed Salahuddin, head of Hizbul Mujahideen, which has claimed responsibility for dozens of attacks on Indian forces in Kashmir. He currently lives and operates from Muzaffarabad, Pakistan.

Ibrahim Athar, an associate of Maulana Azhar Masood and one of the hijackers of Indian Airlines flight IC-814 from Kathmandu to Delhi in 1999. He is a member of Jaish-e-Mohammad and is wanted in hijacking, kidnapping and murder cases. He currently lives and operates from Bahawalpur, Pakistan.

Zahoor Ibrahim Mistri, a member of Harkat-ul-Ansar, which later changed its name to Harkat-ul-Mujahideen. He is wanted in connection with the hijacking of IC-814 and in cases of kidnapping and murder. He lives and operates from Karachi, Pakistan.

Shahid Akhtar Sayed is wanted for the IC-814 hijacking and kidnapping and murder. He lives and operates from Karachi, Pakistan.

Azhar Yusuf, wanted in the IC-814 hijacking case and in cases of kidnapping and murder. He lives and operates from Karachi, Pakistan.

Abdul Karim, a Kashmiri terrorist responsible for more than 30 bomb blasts in Delhi and parts of northern India in 1996–97. He lives and operates from Lahore, Pakistan.

27

THOUSAND CUTS

Warning to "Filthy" Hindus

With so many terrorist outfits — Pakistani as well as Indian — at its beck and call, it is no wonder ISI has an impressive Indian record—one blast in less than every two days. There were as many as 270 bombings across India in 2006, of which Kashmir topped the list with nearly 80, according to the National Bomb Centre. And in 2007, Assam alone saw over 60 explosions.

Inevitably, terror took its toll : 7,000 dead, including more than 1700 security men in Kashmir, the North-East and elsewhere in the country since 2004. Add to this another 450, the number of citizens killed, including the Mumbai, Hyderabad and Delhi bomb blasts. Assam reported over 400 deaths in 2007, up from over 170 the previous year, while in the North-East the central home ministry's own figure of civilians killed was more than 500.

To date this situation continues. For in his inaugural address at a police officers' conference in October, 2007 in New Delhi the home minister admitted that sleeper cells of terrorists existed in the country's mega cities and were being activated as and when required.

His admission came stunningly true when two big cities were bombed on two consecutive days, July 25 and 26, 2008. There were an unbelievable 21 bomb blasts in Ahmedabad on July 26 and 10 in Bangalore the day before, killing over 50 people and injuring 200.

In less than a month, the Gujarat police nailed SIMI as the perpetrator of the Ahmedabad blasts, busting a SIMI module. It arrested 10 persons, including one of two masterminds behind the strike, Mufti Abu Bashir. Tracking the plot the police discovered that it began with a terrorist training camp organised by Nagori in Kerala in December 2007, in which SIMI cadres were given training in such diverse skills as explosives making, shooting, map-reading, motorcycle racing, trekking, mountaineering and river-crossing. A story to mislead the police was also read out to all activists in case they were arrested and interrogated. "The idea to trigger the blasts in various parts of the country including Ahmedabad was conceived in a terror training camp in Kerala, where Safdar Nagori and his brother Kamaruddin Nagori delivered instigating speeches," said Gujarat Jt. Commissioner of Police Ashish Bhatia.

Next month another terrorist camp, this time in Gujarat, was held in January 2008 in the Pavagadh jungles in Halol Taluka, in which the Ahmedabad blasts plan was finalised. The planners visited various Gujarat towns such as Ahmedabad, Vadodara, Surat and Bharuch several times, holding their final meeting in Ahmedabad on June 20 to finalize minute details like who would plant the bombs and where.

Mufti Bashir, one of the two masterminds behind the plot, is a *madrasa* teacher from Azamgarh in UP and spent a year and a half teaching Arabic at a *madrasa* established by Maulana Abdul Aleem Islahi, a known SIMI activist. The other mastermind of the strike was Mumbai-based IT professional and explosives expert Abdus Subhan Qureshi *alias* Tauqeer, who remains untraced.

A particularly vicious feature of the Ahmedabad bombing was that for the first time even hospitals had been made targets. (Incidentally, the idea of bombing hospitals after striking other parts of the city forms part of a terrorist plot in the Hindi film *Contract*).

In the investigation into the Bangalore blasts it was found that the basic design of the bombs used in Bangalore, Ahmedabad and earlier in Jaipur was the same. Karnataka DGP Srikumar said the Bangalore bombs were locally and professionally assembled.

Commenting on the serial bombing in Bangalore a senior Karnataka police officer involved with terrorism in the past observed that investigations into the blast in an empty Hubli courtroom in May that year could have been a deterrent to it. "Terrorism and blast-related cases need sustained investigations. Even if results are not forthcoming, the constant process of inquiry helps in many ways. Findings into a terror strike can prove to be a deterrent to attacks," the officer said.

On May 10, 2008 a low-intensity blast had rocked an empty courtroom in Hubli. Two days later the court was scheduled to hear a case against 12 terror suspects, including SIMI leader Safdar Nagori, who was arrested from Indore in March. The blast "skipped under the radar of a police force caught up with the election process", the media reported.

Apropos the bombings in Ahmedabad and Jaipur the arrested terrorists revealed that Tauqeer had prepared as many as three e-mails which proclaimed the role of Indian Mujahideen, SIMI's "hardline version". The highly provocative 14-page document said the Ahmedabad blasts were an answer to the tyranny and oppression of the Hindu community. "This is our beginning! Our commencement! Our opening launch! To burn you alive in your own Hell—your own Gujarat," said the e-mail.

The mail, written in fluent English and quoting extensively from the Quran, named Gujarat Chief Minister Narendra Modi, RSS and rest of the Sangh Parivar as targets. It threatened the then Maharashtra Chief

Minister Vilasrao Deshmukh and his Home Minister RR Patil and Reliance Industries Chairman Mukesh Ambani as well. It put forth five demands, including the release of those arrested in connection with earlier terror attacks. Curiously, the mail said Indian Mujahideen claimed sole responsibility for the Ahmedabad blasts, planned and executed by Indians only and requested other terror outfits like the Lashkar-e-Toiba not to claim any responsibility. The third city planned to be made a terror target at the same time was Surat. Here two cars were found laden with explosives and 30 live bombs were found planted around the city. They were discovered between July 27 and August 3, and defused. The electronic circuit for the Surat bombs was programmed from a laptop belonging to Usman Agarbattiwala, one of the terrorists of the Ahmedabad plot.

In an e-mail specifically relating to Surat, Indian Mujahideen claimed ownership of the bombs but denied that they did not explode because of faulty circuits. Their purpose, claimed the e-mail, was not to kill but to terrorise. "How many micro-chips can be faulty? One? Or two? Or all 30 at the same time?" The e-mail said the bombs were a warning to filthy Hindus.

The substantial backup for the Surat operation was revealed by the fact that 70 possible suspects were charge-sheeted by the police, of whom as many as 61 are absconding. The IM network has Riaz Bhatkal at its helm, and his close associate, Abdul Sattar, is believed to be a key figure in a network spanning the country.

Urban Terrorism

Targeting major Indian cities is a major feature of Pakistan's war of terror on India, and Mumbai continues to be at the top of the hit list even after two horrendous serial bombings of the past. This came to light when, in February 2008, a module of 7 LeT *fidayeen* (suicide squad members) was found planning to attack as many as 12 sensitive locations in the city. For this purpose an LeT operative by the name Fahim had conducted a recce of all spots on the hit list, which included "Churchgate and Chhatrapati Shivaji Terminus railway stations, Mumbai police headquarters, Gateway of India, and the Bombay Stock Exchange building," said the then Anti-Terrorism squad chief Hemant Karkare.

Delhi Again

A recent high point in the reign of terror came with the capital again– 5 bomb blasts in New Delhi within 30 minutes, killing more than 20 people and injuring over 100. Three more bombs were found and defused. The attack came just a week after Intelligence Bureau (IB) wrote to Delhi Police warning that Delhi could be next in line on the hit list after Jaipur and Ahmedabad. Ahmedabad had also given Delhi many pointers indicating that Delhi was definitely on the terrorists' priority list. The

Indian Mujahideen e-mail after the Ahmedabad blasts had unambiguously threatened that the crusade would continue.

The rabid mail, which poured vitriol on Indian authorities, contained references to some very local Mumbai incidents like a police raid on some Muslim colonies in Andheri that were hardly noticed or reported even in the city. This, investigators said, showed that the perpetrators had good knowledge of events in Mumbai, possibly through a local network. The 13-page e-mail devoted considerable space to investigations carried out by the Gujarat and Rajasthan police and also the Mumbai ATS. Calling the Gujarat police's crackdown a forged story, the mail taunts the police, asking them that if the masterminds had been nabbed, then which mastermind executed today's attack?

The e-mail, signed off by 'Guru Al Hindi' and 'Al-Arbi', finally said: "The Indian Mujahideen accepts the sole responsibility for the Delhi serial blasts and we claim this through our third consecutive e-mail, which is unfortunately still a mystery for you. It is very sad to see the bad condition of your cyber forensics who have still failed to find out our technique of sending the message of death."

The 2002 Gujarat riots were given as an excuse for the serial bomb blasts in Ahmedabad in July. For the recent bomb blasts in Delhi, it was the 1992 demolition of Babri Masjid. An e-mail sent by Indian Mujahideen to television channels, which has almost become its signature move before an attack minutes before the five bomb blasts shook Delhi, sent an ultimatum to the authorities: Vacate the land of Babri as soon as you can. Never assume that we have forgotten the demolition of Babri Masjid, and by Allah we can never forget it! It is that grave mistake of yours which will make you taste humiliation for generations to come, the 13-page e-mail titled *Eye for an Eye: The Dust Will Never Settle Down* said.

The mail in pdf format, written in flawless English, was very similar to the one sent ahead of the Ahmedabad blasts – titled *The Rise of Jihad: Revenge of Gujarat* – in its tone, tenor and rhetoric, but was much more analytical and packed with facts. There is a lot of abuse and vitriol directed against the usual suspects – Narendra Modi, RR Patil, VHP, RSS, Congress. The Congress "continues to cheat the Muslims under the label of secularism", the mail said. "These serial bomb blasts at Delhi are yet another intimidation to the Congress Government to desist from agitating the Muslim sentiment anymore".

Almost three pages of the e-mail had been devoted to a careful analysis of media reports to make the point that newspapers are biased in their coverage of terrorism. The mail carefully tracked news stories published in leading English dailies and mentioned the stories which got covered on the front page or were relegated to the inside pages. It also noted which stories got single or double column space and which were completely ignored.

The mail just before the Jaipur blasts was written in broken English and mostly incoherent. Thereafter, the Indian Mujahideen sent three mails: one just before the Ahmedabad blasts, the second when the Gujarat police claimed to have cracked the blasts case, and the third just before the five blasts that shook Delhi. All the mails have an overdose of rhetoric. "In the light of the injustice and wrongs on the Muslims of Gujarat, we advance our jihad and call our brethren to unite under it and answer these irresolute *kafireen* of India. We call you, O Muslims of Gujarat, to elevate yourselves from the fear of these wretched Hindus, to unify all your courage and bravery that you have in your hearts," said the mail before the Ahmedabad blasts. "By this attack we intend to prove to you the ability and potential of Indian Mujahideen to assault any city of India at any time with the help and permission of our AlmightyAllah."

Ridicule

The last two e-mails ridiculed the investigating agencies and rubbished the claims of Gujarat Police chief PC Pandey on cracking the blasts case. In the mail sent after the arrests made by Gujarat Police, the Indian Mujahideen refers to IB (Intelligence Bureau) as "Ignorance Bureau "and forensic experts as 'foren-sicks'. The mail ridicules the police's 'success' in defusing the bombs in Surat. "Just think, O numbskulls! How many microchips can be faulty? One? Or two? Or all the 30?" Then it goes on to declare, "Not even a single *mujahid* from our ranks who played even a minute role in the blasts has been arrested to date".

War on Mumbai

While the third big hit on Mumbai planned by LeT in February 2008 failed to take off as the 7 cadres who were to carry it out were caught in UP, this failure was more than made up when, in the last week of November 2008, a team of ten terrorists came by sea from Karachi, penetrated three layers of coastal security to reach Mumbai, and mounted one of the most deadly multiple terror attacks the country has seen to date. And for the first time it was open war. The terrorists landed openly near the fishermen's colony in South Mumbai, and a woman selling waste material in a small shop nearby actually watched them come ashore and even asked them what they were doing there. One of them said, *"Tumhe Kya? Tum apna kaam karo."* This was just an hour before the terror began.

The terrorists, in batches of 2 each, then fanned out and struck at 9 places, including two five-star hotels, Taj Mahal and Oberoi/Trident, and the Chhatrapati Shivaji Terminus (CST), Mumbai's biggest and busiest railway station. For the first time the *fidayeen* fought an open battle with security forces which lasted for 2 days and 2 nights and came to an end after 60 hours when all but one were killed. Total toll: Nearly 200 killed, more than 300 wounded. All the terrorists were so heavily armed that they had reportedly enough ammunition to kill 5000 people.

The whole operation was planned in such secrecy that the terrorists were told about their targets only a week before the assault, when they were given data like Google images of their assigned locations, access and exit points, and area maps. Modules were formed and the entire operation was explained to them only at that time. According to Mumbai Police the terrorists had a fairly good idea of their respective target locations through the Google maps supplied to them but had not visited Mumbai before November 26, the day of the attack.

The sole survivor of the terror team, Azam Ameer Kasab, a resident of village Faridkot in Okara district of Pakistan's Punjab, admitted he was trained along with several others at two separate camps in Pakistan. The first camp lasted for nearly 3 months and involved training in the use of firearms and explosives. After a short break of a few weeks the second camp focussed on marine drills for landing on the shore. Most probably this training was given at the Pakistani naval base in the Mangla dam area. According to police sources it was intensive and was given for almost a year and a half to more than 30 terrorists, out of whom 10 were hand-picked.

Kasab admitted the attack was an LeT operation. The Okara district from where he hailed is an active recruiting ground for LeT. Kasab even named LeT commander Zaki-ur Rehman Lakhvi as the man who briefed them on the sites to be attacked and the *modus operandi* of the attack. Indian intelligence agencies confirmed that the Pakistani handlers with whom the terrorists were in constant touch on the telephone during the siege at the Taj Mahal Hotel and Nariman House were top LeT leaders Lakhvi and Yusuf Muzammil. The confirmation was based on voice match done by experts of the Pakistan desk in New Delhi with voice in its data bank.

The Pakistani ship *Al Hussaini* on which the terror team of ten left for Mumbai from KT Bandar near Karachi was initially thought to belong to LeT. While records of vessels entering Indian waters were checked to find out who owned the ship, inquiries revealed that the ship is not registered with marine insurance companies in London. Later, Russia asserted that logistic support to the terrorists was provided by Pakistan-based Indian underworld don Ibrahim Dawood's D Company. Indian intelligence agencies tracing the antecedents of *Al Hussaini* believe it was under the control of a Dawood aide.

Even otherwise the Pakistan connection with the attack was quite clear. After setting sail from Karachi on a Pakistani ship the terrorists hijacked Indian trawler *Kuber* to reach Mumbai, and on this vessel the

Mumbai Police found many items with Pakistani markings. These included a diesel can with an office address in Karachi, clothing items with Pakistani tailor's tags, toilet paper of a Karachi company, a packet of wheat flour bought at a Karachi shop, shaving cream and dental gel made in Pakistan, a Namaz cap from a shop in Multan, and a metal plate with the picture of a gun and instructions in Urdu.

On a much more serious level it was found that most of the guns and grenades used for the attack had their source in Pakistan. Some of them were actually from the Pakistan Government's ordnance factories in Wah city in Pakistan's Punjab. This was the same source of grenades and explosives used in the 1993 Mumbai serial blasts, the 2001 Parliament assault, and the 2008 Kabul embassy attack.

Apart from the overall Pakistani connection, the attack also showed that LeT and ISI were hand in glove in the whole operation. When LeT's chief military commander Zaki-ur-Rehman was arrested for the attack and lodged in Rawalpindi Jail, ISI chief Lt. Gen. Shuja Pasha went there to call on him.

In fact, Home Secretary GK Pillai flatly said ISI was behind 26/11 from start to finish. "ISI has had a much more significant role to play (in the attack than was earlier thought). Then (ISI) were literally controlling it (the attack) from the beginning till the end," Pillai said in an interaction with *Indian Express*.

Although LeT is already a banned organisation, the recent open Pakistani terror war on Mumbai raised an international demand for dismantling of the whole LeT network, which includes its front organisation, public face, Jamaat-ud-Dawa. Reacting to the Mumbai carnage the UN Security Council imposed sanctions on Jamaat-ud-Dawa and declared JuD chief Saeed and Mumbai terror mastermind Zaki-ur Rehman as terrorists. Two other top LeT leaders to be similarly declared terrorists were Haji Mohammad Ashraf and India-born Saudi citizen Zaki-ur Bahaqiz, both financiers of JuD. Bahaqiz raised funds for JuD in Saudi Arabia and was leader of LeT there.

Despite Pakistan's character certificate for JuD its charitable cover was blown and it was banned in Pakistan as well as internationally. The US not only rubbished the Pakistani claim of JuD's innocence but warned that it had learnt the hard way that charitable organisations are also intertwined with entities that have terror links. The bottom line is whether Pakistan abandons its Jihadi links and stops making distinction between the good and bad Jihadis.

Actually, the Jihadi link between LeT and JuD is very much a fact, especially *vis-a-vis* India. This was forcefully highlighted when thumbing its nose at the UN ban JuD rallied virtually every religious party in Pakistan in a rally in Lahore to issue a ten-point charter of demands that included an "immediate end to military operations along the Afghan border so that tribals can defend (Pakistan) against an Indian invasion..." The conference was attended by Jamaat-ud-Dawa's central leaders Maulana Shamshad Ahmed Salfi and Maulana Saifullah Khalid, its public relations heads for Frontier Province and Punjab Ateeq Chouhan and Khalid Bashir, and its spokesman Abdullah Muntazir. Also present were senior leaders of Jamaat-e-Islami, Jamiat-e-Ulema-e-Islam, Jamaat-e-Ahle Sunnat, Majlis-e-Ahrar-e-Islam, Jamia Manzoor-al-Islamia, Al-Khidmat Foundation, Tahreek-e-Khaksar, Tehreek-e-Istiqlal, and Imran Khan's Tehreek-e-Insaf. The chief of Pakistan's ex-servicemen society, Maj. Gen. (retd.) Shafeeq and president of National Labour Federation Rafiq Ahmed Khan were also present. In addition to defence against an Indian invasion the charter demanded that India be declared an enemy country, and all links (with India) be snapped.

Similarly, strident anti-Indianism was in evidence on the JuD's website even many days after it was banned. Some examples: One post said, "A few more shoes please for Indian copycats, equating the Indian Prime Minister with US President Bush, who is responsible for killing over a million Iraqis shamelessly". In another post, titled "Pakistani leaders decry proposed ban on JuD" the website said, Pakistan's Foreign Minister Shah Mehmood Qureshi said India has yet to provide us with evidence that Pakistani nationals were involved in the Mumbai attacks. He said the fact of the matter is that "some Indian politicians want to gain political mileage out of the Mumbai events." Yet another post, titled "India: The unneighbourly neighbour", said Atma Ghati Pathak ("Suicide Squad") members carried out the Mumbai suicidal mission to derail Karkare investigations into the Army-terrorist nexus. Quoting the Pakistani paper *Daily Mail's* latest findings it said, the saffron terrorist groups belonging to Sangh Parivar were behind the recent Mumbai carnage and several suicidal attacks and assassinations in Pakistan and India.

In the meanwhile, after JuD was labelled a terrorist organisation by the UN it was able to transfer money out of most of its bank accounts, negating the impact of the so-called crackdown by the Pakistan government. The *Wall Street Journal* reported that the organisation has stashed millions of dollars in banks in Pakistan as well as abroad. The public outcry on the UN action gave the organisation ample time to transfer its money out of most bank accounts, admitted a Pakistani finance ministry source. "The money in Pakistan is hidden now. We won't find it," he said.

In Pakistan, Europe and the US JuD had asked donors since 2005 to deposit funds in a Pakistani bank, Bank Alfalah, in the name of a separate charitable body called Idara Khidmat-e-Khalq. In 2006 the US State Department identified it as an *alias* for Jamaat. Donations were solicited in the US through a German bank.

There was incontrovertible evidence with the Government of India that pointed to the complicity of ISI and the Pakistan Army in the attack, it was the civilian government that was kept out of the loop. While Kasab confessed that he was trained at two LeT camps, some intercepts of the terrorists' communications, mostly voice-over Internet protocol, used pathways often used by ISI. In fact a US repot even asserted that former ISI men trained the Mumbai attackers. A former defence department official said ... "American intelligence agencies had determined that former officers from Pakistan's army and its powerful ISI helped train the Mumbai attackers", the *New York Times* reported. These agencies have documented regular meetings between ISI and LeT operatives. "It goes beyond information-sharing to include some funding and training," said a US official. "And these are not rogue ISI elements. What's going on is done in a fairly disciplined way." "If there's anything that is a 64 million dollar question today," it is finding out the extent of its (LeT) current ties to the Pakistani intelligence service," said veteran CIA analyst Bruce Riedel. Contesting the Pakistani government's denials that its intelligence agency has no links to LeT, Riedel said it is difficult to believe the Pakistani government's assertions "given the size of LeT activities in Pakistan." The Mumbai terror plot was carried out by professionals who were trained by professionals that were given a professional plan," Riedel said, adding there was clearly considerable planning involved over a protracted period and the attacks were not a plot by amateurs or by a pick-up group. Reacting to the ISI role in the attack the US tried to impose sanctions against some former ISI top guns including former ISI boss Lt. Gen. Hamid Gul, but Pakistan blocked the move.

Experts felt ISI would shield the terrorists and give them enough time to go underground. This was done when LeT, which has been running terror camps, was banned by the UN Security Council in 2005. "They will resurface under another banner...They will restore functions the moment pressure eases. They have detained them before and then released them through the court process by not giving any evidence," said Ajai Sahni, anti-terrorism expert and executive director of the Institute for Conflict Management. That this re-emergence was a strong possibility was underlined by an *Economic Times* report titled *Coming soon: Jamaat by another name*. It reported from Islamabad Maulana Abdul Aziz Alvi, chief of JuD in PoK, saying his organisation does not take permission from UN to carry on its activities.

A first-time feature of this LeT operation was that the by now expected terror e-mail used Hindi words (with a Punjabi accent). Ostensibly sent by some outfit called Deccan Mujahideen, it came from a computer based in Pakistan. The two-page e-mail was headlined *Chetavani nahi, haqeeqat*. It said: "We today want the India government to bring an end to atrocities against Muslims. We want them to return all the states taken away from Muslims. We want an explanation of all the atrocities committed on us. We know that the Hindu community is that of Baniya that only knows how to seek an explanation but never gives one. This attack is in reaction to the attacks started by the Hindus since 1947. Now there won't be any action but only reaction. Such reactions would keep on happening till we take revenge for each and every injustice perpetrated on us."

The Flying Jehadi

After long years of Pakistani terror coming to India by land, the other day it arrived by sea, and now three different official sources have warned of terror from the sky. Jolted by the latest terror attack on Mumbai, Defence Minister Antony asked the three armed forces to beware of the flying Jihadi and take steps to prevent him from striking from the air.

The Intelligence Bureau (IB) cautioned about a Fidayeen (suicide) attack at a major airport. Mumbai airport already had a terror alert in December 2008, while the Bureau of Civil Aviation Security issued warning about terrorists planning to strike at the airports of New Delhi, Bangalore and Chennai.

Intelligence agencies suggested that unused airstrips could be used to mount airborne terror strikes in the country. They could be used as base by terrorists planning suicide attacks using small airstrips. All this makes one central point that even as per official threat perception Pakistani terror in India is far from contained, much less overcome, rather, it is on the increase.

The modern sophistication of e-mails and Google maps apart, such plots are more than a decade old. For a report in March 1994 of the arrest of a group of six agents of a terrorist outfit called Islami Inqalabi Mahaz (IIM), backed by ISI, and its disclosures showed that ISI was even then engaged in setting up its network in Indian cities countrywide. Floppies recovered from these suspects, first-ever such seizure, contained detailed instructions on improvising explosives, RDX and TNT, shaped charges, incendiary bricks, disposable silencers, and secret inks. This showed the group's meticulous preparation for terrorist acts. The instructions also included renting safe houses in Delhi and Mumbai and establishing alternative Indian identities by taking identity cards of health clubs.

Even earlier in 1993, Delhi police had arrested a notorious ISI operative Mohammad Sharief. He was in charge of "K2" operations and was working to bring together Kashmiri and Khalistani militants together. He was also the handler for Lal Singh, the mastermind of the Kanishka air crash in June 1985. Sharief operated out of Aligarh and had set up a big network across India. Mahaz was operating with recruits mostly drawn from Pakistan and Afghanistan. Many of them were mercenaries and had been sent to various countries to carry out specific missions. Mahaz had close relations with Markaz Dawah-ul-Irshad, Ahle Hadis, and Jago Mujahideen, and in turn all these were closely linked with ISI.

The six arrested persons revealed that they had been in touch with a Maj. Ehsan-ul-Haq in Lahore, and used to receive day-to-day instructions from him. Haq in turn was in close touch with Markaz members. The arrest of Dr. Mohammad Ansari in Mumbai in January 1994 revealed that his gang had engineered as many as 52 explosions. ISI was also responsible for the bomb blasts at the RSS office in Madras in 1993.

According to the then Delhi Police Commissioner the IIM terror group was in Delhi with long-term plans to sabotage the country's communication and transport network by planting explosives on railway tracks and at bus stands, communication installations as well as government and commercial buildings throughout the country. Apart from high explosives, the material seized from them included Pakistani passports, diaries, and floppies. The diaries contained various contact numbers in the Middle East and Britain. The floppies contained a long and comprehensive account (running into 250 typed pages) on production of high explosives, use of poisons, and elaborate details on how to improvise weapons from locally available material.

In a subsequent raid on a hideout a large amount of chemicals used for making explosives was also recovered. The place was apparently being used as a lab for manufacturing explosives. From another hideout ruled exercise books with Hindi alphabets written on them were recovered. Two of the terrorists were learning Hindi to understand the local dialect. The well-known Fatehpuri mosque in old Delhi was a meeting point for the terrorists.

IIM had links with JKLF, Al-Jehad, and Harkat-ul-Ansar, and gave arms training to cadres recruited from various Islamic fundamentalist and militant outfits in Pakistan and Bangladesh. It was also closely involved with a group called Hizb-Islami. The Pakistani terrorists in this group had received extensive training in Afghanistan in guerrilla tactics, use of explosives, rockets and other artillery.

ISI has also been setting up dumps of readily available arms within India since more than a decade for use on appropriate occasions. And even now Pakistan is pushing both regulars and Mujahideen into India, equipped with sophisticated, deadly, man-portable weapons. There is heavy influx of such weapons all over India. For this traffic, in addition to Bangladesh and Nepal, Pakistan is presumably using countries of the Middle East and South-East Asia as cutouts to mask its own involvement. This was stated by National Security Advisor Narayanan in his address at a police officers' conference in October 2009 in New Delhi. Such countries include Indonesia, Thailand and the Maldives in addition to Gulf countries like UAE.

And the terrorists who would use these weapons are being continuously trained in Pakistani camps, said a special investigation report of the Pakistani journal *Herald* published in August 2007. More than a thousand militants from Jammu and Kashmir are at such camps. (As per available figures, in 2005 there were as many as 54 training camps across Pakistan.) In addition to hefty donations from Pakistanis and Kashmiri Muslims living abroad to the tune of millions of dollars, these camps are funded by the Kashmir Liberation Cell, an entity of the Pakistan government, which operates a secret fund for the purpose.

All this amply shows that the anti-India Jehad goes on, and it is going on to date. Supervised, guided and aided by ISI, every Islamic terrorist body, big or small, national or international, is engaged in it, as the media reports day in and day out. For instance, there is evidence showing ISI helped plan the July 7, 2009 bombing of the Indian embassy in Kabul in which, just like 26/11, LeT gunmen went from room to room and killed. This conclusion of US investigators is based on signals between Pakistani intelligence officers and the terrorists. "In October 2009, Davood Moradian, senior policy advisor to foreign minister Spanta said that the British and American governments were fully aware of ISI's role, but lacked the courage to confront Islamabad. He claimed that the Afghan government had given British and American intelligence agents evidence that proved ISI involvement in bombings." (*Wikipedia,* online encyclopedia.) US intelligence says ISI officers involved in the Kabul attack "had not been renegades," indicating that their actions might have been authorised by superiors.

According to Saeed Ansari, spokesman for Afghanistan's intelligence service, this same terrorist group was also involved in the attack in February 2010 on guest houses in Kabul where Indians stayed.

ISI even paid Taliban to hit Indians in Kabul. It paid the Haqqani network 15,000–30,000 dollars to kill Indian nationals working on a key road project, and kidnap Indian engineers, doctors and officers. According to leaked Af-Pak documents ISI also supplied explosive-laden motorcycles to suicide bombers in Afghanistan, and listened in on telephone networks to supply them critical information – right under the nose of CIA, while it watched.

Actually these Kabul attacks are a part of a large-scale anti-India operation in Afghanistan by the ISI. The targets are a range of Indian assets including the Indian embassy, its consulates across the country, Indian companies, and their projects. A detailed dossier prepared by the Afghan government on ISI activities in Afghanistan contains a special section on ISI's anti-India activities in Afghanistan.

And now, as reported on March 24, 2010, LeT and HuM have renewed their call for Jehad against India. Pakistan-based terror groups, including Lashkar-e-Toiba and Hizbul Mujahideen, met in Kotli in PoK and pledged to step up their Jihad to liberate Kashmir from India. They asked the Pakistan government to devise a concrete strategy for this purpose since diplomacy, talks and negotiations have not worked. The meeting, organised by JuD, sought lifting of a ban on Jehadi groups so that they could press on with their movement for independence of Kashmir.

A declaration unanimously adopted at this Kashmir Solidarity Conference in Muzaffarabad said the region's status as a base camp for terrorist groups should be restored and the ban on Kashmiri Jehadi groups should be lifted. If the rulers cannot help the Kashmiris, they should open the field for Kashmiri *mujahideen*. The *mujahideen* will deal with India, said the declaration.

Within Pakistan the same month two arrested Pakistanis, Noor Jehan Khan and Rehmat Gul, described as deserters from the Frontier Constabulary, revealed that Taliban had drawn up specific plans to abduct Indian diplomats, including the High Commissioner, to exchange them for terrorist commanders currently in jail in Pakistan.

As for al-Qaeda, its No. 1 and No. 2 top leaders had both threatened India in general and Hindus in particular in the past. Its No. 3, reportedly recently killed, had also repeated the threat. In a direct message to India Mustafa Abu al-Yazid, commander of its operations in Afghanistan and at the time ranked behind No. 2 Ayman al-Zawahiri, had warned of more attacks like the one on Mumbai if it retaliates against Pakistan. In a video seen by Reuters in Feb. 2009 al-Yazid said: "If you make that mistake, then with the command of Allah, you will have to pay a heavy price. The Mujahideen will asunder your armies into the ground." "We will bring *mujahideen* and *fidayeen* from the whole Islamic world to confront you and target your economic interests everywhere until your entire system collapses," he said.

Actually, these threats and warnings, recent though they are, have a long history, as shown by al-Qada's complicity in Kashmir. Bin Laden and Ayman al-Zawahiri considered India to be a part of the 'Crusader-Zionist-Hindu' conspiracy against the Islamic world. According to the 2005 report *'Al-Qaeda: Profile and Threat Assessment'* by Congressional Research Service, Osama bin Laden was involved in training militants for Jehad in Kashmir while living in Sudan in the early nineties. By 2001 Kashmiri terrorist group Harkat-ul-Mujahideen had become a part of the al-Qaeda coalition. According to the United Nations High Commissioner for Refugees al-Qaeda established bases in Pakistan-occupied Kashmir during the 1999 Kargil War, and continues to operate and thrive there with tacit approval of ISI.

Many terrorists active in Kashmir were trained in the same *Madrasas* as Taliban and al-Qaeda. Fazlur Rehman Khalil of Harkat-ul-Mujahideen was a signatory of al-Qaeda's 1998 declaration of Jihad against America and its allies. In a Letter to American People written by Osama bin Laden in 2002 he stated that one of the reasons he was fighting America was because of her support to India on the Kashmir issue. In November 2001 Kathmandu airport went on high alert after threats that Osama planned to hijack a plane from there and crash it into a target in New Delhi. In 2002 a special US team called Delta Force was sent into Indian Kashmir to hunt for Osama bin Laden after reports that he was being sheltered by Harkat-ul-Mujahideen.

Maulana Masood Azhar, founder of Jaish-e-Mohammad, reportedly met Osama bin Laden several times and received funds from him. According to American counterterrorism expert Bruce Riedel al-Qaeda and Taliban were closely involved in the 1999 hijacking of Indian Airlines Flight 814 to Kandahar which led to release of Maulana Masood Azhar from prison in exchange for the passengers. Osama bin Laden personally welcomed Azhar and threw a lavish party in his honour after his release, according to Abu Jandal, bodyguard of bin Laden.

Lashkar-e-Toiba, mastermind behind the 2008 Mumbai attacks, is also known to have strong ties with al-Qaeda leaders living in Pakistan. FBI believes al-Qaeda and Lashkar have been intertwined for a long time, while CIA said al-Qaeda funds Lashkar-e-Toiba. Jean-Louis Bruguiere, top French counterterrorism official, told Reuters in 2009, "Lashkar-e-Toiba is no longer a Pakistani movement with only a Kashmir political or military agenda. Lashkar-e-Toiba is a member of al-Qaeda."

In a video released in 2008 senior al-Qaeda operative Adam Yahiye Gadahn stated that victory in Kashmir had been delayed for years, it was the liberation of the jihad there from that interference which, Allah willing, would be the first step towards victory over the Hindu occupiers of that Islam land.

One may well conclude with an apt quote from *Frontline* that sums up the whole sorry scenario – of groups with the intention and the ability to carry out terror attacks across India, there is no shortage. To paraphrase this in figures, in the year 2008 alone there were 48 terrorist attacks in 18 Indian cities. So successive home ministers' repeated claim that the UPA government had a zero tolerance approach to terrorism was worth a big zero.

28

MANY FRONTS

Multiple Facets of Proxy War

Although the proxy war that Pakistan is waging on India through ISI is mainly fought with bombs and bullets, there are other fronts as well. Prominent among them are:

- Infiltration,
- Espionage,
- Economic subversion,
- Political subversion,
- Social subversion,
- Intellectual subversion,
- Media "management",
- Nexus with the underworld, and
- The drug trade.

Infiltration

It is an open secret that Pakistan has been relentlessly pushing in terrorists, subversives, spies and even regular armymen across India's soft borders. Over the years this infiltration has assumed such massive proportions that it has again exposed the UPA dispensation's peace talks with Pakistan as an exercise in futility. Just days before yet another round of talks was scheduled for May in 2010 the Pakistanis resorted to heavy firing in Jammu & Kashmir as a cover for infiltrating militants. While the UPA powers that be are wondering why the post-Musharraf regime in Pakistan should do so, B Raman, an expert on Pakistan affairs, gave a blunt warning – "PPP has always been unreliable, and India should be careful. They are working out a deal with the Tehrik-e-Taliban, and one of the spin-offs may be that Jehadis would be let loose in Jammu and Kashmir again." Former intelligence agency chief Ajit Doval echoed the sentiment. "The manner of infiltration, holding villagers hostage, is an old tactic. This is not a good portent."

Actually, the rise in infiltration is a developing phenomenon. In 2004 when the so-called peace process was supposedly at its peak, the figure for infiltration was nearly 120. The following year, 2005, it rose above

170 by July. According to a credible report, later that year at least 400 to 500 infiltrators were waiting to cross over. In 2006 the Central Government had admitted that crossborder terrorism had spread to the country's hinterland, and infiltration, in comparison to the previous year, had trebled.

The agenda paper for the 2006 chief ministers' conference also pointed to the rise in grenade attacks in Kashmir and continued insurgency in the North-East. The Government claimed it had taken steps to take forward the "peace process" in Kashmir, but, as the media put it, the result was missing on all counts.

The fact of the matter is that even according to Indian intelligence agencies the number of Pakistanis openly entering India and then surreptitiously exiting is on the increase. Even as far back as in 1994 a home ministry report said nearly eight lakh Pakistanis had entered India (with valid papers), out of which nearly 11,000 had just vanished.

As for militants, hundreds of them have sneaked into the Kashmir Valley since 2006. This number is estimated at 500. The infiltration took place group by group. One of these was organized by HuM, while another was led by an LeT commander. Comparing 2007 with 2006 Army chief J J Singh said there was a 3-fold increase in infiltration bids across the LoC. Curiously enough, while the Jammu and Kashmir police feared that the infiltration situation is fast deteriorating, a defence ministry spokesman said, "We cannot say infiltration is on the rise."

At the same time the dangerous dimensions of infiltration were highlighted by the candid statement of Pranab Mukherji that ISI may well have deeply infiltrated the defence forces and corrupted a sizeable section of the lower ranks. Admitting the presence of spy rings in the Army, he said ISI has moles in different defence organisations, and has even managed to reach New Delhi via Kashmir and Kathmandu. It is also known that ISI has even infiltrated Indian intelligence agencies. (On the other hand RAW has not had much success in placing its operatives in ISI.)

ISI's allies, associates and affiliates are also actively engaged in infiltration. In Kashmir, sleeper agents of these bodies are systematically trying to infiltrate the political, bureaucratic and security establishments in the state. A Srinagar lawyer and political activist ShabbirAhmed Bukhari was caught providing fake ID cards of the youth wing of the National Conference to three LeT terrorists. Shakeel Ahmed Shafi, a member of the State Youth Congress, facilitated LeT cadres to smuggle arms and communication equipment through high security zones by providing them with party ID cards.

In just one year (2007) at least seven LeT sympathizers were discovered to be serving Armymen. In June 2007 one such man in an LeT module in the Poonch area even had his wife with him. National Security had also admitted the possibility of LeT attempting to infiltrate the Air Force.

The ISI gameplan to infiltrate the Indian armed forces came to light when the UP Police Special Task Force nabbed in September 2006 a Pakistani, Tasin Azim, who was sent to India by ISI to develop a base for recruiting their youth into the Indian Army. Actually this plan has been in operation since 2002. Some junior-level army personnel were discovered to be helping Pakistan. A mere signalman recruited three years ago could obtain sensitive documents and pass them on to the Pakistan Army. Before that he had done so thrice and was every time paid by ISI. A bribe of a mere Rs. 20,000 was enough for him.

Now, as of 2010, nearly 2,500 militants are waiting to sneak into J & K from across the border, Army Chief General Deepak Kapoor said early this year. He said militants were waiting at various training camps in Pakistan-occupied Kashmir for the opportune moment to cross into Indian territory. "According to our inputs, there are 42 militant training camps still intact across the border in PoK", the Army Chief said. A year ago Defence Minister Antony had said there was no serious attempt to dismantle the terror infrastructure in Pakistan.

How systematically the entire infiltration operation was handled by ISI was openly reported by the Pakistani newspaper *Friday Times* long back. On May 17, 1990 it wrote: "The terrorists arrive at the LoC bearing code letters from their organizations, and are taken over by Field Intelligence Units, the main grassroots units of ISI."

Espionage

ISI is engaged in espionage in India on a wide scale. When, for instance, Home Minister Shivraj Patil rang the alarm bell in November 2006 over threats to critical installations and nuclear power stations in various parts of India, he had good reason to do so. For as many as 51 spy rings involved in gathering sensitive information on such installations had been busted in the last two years. They were dealing with nuclear installations, missile technology, communication systems, space programmes, and defence establishments. This information was disclosed early last year at a conference of Directors General of Police (DGPs) from all states in the country.

While inaugurating the conference the Home Minister underlined the threat posed by Pakistan-based groups to such critical installations, especially along the coasts. A committee led by Director General of Maharashtra Police PS Pasricha had assessed these threats, and its report was discussed at the conference. The committee found that threat levels against nuclear installations increased after the (then proposed) Indo-US nuclear deal. In 2005 it was revealed that 18 espionage modules were busted, and 30 agents were found to be Indians. In 2006, till mid-September 17 such modules had been detected. They had been tasked with providing information that would facilitate attacks in the hinterland.

That this plan continues to date was proved by the arrest of an ISI agent Afghani in Mumbai in October 2006. He had already passed on information and photographs of vital installations in Mumbai to his bosses in Pakistan during the previous six months. Afghani had shifted to suburban Mankhurd two years ago possibly due to its proximity to strategic installations (Bhabha Atomic Research Center), according to Anti Terrorist Squad (ATS) chief Raghuvanshi. Although only "tenth standard pass", Afghani was tech-savvy enough to send the information by e-mail. "Although sensitive information sent through e-mail can be monitored, his *modus operandi* was to create temporary accounts which he would delete after sending each mail. So his mails could not be traced," admitted Raghuvanshi. Afghani had gone to Pakistan in 2006 and 2007 for month-long training in talent-spotting – to identify and recruit youths with potential as terror operatives. He was given five credit cards by ISI for operational expenses in India and had spent 2 lakh rupees in six months before getting caught. He also admitted to having visited Kashmir "to seek inspiration and motivation from militant activities." In addition to a CD containing sensitive information, the ISI agent was in possession of documents containing contact numbers and ranks of several senior officers of the Indian Navy's Western Command.

Another, rather curious case of espionage for information was that of a Hindu in love with a girl in Karachi, Pakistan. He is Vishal Kumar Upadhyaya, who had converted to Islam two years ago and had been operating under the name Bilal. Upadhyaya had visited Pakistan in 2004 to meet his girlfriend, where he was approached by ISI officials and offered money for providing information about defence establishments in and around Pune. He had met his girlfriend through the Internet. Upadhyaya accepted the offer. It was then that he converted to Islam. In his interrogation after arrest Upadhyaya told the police that he had been transferring information to ISI officials through seven Internet chat accounts that were exclusively connected for the purpose. He kept changing cyber cafes and used his Hindu identity. He received thousands of Rupees for espionage through an international money transfer firm.

Economic Subversion

G Parthasarthy, former High Commissioner to Pakistan, wrote in a newspaper article on September 12, 2008: "At a recent meeting that I had with a group of prominent Pakistanis in a South Asian capital, a close associate of Gen. Musharraf bluntly remarked that if India believed that it could ignore differences with Pakistan and move ahead economically, his country would have no difficulty in taking steps to retard Indian economic progress." What the Pakistani meant was India's economic subversion, which was being carried on long before 2008.

The main method used for this purpose since more than a decade is to pump fake money into the Indian economy through different routes, even different neighbouring countries. As long back as in 1996 a large number of fake currency notes were being pumped into India by terrorists and smugglers as per an economic destabilisation plan drawn up by ISI. Significant amounts of such notes were seized in New Delhi, Bhuj, and Jammu. The notes were being printed in Quetta and Peshawar, and were good enough in appearance to fool an unsuspecting eye.

Since then this technique of economic subversion is being put to use on a massive scale. For when a man from Jammu (a selfconfessed HuM cadre for 15 years !) was arrested in district Idukki of Kerala in January 2010, the terrorist disclosed to the police that militant groups in Pakistan had been regularly bringing in crores worth of counterfeit Indian currency into India.

In February the same year, fake notes were found even in ATMs when the branch manager of Citibank in Gurgaon took to the police a bundle of 500-rupee notes amounting to Rs. 5000 which had been collected from the bank's ATMs in the National Capital Region (NCR) over the previous two months. HDFC Bank had also registered a similar case with the police some months before that. This has raised the apprehension in police circles that a large amount of fake currency may have gone into circulation throughout the Capital.

Further, when the Anti-Terrorism Squad (ATS) of the Mumbai Police, in collaboration with the Kutch police, busted a sleeper cell of the Pakistani terrorist outfit Al-Badr operating from the Muslim pocket of Bhendi Bazar in the city, they arrested prime operative Mohammad Salim Memon, a Pakistani, and found that he had set up the Mumbai cell of the Al-Badr module after being recruited by ISI in June 2006 and was engaged in sneaking into the city a consignment of Rs. 24 lakh in fake currency which had been smuggled into India by the Kutch cell in March last year. Half this amount was sent to Hyderabad for circulation.

Investigations by the Kutch police and Central intelligence agencies revealed that the Al-Badr module was planning to smuggle into India over one crore rupees in fake currency in August *via* the sea route. According to the plan an Indian boat was to set sail from Mandvi port in Kutch and by using a Global Positioning System (GPS) device provided by ISI reach a predetermined location in international waters where it was to have a rendezvous with a Pakistani boat carrying the consignment. Mumbai being the financial capital of India ISI has apparently concentrated its economic subversion strategy here. For when an ISI agent and key supplier of counterfeit currency to Mumbai, Delhi and Kolkata was caught in Mumbai in August 2009 with fake notes of Rs. 1.5 lakh, it was the 14th such seizure in the city during a period of eight months. Counterfeit king Aftab Bhatki of the Dawood Ibrahim gang, who is based in Karachi in Pakistan, is the source of the supplies being shipped to India through Nepal and Dubai. Bhatki's lieutenant Bilal reportedly supplied the consignment to Suleman Shaikh, the Mumbai agent who was caught with it. Shaikh is believed to be a member of a group controlled by an unknown woman based in Delhi. Police interrogation of the arrested agent led to their laying a trap resulting in the arrest of four more gang members who had fake currency worth Rs. 19.5 lakh with them. The Bhatki network of Dawood is known to be an ISI instrument for pumping large amounts of fake money into India. "The quality of the fake notes is so fine that one cannot make out the difference. The only thing missing is the water mark, which can only be checked through laser light," JCP Rakesh Maria said.

In the wake of the twin blasts in Hyderabad on August 20, 2007 the four suspects arrested for the bombings included one Shadab Khan, who had close links with ISI and was in touch with the suspected mastermind Shahid Bilal, commander of HUJI. A former police informer, Shadab was actually a double agent for terror groups in Bangladesh and Pakistan. Shadab and the three associates arrested with him in Hyderabad were all members of a fundamentalist Islamic organization called Darsgah-Jehad-o-Shahadat, and were also involved in the fake currency racket busted in Kerala.

Just two days before the Hyderabad blasts fake currency worth Rs. 2.5 crore was seized in the city. Follow-up investigation led to the arrest of a Mumbai businessman by name Satish Datwani, based in Hong Kong till his return to Mumbai in 2006. He was suspected by the police to be a part of the counterfeit conspiracy and had received part of the consignment for circulation. This was given to him on orders from Dawood aide Khuda Baksh, suspected to be one of the brains behind the racket. The Hyderabad police had already discovered close links between ISI and Dawood-backed networks in smuggling high-quality fake currency into the city from the Middle East using the sea route.

The same month, in September, there were two seizures of fake currency in Mumbai. On September 11 a gang of four, including a Bangladeshi woman, was caught carrying such money worth Rs. 1.3 lakh. Their interrogation led to the second seizure in less than 10 days, on September 20, when five more Bangladeshis, including two women, were arrested with over 9 lakh worth fake currency.

Apart from the prime commercial target Mumbai, the terrorist-infested city of Hyderabad and the state of Kerala, even interior Indian cities like Pune in Maharashtra are being targeted by terror outfits from Pakistan and Bangladesh with a vast banking network for circulation of counterfeit currency. Counterfeit notes have been seized from a number of suspected terror outfit members arrested in Pune, an indication of the currency racket flourishing in the city. It is beginning to manifest itself to such an extent that the banking sector has expressed concern. Recently, when the Pune unit of state Anti Terrorism Squad (ATS) arrested suspected Indian Mujahideen member Hussain Shabbir Nasiruddin Gangavali from a mosque in the city, he had in his possession counterfeit notes worth Rs. 25,000. In March 2008, the Mumbai ATS had gunned down two Bangladeshi terrorists linked to members of the fake currency racket in the state. Earlier, the state ATS had recovered fake notes in Rs. 500 denomination from Ayaz Khan and Nadim Shaikh in Pune, both members of the banned SIMI. Large volumes of counterfeit notes are brought into the country from the Bangladesh border through illegal channels. Shashikant Bugde, Managing Director of Cosmos Bank, admitted that the fake currency issue was serious. "A huge number of counterfeit notes is being deposited in the banks. It is getting hard for the banks to identify the counterfeit notes," Bugde said.

B Shivkumar, state head of IDBI Bank, said, "The problem is taking on serious proportions." Addressing the media in November 2008 RBI Executive Director Gopalkrishnan admitted the rise in incidents of fake notes recovered from the currency chests of banks in the country, and expressed the need for the central government to set up a separate agency to deal with such cases.

And now the latest development in Pakistan's counterfeiting strategy is that fake notes are being made even in India. In the first instance of its kind in the Kashmir Valley, the state police raided and busted operations of a mini-printing press in the Pampore area of Anantnag. The 'prize catch' came even as law enforcement agencies and Opposition leaders bemoaned that the economy was being destablised by the printing and distribution of large quantities of fake Indian currency notes (FICN). Another implication is that the actual printing of FICN in the Valley fits in with a new trend in militancy. The printing press operators are Abdul Hamid, Gulam Nabi Malik and Muzzafar Ahmad Bhatt, and their mini mint was raided even as they were printing FICN of Rs 500 denomination. Experts who examined the seized FICN in Srinagar opined that it was of very sophisticated quality and could easily be mistaken for genuine currency. Along with a sophisticated printer, the raid yielded nine freshly printed Rs. 500 notes and 44 plain currency sheets, with the Reserve Bank of India seal. The three accused admitted to having printed FICN totalling Rs. 6 lakh, which has since been distributed to cadres of the Hizbul Mujahideen and Lashkar-e-Toiba.

Intelligence agencies in Srinagar feel that the actual printing of FICN in the Valley fits in with the latest trends of militancy, with inputs about militant groups facing a serious crunch of hard currency and a depletion of FICN stocks from Pakistan and Nepal. Along with this, the recovery of consignments of FICN from infiltrators, whose bid to cross the Line of Control has been foiled by security forces, has also been drastically reduced, thus, perhaps, forcing operatives to take the next best step, to set up printing shop in their own backyard. Police officials are now working on at least two more suspected cases of FICN printing, again in the heart of the Kashmir Valley.

Although officially a mere Rs 10 crore worth of fake currency was seized across the country in 2007, this amount is only the tip of the iceberg. Even conservative estimates put the amount of fake currency in use at several hundreds of crores in the country. The latest crop of fake notes are so well forged that even investigators trained to detect them find it hard to differentiate them from the real currency. Printed in sophisticated presses across India's western and eastern borders, this money is entering India through a myriad of air, land and sea routes. Investigations reveal that Jehadi outfits located across the borders have emerged as principal carriers of fake currency into India. A large amount of this currency is funding terror networks in the country.

Now, for the first time, in April 2010, Indian investigators produced forensic evidence in court showing that counterfeit currency seized across the country last year had a common raw material and production source: Pakistan. In fact, the pulp used to make the fake Indian currency bills as well as a synthetic fibre added to the pulp were exact matches of their counterparts in the legal tender of Pakistan, according to a three-page forensic report submitted in a National Investigation Agency (NIA) court in Mumbai. The court was further informed that the forensic team had found that the sophistication shown in making these notes, right to the security characters in the tender, has shown that the manufacturing units could not be owned by an individual but only a state.

Explaining this economic terrorism at greater length in an article in *Organiser* in 2009 Joginder Singh, former Director of CBI, wrote *inter alia*: Of late, Pakistan has been procuring currency-standard printing paper in huge quantities from London-based companies, much higher than normal requirement of the country for printing its own currency. It is diverting it to print fake Indian currency notes. It is believed that the Pakistan Government printing press in Quetta (Baluchistan), Karachi's security press, and two other presses in Lahore and Peshawar are being used for this.

ISI has been using Pakistan International Airlines (PIA) to transport the counterfeit currency to its conduits in Nepal, Bangladesh and Sri Lanka. The *modus operandi* of the ISI was revealed by two Nepali counterfeit currency traffickers who were arrested by Thailand police sometime back.

Diplomat Smugglers

The first such exposé was made when Pakistani diplomats were caught distributing fake Indian currency notes. The racket was being carried out by using the network of underworld kingpin Dawood Ibrahim not only in India but also in Sri Lanka, Bangladesh and Nepal in close association with different terror outfits. The menace of finely printed fake currency has grown to such proportions that often people get fake notes even through ATMs.

According to a government committee estimate counterfeit currency amounting to Rs. 169,000 crore is floating around in the Indian financial system. From real estate transactions to ordinary grocery shopping, these bogus notes are being used. According to the National Crime Record Bureau (NCRB), between January and August 2008, 1,170 cases had been registered across the country in connection with fake currency.

Investigations into the Mumbai 26/11 attacks also revealed that a large part of the money to fund the terror operation was obtained through fake currency rackets and hawala channels. ISI raises Rs. 1,800 crore annually to fund terror operations, and a major chunk of this amount comes in through fake currency rackets.

Summing up the counterfeit conspiracy *Organiser* columnist MD Nalapat recently wrote: "While the Reserve Bank of India (RBI) estimates that counterfeit notes (60 per cent of which are printed by foreign terrorist networks to fund operations in India) account for only Rs. 40,000 crores, the actual figure may be close to Rs. 1,20,000 crore. (According to some, 1,69,000 crore.) Today, fake currency is in circulation throughout the country, and is being handed out even by banks, especially in smaller towns."

Hawala Racket: Another strategy for India's economic subversion that ISI has adopted — one in which the Dawood gang of international criminals is its active partner — is the Hawala racket, used for terror money transactions. In 2007–08 the Government's Financial Intelligence Unit received 133 Suspicious Transaction Reports (STRs) from banks, mostly relating to suspected terror financing.

An example in point was the amount of Rs. 1,14,000 recovered from Hawala racketeers in Rajouri, Jammu. This money was meant for the top commander and financial chief of the Hizb-ul Mujahideen (HuM) terrorist outfit in Jammu and Kashmir, Mohammad Zulf, and for Saqib *alias* Abbas Bhai, divisional commander of HuM for three districts — Rajouri, Poonch and Reasi – and its seniormost militant commander in the state. Zulf *alias* Munshi belongs to a family with a history of producing financial chiefs for various militant outfits. His elder brother Abdul Qayoom was the chief of Muttahida Jehad Council (MJC), an amalgam of militant outfits in the state, until he was eliminated by the Rajouri police on June 27, 2009. His diaries revealed the transaction and distribution of lakhs of Rupees between various outfits.

Monetary Infiltration: Yet another means of infiltration into the Indian economy — one that is not easily noticed — is what can be called Muslim money. For according to media reports in January 2010 money from the Islamic World is flowing into Dalal Street, the investment hub of Mumbai, India's commercial capital. A relevant and noteworthy factor here is that about 840 Indian shares are compliant with the Sharia system of investing laid down in the Quran. Even if a fraction of Arab oil money comes in, it would run into billions of petro-dollars. One wonders – how long before these Arab billions initially affect and eventually dominate the Indian economy?

The recent terror targets i.e. Bangalore, Ahmedabad and Surat, all in quick succession, also clearly suggest that the real target is India's economic progress. Both Karnataka and Gujarat have emerged as promising investment destinations. While Karnataka, especially Bangalore, has been the destination for investment in IT and biotech sectors, Gujarat has become a favoured destination for investment in manufacturing and power over the last five years. In the case of Surat there is a legitimate apprehension that a mass exodus of frightened diamond workers from the Gujarat-Saurashtra hinterland, alarmed foreign buyers cancelling their trips, and suspended investment plans for an upcoming Special Economic Zone (SEZ) in the city, with a gem and jewellery park, would bring the diamond industry to a point which, even if for some time, would cause losses to the tune of thousands of crores of Rupees.

Political Subversion

Yet another ISI tactic was political subversion. The most recent and glaring example of this was the blatantly secessionist statements of Kashmiri leaders like Mehbooba. Actually, this is not a new phenomenon. Subversion of the electoral process in Kashmir (and now right up to Kerala) has been practised by ISI for more than a decade. For in 1996 Awami League chief Jamsheed Shirazi *alias* Kaka Parrey had alleged that scores of J&K MLAs had links with ISI. In the wake of this charge BJP leader Kidarnath Sahni, then in charge of the Party's J&K affairs, had demanded that the state government identify persons also in the state secretariat who had links with ISI.

Here a relevant financial footnote: "Even major groups such as HuM, LeT and JeM cannot sustain themselves without government support beyond a year," a Muzaffarabad (PoK) - based observer once told the Pakistani journal *Herald*. "If our pipelines remain dry, the freedom movement in Kashmir will grind to a halt by 2008," added a Muzaffarabad-based commander. The outfits pay anywhere from Rs. 1000 to 3000 per month per cadre. To raise these funds ISI operations are partly funded through kidnapping for ransom bids. For instance, it was behind the kidnapping of Mumbai-based diamond merchants in August 1991.

The same ISI had told the separatist Hurriyat to sneak into J&K polls. Intelligence information available with the Government of India linked the pro-Pakistan Hizbul Mujahideen with the killing of six domestic tourists in the Kashmir Valley and pointed to a two-pronged ISI plan to sabotage the then proposed assembly elections in Jammu and Kashmir. The kidnapping and subsequent murder of the six tourists a few days after the killing of a former National Conference legislator, Syed Ahmed Sayeed, in similar circumstances was the first part of the ISI design: The objective was to derail the political process by deterring popular participation in the elections. The second part of the ISI plan, according to the sources, was that in case the underground militants fail to derail the elections, their overground political cover — the All Party Hurriyat Conference — should step in by proxy.

The Jamaat-e-Islami, which functions as the politico-ideological instrument for the pro-Pakistan militant groups, was directed by ISI to field `independent' candidates from its strongholds in the Valley and Doda district of Jammu region. The ISI also directed other segments of the Hurriyat, such as the People's Conference, to fight the elections by proxy. The People's Conference, led byAbdul Ghani Lone, has been actively involved in the state's electoral politics for over two decades.

Social Subversion

A more subtle subversion technique that ISI and its fronts are trying to press into service is exploitation of the caste system to promote social discord among Hindu infidels and thus weaken them. For instance a terrorist body called Inqilab-i-Islam Ayatollah, which came up in Gujarat and was engaged in propaganda and disinformation, issued pamphlets calling upon Harijans and Vanvasis to embrace Islam if they wanted deliverance from the clutches and insults of the high-caste Hindus, as Islam is a casteless and creedless society where everyone was equal.

As for ISI itself, by mid-90s it had extended its targeted segment of the Indian society and roped in Dalits and OBCs for training in subversion. The criminal Mafia of Mumbai, Dubai and Nepal were some of the channels used as active aids in the nefarious effort to build up an alliance between Muslims, Dalits and OBCs at ISI's bidding.

ISI also tried to target leaders, teachers and students of fundamentalist Islamic institutions like Dar-ul-Uloom, Deoband, Darul-Uloom Naduatul, Lucknow, Ahle Hadis, and Tablighi Jamaat.

Finally, certain Muslim political parties of India are also vulnerable to ISI's designs because of their dependence on Muslim countries for funds.

Intellectual Subversion

In 2010, there were reports of various separatist and pro-Pak Muslim leaders making frequent visits to the US and other Western countries to sell their anti-Indianism. These people can be called the products of intellectual subversion, yet another subversion technique that ISI has been using for long years. For it was as far back as in 1994 that it had launched this type of strategy to win over influential persons all over the country for the success of its gameplan in Kashmir.

According to sources, the ISI is making a serious bid to create fresh contact points in Jammu, Srinagar, Amritsar, Delhi and Bombay focussing its attention on some pro-militant intellectuals, media-persons, overground leaders and sympathisers of militants in universities, colleges and other professions with the object of highlighting human rights abuses by security forces in Kashmir. Having failed miserably at the meeting of the United Nations Human Rights Commission (UNHRC) of Geneva, the Pakistani gameplan now is to use these contact points for accusing security forces of excesses in Kashmir in order to lessen the pressure on militants and also to keep the issue of human rights abuses alive.

The interrogation of some of the arrested militants and smugglers including drug smugglers revealed that foreign currency smuggled into Jammu and Kashmir would be made available to these contact points for sponsoring their tours to USA, UK, Iran, Canada and other important countries on ISI missions. Intelligence sources said the recent recovery of a consignment of Rs. 1.15 crore in US and Canadian dollars, Pounds and Riyals in the Samba sector by the Border Security Force was meant for distribution among ISI's contact points. It was the biggest ever cache of foreign money recovered near the Indo-Pak border, and it included 74,019 US dollars, 35,775 Canadian dollars, 55,205 Pounds, 27,48,555 Riyals, and 7755 UAE Dinars.

Media "Management"

"Management" of the media, the time-tested device of *suppressio veri, suggestio falsi,* has been used by the Pakistani masters of terrorism since long. This was extensively described by *Facets of a Proxy War*, a document prepared by the Government as far back as in 1993 but released only abroad.

One of the primary targets of these militant groups is the local Press which they threaten constantly to obtain their backing for their nefarious activities, as also to block out the truth. Editors of newspapers have been shot dead, offices of newspapers have been attacked or burnt, independent-reporting correspondents have been asked peremptorily to leave the Kashmir Valley, and pliable reporters and stringers who will toe the line have been appointed to produce tailored reports.

Incidents of violence and intimidation against the Press have been recorded for the last 3-4 years. The pro-Pakistan Hizb-ul-Mujahideen has been the most active against the media. It imposed a ban on the circulation of the national and Jammu newspapers in the Kashmir Valley. Agents of such newspapers were threatened and asked to stop the sale and circulation of their newspapers and periodicals. Similar ban was imposed on the entry and distribution of English dailies *Kashmir Times* and *Excelsior* published from Jammu. The entry of the Delhi edition of the *Indian Express* was prohibited and local correspondent of the paper, George Joseph, was asked (April 1, 1992) to leave Kashmir within 48 hours. Joseph was accused of publishing 'anti-movement' articles.

The Jammu and Kashmir Liberation Front banned the circulation of the *Sunday* weekly published from Calcutta. The correspondent of the weekly, Ms. Shiraz Sidhva, was barred from visiting the Kashmir Valley. (This order was later withdrawn.) The Al Umar Mujahideen imposed a ban on the entry of the periodical *Sunday Times* into the Kashmir Valley. Twice the residence of the Srinagar correspondent of the BBC, Yusuf Jameel, was subjected to grenade attacks. Restrictions on what could be published in the newspapers were imposed by the Hizbul-Mujahideen (HuM): No suggestions were to be made that the Kashmir issue could be settled through negotiations. Stern action was threatened if the Press did not provide bold coverage to the activities of the HuM. A letter to this effect was sent on September 10, 1991 to the newspaper offices in the Pulwama district.

The Editor of the Urdu daily *Alsafa*, Mohd. Shaban Vakil, was shot dead in his office (April 23, 1991). A powerful explosion damaged the printing press of the daily *Aftab* (November 4, 1990). There was extensive damage and the loss was estimated at over Rs. 50 lakh. Again, copies of the same newspaper were set ablaze by militants at Pampore, Pulwama, on May 2, 1992. An explosion took place at the Dalgate residence of Sofi Ghulam Mohd., Editor, *Srinagar Times*, causing extensive damage to the residence and his car. This happened on October 2, 1990. Thereafter, on October 5 and 10, 1990 the city office of the *Srinagar Times* was burnt.

The Station Director of the Srinagar Television Station, Lassa Kaul, was shot dead by the militants on February 13, 1990. The Station Director, All India Radio, Leh (Ladakh), BashirArif, was kidnapped by the militants on November 2, 1991 and kept hostage for eleven days. The Assistant Director of All India Radio, Srinagar, was kidnapped on March 7, 1992.

The language Press in the Kashmir Valley has also been stifled by the militant groups. Facing the gun, there is little choice for them except publishing distorted and doctored stories to please the masters. Stringers, controlled by the militant units, put out colourful and contorted reports which are travesty of truth. Disinformation, false reports and rumours are floated by the militants and their agents to suit their designs.

Pakistan Press Backing Militancy: On the other hand, the Press in Pakistan has been openly espousing the cause of the extremist and terrorist groups operating in the Kashmir valley. Various news items, comments, articles and editorials in the Pakistan newspapers and periodicals reveal the extent of Pakistan's involvement and collusion in the militancy prevailing in the Valley. As Pakistan sees it, their two-nation theory remains truncated without the accession of Kashmir to Pakistan.

No less a person than the then President of Pakistan, Ghulam Ishaq Khan, had been reported by the Pakistan Press as commenting that the issue of Kashmir is the unfinished agenda of Partition. Later Pakistan Press International (PPI) in a news item put out on April 30,1992 said that Prime Minister Nawaz Sharif expressed the view that the success of the Afghan Mujahideen struggle would prove an eye-opener for those who thought they could subdue the spirit and struggle of the Kashmir people for their liberation and then accession of Kashmir to Pakistan.

On the same lines, the *Nation* reported on May 3, 1992 that Prime Minister Nawaz Sharif had said that the victory of the Mujahideen in the Afghan Jehad after fourteen years of struggle was the success of Islam and hoped that it would pave the way for the liberation of Kashmir. He said that Kashmir would become part of Pakistan and thanksgiving prayers would be offered in the mosque of Srinagar like he offered the *Namaz Shukrana* in the mosque in Kabul.

The former prime minister of Pakistan, Benazir Bhutto, had also given a provocative call to the extremists. Speaking at Muzaffarabad (March 13, 1990) she had exhorted the Kashmiri Hurriyat Pasands to intensify their fight against Indian subjugation. She was confident that they would succeed as "they were Muslims and had the blood of Ghazis running in their veins".

There are several press reports revealing Pakistan's approach to Kashmir. Shireen M. Mazari writing in the *Muslim* (April 2, 1991) said: "Whether Pakistan wants to or not, it will, in fact it must, get involved in the Kashmir insurgency". Mushaid Hussain wrote in the *Frontier Post* (May 29, 1991) that the approach which Pakistan had adopted in regard to Kashmir was an Afghan model, essentially a protracted war, which has made Kashmir into a bleeding wound for India..." More emphatically, it was confirmed by Javed A. Malik in his article which appeared in the *News* (December 4, 1991): "As the right of self-determination and the annexation of Kashmir to Pakistan is a part of the two-nation theory, Pakistan is not complete till Kashmir is annexed to it".

Several Pakistani journalists, columnists and newspapers have openly demanded or supported the supply of Pakistan arms to militants in the Kashmir Valley, as also their training in Pakistan. Brig. Bashir writing in the *Nation* (October 1, 1991) called upon the supporters of the movement to supply the terrorists surface-to-air missiles.

Later, in December 1996, the Jammu and Kashmir government had warned local daily newspapers against ISI designs to twist press reports in order to help the continuance of terrorist and subversive acts in the state. This was done following reports from across the border that ISI had adopted a systematic plan to keep militancy alive in the Kashmir Valley which would involve the local press on a large scale. Under this plan ISI had asked the militants to issue diktats to the local media to highlight their activities and blow out of proportion even a minor incident.

The latest update on the media situation is that in the aftermath of the recent 60-hour-long war of terror on Mumbai the Pakistani press loudly played up the Pakistani politicians' lies, which were exposed as soon as told, making their government leaders eat their words.

Nexus with Underworld

ISI's nexus with the Indian underworld, described earlier in the context of economic subversion, is more than a decade old. Two huge drug seizures— 50 kg of *charas* on September 8, 1996 and 170 kg of hashish just a week earlier, on September 1— convinced the police that even then ISI had entrenched itself in Mumbai's underworld. Police Commissioner Ramdev Tyagi told the media, "We have definite evidence of ISI's collaboration with Mumbai's underworld." JCP Sharma added, "The huge seizure of hashish is a clear indication that the ISI is using the underworld for its subversive activities". The contraband had originated in Afghanistan and had reached Mumbai *via* Pakistan. Abdul Samad Khan, who hid the stock for two months in a suburb, was a known lieutenant of Dawood Ibrahim.

In the wake of the Ayodhya demolition in December 1992 ISI brokered a truce between the underworlds of two port cities, one in Pakistan, the other in India — Karachi and Mumbai. Before that the two were constantly locked in a game of oneupmanship and the Karachi dons were baying for Dawood's blood. But on December 9, 1992 the dons of the two cities met for the first time ever under the auspices of ISI.

"It was at this meeting that the most heinous and diabolical plan to avenge the Hindu aggression was chalked," wrote *Indian Express* in its story titled *ISI- Underworld Link Exposed* on September 10, 1996. Educated Muslim youths from different fields like engineering, medicine, literature and travel were roped in for the task.

According to senior police officers sometimes Indian Muslims did not even know they were being unwittingly used by Pakistan's ISI. A classic example of this was Delhi's Dr. Jalees Ansari, India's unibomber. Belonging to the fundamentalist Muslim sect Ahle Hadis, Ansari was a self-styled `Mujahid' (crusader). He was charged with planting bombs in suburban as well as long-distance trains, and was arrested with as many as 53 bombs in his possession. "The man was so engrossed in his community service that he did not even know that in fact he was serving the ISI", the police officer who arrested him said.

"Mumbai remains ISI's main target in their gameplan to destabilize the country. The fact that they have managed to secure more than a foothold in the underworld makes this task even easier," concluded the *Indian Express* report.

Pak Guest Dawood: With the passage of time the ISI-Dawood nexus has strengthened to such an extent that the formerly Dubai-based don is now a guest of honour in Pakistan, his precious person under armed protection, his multi-national criminal reputation notwithstanding. Dawood Ibrahim Pakistan's biggest don, has figured in *Forbes* magazine's first ever list of the world's 10 most wanted fugitives, then headed by al-Qaeda chief Osama bin Laden. Dawood ranked fourth in the list. The magazine said, though the Pakistan Government denied it, Dawood is probably in that country. He is believed to have close links with ISI and travels on passports from India, Pakistan and Yemen. The magazine also mentioned reports that he has had plastic surgery to alter his appearance. *Forbes* said it consulted law enforcement agencies in the US and around the world to identify these 10.

Forbes' 'belief' about Dawood being in Pakistan was confirmed by Karimullah, accused in the Mumbai local trains serial bombing in 1993 and arrested in August 2008, who told the police that the fugitive gangster lives in Karachi in the posh Clifton area, and his residence is guarded by retired Pakistan Army officers. Karimullah also provided the police some incriminating photographs to back the information he gave. He added that Dawood is extremely well-connected in Pakistan's political circles. He has also invested heavily in the Karachi stock market. Karimullah, however, said that the report (which *Forbes* has mentioned as a rumour) that Dawood has gone under the scalpel to change his appearance is baseless. While Dawood is living in style in Karachi half a dozen of his associates have also been sheltered in the city, and the don has set them up well. According to Karimullah some of them have been given property, while others have been given supermarkets. Dawood's trusted lieutenant Tiger Memon has become one of the biggest builders in Karachi with several construction projects to his name.

The US has declared Dawood a global terrorist, even as showing remarkable lack of interest in his deportation from Pakistan to India. In his memoir *My Country My Life* former Deputy Prime Minister LK Advani expresses his deep disappointment with reluctance in pressing Pakistan to hand over Dawood to India, writing in detail about his fruitless efforts in this direction with the then US Secretary of State Colin Powell and National Security Advisor Condoleeza Rice.

A recent update in this murky liaison is the Russian assertion that the Pakistani terrorists who mounted the latest assault on Mumbai used Dawood's D-Company network and showed his direct involvement in the multiple attacks. Russia has gone public with its intelligence inputs that point to the involvement of Dawood Ibrahim, who is believed to be operating his vast network from Karachi, in the Mumbai terror attacks. "The gathered inputs testify that infamous regional drug baron Dawood Ibrahim had provided his logistics network for preparing and carrying out the Mumbai terror attacks", director of Russia's federal anti-narcotics service Viktor Ivanov said in an interview to Russian government daily *Rossiskaya Gazeta*. He said the Mumbai attacks were a burning example of how illegal drug trafficking networks were being used to carry out terror activities.

Linkages between LeT's chief operational commander Zaki-ur-Rehman Lakhvi and Dawood were forged through Kerala-born software engineer EM Bashir in early 2000.

Now the Russian assertion on Dawood has been backed by the Americans. Dawood Ibrahim had an important role in the 26/11 carnage by providing logistic support to the LeT operatives to carry out the deadly operation, stated a report on Lashkar-e-Toiba (LeT) released by the Strategic Studies Institute of the US Army War College, Department of Defence. In exchange for his refuge in Pakistan, the report says, Dawood diverts a percentage of D-Company's profits to ISI-supported Islamic terrorist groups, such as LeT. "Evidence demonstrates that these links were formed in late 1993 or early 1994. Photographs of Tiger Memon posing with leaders of the Jammu and Kashmir Islamic Front (JKLF) at an ISI safe house in Muzaffarabad surfaced and served as the first proof of the involvement of mafia money in Kashmir," the report notes.

The 117-page report, *Lashkar-e-Toiba: The Fallacy of Subservient Proxies and the Future of Islamist Terrorism in India* authored by Ryan Clarke, says the D-Company has now extended its base to Saudi Arabia too. "LeT, which is responsible for 60 per cent of terrorist killings in India, has been able to establish cells in several parts of the world as a result of assistance received from elements within the ISI and Dawood's network within India and in the Gulf," the report adds.

When LeT's partner in the Islamic Front for Jihad, al-Qaeda, expressed a desire to expand its operations in East Africa and were willing to offer cash for D-Company's networks, "Ibrahim accepted al-Qaeda's offer, and Anees Ibrahim, Dawood's younger brother, made sizeable investments in the shipping industries of East Africa and the United Arab Emirates (UAE) to underwrite D-Company's narcotics trafficking activities". The report warns that India's transportation, economic infrastructure and political establishment are on LeT's radar.

Drug Trade

The money ISI makes with its huge drug trade has been consistently used to fund Kashmir militants over a long time. As far back as in May 1994, ISI, with active participation of drug lords, had pumped in a whopping Rs. 100 crore in foreign currencies to various terrorist outfits in the Kashmir Valley to keep the proxy war on India going in its primary theatre.

The presently extensive drug empire of Pakistan has also a long past, as indicated by Zia's contacts. The first Pakistani drug smuggler-cum-gunrunner, Iqbal Beg, started his career in the 1960s by smuggling gold from Pakistan to India and gems from India to Pakistan. in the 70s he expanded his operations to the Gulf, Iran and Turkey, and in the 80s went into the more profitable heroin trade. Eventually he became known as the baron of the Lahore drug consortium. One of his employees was Nawaz Sharif's brother-in-law Sohail Zia Butt.

Even in those days Beg had developed extensive contacts in Delhi and Mumbai that are now used by ISI. According to a CIA report Beg was known as the king of the India route and was a major player in the world of intelligence, insurgency and arms smuggling. His lieutenant Shaukat Ali Bhatti emerged as one of the chief arms deal brokers for terrorists operating in India.

A natural factor facilitating ISI involvement in the murky drug trade was convenient geography. Large tracts of poppy fields on both sides of the Durand Line continued to exist despite decades of war, and the local drug mafia worked in tandem with ISI to ensure supply of weapons and ammunition to the Afghan Mujahideen. So deep was their involvement in drug deals that ISI was reportedly using vehicles of an official agency, the National Logistics Board, to ferry drugs across the border into Pakistan for export to the West.

ISI's Drug Cartels: Pakistan's tribals play a crucial role in running ISI's drug cartels. For a decade and a half, ISI has been nurturing a large number of tribal communities living in the Federally Administered Tribal Areas (FATA) of North-West Frontier Province (NWFP) for drugs meant for being smuggled into India. This was stated in a top-level US report published in 1994. These tribals, who also acted as couriers, were sponsored by leading drug cartels of NWFP and Punjab.

According to a CIA report, around the same period a large number of these tribals, who were veterans of the Afghan War, had been coming into the Kashmir Valley carrying heroin. Smugglers' bazaars for narcotics, mainly heroin, were held in the Khyber Agency with the tacit permission of the Pakistan Army. Their consignments filtered into India through porous north-western borders with the help of ISI front organisations in Karachi, Lahore and Pakistani Punjab. These fronts were the Afridi Mafia, the Mohmand Network, the Gandaj Traders, and the Yusufzai and Khatak Elites. The Afridis, a 40,000 strong community centred around Peshawar, took to the heroin business from the very beginning, and engaged in all its phases, from growing opium to transporting heroin into international channels. The powerful Yusufzai Khans, said the CIA report, had firm political entrenchment in Islamabad. The Mohmands controlled opium movement but lacked refining capacity, however, a large number of heroin laboratories functioned in and around Jalalabad, their area.

The gigantic proportions of this whole business came to light when, in March 1994, the Kutch police busted one of the biggest drug cartels operating in India's western region along the Gujarat border with the active support of ISI and involving the trafficking of narcotics worth over Rs. 150 crore. Investigations revealed that the Field Intelligence Unit, a branch of ISI, was funding the smuggling operation. The cartel was supplying the drugs to peddlers in Gujarat, Mumbai, and Rajasthan.

How pitifully inadequate the security of the Kutch border was, became evident from the fact that the arrested kingpin of the operation, Suleman Hamid, was operating on the Kutch-Pakistan border for the past 15 years and had crossed it 30 times with large consignments of drugs.

The drug mafia in Pakistan has an annual turnover of 2.5 billion dollars, and not only ISI officials, top Pakistan Army generals as well as political leaders are involved in it. In fact, Pakistan's clandestine drug trade is such a big business that the phenomenal growth of the ISI, from its modest origins to an enviably extensive intelligence network with global operations has been made possible with drug money", wrote *Observer* (now defunct) columnist D R Ahuja in an article titled *Drug money in Pakistan's army and politics* on November 24, 1994. It opened with a *Washington Post* report on September 12, 1994 saying Gen. Aslam Beg, the then Pakistan Army chief, and Gen. Asad Durrani, the then ISI chief, had produced a blueprint for using drug money for their clandestine operations. In the wake of the story two Pakistani journalists, Ilyas Khan and Owais Tohid, brought out a detailed investigative report citing actual cases of the involvement of individual officers and use of army vehicles in heroin trafficking over the previous several years. According to their investigations there were about 100 heroin refining laboratories since 1991. Seventy tons of heroin were annually passing through Pakistan to various international destinations.

The report suggested that former dictator Zia-ul Haq had been counselled by an advisor in 1974 to capitalize on drug money in the absence of foreign assistance. By mid-eighties the involvement of a large number of army officers in heroin smuggling was too widespread for concealment. As early as 1976, just three days before a state visit by Prime Minister ZA

Bhutto to Sweden, large quantities of hashish were seized from two Pakistan Air Force planes by Swedish authorities.

The involvement of the armed forces in drug smuggling became more pronounced during Zia's rule. During the entire 11 years in power, Zia spent considerable time in close proximity with drug barons. Many of his own proteges were also engaged in the clandestine business, and the most well-known of them, Gen. Fazal, was once called the world's richest General.

Individual ISI officers participated in the trade, either as part of sanctioned operations or to enrich themselves. Some Army officers, like Maj. Afridi, Maj. Javed and Maj. Zahoor, who indulged in drug-running during the Zia regime for lining their pockets but escaped penalty in the post-Zia clean-up, delved deeper into the drug trade and were roped in by ISI for their dual expertise.

During this same period came the revelation by former Prime Minister Nawaz Sharif of a plan by the Pakistan Army and Intelligence chiefs to orchestrate large-scale drug deals to finance covert operations abroad.

By tapping into the drug bonanza ISI could garner a source of funds that would more than make up for the loss of the largesse it used to receive from the CIA at the height of the Afghan operation. Some estimates of the money earned by Pakistani drug cartels were mind-boggling. According to a study reported in September 1994 the Pakistani share of the world narcotics trade was about 120 billion dollars a year.

Earlier in August 1992, Pakistan's National Development Finance Corporation had estimated that the black economy of the state gained 32.5 billion dollars annually from the cultivation, production and smuggling of illicit narcotics from the Golden Crescent.

A CIA report of 1992 said such huge profits enabled the drug mafia to penetrate the Pakistani state and economy at all levels. Even Pakistani experts believed that drug money fuelled the political system, supporting party organizations and election campaigns, and buying protection for the drug mafia at the highest political levels.

Despite Nawaz Sharif's revelation about drug deals his own reputation with regards to the drug mafia was not clean. For during the 1990 election campaign Sharif's Islami Jamhoori Ittehad (IJI) openly embraced Haji Ayub, reputed to be Pakistan's biggest drug baron, putting him in charge of the election campaign in tribal areas. The CIA report said, "In Punjab, where blood and kinship ties are often the key relays along which wealth and power flow, it is difficult for Pakistanis to believe the Sharifs are not involved in narcotics — or at least benefiting from the enormous capital generated by the drug trade."

Thanks to India's invitingly porous borders, this country provides a convenient conduit for a substantial portion of Pakistan's huge, illicit drug trade with the West. Recent seizures showed that the smuggling of heroin along the Indo-Pak border is even growing. The latest report of the International Narcotics Control Board (INCB) has confirmed what is more or less an open secret, that a substantial portion of this heroin originates in Afghanistan and passes through Pakistan and India on its way to Europe.

Another recent report, the International Narcotics Control Strategy Report (INCSR) by the US Department of State, pointing to India's strategic location between South East and South-West Asia said, "The two main sources of illicit opium make the country a heroin transshipment area". What is of concern is the trend of India being used not only as a major transit route but also a destination for the drugs. "West African traffickers have targeted South-Asian countries, mainly India, for cocaine trafficking," the INCB said.

For ISI drugs are also a weapon of the proxy war. It has smuggled narcotics into Jammu and Kashmir and Punjab to utilise the sale proceeds to step up militant and subversive activities in various parts of India. The Border Security Force has nabbed many transborder drug smugglers at the Indo-Pak border and seized large quantities of opium, brown sugar, and heroin. ISI has also used the strategy of packaging drugs with arms consignments. Seizures of heroin, hashish or similar drugs along with RDX explosives have been made in Rajasthan, Kutch, and along the coast of Gujarat.

In this business the Indian underworld ruled by Dawood Ibrahim is a willing henchman of ISI. Home Ministry sources confirmed that the don-in-exile is invaluable to ISI in the smuggling of drugs and arms into India through the borders of Rajasthan and Gujarat. ISI had once persuaded him to pack in 400 kg of Pakistani heroin, valued at a staggering Rs. 400 crore, along with an arms consignment meant for Mumbai. Now the don is used for pushing drugs and arms into the country through his underworld contacts in the Western region.

A new twist in the drug-smuggling operations is the D-Company's hand in ship-breaking deals. A recent, confidential report by naval intelligence has pointed out that the gang is involved in most deals going around in the ship-breaking business. It said the dead ships coming to India under flags of convenience are not only an environmental threat but also pose a threat to India's maritime security.

"The high stakes of profit margin, cheap labour, corrupt practices, and a large floating population have made the labour settlement at Alang (the biggest Asian ship-breaking yard, based in Gujarat) an ideal breeding ground for mafia and anti-national elements to indulge in nefarious activities almost unhindered," the intelligence report observed.

Earlier media reports had described how a 2000-seater luxury cruise ship, *SS Norway*, also called *Blue Lady*, had been officially sold to a Liberian company for 10 dollars! It was then bought by an Indian company for scrapping at Alang. Scrap steel prices are shooting through the roof these days.

"Apparently, a large number of cash buyers are Pakistani nationals based in London and the UAE. Due to large profit margins the Dawood group appears to have invested heavily in cash buyers, thus having a stake in most deals," naval intelligence said. It also warned that the involvement of the D-Company and Pakistani nationals means the ship-breaking industry has become a route for landing contraband and explosives. In other words, ISI's drugs-and-arms mixture has now an additional route.

All in all, Pakistan has acquired international notoriety as a merchant of narcotics and drug trafficking. Years ago *Dawn* wrote: "Let us face it. People living in the rest of the world are fed up with our unabated efforts to get their children addicted to heroin. Americans, Europeans and Arabs have been sending clear signals that their patience is running out." Seventy per cent of the heroin which reaches the streets of North America and Europe goes from Pakistan.

American Contribution

Finally, to these multiple facets of ISI's proxy war on India a factor that needs to be newly added is the American contribution. The way the US administration in general and its intelligence apparatus, headed by the CIA, in particular swallow anti-India disinformation that ISI feeds them has acquired serious propotions. In a scathing analysis of this scenario *Organiser* columnist M D Nalapat wrote on May 30, 2010:

"The quality of chutzpah is exemplified by the twins who murdered their parents and then asked for mercy on the ground that they were orphans. In other words, it means a situation where an individual creates the situation, and then claims himself to be a victim of it. No other word can describe the outburst of US Secretary of State Hillary Clinton on Pakistan, that the country will have to pay dearly should a terror attack on the US get traced back to its shores. This is the exact opposite of the course Clinton is urging on India. In our case, her advice is to ignore Pakistan-directed terror attacks and continue on the path of giving concessions to the only military that has Jehad as its motto, the Pakistan army".

"Had the US backed him, Zardari would have removed from office more than thirty officers who are in league with the Taliban. President Zardari is a Shia rather than a Wahabi, the way Kayani and Gilani are.

Both have roots in the Jamaat-i-Islami Pakistan, which has been taken over by the Wahabis since the 1980s and has very close links with both the military as well as the Taliban, often serving as the go-between. Most of these linkages are invisible to the CIA, the Defense Intelligence Agency and other US intelligence agencies, because of the fact that these have outsourced much of their field activity to the Pakistan army. The overwhelming majority of CIA and other US assets in Pakistan (and in Afghanistan) are double agents, with their primary loyalty being to the ISI and its agenda of ensuring that the Taliban return to power in Kabul by 2013-15".

"Most of what passes for field intelligence in the US–especially that culled from human sources, is in fact disinformation created and disseminated by the Pakistan army. The purpose of such deceit is to ensure that those inconvenient to Kayani and his allies (including the Taliban) get picked up by the US, while those who are secretly in league with the ISI and its Taliban-centred gameplan are presented as moderates deserving of the huge cash handouts that the US regularly disburses in Afghanistan to keep moderate tribal leaders happy and out of the clutches of the Taliban. The fact is that more than 80 per cent of the present Taliban leadership has been the recipient of US cash and assistance, funnelled to them on the advice of the ISI. In exchange, more mock Taliban get arrested or killed, and desultory sweeps get conducted in those areas where the Taliban are known to be concentrating. Of course, few get caught, given that they are warned in advance of the approaching raid".

"Most of the independent analysts in the US of Afghanistan are dependent on the ISI for logistics and contacts, and faithfully sing the song that has been scripted for them, which is that cooperation with the Pakistan army is essential to success".

"Since the time of Zia, the Sunni Punjabi component that dominates the Pakistan military has cast its fortunes with Jihadists. And because of the backing they have got from Hillary Clinton (who was known as the Senator from Punjab some years ago), they have administratively finished off President Zardari, thus leaving Army Chief of Staff Kayani as the paramount authority in the country. Small wonder when US officials visit Pakistan, they spend far more time at Army HQ than in offices nominally controlled by civilians".

"The ISI has been extremely effective in using the CIA and other foreign intelligence agencies to spread a global panic about India. A week ago, one more of a long list of US Terror Advisories was issued, which warned of an imminent attack in Delhi on May 1 or May 2. This columnist spent most of those two days going to several shopping malls in Delhi and Gurgaon, and was happy to see the contempt with which this warning was treated. On cue, Australia, Canada and the UK joined the US in portraying India as a country prone to terrorism".

"Clearly, the bogus information about the imminent threat was given to the CIA by the ISI, which, as has been the case for fifty years, swallowed it entirely".

"The reality is that not a single one of the many US terror advisories about India has been followed by a terror attack. Clearly, when it does execute an attack, as in Mumbai two years ago, the ISI takes care to ensure that no foreign agency gets warned about its plans. In the case of the May 1-2 advisory, it transpired, the Terror Advisory was right about the attack, but wrong about the city. For an attempt was made not on Delhi but on New York. Thanks to the benign neglect by the US of the Jehadi core of the Pakistan army leadership, the Taliban have been facilitated in setting up a network across the US that is estimated to become fully operational within the next two years. Once this terror network establishes roots across major cities, it would be able to carry out mass terror attacks almost every month. Such are the fruits of the Clinton-Bush-Obama policy of relying on the Pakistan army to fight the very terrorists that this force has created and continues to nurture. It will take more than synthetic tough talk from Hillary Clinton to retrieve the US from the abyss into which it is being pushed by the proliferation of Pakistan-sponsored groups that nestle in Houston, Detroit, Chicago and Miami".

"Rather than play the ISI game of painting India as unsafe, what Washington needs to do is to understand that the distinction between the Afghan Taliban and the Pakistan Taliban is illusory and that the two together have fused into a machine that endangers the globe. George W Bush made a historic blunder in 2001 when he took the advice of the CIA and the Pentagon and chose Pakistan as his principal regional ally against the terrorists, even ensuring the escape of leading al Qaeda elements at Kunduz into Pakistan. President Barack Obama is making the same mistake".

29

TERROR GOES HI-TECH

Skype, WiFi, Et Al

Technology has contributed substantialy to the success of the recent terror strikes. It is inconceivable that anyone could have coordinated an attack that was so precisely timed without taking advantage of the various easy communication tools that technology offers today. If a determined terrorist really wanted to evade detection, technology today offers him several alternatives. Anonymous software, various encryption techniques, or even just an easily acquired knowledge of the way the Internet works is all a terrorist needs to conceal his tracks. So it is no wonder terrorists now-a-days use bits and bytes of sophisticated technologies to attack their targets and even provide virtual training to recruits through specially-created websites.

CDs for Training

For starters, conspirators of the July 26 blasts in Ahemdabad had gained theoretical knowledge to make bombs from compact discs (CDs) given to them at training camps in Madhya Pradesh. The CDs, which contained both videos and text in Urdu, not only helped the accused learn the bomb assembly technique, but also ways to maximize its impact. The police found 18 such CDs in a Vadodara house.

Ahemdabad Joint Commissioner of Police Ashish Bhatia said a number of youths from Gujarat had attended training camps organised by SIMI in and outside Gujarat. "At one such camp in Madhya Pradesh, the youths were provided CDs which contained various information about making bombs using RDX, ammonium nitrate, H_2O and gas cylinders," said Bhatia. He added: "Based on the informaiton available in the CDs, they tried different things on their own to update themselves in terror activities. The CDs also contained inflammatory speeches of Osama bin Laden, Ayman-al-Zawahiri and other al-Qaeda leaders, and clippings of terror camps in Afghanistan and Iraq.

E-mail

An e-mail from al-Qaeda threatening to target judges and blow up Parliament and the Taj Mahal was received by the Delhi High Court. The

Registrar received the threat a few days after the serial blasts in courts in Uttar Pradesh in November 2009. A senior police official said courts had become a potential terror target in the wake of the Uttar Pradesh blasts which were suspected to be carried out to avenge the beating up of three terrorists by lawyers in a Lucknow court. Advance e-mails have become a signature of recent IM strikes.

Cell Phone Detonation

Terrorists operating in India have now switched over to cell phone-driven detonation of improvised explosive devices (IED) across the country. A recent recovery of IEDs fitted with a mobile phone in a pressure cooker in Srinagar has forced the Mumbai investigating team to re-examine the 7/11 serial blasts whether the pressure cooker bombs placed in the trains were triggered by mobile phones. "This recent change in tactics has opened up a different front altogether, we use jammers only when VIPs move," a senior police officer said, adding even jammers could be futile if the terrorists start using satellite phones to detonate bombs.

In all these blasts the terrorists had filled explosive chemicals or IED in steel boxes or pressures cookers. The detonator was connected to a cellular phone, and after planting the bomb they called up from elsewhere, which could be as far as the US, and as the mobile rings the circuit gets completed, which triggers the explosion.

SIM Cards

A recent routine input received by the security agencies from the Gujarat Police intelligence department showed a sudden spurt in the sale of mobile phone SIM cards in the border areas. It was not proportionate to the increase in the number of cellphone connections.

"A large number of these fixed validity Indian SIMs are being smuggled into Pakistan by Pakistani nationals so that they can be used during their later visits to India," said a senior state intelligence officer. Some of these SIM cards are also being used from certain points in Pakistan to communicate with people in India and for that purpose the callers are availing the services of Indian cellular service providers. In Gujarat "cell phone services have reached even the most remote villages, some of which are located very close to the international border. Therefore, tower signals spill into some places in Pakistan as well," the officer added. Intelligence officials have also listed names of villages, like Koteshwar, Lakhpat, Dayapur, Khavada on the Indian side of the border, from where the possibility of spillage is the highest.

"Excellent connectivity and readily available Indian SIMs in Pakistan may soon turn out to be a useful means of communication between ISI agents in Pakistan and their sleeper agents here," the officer added.

Worried about the finding, GS Gill, Additional Director General (West) of BSF, said: "Transborder cellular communication is an issue of concern."

Skype

Enforcement agencies are now spending more time patrolling the World Wide Web as terrorists and drug syndicates have increasingly taken to using encrypted chatrooms and e-payment gateway to transfer key documents and carry out transactions.

In a recent drug bust case in Delhi, it was found that the syndicate was using Skype chatroom, an encrypted chat forum difficult for intelligence agencies to crack, to transfer documents. Transfer of files over Skype is encrypted end to end and protects privacy when transferring information. "We now spend more time patrolling the Net and doing electronic surveillance than snooping on physical targets," confessed a senior intelligence official. He said there was a need for all enforcement agencies to create exclusive cyber cells and dedicate a fixed time for Net patrolling. To avoid transactions of dirty money through their gateways, many online e-payment companies keep away from deals relating to lotteries, Internet pharmaceutical purchases and memberships of pornographic websites. However, a Sweden-based e-payment firm, Penova, is under investigation jointly by Indian and US authorities over huge transactions of dirty money.

WiFi Network

The recent incident involving US national Kenneth Haywood, whose Internet Protocol (IP) address was allegedly used to send the terror e-mail prior to the Ahmedabad serial blasts, should be regarded as a wake-up call. While this incident of wireless hacking took security agencies by surprise, lakhs of individuals and companies are actually exposed to a similar risk. Incidents of such hacking are common, but go unreported since they may not have such grave implications.

The police version of the Haywood incident, as reported in the newspapers, is that suspected criminals allegedly hacked into the Wi-Fi network of his laptop and used it to send the terror e-mail. Prior to this hacking Haywood is said to have complained of high browsing bills. If this is to be believed, then one possibility is that Haywood may have left his access point open. The suspected terrorist could then have hooked on to this access point and sent the e-mail, which then showed Haywood's IP address as the originator. This is regarded, in hacking terminology, as stealing of bandwidth while impersonating Haywood.

Kir-n Deshpande, president, AirTight Networks, a company engaged in wireless vulnerability management, said: "Wireless or WiFi works in the unlicensed and unregulated radio spectrum. Wireless access is free and wireless security becomes a sericus issue, because these waves are invisible. Ignorance about radio waves, too, is a serious concern."

This was forcefully highlighted byAjey Lele, a researcher in non-traditional threats to national security at the Institute of Defence Studies and Analyses, Delhi. In a newspaper piece on how the terrorists used modern technology against a modern city during the latest attack on Mumbai, Lele wrote: First, their sea journey, a complex endeavour in itself was accurately navigated using state-of-the-art GPS (geographical positioning system) gadgets. They stayed in touch using satellite phones. They also used the GPS maps to chart entry and escape routes: a GPS map of South Mumbai was found in their possession. Given how crucial it was to reach their targets in time, and without getting noticed, GPS proved very handy. Ironically, GPS was initially devised by the United States mainly for military requirements: a constellation of 24 or 28 satellites which, with the assistance of an earth-borne receiver unit, help to pinpoint one's ground location accurately. Today, these systems can easily be bought at any marine store for as little as 100 dollars.

Satellite phones were used as well. While on the high seas, they are essential for communication and coordination, even afterwards, terrorists were in touch with their handlers over the instruments. Such phones are available for between $200 to $1000 a piece. They connect to orbiting satellites and are mainly used in remote areas where cellphone services are not available. The satphone was used to make 4/5 calls to Sialkot and Karachi in Pakistan. Made by the Thuraya Company, based in Dubai, it was traced to a distributor in Karachi. In addition the terrorists carried hi-tech gadgets like BlackBerrys, CDs holding high-resolution satellite images like those used for Google Earth maps, and multiple cellphones with switchable SIM Cards that would be hard to trace. While communicating with their contacts or handlers, the terrorists called voice-over-Internet protocol phone numbers, making them harder to trace. Kasab told the police that he was shown video footage of the targets and satellite images before the attack. Even the e-mail was hi-tech. It used Urdu-language voice-recognition software that could type it in Devnagari and even made it jump from one server to another in order to hide its ethnic or geographic origin.

A still newer terror technique is that al-Qaeda bombers can now carry explosives in the stomach. Al-Qaeda has developed new devices that enable suicide bombers to carry them hidden in the stomach to breach airline security. An al-Qaeda terrorist called Al-Asiri passed through airline security checks with a bomb hidden in his intestine and made an abortive bid to assassinate a prominent Saudi prince. Security experts believe the explosive, with an electronic detonator, was probably contained in a long thin animal gut casing to protect it from stomach acid.

At the same time al-Qaeda continues to regularly use the common computer tool of an internet website. In fact, the organisation's use of the Internet has grown more sophisticated, encompassing financing, recruitment, networking, mobilization, publicity, as well as information dissemination, gathering and sharing.

Al-Qaeda in Iraq regularly releases videos glorifying the activity of jihadist suicide bombers. In addition, both before and after the death of Abu Musad al-Zarqawi (the former leader of al-Qaeda in Iraq), the umbrella organization to which al-Qaeda in Iraq belongs, the Mujahideen Shura Council, has a regular presence on the Web. The range of multimedia content includes guerrilla training clips, stills of victims about to be murdered, testimonials of suicide bombers, and videos that show participation in *jihad* through stylized portraits of mosques and musical scores. A website associated with al-Qaeda posted a video of captured American entrepreneur Nick Berg being decapitated in Iraq. Other decapitation videos and pictures, including those of Daniel Pearl, were first posted on jihadist websites.

In December 2004 an audio message claiming to be from bin Laden was posted directly to a website, rather than sending a copy to al Jazeera as he had done in the past. It lasted for over an hour and was much more virulent than usual. In the past, Alneda.com and Jehad.net were perhaps the most significant al-Qaeda websites. Alneda was initially taken down by American Jon Messner, but the operators resisted by shifting the site to various servers and strategically shifting content. The US is currently attempting to extradite a British information technology specialist, Babar Ahmad, on charges of operating a network of English-language al-Qaeda websites, such as Azzam.com. Ahmad's extradition is opposed by various British Muslim organizations, such as the Muslim Association of Britain.

Websites can now even be rented, as Taliban has shown. Last year a Taliban website claiming to be the voice of the Islamic Emirate of Afghanistan boasted of a deadly new attack on coalition forces in that country. The most remarkable feature about the message was how it was delivered. The words were the Taliban's, but they were flashed around the globe by a US-owned firm located in Houston. The Company, a web-hosting outfit called The Planet, said it simply rented cyberspace to the group and had no clue about its Taliban connections. For more than a year the terrorist group used the site to rally its followers. The cost of the service: roughly $70 a month, payable by credit card.

Finally, although all this sophistication in the technology of terror is a new advance, ISI has been using the terror tool for years. For instance, when a group of terrorists trained in Pakistan infiltrated into India a decade and a half ago with a plan to bomb government buildings, strategic installations, railway tracks etc. but was nabbed by the Delhi Police in March 1994, a search of their Delhi hideout revealed sets of computer floppies of "*Win Word*" software which contained "*how-to*" instructions on handling RDX, TNT, shaped charges, and even secret inks.

30

NUCLEAR TERRORISM

The ISI Connection

Pakistan is a terrorist state. Nuclear terrorism is a real threat. Put these two facts together, and the combination becomes deadly. With this realisation in mind Prakash Singh, former Director of the Border Security Force, wrote an article in a newspaper in September 1994: "I am not an alarmist, but let it also be on record that Pakistan would have no scruples about dropping the Islamic nuclear bomb on India. The theory of deterrence would not apply. It is reasonably certain that in such a situation Pakistan would get substantial help from certain West Asian countries."

Khan's Nuclear Scam

The way things have developed in Pakistan since then, this dire possibility cannot be wished away as alarmism. For the "Islamic bomb" originally conceived by ZA Bhutto was not only fathered by AQ Khan but made a pan-Islamic bomb through his clandestine business of selling nuclear technology on the international black market. With Khan exposed, humiliated and put under house arrest and his associates rounded up, it was thought the murky business had closed down. Apparently that is not the case. For it was reported in mid-2007 that the AQ Khan network may start business again. A new study said the Pakistani nuclear smuggling network that was crippled three years ago could resume business in view of a strong demand for atomic technology from governments and terrorist groups. The US had declared at the time that the network led by AQ Khan had been rolled up, actually only a few of the 40-odd individuals identified as having worked with him are in prison, said the report by the London-based International Institute for Strategic Studies. "At least some of Khan's associates appear to have escaped and could, after a period of lying low, resume their black market business," said a 176-page dossier titled *Nuclear Black Markets: Pakistan, AQ Khan and the Rise of Proliferation Networks.* Meanwhile top Pakistani scientist Samar Mubarakmand, Chairman of the National Engineering and Scientific Commission, declared in December 2007 that Pakistan's nuclear programme has not been capped, and the removal of AQ Khan did not mean the government planned a rollback.

Zardari Mental Case

The same month President Musharraf took charge of Pakistan's nuclear arsenal by issuing an ordinance that made him the head of the National Command Authority, which is responsible for the development of atomic weapons. And now that President Musharraf has been succeeded by President Zardari, the matter of nuke control in Pakistan is causing worry in the US. For Zardari's medical records have come to light that show that as recently as 2007 Zardari's doctors had diagnosed him with mental problems such as stress, depression and dementia. In March 2007, reported the *Financial Times*, New York psychologist Stephen Reich concluded that Zardari was chronically anxious and apprehensive and had thoughts of suicide, though he had not acted on them. While Zardari's spokespersons claim he has been cured, many US officials, among them Rep. Pete Hoekstra, the ranking Republican on the House Intelligence Committee, told *Newsweek* that word of Zardari's mental health history took them by surprise. "Typically," said Hoekstra, "(the US) wouldn't want that kind of person involved in a nuclear chain of command." So the US sought direct access to Pakistani nukes. The State Department proposed to the Pakistan government that an official who would be permanently posted in the US Embassy in Pakistan to deal with nuclear issues should have direct access to the National Command Authority.

That this alarming situation is actually the doing of the Americans themselves is now coming to light. For four years before AQ Khan was exposed and publicly humiliated, British and US authorities had been briefed about his role in selling nuclear weapons technology to North Korea, Libya and Iran, but were told to keep quiet about the findings, which were only revealed several years later when the risk of nuclear weapons falling into the hands of rogue states and terrorists became more real than it ever was.

Open Nuclear Bazaar

Actually the Pak nuke story began with China almost three decades ago. It was China that provided Pakistan with the blueprint to build a nuclear weapon in early 1980s, a small, reliable armament that could be delivered on India by attack aircraft or missile. The blueprint was delivered as the desperate Pakistani nuclear scientists led by AQ Khan were unable to build the weapon they wanted, said a book by David Albright, a former UN weapons inspector. The book, *Peddling Peril: The Secret Nuclear Trade Arms America's Enemies,* gives an in-depth account of how the AQ Khan network, through espionage and stealing, built the nuclear plant and finally the weapon for Pakistan, the secret technology of which was later passed on to several rouge nations.

In 2004 Khan publicly admitted to selling nuclear weapons technology to Libya, but now it turns out that Libya was just the tip of the iceberg. For a British customs investigator has uncovered a huge black market in nuclear technology, presided over by Khan, that sold sensitive components to whoever was willing to pay for them. The astonishing detective work of the investigator, Atif Amin, is painstakingly described in a book titled *America and the Islamic Bomb,* written by Washington-based authors David Armstrong and Joe Trento, who say the findings had been passed on to both MI-6 and CIA.

Armstrong said that both US and Britain connived in Islamabad's nuclear programme, as "Pakistan got a get-out-of-the-jail-free card, because they were always doing favours for everybody. If it's not Afghanistan, it's the Taliban, if it's not the Taliban, it's always something. They always have some execuse, so they can argue that we are too indispensable to you guys to shut down our nuclear smuggling."

Bribed US Officials

A new twist to the whole murky story that came to light in January 2010 was the stunning revelation that corrupt US officials had actually helped Pakistan steal N-weapons secrets. Senior US officials helped Pakistan steal atomic weapons secrets through Turkish agents in exchange for money and other benefits, with ISI passing on the sensitive information to the now-disgraced AQ Khan, reported the British newspaper *Sunday Times.* According to the paper, intercepted communications showed that former ISI chief Mahmoud Ahmed and his colleagues stationed in Washington were in constant touch with attaches in the Turkish embassy. It reported the account of whistle-blower Sibel Edmonds, former Turkish language translator for the FBI, who listened in to hundreds of sensitive intercepted conversations while based at the agency's Washington field office.

Edmonds described how foreign intelligence agents had enlisted the support of US officials to acquire a network of moles in sensitive military and nuclear institutions. According to Edmonds, she heard evidence that one well-known senior official in the US State Department was being paid by Turkish agents in Washington, who were selling the information to black market buyers, including Pakistan. In one such taped conversation Edmonds heard this official arrange to pick up a 15000-dollar cash bribe, which was to be dropped of at an agreed location by a Turkish diplomat. The Turks, she revealed, often served as a conduit for ISI, as they did not attract so much suspicion. The American Turkish Council in Washington was used for these clandestine transactions. Thus, while it is conventional wisdom that AQ Khan made a fortune selling atomic secrets to Libya, Iran and North Korea, which he acquired *via* a network of companies in America and Britain, it now transpires that Ankara in Turkey was the main transit point and a very senior US official the chief salesman. Khan was close to ISI and its chief Gen. Ahmed. The ISI was also close to al-Qaeda both before and after 9/11, and the ISI chief is believed to have sanctioned a 100,000-dollar wire payment to hijacker Mohammed Atta immediately before the attack.

All in all, ISI played a crucial role in Pakistan's quest for the nuclear bomb. In this it was in association with the infamous Bank of Credit and Commerce International (BCCI), as also in league with many well-known arms smugglers like Victor Bout, subsequently participating in the elaborate AQ Khan scam.

Benazir Nuclear Smuggler

A final, most curious, twist in the already murky Pak nuke story was provided by AQ Khan's reported role in selling the technology to North Korea. Actually, his was not the prime role, it was that of Benazir Bhutto herself while in power. Shyam Bhatia, a London-based Indian journalist with whom Benazir was quite friendly, wrote after her assassination the extraordinary story of how Benazir Bhutto smuggled nuclear secrets out of Pakistan:

"The most extraordinary part of our conversation (in Dubai in 2003), which I promised never to reveal in her lifetime, was Benazir's role in exporting her country's nuclear secrets to North Korea. She had participated in the negotiation to give Pakistan's nuclear bomb details to North Korea in exchange for missile technology. The solution to the problem of keeping the deal secret from the Americans was to find an overcoat with the deepest pocket possible, in which she could carry warhead designs on a series of CDs during a state visit to Pyongyang... And nobody guessed. Indeed, everyone to this day has wondered how it was possible for the information to be relayed."

Even apart from Pakistan's nuclear scams, the fact stands that nuclear terrorism is a real threat, primarily because the global nuclear weapons stockpile is not uniformly secure (and Pakistan's is definitely insecure), and because fissionable material is relatively available. From 1993 to 2006 the IAEA documented 175 cases of nuclear theft. Nuclear know-how instructions on how to assemble a weapon, floor plans for a terror farm is accessible to anyone with a basic understanding of physics.

Of far greater practical importance, transportation is not very difficult. For terror organisations can use cargo containers to transport nuclear weapons into the country using the sea route, Navy Chief Admiral Sureesh Mehta warned. "It has been acknowledged widely that the container would be the most likely means for a terrorist organisation to illegally transport a nuclear weapon," stated the Navy Chief at the inauguration of a seminar on port security organised by the National Maritime Organisation.

Easy transportation apart, the clearly insecure storage conditions of Pakistan's nuclear stockpile throws up a deadly possibility — its possible use by al-Qaeda. If it were in a position to do so, al-Qaeda would use Pakistan's nuclear weapons in its fight against the US, a top leader has said not long back. "God willing, the nuclear weapons will not fall into the hands of the Americans and the *mujahideen* would take them and use them against the Americans," Mustafa Abu al-Yazid, leader of al-Qaeda in Afghanistan, said in an interview with Al Jazeera during the Swat battle. "We expect that the Pakistani Army would be defeated (in Swat)... and that would be its end everywhere, God willing," he declared.

Osama bin Laden had indeed sought and wanted to use nuclear arms, former bodyguard Nasser al-Bahri once said in an interview with an Arab daily. "Sheikh Osama used to dream of possessing nuclear weapons, and I am sure that if he were to get his hands on a nuclear weapon, he would not have hesitated to use it," the Yemeni guard told the London-based *Al-Quds AI-Arabi*.

To conclude with a sobering thought, Pakistan now has more and better nuclear weapons than India. Close on the heels of revelations that Pakistan has been illegally modifying US-made Harpoon missiles with the objective of targeting India, two reports have come from Washington asserting that Islamabad has been steadily working towards increasing its nuclear capabilities, both in terms of numbers as well as quality. These reports — one published by the Congressional Research Service (CRS) and the other in the *Bulletin of Atomic Sciences* — differently estimate the number of nuclear weapons in Pakistan's possession between 60 and 90, but both agree that the country has been engaged in enhancing its nuclear arsenal and capacity to produce fissile material.

Pakistan had doubled its stock of nuclear weapons in the last ten years. In fact the infamous AQ Khan is on record as saying in May 2011 that Pakistan's nuclear programme continued "without break" during the last decade. As a result Pakistan has doubled its n-arms stockpile, while India has fallen behind. It now totals more than 110 deployed nuclear weapons, the *Washington Post* reported quoting David Albright, President of the Institute for Science and International Security. Quoting Pakistan's defence attache' at its embassy in Washington, Brig. General Nazir Butt, the paper said a number of Pakistani nuclear weapons are heavily deployed near the border with India. It also quoted Peter Lavoie, US national intelligence officer for South Asia, as saying, "Despite pending economic catastrophe, Pakistan is producing nuclear weapons at a faster rate than any other country in the world".

That this formidable nuclear arsenal of Pakistan is in far-from-safe hands is an open secret. For Pakistan is a "very dangerous" country, its own former President Parvez Musharraf has admitted in an interview to the *Time* Magazine. This truth was underscored by the daring commando-style raid by Pakistani Taliban on the Karachi naval base in the last week of May 2011, which lasted for 17 hours.

To this scenario Pakistani terrorist leaders have added a fell footnote by now calling for nuclear war on India. At a Jamaat-ud-Dawa rally in Lahore to mark "Kashmir Solidarity Day", JuD Chief Hafiz Saeed declared that the Jehad for Kashmir should be stepped up even if it led to a "nuclear war" with India. JuD's deputy chief Abdur Rehman Makki called upon the Pakistan government to set up a separate ministry for Jehad in Kashmir. "The JuD will provide the budget for this ministry," he declared.

31

ISI INTERNATIONAL
Global Terror Trail

The Soviet invasion of Afghanistan provided ISI a golden opportunity to spread its international wings for the first time. It trained and armed (with US-supplied weapons) more than 80,000 Mujahideen and sent them into battle. As a result a formidable international fighting force became available to ISI. Moreover, during the course of the war it could develop links with fundamentalist Islamic terror groups of the world, as well as with the international underworld of drug-smugglers and gunrunners.

It was against this background that ISI developed its Kashmir plan mentioned earlier, in four stages, which began in 1987 with a low-intensity conflict between locals and the State government. The final, fourth, phase of the plan was launched in 1992 with the infiltration of 500 Afghan Mujahideen into Kashmir. To this was later added a large number of volunteers recruited by Harkat-ul-Jehad-e-Islami (HUJI), which was originally founded in Pakistan but later shifted to Bangladesh.

This was the beginning of ISI's widening links abroad. Then a 1994 US report revealed ISI connections with Sudan and Libya. The report of the Task Force on Terrorism and Unconventional Warfare of the US House Republican Research Committee stated that Sudanese terrorist leaders Turabi and Mustafa Uthman visited terrorist training camps and trained various terrorist outfits, including Jamaat-i-Islami of Pakistan, Hizb-ul-Mujahideen of Kashmir, and Hizb-ul-Islami and Jamiat-i-Islami of Afghanistan.

"The spiral of hatred and violence between the security forces and the people served the interests of the terrorists and secessionists admirably. They achieved the aim of morally and physically isolating the people from the state without too much effort on their part. Mass discontent and alienation is a critical requirement and integral to the plans of the separate movement. "This was the simply worded sermon of Turabi and Uthman, "Badshahs of terrorism", to ISI operatives working "K-2", the Kashmir plan against India.

Several Sudanese were also sent to Peshawar in Pakistan from November 1991 onwards to train national liberation forces in Mujahideen camps. Later, a large number of Libyans too joined these camps. All these terrorist outfits became members of the Turabi-led Popular International

Organization (PIO) and helped Islamists in Egypt, Algeria and Sudan. By early 1992 Turabi had consolidated arrangements to send trainee to Muslim Brotherhood sites in Peshawar.

This coincided with the Libyan intelligence agency's shifting its training centres to other countries including Pakistan and Afghanistan, where active training of Islamist terrorists was already taking place. The Libyans also assisted in upgrading the terrorist infrastructure in these countries.

The Sudanese and Libyan experts educated ISI operatives of the Kashmir Desk on a four-point programme:

1. Religious fundamentalism propagation in small but lethal doses to promote separatism and a communal outlook.
2. Training and indoctrination of selected leaders from the Valley and to create militant cadres.
3. Youth mobilisation from the Valley and Poonch sector for training in arms and urban terrorism.
4. Creation of special political fronts in the Valley for organising agitations.

Another revelation in the US report was that Algerian terrorist leaders Tayib-al-Afghani, his brother Murad-al-Afghani and Haj Banua regularly visited Pakistani camps for Kashmiri youth. The Afghani brothers and Banua were known for their brutality and extreme violence. Considered legends, they were conducting classroom teaching of Islamic interpretation of terrorism.

It is estimated that the Libyan-assisted camps trained thousands of brethren from all over the Muslim world, while, according to the US report of 1994, about 26,000 Kashmiri Muslims were trained in Pakistani sanctuaries under Turabi's guidance. But whether it was the Sudanese or the Libyans who conducted terrorist training on Pakistani soil, ISI's links with them was underlined by the fact that ISI bosses directly involved in the programme were all top brass of the Pakistan Army. They were Lt. Gen. Akhtar Abdul Rehman, Maj. Gen. Durrani, Maj. Gen. Naseer Khan, and Lt. Gen. Javed Nasir.

ISI Terror Abroad

With ISI's demonstrable ability to perpetrate terrorism across a huge country like India, no wonder it participated in international terrorism post 9/11. According to Zahid Hussain, a senior Pakistani journalist and author of a book on Islamic Militancy, some terrorist attacks on Western countries were actually planned in Pakistan:

1. *9/11:* To start with 9/11 itself, US intelligence suspected ISI was at least partly involved in the WTC strike in New York. On September 11, 2001 three hijacked aircraft were used as bombs and rammed into the World Trade Centre and the Pentagon. A fourth hijacked airline crashed into rural Pennsylvania. More than 3000 people were killed. The Pakistani connection in this horrendous act was that six main suspects, including

mastermind Khalid Sheikh Mohammed, were arrested in Pakistan. They were hiding in the cities of Karachi and Faisalabad.

2. *Kidnapping of Daniel Pearl:* On January 23, 2002 *Wall Street Journal* correspondent Daniel Pearl was kidnapped in Karachi by terrorists of the Jaish-e-Mohammed. The Pak link with the act was that it refused to extradite Omar Saeed Sheikh, convicted of killing Pearl, to the US government. Here it may be recalled that ironically enough ISI was initiated into international terror by the Americans when it worked as CIA's B team during the Afghan war. *Apropos* this connection, a very recent and pithy one-liner by an *Indian Express* columnist is worth quoting— "Intelligence agents around the world share a complicated relationship, like the CIA and ISI, which cannot live with or do without each other."
3. *Terror attack in Mombasa:* On November 28, 2002 three suicide bombers in a car attacked a hotel in Mombasa, Kenya, killing 15 and injuring 40. The Pakistani connection was that although al-Qaeda claimed responsibility for the car-bombing, six Pakistanis were arrested.
4. *Bomb explosion in London double-decker:* On July 7, 2005 bombs exploded on a double-decker bus in London and also on three underground local trains. Fifty-six people were killed. The Pak link was that three of the bombers were either trained in or had been to Pakistan. Pak connection: Abdullah Azam Brigade, with ideological links in Pakistan, claimed responsibility.
5. *Plot to blow up Ontario Intelligence headquarters:* On June 3, 2006, 17 al-Qaeda terrorists were arrested in Ontario, Canada. They were accused of planning to storm Parliament and also blow up the Canadian Intelligence headquarters in Toronto. Twelve of the arrested were from Pakistan and Bangladesh.
6. *Targetting Aircraft in the U.K.:* On August, 10, 2006 a bomb plot targetting multiple aircraft in UK was foiled. All main suspects had links to Pakistan, including Rashid Rauf arrested there.

Elsewhere in the world, according to a paper prepared in 1993 by Youssef Bodansky, Director, US House of Representatives Republican Task Force on International Terrorism and Unconventional Warfare, the subversive energies of former Mujahideen were being used to transform South Asia into a centre of Islamic terrorism. Clearly it was ISI who had a force of idle former Mujahideen at its disposal. In fact, it is an open secret that ISI has strong links with most terrorist outfits in South Asia. ISI has also been systematically exporting terrorists even to far-away territories such as Chechnya and Sudan, not to mention nearby Sri Lanka. The Sri Lankan island of Delft was a location of arms and explosives training camps conducted for terrorists by ISI and LTTE. Not long ago a prominent newspaper reported a top-ranking military intelligence official saying it is an open secret that ISI was giving all help to LTTE in Sri Lanka.

To round off this terror trail, of the 14 top terrorists held by the US at Guantanamo, seven had links to Pakistan.

And now the recent (July 2010) bomb attack on the Indian embassy in Kabul, post-Taliban Afghan capital, has provided the final touch to ISI's international terrorism. The Karzai government confirmed to Indian authorities that ISI was involved in the attack, while the US too held it responsible for masterminding it. The presence of mines and even tank shells to cause maximum damage clearly showed to the investigators a terror trail leading to ISI.

Another fact strongly suggestive of the Pakistani hand in the event was that US agencies picked up intercepts of conversation happening on the Pakistan side of the Pak-Afghan border on the day of the bombing describing the blast as a *mazedaar* attack. These intercepts were also picked up by French and Afghan agencies and passed on to India.

The new Army Chief Gen. Kayani was himself in the know of the plot, the *New York Times* reported. "It's very difficult to imagine that he was not aware," a senior American official said.

Actually, ISI's involvement in Afghanistan has been a long and continuing story. A LAT-WP dispatch from Afghanistan had described how even while Musharraf was proclaiming his alliance with the US war on terror many in his army and security agencies were wedded to the Taliban, according to independent American analysts including Boston University's Pakistani scholar Hussain Haqqani. Parts of ISI, the Army and political and religious elites formed a network to help the Taliban and allied guerrillas recruit and train fighters, raise money, and infiltrate Afghanistan. ISI had hundreds of men who served as handlers for its guerrilla clients. It had to shut down many of them under US pressure, but the purge was far from effective. For instance al-Qaeda used its connections twice to bomb Musharraf's highly secured motorcades in 2003, coming close to killing him.

In October 2006 the Commander of NATO forces in Afghanistan had met Musharraf in Islamabad and asked him to rein in ISI, confronting him with evidence that it was training Taliban fighters to attack British troops. Lt. Gen. David Richards, the British General commanding the NATO troops, had satellite pictures and videos showing the training camps. He also gave Musharraf the address of the Taliban leader in the Pakistani city of Quetta, where he was living quite openly, and asked that he be arrested. What actually happened was that journalists inquiring into Taliban activities in the city were beaten up or jailed.

Another aspect of the internationalisation of ISI terror is that its prominent extensions Lashkar and Jaish have acquired recognition as 'al-Qaeda elite' and have joined a growing Asian terror conglomerate. Former National Security Advisor MK Narayanan has said that Lashkar-e-Toiba, Jaish-e-Mohammed, Harkat-ul-Jehad-i-Islami are now part of al-Qaeda's elite terrorist network along with groups in Central and East Asia. Speaking at an annual Munich Security Conference, Narayanan said this intricate web of terror groups had common resource structures.

"Al-Qaeda's elite terrorist network such as the Islamic Movement of Uzbekistan and Islamic Jehad Group (in Central Asia), the Lashkar-e-Toiba, Jaish-e-Mohammed, Lashkar-e-Jhangvi and Harkat-ul-Jehadi-Islami and the Taliban (in South Asia), the Jemiah Islamiah and the Abu Sayyaf Group in South East and East Asia represent an intricate web of terrorist networks. They have forged common funding structures, common training curricula and have a common resource for obtaining explosives and weapons," he said.

Narayanan said that there were credible reports suggesting that this region was also the source and destination for proliferation of weapons of mass destruction (WMDs). Threats to stability from nuclear weapons in the hands of volatile states could not be discounted. At the same conference Narayanan spoke of terror outfits manipulating the Indian stock markets to raise funds.

Here it is relevant to recall that according to a secret Government report of 1996 militants in Kashmir had developed a well-entrenched nexus with foreign sources for financial and ideological support. Indeed, foreign funding is the prime mover of secessionist and terrorist violence in the Valley, in Punjab, and the North-East. According to a report compiled by the Joint Intelligence Committee (JIC) ISI was then spending about Rs 2.4 crore per month to sponsor its subversive activities in Jammu and Kashmir. The JIC identified Pakistan, Syria, Iran and Libya as countries selectively supporting militancy for regional gains, and Saudi Arabia, Kuwait, the United Arab Emirates (UAE), Bahrain and Bangladesh as countries backing pan-Islamic activities. Linking the insurgency in Punjab and Jammu & Kashmir to drug money being generated in Pakistan the report claimed that there was sufficient evidence pointing to the definite involvement of ISI.

A curious twist to ISI's international presence was recently given by some British MPs who called for a probe into allegations that the British intelligence agency MI-5 was outsourcing to ISI the torture of Pak-origin Britons detained during counterterror operations in that country. The allegations, made by four British citizens, were published by the *Guardian* newspaper. One of them was quoted as saying that for several months ISI kept him in a pitch-dark cell not much bigger than a coffin and brought him out to be beaten, whipped, and given electric shocks.

Meanwhile a study titled *Hearts and Minds and Eyes and Ears: Reducing Radicalisation Risks through Reassurance-oriented Policing* warned "The threat to the UK from Jihadist terrorism may increase in the future." And the British are convinced that ISI would be largely responsible for this development. For when the plot to blow up British planes brought to light ISI's important role in helping al-Qaeda and Taliban in this conspiracy MI-5 had said in its report that before fighting al-Qaeda and Taliban it would be necessary to deal with ISI.

In the past, a report issued by Britain's defence ministry once said with typical British humour: Whether it is the event of two crocodiles in the Indus in Pakistan being found injured, or Benazir Bhutto's marriage, or the government in Pakistan falling, or the prime minister being appointed or dismissed, or communal riots, followed by linguistic bloodshed, or packing off Gulbuddin Hekmatyar and Altaf Hussain to London ... behind all such incidents the ISI hand can be seen somewhere.

On a much more sombre note in recent times, the British Government expressed the feeling that if the world is to be saved from terrorism, it would be necessary to put an end to ISI.

Almost in a similar vein KPS Gill recently wrote a hard-hitting article on ISI in the *Pioneer* titled *West Ignoring ISI's Deadly Role* which merits an extended quote: "For decades now, the West has systematically misread what it perceives as 'Islamic' or 'Islamist' terrorism. There is a studied neglect of the realities on the ground, particularly of the fact that Pakistan's Inter Services Intelligence as an organ of the country's military and political establishment has been, and remains, the principal source of the impetus, the infrastructure and the organizational network of Islamist terrorism across the world. Historically, it is now common knowledge that it was the ISI that created virtually the entire structure of Islamist terrorist groupings behind the global jihad, which has now proliferated in new areas through the agency of various proxies. This includes al-Qaeda, and the entire spectrum of affiliates that continues to operate, with varying degrees of freedom, from Pakistani soil more than six-and-a-half years after 9/11."

"Of the numerous cases of arrests, conspiracies and terrorist attacks related to Islamist groupings across the world (which I have documented in some detail in *Pakistan: The Footprints of Terror*, www.satp.org), connections that are generally attributed to the 'al-Qaeda', have been found, on closer scrutiny, to be more correctly ascribed to a range of other groupings, prominently including Lashkar-e-Toiba, Jaish-e-Mohammed, Harkat-ul Mujahideen, Harkat-ul Jihad Islami, Sipah-e-Sahaba Pakistan and various factions of the Taliban, everyone of which, was a *sarkari* (state-sponsored) jihadi group in its origin, and most of which continue to receive state patronage in Pakistan."

"In the immediate aftermath of Operation Enduring Freedom, when the Afghan infrastructure of Islamist terrorism was uprooted, Indian intelligence sources and various analysts, including this writer, had repeatedly asserted that Osama bin Laden, the al-Qaeda leadership and remnants, and the defeated rump of the Taliban had all been relocated in

Pakistan with the active cooperation and collaboration of the ISI and the Pakistan Army".

"Pakistan has, par excellence, harnessed terrorism as an instrument of state policy for well over two decades. Today, Pakistan is in the grip of a violent "blowback", what the Italian magazine *Limes* has described as *Il Boomerang Jihadista*."

"Nevertheless, the fact that the Pakistan establishment continues to use Islamist extremism and terror as a principal instrument of state policy, despite the disastrous implosion within the country, is equally inescapable. This is most visibly the case across Pakistan's Afghan and Kashmir borders — as well as in the substantial infrastructure of support of Pakistan for the terrorists operating in these theatres – but is equally true of the far more dispersed incidence of Islamist terrorism in Western countries. Despite the internal turmoil they have contributed to, the Islamist fundamentalist and extremist groupings in Pakistan remain a necessary element of the state's instrumentalities of domestic management and external projection giving the country leverage far beyond its natural means, in every concentration of Muslim populations across the world. It is Pakistan, through its state agencies, and loosely-controlled radical and jihadi affiliates, that continues to propagate Islamist jihad among the Muslim youth across the world, and that offers opportunities for training and absorption into terrorist organizations headquartered on its soil."

In conclusion, the forthright KPS Gill bluntly observed: "The reality is, there is no such thing as Islamist terrorism. There is only ISI terror that has been dubbed "Islamist terror". Were the al-Qaeda to be completely destroyed at some (improbable) stage in the foreseeable future, Islamist terrorism would continue to thrive on and from Pakistani soil."

A footnote to this fact was provided by Zardari's observation that Pakistan is now the "Petri dish of international terrorism". He made this statement in his address at the Socialist International Conference at Athens in Greece in July 2009, but explained away this reality as a "product of failed international politics".

Actually Zardari was not saying anything new, because Pakistan's credentials as "A Terrorist State" are more than a decade old. In an editorial with that title in January 1996 *Hindustan Times* pointed to the Ethiopian complaint to the UN Security Council that most of the potential assassins of Egyptian President Hosni Mubarak nabbed in Addis Ababa the previous year were recruited in Pakistan, and concluded that "Pakistan has evolved itself as the fountainhead of international terrorism".

Long before the abortive attack on Mubarak in June 1995 Egypt and Algeria had accused Pakistan of training terrorists fighting the regimes in Cairo and Algiers. It was widely known even during those times that Pathan, Arab and mercenaries of other nationalities were being trained in Pakistan for terrorism in India. Pakistan-trained terrorists were arrested in the Philippines for helping local Muslim terrorists, while others were openly fighting in Bosnia and Chechnya. Pointing all this out the *HT* editorial concluded: "The point to note is that most of the Islamic terrorist acts across the world can be traced to Pakistan. The cradle of Islamic terrorism is the Islamic University in the Pakistani capital built with Saudi funds."

32

ISI STRUCTURE

Elaborate Form, Deadly Effect

ISI's prolonged and multi-pronged proxy war on India can obviously not be conducted with such deadly effect without detailed division of responsibility laid down in an elaborate structure on the organizational and operational levels. ISI has such a structure, and it is impressively elaborate, as per the information with knowledgeable Indian personalities – Parthasarthy, former High Commissioner to Pakistan, B. Raman, a former top-ranking Indian intelligence officer, and Maj. Gen. (retd.) Rajendra Nath.

ISI HQ are located in Islamabad, and the head of ISI is called its Director General. He has to be a Lt. General in the Pakistan Army. The DG has three Deputy Directors General below him, who are in charge of three separate areas of ISI activity, which are Political, External and General.

The general staff of ISI mainly comes from police, paramilitary forces, and some specialized units from the Army, such as SSG commandos. The total work force of ISI has never been made public. According to an expert estimate it is around 25,000, while according to a media estimate of 1997 it is over 40,000.

ISI is divided into several (most probably 11) departments, which are assigned separate functions as follows:

1. **Joint Intelligence X (JIX):** Co-ordinator of all other ISI departments. Intelligence gathered by them is processed by it for preparing reports.
2. **Joint Intelligence Bureau (JIB):** Largest and most important part of ISI. Main area of responsibility gathering intelligence on political parties. Also has a sub-section for operations in India.
3. **Joint Counter-Intelligence Bureau (JCIB):** Pak version of NOCs of CIA. Pakistani diplomats who conduct intelligence gathering operations report to it. Main area of operation: Middle East, South Asia, China, Afghanistan, and Central Asia. Reportedly extended to Europe, Africa, and South America.
4. **Joint Intelligence North (JIN):** Exclusively responsible for Jammu and Kashmir, especially Indian troop movements along LoC.

Responsible for the proxy war in Jammu and Kashmir, and control of Afghanistan through Taliban. Controls Army of Islam comprising organizations like al-Qaeda, Harkat-ul-Mujahideen, Lashkar-e-Toiba, Al-Badr, and Jaish-e-Mohammed. It also controls all opium cultivation and heroin refining and smuggling from Pakistan and Afghan territory.

According to Raman, Lt. Gen. Mohammed Aziz, presently a Corps Commander at Lahore, is the clandestine chief of the Army of Islam.

5. **Joint Intelligence Miscellaneous (JIM):** Responsible for espionage and related activities in wartime. This includes covert activity in foreign countries, and clandestine procurement of nuclear and missile technology. Maj. Gen. Sultan Habib, an ISI operative of JIM, had distinguished himself in the theft of nuclear material while posted as Defence Attache in the Pakistani embassy in Moscow from 1991 to 1993. At that time he had concurrent accreditation to the Central Asian Republics, Poland and Czechoslovakia. He was later posted as Ambassador to North Korea to oversee the clandestine nuclear and missile technology cooperation between the two countries. After completing his tenure in Moscow, Habib had coordinated the training of Pakistani personnel in missile production facilities of North Korea, and, in turn, the training of North Korean scientists in the nuclear establishments of Pakistan.

   This two-way liaison was organized through Capt. Shafaqat Cheema, acting head of mission in the Pakistani embassy in North Korea from 1992 to 1996. Before Habib, the North Korea-Pakistan cooperation project was handled by Maj. Gen. Sajjad, who worked in the clandestine procurement division of ISI for five years. On Capt. Cheema's return to HQ in 1996, ISI discovered that in addition to acting as the secret ISI contact with the North Korean nuclear establishment, he was also making money on the side from Iranian and Iraqi intelligence by helping them steal nuclear technology and material not only from North Korea but also from Russia and the CARs. When Cheema learnt that ISI was investigating his scam he fled to Xinjiang in China and sought asylum, but the Chinese arrested him and handed him over to ISI. What then happened to him is not known.

   Here it is interesting to note that even before India's first nuclear test at Pokharan in 1974, ISI had set up a division for clandestine procurement of military nuclear technology from China and North Korea. This division was funded partly by concealed allocation in the State budget, partly with dollars earned in the illicit drug trade, and partly with donations from Saudi Arabia and Libya.

6. **Joint Signal Intelligence Bureau (JSIB):** Wireless communication intercept, monitoring enemy agents, reconnaissance operations such as photographs.

7. **Joint Intelligence Technical (JIT):** Developing gadgets, monitoring equipment, explosives. JIT has a chemical warfare section too.

To this list Maj. Gen. (retd.) Rajendra Nath adds another important division, namely, **Inter-Services Federal Intelligence**. There is also a **Covert Action Division** that was tasked with assisting insurgents in the North-East as far back as in the 1950s.

Each of these divisions has a large staff that is mainly made up of army officers. At the same time ISI also has advisers drawn from various human resources such as foreign service officers, journalists, businessmen, religious leaders, and intellectuals. Finally, there is an ISI school for basic training for recruited agents.

33

ISI TODAY

Terror Business As Usual

ISI under Musharraf for nearly a decade, continued to be the dominating factor in Pakistani politics. Musharraf used it for his power play at home and as an instrument of foreign policy abroad. In this respect it progressed along expected lines. On the other hand, however, this period, especially the last couple of years, saw a series of extraordinary events such as the 'civilianization' of the military dictator, the face-off with the judiciary at the highest level, the assassination of Benazir Bhutto, the coming of the coalition, and, finally, the political downfall of Musharraf. He had been even threatened with a revolution if he did not quit. In an interview to Canadian Broadcasting Corporation former ISI chief Hamid Gul once said "If Musharraf does not step down we may have to think (about forcibly removing him)... a civil war, or, if we are lucky, a revolution, something like the Iranian revolution (against the Shah in 1974)... Pakistan is ripe for such possibilities," he said.

Invisible Government

Five years ago Vikram Sood, former secretary of RAW, described ISI as the Agency that runs Pakistan in an article in the *Tehelka* journal in its issue ofAugust 12, 2006. Pointing out that one of its former chiefs did not hesitate to admit that ISI is a state within a state, he wrote: "Other similar honorifics have been bestowed upon this powerful agency over time, and not without reason, the most common being "Invisible Government" or Pakistan's "Secret Godfathers".

Examples of Benazir Bhutto and Nawaz Sharif show that "whenever Pakistan's prime ministers tried to have their own man as the ISI chief, the Army ensured that it was the prime minister who lost his job." "Domestic political gamesmanship has become a way of life for the ISI." "The Army is to remain supreme domestically, and the ISI is the handmaiden."

For instance when, during his second tenure as Prime Minister (1997-99), Nawaz Sharif appointed Lt. Gen. Ziauddin, an engineer, as ISI head (DG), overriding the objection ofArmy Chief Gen. Musharraf, as a counter-move Musharraf transferred Lt. Gen. Mohammed Aziz, the then DDG,

ISI, on promotion to GHQ and transferred ISI's entire Jt. Intelligence North division, responsible for covert actions in India and Afghanistan, to Military Intelligence to be supervised by Aziz.

He even made ISI chief Ziauddin *persona non grata* and kept him totally out of the picture in the planning and implementation of the Kargil operation. After the Kargil war Nawaz Sharif sent Ziauddin to Washington on a secret visit to inform the Clinton Administration of his concern over the loyalty of Musharraf. On his return from the US Ziauddin went to Kandahar, on orders from Sharif, to pressurise Taliban *amir* (chief) Mullah Omar to stop helping the anti-Shia outfit Sipah Sahaba and cooperate with the US in the capture and deportation of Osama bin Laden. On coming to know this Musharraf sent Aziz to Kandahar to tell Omar not to listen to Ziauddin. During the period of the face-off Musharraf saw to it that not only was the Sharif-nominated ISI chief sidelined but also that his man Aziz was in operational control of ISI and was directly answerable to him.

200 Per Cent

How heavily Gen. Musharraf, as Pakistan's military dictator, depended on ISI was seen when in the BBC *Newsnight* programme on September 27, 2006 a research paper prepared by the British ministry of defence was quoted linking ISI with support for Taliban and other terror acts in the West. The report stated: "The US/UK cannot begin to turn the tide until they identify the real enemies from attacking ideas tactically and seek to put in place a more just vision. This will require Pakistan to move away from Army rule and for the ISI to be disbanded..." Musharraf not only rejected this call but proclaimed, "I totally, 200 per cent, reject it. I reject it from anybody... who tells me to dismantle ISI."

In a similar vein he had once declared that the West could be brought to its knees if Pakistan withdrew its cooperation in the so-called war on terror. In a finger-wagging attack on the West's growing doubts about Pakistan's role in fighting Islamic terrorism Musharraf said the US and UK had to understand that Pakistan was the West's "main ally" — "You'll be brought to your knees if Pakistan doesn't cooperate with you... If we were not with you, you won't change anything. Let that be clear. And if the ISI is not with you, you will fail."

Actually Musharraf's politicking throughout his reign was based on the realization that if ISI was not with him, he would fail. So he not only depended on it, he even clandestinely worked through it. For instance, during Benazir Bhutto's exile, having failed in his efforts to weaken the PPP by taking advantage of her absence from the scene, and faced with the growing unity of action between Altaf Hussain's MQM and Sindhi nationalists, Musharraf had constituted a secret task force in ISI headed by its Director General Lt. Gen. Mehmood Ahmed and consisting of Lt. Gen. (retd.) Moiuddin Haider, Interior Minister, and Lt. Gen. Muzaffar Usmani, Deputy Chief of Army Staff, to break all three — the PPP, the MQM, and the Sindhi nationalists. This task force had encouraged not only fundamentalist religio-political organizations like the Jamaat-e-Islami (JEI) and Jamaat-ul-Ulema (JUU) but also rigidly sectarian outfits like Sipah Sahaba and Lashkar-e-Jhangvi.

As a result there was resurgence of the street power of the JEI and JUU, leading later to anti-Shia massacres of the kind caused by Musharraf in Gilgit in 1988. Over 200 Shias were gunned down. There were also assassinations, for which Lashkar-e-Jhangvi claimed responsibility.

Wahabi Poison

ISI's divide-and-rule policy even led to intra-sectarian violence erupting for the first time within the Sunni community itself between Deobandi Sunnis belonging to Sipah Sahaba and Lashkar-e-Jhangvi and Barelvi Sunnis belonging to the Sunni Tehrik organisation formed in the early 1990s to counter the growing Wahabi (Arab) influence on Islam in Pakistan and another organisation called Almi Tanzeem Ahle Sunnat formed in 1998 in Gujrat (Pakistan), to counter the activities of the Deobandi "Army of Islam" headed by a top-ranking Pakistani Army officer. The Tanzeem accused the Army of Islam of injecting what it considered the Wahabi poison into the Pakistani society.

ISI, on its part, was reluctant to have a direct confrontation with the Barelvi organizations and so pitted Sipah Sahaba and LeJ against them. This led to frequent bloody clashes between rival Sunni groups in Sindh. The most horrifying such incident was the gunning down of a prominent Maulana of Sunni Tehrik and five of his followers in Karachi on May 18, 2001 by Sipah Sahaba. This gory incident had caused a major breakdown in law and order in the city for days.

Despite such tactics the situation in Pakistan under Musharraf went on worsening till it deteriorated to the point where the Americans (as well as some in the Pakistani media) began to talk and write about Pakistan being a failed state and becoming the most dangerous place in the world, about terrorists running a mini-state in an annexed territory within Pakistan, and finally about a question mark on the very survival of Pakistan.

The murky goings on in Pakistani politics during the later years of the Musharraf regime culminated on a dark note. Benazir Bhutto said in 2007 in one of her last interviews, "it's not just the intelligence services who were previously called a state within a state. Today it's the militants who are becoming yet another little state within the state, and this is leading some people down the slippery slope of being called a failed state".

It was indeed a failed state, and it failed to protect her life. Benazir Bhutto was assassinated in Rawalpindi on Dec. 27, 2007. The political air became thick with charges and countercharges, which ended up in the institution of a United Nations investigation. The UN report, released in April 2010, made two basic points. The first was that ISI used Lashkar-e-Toiba (LeT) to whip up anti-India passion, and it was such links and connections between elements in the intelligence agencies and militants which most concerned Bhutto and many others who believed that the authorities could activate those connections to harm her. The second, and concommitant, part was that the Musharraf regime failed to protect her.

The 65-page report by a panel headed by Chile's UN ambassador Heraldo Munoz said the assassination could have been prevented, but Pervez Musharraf's government failed to protect her despite serious threat. It added that ISI and the police deliberately failed to properly probe the killing. Finally, the UN panel held that Benazir Bhutto's assassination was still shrouded in mystery, and concluded with recommending the setting up a truth commission to find out who really murdered her.

Expectedly enough some selected officials were made scapegoats and sacked, while some top guns in intelligence were placed on the Exit Control List, that is, they could not leave the country. They included former ISI chief Hamid Gul and ex-Intelligence Bureau head Ijaz Shah. That done, the government said that it would also take action against former military ruler Pervez Musharraf.

In another instance, after 9/11 ISI was supposedly purged of members who did not support President Pervez Musharraf's stance towards the Taliban and al-Qaeda. News reports in July 2008, however, indicated that ISI may instead have chosen to merely suppress the activities of these individuals rather than remove them from office. Initially, the decision of the ISI to suddenly switch support to the United States went almost unnoticed. Several years later it was revealed that the US Deputy Secretary of State Richard Armitage had allegedly threatened to bomb Pakistan back to the Stone Age if Pakistan did not support the US-led War on Terror. This was according to President Musharaff and the ex-CIA chief George Tenet. It is known that Richard Armitage invited Pakistan's Ambassador Maleeha Lodhi and the then ISI chief Mahmood Ahmed, who was in Washington, to his office on September 13, 2001, two days after the 9/11 attacks for talks, but Richard Armitage has denied using those words.

Clearly all this had already put a question-mark on Musharraf's own political survival. To avert his nemesis he promulgated the Emergency — a response typical of a dictator. Pakistan was turned into what *Dawn* condemned as a garrison state, but the emergency proved so ineffectual in shoring up the General's sliding political fortunes that it had to be done away with within six short weeks.

The other remedy he tried was to change his clothes. He decided to doff his military uniform and become a civilian President and even promise an election, which, as in the past, he depended on ISI to rig. And finally, as a last-ditch attempt to keep his hold on the Pakistani state's two main pillars, the Army and ISI, he handed over the Army to his trusted loyalist Gen. Ashfaq Kayani and ISI to another loyalist, Gen. Taj (who was with him in the plane from Colombo to Karachi on the day of the coup in October 1999).

In a harsh commentary on this dismal scenario Murtaza Rizvi, an editor with *Dawn*, opened his article titled *Pakistan's been here before* in *Indian Express* of 30.11.07 thus: "What ails Pakistan today is not Pervez Musharraf, in or out of uniform, nor indeed the lack of a stable political system. These are but symptoms of the graver malaise eating away at the heart of the state: The continued stranglehold of the armed forces over all power. The Army will continue to pull strings from behind the scenes. So here's to the Pakistan Army first!".

Even after ISI's complicity in the bomb attack on the Indian embassy in Kabul came to light, Musharraf came to its rescue and declared that ISI is the first line of defence of Pakistan. In a speech in Karachi in August 2008 he said weakening ISI would weaken Pakistan and its Armed Forces. He also dismissed the allegations levelled against ISI as a conspiracy and certified it as a patriotic institution.

All this goes to show the position of strength in which ISI was ensconced during the Musharraf era. With President Musharraf finally becoming former President Musharraf, it continued there. So far as ISI is concerned, the more political things changed, the more they remained the same. In fact, for ex-Prez Mush 2009 was a year of confessions. He confessed that ISI maintains links with terrorist commanders like Sirajuddin Haqqani, suspected of having masterminded the attack on the Indian embassy in Kabul. In an interview to a German weekly Musharraf said the ISI used Haqqani's influence to secure the release of Pakistan's Ambassador to Afghanistan who was kidnapped by Tehrik-e-Taliban chief Baitullah Mehsud.

Then he said military aid provided by US to Pakistan for the war against terror during his tenure had been used for defence against India, the first such admission by any top Pakistani leader. Musharraf admitted he had violated rules governing the use of the military aid, and justified his actions by saying he had acted in the best interest of Pakistan. In an interview with a news channel he even said that he did not care whether the US would be angered by his disclosure. Later he backtracked and said Pakistan never misutilised US funds.

In yet another confession, ISI has influence over every terrorist group and it uses these contacts to its own advantage, Musharraf said in a rare admission. Debunking Pakistan's oft-repeated position that ISI had no role in terror activities across the border, Musharraf claimed that the intelligence agency's effectiveness was through such ingress. Always, in every group, there is an ingress of the ISI. And that is the efficiency, the effectiveness of the ISI.

MK Dhar wrote in his review of the book *Profiles of Intelligence* by ISI officer Syed Tirmagi, released in Pakistan in 1996: Tirmagi's long innings with the ISI has given him a deep insight, and he confirms that the ISI is the strongest leg of the power tripod in Pakistan: the Punjabi-dominated armed forces, the bureaucrats, and the ISI. All of them have long memories and are stuck in pre-1947 grooves. They have taught the people of Pakistan that India is a demon, and its disintegration is a must for survival.

Military Economy

A relevant point here is that in the case of the Pakistan Army power and pelf go together, because with 20-billion dollar assets, the military is Pakistan's biggest corporate. According to a book released in London in mid-2007, Pakistan's biggest corporate entity is its military, running businesses ranging from sugar mills to banks and TV channels worth 20 billion dollars. Written by Pakistan Navy's former research directorAyesha Siddiqa, it puts the value of the land under military control alone at about 12 billion dollars. (The book, *Military Inc., Inside Pakistan's Military Economy,* was banned in Pakistan on the day of its launch.) The author says, "If you factor in all segments of the military economy, it is perhaps the largest corporate group." Asked if General Musharraf could be considered the ultimate patron of this huge wealth, Siddiqa said, "Every Army Chief is the chief patron of this economy. Not for nothing was a Pakistani general once called the world's richest General and the Army's corps commanders called crore commanders".

Musharraf himself has now been charged by PPP with having gobbled up 700 million dollars. PPP chief (and now President) Zardari has accused him of misappropriating 700 million dollars of anti-terror aid provided by the US. (A relevant update here: US President Obama had charged publicly that Pakistan was using American money to prepare for war on India. Obviously this charge was based on the admission of the US administration and military officials that much of the American money was being used for weapon systems for countering India, not for fighting al-Qaeda and Taliban.)

Writing about the new Pakistan Army chief Gen. Kayani the Indian media, as is its wont, made some hopeful noises, but they don't mean much. For, in the first place, he views India, like all senior officers, with deep distrust, says Pakistan-watcher Stephen Cohen. Secondly, and far more importantly for India, he was the chief of ISI.

Euphemistic Verbiage

The *Indian Express* comment on Kayani was a typical, soothing exercise in euphemism. On November 30, 2007 it wrote: "What made the Indian security establishment sit up was when Kayani took over the powerful ISI in October 2004. The interest was primarily due to the unique task assigned to him by President Musharraf— a thorough crackdown on extremism, the first of its kind by Pakistan's security forces in six decades. At the same time the former spy chief is known for his thorough understanding of the Kashmir issue and has been the key figure formulating Pakistan Army's policy for the region in the past decade. Indian analysts feel that as the Army chief he will be walking on a thin line on the crackdown on terror." "One thing that is clear," the paper quoted a senior officer as saying, "is that he will crack down on terror. However, the priority will be to eliminate anti-Western terror, and a crackdown on Kashmir militants is not likely in the near future."

Shorn of the euphemistic verbiage, this means, in the first place it was Kayani who was guiding Pakistan's terror war on India for a full decade including the period of his tenure as ISI boss, and secondly he would be in no hurry to crack down on terrorism in India. In other words, so far as India is concerned, it will be business as usual for ISI, Pakistan's export house of terror.

Post-Musharraf

"What happens post-Musharraf?" asked Ejaz Haider, op-ed editor of the Pakistani *Daily Times* and consulting editor of *Friday Times*, Lahore, in his piece in *Indian Express*, and then proceeded to give the answer in a lighter vein in the opening paragraph:

"The new parliament is in. Pakistan has a female Speaker of the National Assembly, a first, arch rivals PPP and PML-N are in the kip having solemnised the marriage in Murree on March 9, the erstwhile King's Party has conceded defeat, and everyone, including Bertie Wooster and Aunts Agatha and Dahlia, is calling the slain Benazir Bhutto a martyr. Is this the Garden of Eden? No, if we go by Ted Hughes' Apple Tragedy, utopias have a way of going to hell, and in this garden slither many a serpent..."

As per a typical American expression, Zardari is a loser. In fact, he has been listed the fifth biggest loser in the world by the prestigious *Foreign Policy* magazine. "Zardari was known to be a bad guy long before he became Pakistan's President. Many of the closest friends of his late wife Benazir Bhutto could not stand him. Now, as it turns out, neither can most of the Pakistani people," read the citation by the US-based magazine. *Foreign Policy* listed 12 other leaders from headlines ranked by just how little sympathy we should have for them. The Pope was declared "the second biggest loser because he is out of touch with the real world and his papacy is a disaster," the magazine wrote.

By a quirk of fate, this loser became a leader. He became the leader of Benazir Bhutto's PPP and led the party in its ensuing power struggle with Nawaz Sharif's Muslim League. The struggle ended in a patch-up and the PPP leader became President of Pakistan. This solemnised marriage, mentioned earlier by columnist Ejaz Haider, was soon on the rocks. The ruling PPP and opposition PML-N engaged in a war of words over the sweeping powers wielded by President Zardari, with former premier Nawaz Sharif describing his dispensation as no different from dictatorship. "Nothing has changed after the general election last year. The status quo still exists. The same judges (appointed during former President Pervez Musharraf's tenure) and courts are still there. The system is the same and Pakistan's Constitution and laws remain unchanged," he said.

This downturn in Zardari's political fortunes was compounded by Musharraf's legacy of a confrontation with the court. Musharraf had not only sacked judges hostile to him but issued an ordinance called National Reconciliation Ordinance by which cases in Switzerland against Zardari for using Swiss bank accounts to stash away millions of dollars were withdrawn. Zardari gained billions of dollars when the graft cases against him were dropped under a law that has now expired. Zardari was accused of amassing assets worth $ 1.5 billion and Rs. 22 billion during the period when his wife Benazir Bhutto was PM.

Commenting on the situation in an article titled *In disrepute* (alluding to Zardari) on Jan. 27, 2010 *The Economist* observed:

"The Supreme Court of Pakistan has made its intention clear. It wants to turf Asif Zardari from the presidency and compel him to return the wealth that he has allegedly looted and stashed away in Switzerland. In a 287-page judgment the court explained why it had ruled the National Reconciliation Ordinance (NRO) unconstitutional. The NRO, promulgated by the ousted dictator, Pervez Musharraf, in 2007, cleared Mr Zardari and his wife, the late Benazir Bhutto, of all corruption cases against them. It has ordered Mr Zardari's government to apply to the Swiss authorities to reopen the money-laundering case against Mr Zardari and Ms Bhutto".

"Political pundits foresee the end of Mr Zardari's presidency. He has thundered about a conspiracy against his people's government, alluding to a nexus between the army, the judiciary and a section of the press. The army resents him as too soft towards both America and India. His efforts to bring the generals under civilian control have earned their hostility. The judges are on the warpath. And the opposition is fanning the conflict, hoping for a mid-term election and the rout of Mr Zardari's party. The court battles ahead are going to be nasty. Sooner rather than later, the army is likely to step in to try to break the deadlock between the judiciary and the executive. Pakistan's enduring tragedy, however, is that its (the Army's) record is no better than that of the civilians."

In short, Zardari found himself defeated by the situation. In a sort of last-ditch move his government had told the court it would not reopen the graft cases against him, as the matter has been closed. The court retaliated by putting aside Musharraf's NRO itself. The inevitable result was the damning verdict.

Left with no choice, and not waiting for the ignominy of being dethroned, Zardari chose to sort of self-destruct. On April 19, 2010 he signed away his sweeping powers. To quote an Indian media report of that day: "Pakistan's President Asif Ali Zardari on Monday signed into law sweeping constitutional reforms that strip him of key powers in a move to bolster parliamentary democracy weakened by military rule. The amendment rolls back decades of meddling by military rulers and removes the head of state's power to sack the prime minister, appoint heads of the armed forces, unilaterally declare emergency rule and dissolve parliament. Prime Minister Yousuf Raza Gilani will assume executive power in a move that could help ease simmering political instability in the nuclear-armed country. A grinning Zardari signed the amendment at a ceremony attended by Gilani and opposition leader Nawaz Sharif — a sign of the rare cross-party support for the bill in the fractious world of Pakistani politics. "It is my hope that the doors of dictatorship are closed forever," he said after signing the 18th amendment to Pakistan's 1973 parliamentary constitution. The package removes many of the sweeping powers amassed by military dictators Pervez Musharraf and Zia-ul-Haq, although the army remains a powerful force in Pakistan. No senior military officials attended Monday's ceremony."

The concluding sentence of this glowing report gives the whole show away. The fact of the matter is that Pakistan was not a democracy in the past and there are no signs that it will be a democracy in the future. The Army top brass did not think it necessary to come and see the President closing the doors of dictatorship for ever, because, as the report itself admits, the Army remains a powerful force, all constitutional amendments notwithstanding. As a Pakistani journalist had already put it, power in Pakistan lies not in the presidential mansion, nor in the prime minister's office, but in the army headquarters in Rawalpindi and its instrument, the ISI. And all Pakistanis know this.

In attempting to explain why so many attacks — abortive and successful— can be traced back to a single country, analysts tend to dwell on the 1980s, when Pakistan acted as a staging ground for the successful American and Saudi-funded jihad against the Soviet Union in Afghanistan.

But while the anti-Soviet campaign undoubtedly accelerated Pakistan's emergence as a jihadist haven, to truly understand the country it's important to go back further, to its creation.

Pakistan was carved out of the Muslim-majority areas of British India in 1947, the world's first modern nation based solely on Islam. From the start, the new country was touched by the messianic zeal of pan-Islamism. The Quranic scholar Muhammad Asad — an Austrian Jew born Leopold Weiss — became an early Pakistani ambassador to the United Nations. The Egyptian Said Ramadan, son-in-law of Muslim Brotherhood founder Hassan al-Banna, made Pakistan a second home of sorts and collaborated with Pakistan's leading Islamist ideologue, the Jamaat-e-Islami's Abul Ala Maududi. In 1949, Pakistan established the world's first transnational Islamic organization, the World Muslim Congress.

What about today, 63 years later? ISI's reluctance to dismantle its structure of terrorism – training camps, a web of ultraorthodox *madrassas* that preach violence, and terrorist groups such as the Lashkar-e-Toiba ensures that Pakistan remains a magnet for any Muslim with a grudge against the world and the urge to do something violent about it.

"The choice of the rather inelegant civilianising over democratisation is more apt, and that is the expression many Pakistanis prefer to use, the nuance is important," recently wrote *Indian Express* editor Shekhar Gupta in his *National Interest* column. He went on to add: "I once asked a prominent Pakistani thinker when it would be that an elected government in Pakistan acquires real control over its foreign, Kashmir and India policies and its nuclear weapons. His answer was quite brilliant: When three Army chiefs have retired and gone home to play Golf, and when two elected governments have completed their full terms without being dismissed."

Against the background of such a bizarre possibility the two new leaders of Pakistan, Nawaz Sharif and Asif Zardari, are making some brave talk in order to establish their credentials. For instance, when two top US State Department officials met them in March, Sharif accused the US of making Pakistan a killing field, while PPP leader (not yet President) Zardari did not tell what he said but he had Husain Haqqani (now his advisor) with him in the meeting who said the Americans had been given notice that the old days were over. "If I can use an American expression, there is a new sheriff in town," he said.

Subservient President

However there are clear pointers that discretion is the better part of the bravery of such words, especially where ISI is concerned. One of them was that the brand new Prime Minister Geelani and PPP co-chairman Zardari (not yet president) visited the ISI HQ while Musharraf loyalist Taj was still the ISI boss and had not yet been shunted out. And even after becoming president, Zardari's subservience is very much in evidence. For the joke of Indian Prime Minister Manmohan Singh inviting the ISI chief to India to help investigate the Mumbai carnage apart, when President Zardari agreed and decided to do so, he had to promptly reverse his decision after a post-midnight call to him by Army chief Gen. Kayani. The Army chief even sent his plane to bring back Foreign Minister Shah Mehmood Qureshi who was in Delhi at the time of the attack.

Now Zardari is defending ISI as desperately as Musharraf did. *Apropos* the terror war on Mumbai he declared in an interview to *Newsweek* that ISI had no links with LeT and that any linkages were a thing of the past. "We are talking about an age-old situation. This is something (that happened) in the old days when dictators used to run the country. Maybe before 9/11 that may have been the position. Since then things have changed. "At the same time Zardari expressed helplessness in clamping down on banned outfits' terror, saying they keep re-emerging in different forms".

As against this far-from-reassuring scenario, the Americans keep hoping against hope for a better shape of things to come. President Obama may reportedly ask Pakistan to reform a "rogue" ISI and bring it under firm civilian control. As for President Bush, when, during his first visit to the US the new Pak Prime Minister Yousuf Raza Geelani called on him, an annoyed Bush had point-blank asked him, "Who is controlling the ISI?"

The plain answer to that question is, no democratic government in Pakistan has ever been able to wield any control over ISI. ISI is a law unto itself. Senior ISI officials listen only to the Army chief and nobody else. They have only one boss, and it is not their prime minister. Not even the present President, the Army could ultimately threaten his government, wrote the Pakistani paper *Nation*.

ISI Mafia

Actually it gets worse. For even within Pakistan there are many who believe that ISI is no longer a government organisation but a mafia run by army officers and the old guard of the agency, who are involved in criminal activities like abduction, extortion, drug trafficking, printing of fake currency, and terrorism.

34

TODAY'S TERRORIST

More Willing for Mass Killing

The ISI terrorist has been operating on Indian soil for decades, aided and abetted by al-Qaeda and Taliban. All three have one and the same agenda–*Dar-ul-Islam*, a world dominated by Islam. This goal has remained constant, but, over the years, the instrument of this goal, the terrorist, has changed, evolved, mutated. The days of the Afghan Mujahideen are behind him. Now he has a different psychology.

Various terrorism experts have tried to map this change. Soon after 9/11, a US professor of psychiatry, Marc Sageman, was asked by CIA to profile an al-Qaeda terrorist. Using a databank of 400 global network terrorists Sageman came to some startling conclusions: The latter-day Jihadi is now a middle class, if not upper crust, Muslim. He is educated – an engineering degree is almost a prerequisite to become a terrorist. He is not single, he is usually married, has children, and sees nothing wrong in watching movies. This was Sageman's latter-day al-Qaeda recruit.

Rohan Gunaratna, author of *Inside al-Qaeda* says, "The original Sageman profile covered the first generation of Islamic terrorists." This was the generation of the stereotypical al-Qaeda cadre – an Arab veteran of the anti-Soviet Jihad in Afghanistan, who probably knew bin Laden in person.

Second Generation

The second generation Islamic terrorist, say most experts, has minimal experience of Afghanistan. "In their case al-Qaeda is a source of inspiration but not much more," says B. Raman, a former RAW terrorism-expert. "They are more likely," says Gunaratna "to be trained by disparate groups ranging from Lashkar-e-Toiba, Jaish-e-Mohammed, and assorted Middle East groups ranging from the Libyan Islamic Fighters to the Tawhidi-al-Jihad of Iraq".

This has made second-generation Islamic terror more cosmopolitan. "Outside the Middle East, in the attacks in London or cells found in Australia, international Jihadis are more often Pakistani, occasionally Bangladeshi," says Raman. Sidney Jones, an expert on South-East Asian Terror for the International Crisis Group, points out that the Afghan veteran, once the heart of the global network, has been replaced by a war veteran of Kashmir, Iraq or the Philippines. "This makes cells more violence-prone."

Generation Three

Islamic terror's Generation Three is now upon us. They are younger, and radicalised by local media and the Internet. 80 per cent of Sageman's examples picked up their militant Islamism overseas. Gunaratna says the recent abortive terror plots in Britain and Canada are an indication of what the future holds. The new terrorist is likely to be wholly home-grown, operationally clumsier, but technically more savvy than his predecessors. This home-grown terrorist, says Dr. Tanveer Ahmed, an Australian psychiatrist, is likely to be of South Asian background, especially Pakistani – tertiary educated, interested in foreign affairs, especially the Arab world and sees himself as a Muslim alone, without nationality.

Indian Terrorist

The Indian terrorist too has changed with the times. He too has acquired the sophistication that makes the modern al-Qaeda product. Take Faisal Sheikh. Called by the police the Commander of LeT for Western India and charged with the Mumbai local trains bombings of 7/11, he is a clean-shaven, handsome young man in his thirties, who spoke English as if it was his mother tongue. He wore denims, spent evenings in a beer bar, even knew a bar-girl, who visited him at his place in Bandra. He had studied engineering for a couple of years. He looked the very antithesis of the traditional *madrasa*-product.

Faisal is no exception. In fact, as updated Jihadi profiles go, he is the prototype. All the men picked up for the 7/11 bombing were similar. Ehtesham Siddique, General Secretary of SIMI in Maharashtra, accused of planting the bomb in the Mira Road suburb, is an engineer. Dr. Tanvir Ansari, who provided logistic support, spent six years in a Nagpur medical college. Naved Khan, alleged planter of the bomb in another Mumbai suburb, Khar, worked in a call centre in Hyderabad. And Rizwan Dawre, who made travel arrangements for Jihadis coming from Pakistan, earned an impressive monthly salary as a senior software professional with a multinational IT company in Dubai.

In fact, today's terrorist is impressively techno-savvy. He can, and does, use advanced information technology like Skype. In the recent LeT attack on Amarnath pilgrims the terrorists could successfully ambush an Army convoy on the Srinagar-Baramula highway despite sophisticated jammers — supposed deterrents to explosives since they block all electronic devices within a certain reach — that were moving with it. The Army and Police said instead of electronic devices the terrorists used the manual-wire technique to trigger the powerful Improvised Explosive Device (IED) used for the attack.

With all this, however, Raman says there is a distinction between the radical Indian Muslim and the pan-Islamic militant. In his opinion Indian Muslims are radicalised by domestic events rather than by pan-Islamic terror talk, but the relationship between the two is dangerously narrowing. The Mumbai bomb blasts of 2006 and earlier of 1993 seem to show that Indian Muslim terrorists are now more willing for mass killings than before —- an echo of bin Laden's decree that Jihadis should not worry about killing innocent infidels.

Jehadist Psyche

Finally, the apparent Indian-International distinction apart, and despite the sophistication of modern terrorism, the concept of *Shahádat* (martyrdom) appeals to the Jehadist's psyche. An extreme example of this was the announcement in December 2008 of Khalid Sheikh Mohammed, the self-confessed mastermind behind the 2001 terrorist attacks on New York and Washington, that he and his four associates standing trial in the US want to plead guilty to their role in the killing of 3000 people in the most deadly assault in America's history. Regarded as No. 3 in the al-Qaeda hierarchy, he confessed to 30 other terrorist strikes. The reason for the confession he gave to the court was that he had wished for *Shahádat* for a long time.

35

NON-RESPONSE

India's Pathetic Record

India has been hit by terrorists at will and with chilling regularity — Mumbai, Delhi, Bangalore, Hyderabad, Malegaon, Varanasi, Kashmir... the list is endless. The reason why India has found itself under such a relentless siege from the forces of terror is apparent from its response (or, more precisely, the lack of it) to the murder and mayhem they perpetrate. In fact, India's track record in responding to terror is pathetic.

The country that has had to face the worst of terrorist attacks on its own soil, barring Iraq, is India. Since the beginning of 2004, India lost almost 4000 lives to terrorist incidents — more than all of North America, South America, Central America, Europe, and Eurasia put together. More than 40 per cent of the total deaths in India occurred in Kashmir alone as a result of Pakistan's proxy war, led by ISI and aided and abetted by al-Qaeda, Taliban *et al*. There are other figures that are still more disturbing. For instance, India lost over 53,000 lives to terrorism over the last decade. In comparison, it lost 8000 lives in all its wars since independence. In other words, terror attacks on India have bled the country much more than conventional wars.

And what is India doing to block this unending death trail? In August 2007 the *Times of India* published a list of 11 big hits between March 1993 and August 2007 that killed 800 people. Ten out of the 11 had the same comment at the end — "mastermind absconding". No wonder this inaction had the tragic consequence of reducing the whole of India to a killing field.

A meaningful response to the Islamic terrorism rampant in the country needs action on three operational levels – BEFORE, DURING, and AFTER. On all three the Indian response has been dismal.

BEFORE

For starters, how disastrously negligent our protectors of the people are on the BEFORE level was revealed by the case of the 60-hour terror war on Mumbai in November 2008. There were warnings galore of the terrible shape of things to come – and they were all ignored.

Some shocking details:

Warnings Galore

"Our coastal areas are coming under increased threat from terrorist groups, which have decided to use the sea route to infiltrate into India. They also plan to induct arms and ammunition through the sea routes!" That was Home Minister Shivraj Patil addressing the Directors General and Inspectors General of Police in November 2006. "We understand they (the terrorists) have been collecting information regarding location of various refineries on or near the Indian coastline... Some Lashkar-e-Toiba (LeT) operatives are also being trained specifically for sabotage of oil installations. There are plans to occupy some uninhabited islands off the country's coastline to use them as bases for launching operations on the Indian coast...".

Minister of Defence Antony had been no less alert. On March 9, 2007, he was asked in the Lok Sabha whether the intelligence agencies have warned about the possibility of terrorists trying to infiltrate through the sea route or trying to target our offshore installations. He answered, "Yes, sir. There are reports about terrorists of various *tanzeems* being imparted training and likelihood of their infiltration through sea routes..." He was asked whether maritime terrorism, gun-running, drug-trafficking and piracy were major threats that India was facing from the sea borders of the country?" His answer? "Yes, sir."

On May 9, 2007, the home minister was again asked in the Rajya Sabha, whether "it is a fact that there are strong apprehensions of terrorist threats to the country through the sea route." "As per available reports," he again answered, "Pak-based terrorist groups, particularly LeT, have been exploring possibilities of induction of manpower and terrorist hardware through the sea route..."

On December 8, 2007, National Security Adviser MK Narayanan was educating the world at the 4th Regional Security Summit organised by the International Institute of Strategic Studies. "According to our intelligence reports," he confided to the assembled sheikhs and experts, "there are certain new schools that are now being established on the Pakistan-Afghanistan border, which now specialise in the training of an international brigade of terrorists to fight in many climes. According to our information, recruits from 14 to 15 countries have been identified as amongst the trainees there... Training has become extremely rigorous, it is almost frightening in nature... Studies are being carried out about important targets, with regard to vulnerability, accessibility, poor security, absence of proper counter-terrorism measures, etc. The sea route, in particular, is becoming the chosen route for carrying out many attacks, even on land. References to this are to be found replete in current terrorist literature."

On March 11, 2008, Defence Minister Antony addressed the

"International Maritime Search and Rescue Conference," in Delhi. He again warned the delegates of dangers of terror attacks from the sea in the region. In fact, he said that he had warned the country at least six times in the past two years about the threat of terrorists using the sea route to infiltrate into the country. Are these gentlemen consultants to the government or the ones running the government? Is their job to issue warnings to others or to see that the warnings are acted upon? Warning given, the job is done? But that has been the fate of all warnings. After all, that very sea route was used to smuggle explosives for the blasts across Bombay in 1993. Were those blasts not warning enough?

Seven years later, in 2000, the warning and lesson were made explicit yet again. Four task forces were set up in the wake of the Kargil war. The one on border management warned, "The long coastline with its inadequate policing makes it easy to land arms and explosives at isolated spots on the coast." It recalled that this is exactly how explosives were smuggled into Maharashtra in 1993. "The situation, if anything, has worsened over the years with the activities of the ISI becoming more widespread along the coast." ISI had started using the Lakshadweep archipelago as a major staging point for smuggling arms and personnel into India. Lakshadweep has 36 islands. Ten of these are inhabited. Talking of one of these islands – Suheli – the task force pointed out that sea vessels of smugglers apart, "there have been instances of twin-rotor helicopters (of the kind used by military) landing at Suheli Island and spotting of unidentified helicopters flying over the waters around the islands".

On November 13, 2008, just a fortnight before the multiple assaults in Mumbai, Prime Minister Manmohan Singh himself warned the BIMSTEC summit "Terrorism and threats from the sea continue to challenge the authority of the state."

On November 19, just about a week before the attack, one of the intelligence agencies had circulated top secret information on the basis of an intercept the previous day that an attack had been planned from sea on Mumbai and would be effected very soon. While November 26 was not mentioned as a precise date, sources said, another date before the day of the attack was specified. It also said the terrorists could probably come by an Indian fishing trawler.

This input was passed on for further analysis to the National Security Council Secretariat and Joint Intelligence Council. Subsequently, this was shared with the Navy and the Coast Guard. Also, it was sent in the form of an advisory to Maharashtra.

By now it was time for home minister to address yet another meeting of the DGs and IGs of Police. Thus on November 22, 2008, that is literally on the eve of the attacks in Mumbai, he told the police chiefs, "To control terrorism in the hinterland, we have to see that infiltration of terrorists from other countries does not take place through the sea routes and through the borders between India and friendly countries. The coastlines also have to be guarded through Navy, Coast Guard and Coastal Police. The states' special branches and the CID should identify the persons forming part of the sleeper cells and lodging in cities and towns and studying in educational institutions and working in industries and professions..."

While India's own government leaders were thus busy issuing warning after warning to the people, warnings also came from abroad. The US said it had issued two specific warnings of attacks on Mumbai. Reports quoting US intelligence officials said their agencies had warned Indian counterparts in mid-October of a potential attack from the sea against hotels and business centres in Mumbai. The reports said warnings were issued not once, but twice. The American network CNN quoted a US intelligence official as saying that the warnings were to the point. "The US intelligence indicated that a group might enter the country by water and launch an attack on Mumbai," said the official. Another network, ABCnews.com was told that specific locations, including the Taj Hotel, were listed in the US warning.

Believe it or not, even a fellow-terrorist had warned that the terrorists were coming. Fahim Ansari *alias* Abu Zarar, who was arrested by UP's Special Task Force after an attack on the CRPF camp at Rampur in Uttar Pradesh on December 31, 2007, had reportedly told the police that Lashkar-e-Toiba planned to execute terror operations in Mumbai. But no one took him seriously. According to a police officer, Fahim had disclosed that the LeT planned to send Fidayeen to Mumbai for carrying out terror operations and that he had been tasked by his bosses to conduct a recce of possible targets and make arrangements for logistical support. "As far as I recall, he had named three places as the targets of LeT: Bombay Stock Exchange, Police Commissioner's Office and Gateway of India," the officer said. Another officer said Fahim had named many places, including the CST railway station, Capitol cinema, Taj Hotel and US Consulate.

To cap it all, less than a month before the attack LeT chief Saeed had himself warned of launching fresh attacks on India. In a speech put out on the terror outfit's official website (www jamat-dawah.org/ Oct 13, 2008), Hafiz had said: "India understands only one language, the language of jihad". "The morale of the Kashmiris is extremely high and it is the time to support jihad. India has failed to suppress the freedom movement of the Kashmiris despite employing every type of atrocity. This proves that jihad cannot be suppressed. In fact, with little support, it can break apart India just like the former USSR".

Finally, all this warning-mongering notwithstanding, just four days after Home Minister's final warning the terrorists, using the same sea route, did the exact same thing of which these worthies had been repeatedly warning all and sundry.

Most Vulnerable Coastline

Intelligence agencies have for long known that the country's long coastline is its most vulnerable border. Its Saurashtra/Kutch patch had come under the scanner about 15 years ago when a consignment of RDX sent by underworld don Dawood Ibrahim and used in the Mumbai serial blasts landed near Porbandar.

The Lashkar men who started off from Karachi in a mother ship could have been intercepted even before they entered Indian waters if the Navy, which forms the first line of defence, had got intelligence updates about their movements. The second layer of security, the Coast Guard, also failed. The unloading of the terrorists, along with a large amount of explosives and ammunition, from the mother ship to the fishing vessel, was not detected by Coast Guard boats. The most serious lapse, a parliamentary panel noted, was a gap in the surveillance capability of both the Navy and Coast Guard due to a lack of aerial platforms like maritime Dornier aircraft that are crucial for surveillance.

Once the terrorists were close to the shore, they breached the third and innermost layer of security, the coastal police. The ease with which they managed to land with a sizeable amount of arms and ammunition confirmed what experts have long known — the marine wings of police forces are woefully short of resources and manpower to guard the shore. While a detailed Coastal Security Plan has been drawn up, most of it has not been implemented.

Intelligence agencies have pointed out the vulnerability of the coastline in various reports and studies. A recent Central Intelligence Report had even warned the Gujarat frontier BSF and the Coast Guard about some new launching pads and getaways for terrorists that had come up in the Thatta and Badin districts of Pakistan in the last one year. Another intelligence report had also alerted security agencies about the possible entry of terrorists into India by sea. "The input received by us specifically mentioned Maharashtra and Mumbai," an officer said. Gujarat intelligence, too, had alerted the BSF and the Coast Guard about the increasing vulnerability of the coast to illegal infiltration and smuggling.

Finally, a 19-page document called the seamen's identity card, used by mechanised boats in India, allows holders to enter and exit ports without any other supporting document. This is the only travel document in the country that is issued without any background check.

DURING

While all these warnings illustrated the sorry BEFORE situation, on the DURING level the pitiably poor preparedness of the police sharply contrasted with the meticulous planning with which the terrorists mounted the multiple attack on Mumbai. Referring to the attack on the Taj Mahal Hotel, Ratan Tata said, "I think in the Taj the first contingent came with three policemen, and they were ill-equipped... In fact one got killed, the other got shot badly, and one remained."

Far more damning was the *Mumbai Mirror* report on the "Night of Terror", which, it said, "completely exposed Mumbai cops' underbelly. It has always been soft, vulnerable and even fools don't believe in the claim that the force is second-best to only the Scotland Yard. How many times have experts reminded policemen of the need for modern weapons and thorough training to fight the new-age terrorists? On the same night the terrorists roamed around freely with their AK-47s and carbines, as the policemen looked on haplessly with their outdated 303 rifles. In front of the horrified eyes of one of our reporters, a policeman asked his colleague if the weapon he was handling was an automatic. He then asked his colleague how it should be loaded. And what about the quality of the so-called bullet-proof vests and helmets that were so easily pierced by the terrorists' bullets?"

Commenting on them, the *Indian Express* added: "The entire force was greatly disadvantaged by heavy bulletproof jackets that didn't halt bullets from AK 47s, and helmets that provided no real protection. The danger of this was brought home by two tragic events – bullets penetrating ACP Ashok Kamte's head in spite of his helmet, and ATS chief Hemant Karkare succumbing to bullet injuries on his chest in spite of his bulletproof jacket."

"The Mumbai police had ordered bulletproof jackets in bulk in 1992. The department purchased another batch of jackets in 2002, but surprisingly, there was no improvement in weight or design. Now it has 885 jackets, of which 109 cannot be used at all, 715 have been distributed among policemen and 61 are lying in the storeroom unused."

On the quality of helmets bought for the police force, Vinay Korgaonkar, Additional Commissioner of Police (protection), said most police personnel deployed in the city wear helmets with a metallic netted veil. "Such helmets are effective only against stone-pelting, not bullets from sophisticated firearms."

To compound the situation, the Maharashtra Anti-Terrorism Squad (ATS) headquarters in Mumbai got its first bulletproof vehicle, for the use of its chief Hemant Karkare, in October, which he checked out once but hardly used it again. On November 26 he and two other officers were shot dead in a regular police vehicle.

The ATS had asked for bullet-proof vehicles earlier this year, and orders were placed for two vehicles, a Tata Safari which was delivered a month before Karkare was killed, and a Mahindra Scorpio which arrived 10 days after the tragedy. Karkare preferred his Tata Indigo or Chevrolet Tavera. Said an officer, "Sir never used this (bullet-proof) vehicle, except once when it had just arrived. He just took one ride to see how it was. After that it was never used." The Maharashtra government has 18 bullet-proof Ambassador cars for the use of VVIPs, including the Chief Minister, his deputy and others with Z category security, but the two ATS SUVs were the first bullet-proof vehicles for the state police.

AFTER

On the AFTER level too things were equally bad. Having failed to prevent the Mumbai terror strike despite being warned that Jihadis would be using the sea route to reach India, the Navy Chief admitted a "systemic failure" on the part of the security and intelligence gathering establishment. At the same time he maintained that the warnings were general in nature and not specific, so there was no actionable intelligence.

Referring to reports that the Coast Guard had intercepted the fishing vessel Kuber but let it pass after a check, Adm. Mehta said there were about 1.5 lakh fishing trawlers registered in India, over 50,000 of them in Gujarat and Maharashtra alone. "Even if one-tenth of that number is in Mumbai, something like 5,000 people are coming in or going out every day," he said. "This vessel was challenged by the Coast Guard, but the ship occupants had shown their valid papers and moved on."

Then again, *apropos* the officially-noticed suspicious flights of unknown aircraft in the region of the 36 Lakshadweep islands, coastal security is a sorry joke. "Intelligence gathering in the islands," the previously - mentioned government task force recorded, "is carried out by one inspector, one sub-inspector, one head constable and three constables working in the special branch at Kavaratti", just one of the 36 islands. "Intelligence gathering in all other islands is carried out by one head constable/constable who reports to the OIC (officer in charge) of the police station, who in turn passes it on to the inspector (special branch) at Kavaratti."

What has happened since, what is the position today? A person who has held the highest posts in intelligence said – exactly what it was then, with one difference. With the upgradation of all posts, the inspector (special branch) at Kavaratti is now designated not as officer in charge, but as joint assistant director or deputy central intelligence officer, depending on his cadre. As for the other recommendations – patrolling, setting up sensors, and a host of other things, they are as they were.

As for bewaring the "Flying Jihadi", after the auditors blew the lid off the country's vulnerable air defence system, A K Antony, our Defence

Minister, (on 25th Oct.) made the glaring admission that India's guards had been down for the last two decades. He corroborated what the Comptroller and Auditor General had highlighted in his latest report tabled in Parliament stating the Indian Air Force has been operating an outdated surveillance system.

The defence minister admitted that military decision-makers have failed to provide adequate number of radars to IAF. What made the matter worse is the fact that acquisition plans for including more radars have been pending for the last 18 years. The 18-year-old files have begun to move only now, he said, explaining the sorry state of affairs of the country's top planners. "We are lagging behind. We could have most modem radars and equipment," he said. The IAF had indicated its requirement of surveillance systems long back. Senior IAF officials have gone on record saying several areas of the country were exposed to aerial threats.

The sum and substance of this whole sorry story is that 26/11 was a systemic failure.

Far more disturbing, while the latest horrendous event so vividly exposed the system's inability to meet a specific challenge, it also exemplified India's dismal failure to fight the war on terror as a whole. This has been extensively dwelt upon by security experts and media analysts. Their emphasis may differ from individual to individual, but one factor is common—scathing criticism.

For instance, MK Dhar, former Jt. Director of the Intelligence Bureau, has bluntly commented on the non-performance of the Indian security apparatus as a whole in his interview to the *Mumbai Mirror*, published on September 2, 2007 under the heading *India has ZERO Intelligence*. Dhar says India is so vulnerable to terrorism and its track record in combating it so pathetic because of the politico-police nexus, compounded by inefficient intelligence agencies. At a deeper level he says the gravity of the terror situation is a reflection of the fact that in India the "secular fence" is very "fragile", as the so-called secular parties tend to blatantly placate certain segments of the society. A couple of excerpts:

"How well prepared are intelligence agencies to combat these frequent blasts?"

Our preparations cover only 20 per cent of the threat quantum. The IB is very thinly spread on the ground. They have very little access into the target community and subversive cells set up by foreign agencies. They are mostly ineffective in tracking down foreign Jihadis.

The cops are busy either with law and order or *bandobast* duties and carrying out assignments given by political masters. The others are busy scavenging *hafta*. Politicians and Mafia sleep under the common bed-sheet in India. It is something that affects our nation's security.

Do you think the IB and RAW continue to be used by politicians for their own personal ends?

Regretfully, I have to admit that the IB, CBI and RAW are political pawns. Similarly, the intelligence wings of state police are used for petty political pursuits. This is the biggest abuse of our democracy. Our police cannot be converted into an armed wing of our ruling political parties.

Harsh Reality

Offering the same analysis of the sorry situation, economist Bibek Debroy writes in his article titled *To Be a Hard State* in the *Times of India* of August 28, 2007: "The harsh reality is that a lethal blend of corruption, inefficiency and political meddling has enfeebled our criminal justice administration and sapped the police of will and strength to take on those killing the innocent." Relating this to the investigation going on in the Hyderabad carnage, he says there are pointers to suggest that the loss of life could have been averted if the police had been allowed to pick up some of the Jihadi footsoldiers who found sanctuary in pockets of Hyderabad's Walled City.

Another very disturbing aspect of the Hyderabad event which Debroy points out is the brazen attitude of the democratic processes by openly anti-national, even subversive, elements. The fundamentalist Muslim body Majlis-e-Ittehad ul-Muslimeen (MIM) had one Lok Sabha seat and four Assembly seats. It supports the UPA at the Centre and the Congress Government in Andhra, and, writes Debroy, "has distinguished itself by opposing a motion in the Andhra Assembly condemning 9/11, and attacking Tasleema Nasreen in August 2007. A few days before the Hyderabad blasts MIM criticised Hyderabad's anti-terrorist squad for adopting a hard line approach to terror... Has anyone from the Central or State government uttered a word against MIM? Not that I know of."

Staggering Explosives Thefts

The two main points Dhar made in his interview to the press were that the police are corrupt and the intelligence agencies are ineffective. This calamitous combination can have no more telling an example than the staggering scale on which deadly explosives are being stolen virtually all over the country. This was revealed in an investigation carried out by the *Indian Express* and published on October 6-7, 2007:

Tonnes and tonnes of explosives are stolen, with no trace. And this from licensed manufacturers across the country. Not only is there no record of what reaches whose hands, even the trail of such material is virtually impossible to trace after a terror attack. There is colossal theft and diversion of explosives from the approximately 22,000 licensed explosives manufacturers in the country. According to official records, in just two years, 2004–2006, for which data is complete, the scale of theft is staggering: 86,899 detonators, 20,150 kg of slurry explosives, 52,740 metres of detonating fuse, and 418 kg of gelatin sticks, plus huge quantities of explosive cartridges and boosters stolen from stores. Added to this, ammonium nitrate, a chemical freely sold in the market, can be mixed with fuel oil and sulphur and used for lethal strikes with devastating effect. It was mixed with RDX for the Varanasi blasts in March 2006, in the Mumbai local trains blasts, in Malegaon, and in Hyderabad.

Days after the serial bomb blasts in New Delhi, the home ministry was sent a reminder by the Department of Industrial Policy and Promotion of the urgency for making amendments in laws to regulate sale of ammonium nitrate. The reminder — and its timing—best illustrates the manner in which the country's top security establishment frittered away the opportunity to come up with a new system of regulation of manufacture and pilferage of ammonium nitrate, the most commonly used explosive in all major terror attacks.

For, ironically, it was the home ministry itself that chaired a "highest-level" committee to examine all aspects of the explosive problem. Its terms of reference were spot on: to put in place an accountable regime for manufacture, supply and movement of explosives, prevention of pilferage and misuse of explosive materials and regulation of manufacture and sale of ammonium nitrate. Deadline for the committee's report: three months. Chaired by Home Secretary Madhukar Gupta, the panel included the top brass of the security establishment – Secretary, Defence, Industrial Promotion and Revenue as well as Chairman of the Ordnance Factory Board, the Director, Intelligence Bureau, and Secretary, Research and Analysis Wing. The report is so far nowhere in sight.

To cap it all, when two correspondents of the *Outlook* Weekly, Saikat Datta and Jaideep Mazumdar, were told – Go, "buy" some RDX, they did just that–bought some RDX ! In a startling report from Murshidabad titled *How We Bought RDX* in the journal's issue of October 2, 2006 they described how they found that this deadly explosive may be more easily available than the police and intelligence agencies would have everyone believe.

Fatal Flaw

The failure of the state's machinery to protect the citizen is certainly a substantial contributory factor in terrorists having a field day in India. However, at a deeper level there is a fundamental reason, which may be called the malaise of the mindset. For winning the war on terror, the Indian mindset is everything that it should not be. Elaborating on this fatal flow, Diwakar of *TNN* wrote in his dispatch on August 28, 2007:

"The response to the latest terror outrage in Hyderabad was followed by the by-now familiar vows to bring the culprits to book, levelling charges, even if well-formed, against Pakistan and Bangladesh, condolences for victims, and review meetings from the Prime Minister down".

For a country that, for more than two decades now, has been bled by relentless terrorist attacks, India has been in a state of denial, first by claiming that no Indian was messed up with al-Qaeda, and when that proved wrong, describing this vicious campaign of violence as the handiwork of a "handful of misguided youth."

A far-more severe indictment of the Indian non-response to terrorism comes from reputed columnist Brahma Chellany. Dubbing it "hand wringing", he wrote in an article in *Hindustan Times* on November 8, 2005: "India has already put the bombings behind it and gone back to what now defines it – partisan politics, scandal, and cricket. It is business as usual." The whole piece damns India's utter lack of a "credible counterterror strategy." Some telling excerpts:

No Political Will

"It does not need an outgoing Chief Justice of India to remind fellow-citizens that "we don't have the political will to fight terrorism." That failing is manifest from India's reluctance to wage it own war on terror... Not only is there no will, the Indian system has also become so effete that the state instruments are unable to deliver even on the odd occasion when the leadership displays a political spine."

"It is as if the Indian state has come to accept terrorist strikes as the products of its unalterable geography or destiny. That may help explain why India's response to Pakistan's strategy of bleeding by "a thousand cuts" has been survival by a thousand bandages."

"Whenever India is tested by the horror of terrorism, it responds in a preset way with brave words that serve as a cover to do nothing."

"To know why transnational terrorists fancy India as an easy target, just compare New Delhi's reluctance to impose costs on terrorists and their sponsors with the declared policy of several democracies not to let any terror attack go unpunished. Indeed, India has advertised itself as a soft target by striking deals with terrorists..."

"If India is not to compound its problems, it needs to shed its lackadaisical ways and take the battle to the springboard of terrorism... For India, terrorism is an existential battle... The only defence against the sly, murderous terrorists is offence aimed at hounding, disrupting, and smashing their cells, networks and safe havens. Against covert, unconventional aggression, counteraction must also employ clandestine, unconventional methods..."

Still more stringent is the reaction of journalist-MP and former Central Minister Arun Shourie. Explaining the "weakened and confused" state of the society he wrote:

"The responsibility lies as much with those who have dissipated national resolve, who have made nationalism a dirty word. That set includes the media as much as politicians. 60-70,000 killed by terrorism and we are still debating whether we should have a federal investigating agency. 60-70,000 killed by terrorists and we are still debating whether we should have a special law to bring them to book. Of course, we must have the agency. Of course we must have the sternest law in the world. But having the law is not enough. We must enforce it".

"And enforcing the law means carrying out sentences that the law provides. The Parliament of India is attacked, guards are killed, one of the killers is tried and convicted, the sentence is confirmed by the Supreme Court, and, eight years after the assault his "papers are still being processed," indeed there are signature campaigns against executing the sentence. Given these circumstances, the best thing for a terrorist is to succeed in his mission and then get caught. He will get the best lawyers to defend him. He will get judges who are ever so solicitous about his rights, ever so finicky about procedures. And, of course, he will get activists to shoot off press statements on his behalf. Lawyers better, judges more solicitous, activists more articulate and better networked than any in his own country".

"The society has to be clear in its mind. This is, it has for 20 years been, war. It can be won only by overwhelming the adversary ... not by running after the terrorist, but by outrunning him, indeed by overrunning him. Not an eye for an eye. For an eye, both eyes. Not a tooth for a tooth. For a tooth, the whole jaw".

Turki ka Jawab

These same points Shourie succinctly summed up in his speech in Parliament. In fact his call for the needed response to Pakistan is robust and manly enough to remind one of Shivaji's famous retort to Aurangzeb: *Turki ka jawab Turki mein milega.*

Shourie's speech in Parliament made 10 points with clarity and force.

"Please," he said –

- Stop running to "mummy"! this business of putting faith that somebody else will do our work for us.
- Stop this miscalled peace process.
- Shed denial. Every time in this House there was a debate on internal security, the home minister was in total denial.
- You have again read out a set of measures. Implement it.
- Prepare for the next form of assault. We are always preparing for the last.
- Stop seeing these incidents, whether in Assam or anywhere else, as single, discreet, isolated incidents.
- They are part of a sequence for a war of attrition. It is a war.
- Do not go by the joint statements that their leaders sign with you.

- No war can be won with a strategy of permanent defence. You must make those who control and orchestrate such a war to pay.
- Realise that no war is won with minimal force. It is won by overwhelming the enemy. Not an eye-for-an-eye, not a-tooth-for-a-tooth. For an eye, both eyes ! For a tooth, the whole jaw !

To this forceful, all-round condemnation by concerned Indians Parthasarathy adds ridicule of the Government's decision to set up an "anti-terrorism institutional mechanism" jointly with Pakistan. Writing in *Blitz* in September 2006 that the proposal defies all comprehension, he added with biting sarcasm: "Agreeing to such a "mechanism" would be akin to setting up a Joint Investigative Team of Dawood Ibrahim and the CBI to investigate the 1993 Mumbai bomb blasts, or setting up yet another "task force" of Maulana Masood Azhar of the Jaish-e-Mohammad and the CBI to investigate the IC-814 hijacking, or the December 13, 2001 attack on Parliament."

36

COUNTERMEASURES

Think Tank Thinking

Enough is Enough

Reacting to the terror war on Mumbai in November 2008 an outraged people across India declared "enough is enough", and proposed a variety of responses, ranging from the typically passive to the refreshingly assertive ... from petition to retaliation.

The passive response expectedly came from the President of India. She expressed the need for adequate security training for the citizen. By way of an organized expression of more or less the same mindset, a "Netizen" of Mumbai by name Umesh Chhajed launched a massive online petition to the Prime Minister demanding destruction of all terrorist training camps, internal terror support networks, and strengthening of police force on the website www.PetitionOnline.com. After reading various media reports and watching "irresponsible comments" of political leaders, Chhajed drafted a pointed agenda. The petition stated: "Three urgent steps need to be taken to send a signal to the perpetrators and the victims that this time round, Indian political leadership will take visible action and walk the talk. Very simply, we want assertive action in response to the recent terror incidents (mini-war) in Mumbai." This is followed by the three points. The petition also says that Mumbai's 26/11 should be treated as India's 9/11.

RR Raina, who works as a financial analyst in Pune and signed the petition said: "This is exactly what I had wanted to do. Though I do not think that the present government will take any strong step, the voice of commoners like me will at least reach the government records through this petition." Like Raina, many others not only from India, but also from the USA, Britain, Japan and Netherlands feel the same way.

Within the first few days of kick-starting, more than one lakh Netizens had already signed the memorandum. The target was one million signatures.

On a more basic level Gujarat Chief Minister proposed the setting up of a Defence University. In a similar vein Mumbai's Rambhau Mhalgi Prabodhini, a deemed university recognised by UNESCO, has been urged by this writer to set up a "Suraksha Vidyapeeth" (Citizens' Defence

Academy) with a comprehensive syllabus ranging from combat training and intelligence-gathering techniques to war history, geopolitics and terrorism-related psychology. He has also urged Prabodhini to prepare a comprehensive database of terrorists and terrorist organisations. (During the investigations into the twin bomb-blasts in Hyderabad the media had reported that the investigators were hampered by the fact that the police had no such database.)

Distinguished legal luminary Soli Sorabjee filed a PIL stressing the distressing fact that Mumbai Police were "woefully underarmed and understaffed". Arm them with modern weapons, his PIL demanded.

Going from defence to offence one citizen's proposed response was training private commandos who could even launch covert action inside Pakistan.

So far as the Government of India's response was concerned, a retaliatory war was ruled out, but, in the opinion of the Americans, retaliatory strikes cannot be. Rather, if Pakistan did not act, India had the right to strike, they said, down from President Obama. When, during a post-Mumbai visit to Pakistan, US senator McCain was asked what the US would do if India decides to take action, he replied, "We were angry after 9/11. This is India's 9/11. We cannot tell India not to act when that is what we did..."

Finally, the response of reasoned retaliation proposed by Subramanian Swamy is worth a quote. In his column in *Organiser* he recently wrote: "Coming to the question of retaliation for the Mumbai 26/11 attack, I advocate US-Israel-India coordinated aerial strikes at all the prominent training bases of the LeT and JeM in PoK, which action, since it would be on a part of India, will not mean an act of war, whatever Pakistan may think. This is the mirror-image of the argument that Pakistan itself had used while invading India in 1999 in the Kargil sector, that is, since they consider J&K not a part of India, hence Pakistan can invade it!"

While these and many other similar responses are generally on the individual level, an organised, systematic, armed response to Pakistan's terror war on India has also been chalked out by a body of experts from military and intelligence agencies. Describing it in his book *Nefarious Activities of Pakistan's ISI,* Col. Shyam Kumar reviews the ISI threat to India by way of some general observations thus:

"We have not yet been able to fully deal with ISI. In fact, we are only reacting to ISI activities...The ISI has, from its small and seemingly innocuous beginnings in 1948, steadily developed into the principal instrument of Pakistan's state-sponsorship of terrorism directed against India. This sinister organization today poses a grave and escalating threat not merely to India's internal security but to our very national fabric...A review of the capabilities and objectives of the ISI leads to the inevitable conclusion that India would have to live with an intractable Pakistan..."

"Taking the ground realities into account," says the author," a Think Tank comprising senior retired officers of the Army, Police and Intelligence organisations be constituted to suggest measures which could supplement the on-going efforts of our security agencies in neutralising the ISI's designs and activities". "This Think Tank," says the book, "has taken note of the proliferation of the ISI network in various parts of the country from UP to Kerala, as also of three potentially explosive factors which, in its view, are likely to further encourage the ISI towards achieving its ambitious plan of promoting transborder terrorism and balkanizing India through the medium of Sikh and Kashmiri militant organisations as well as the North-Eastern Insurgent outfits."

First, with their surrogates, the Taliban, now controlling nearly 90 per cent of Afghanistan, the ISI is in a position to divert a sizable number of highly committed and battle-hardened Mujahideen to the so-called "Jehad" in Kashmir. In fact, such a diversion is not only operationally feasible, but also politically necessary for the ISI, given the destabilizing potential of a large mass of highly trained and motivated mercenaries floating idle within Pakistan itself.

Secondly, in the wake of the humiliating defeat suffered by Pakistan in Kargil, the ISI could be expected to upgrade the level of the on-going proxy war in Kashmir and other parts of the country. History bears ample testimony to this prognosis, since Pakistan's defeats in the 1965 and 1971 wars were followed by significant upswings in ISI-sponsored, violence and subversion in both Punjab and Kashmir. Ominously, the former Pakistan Prime Minister Nawaz Sharif, before he was overthrown by the military coup, had threatened that "there will be many more Kargils" unless the Kashmir problem is solved. Gen. Parvez Musharraf had gone a step further by declaring, "Even if the Kashmir problem is solved, confrontation with India will continue". Another menacing dimension has been added by the "Jehad" call recently given against India and US by Osama bin Laden."

The Think Tank's members have mapped out a comprehensive strategy encompassing the operational, intelligence, administrative, psy-war and economic countermeasures for combating the ISI. This strategy does not envisage systemic changes in the present security establishment, but focuses on mobilising the existing apparatus to deal with the ever-widening and deepening ISI infrastructure.

The recommendations of the think tank, which are "optional," are as follows:

India's operational response ought to be hinged on two clearly discernible premises. First, with ISI-sponsored mercenaries now specially targeting Army campuses, paramilitary installations and killing uniformed personnel with impunity, there is an urgent need to prepare a blueprint for anti-ISI operations with clearly defined objectives. Second, it needs to be recognised that in context and dimension of the proxy war in Kashmir, the para-military forces have a limited role. Instead, the prevailing situation dictates that counter-ISI operations in Kashmir be entrusted to the Army, which is better equipped both mentally and physically.

The NSG was created in 1986 to combat terrorist activities but is now being used extensively for VIP security — a role not envisaged under the NSG Act. The NSG's original role should be restored so that this crack outfit may be used exclusively for combating extremist activities in J & K and North-East in particular, as well as in other parts of the country, whenever required. If this is not operationally possible, a VIP Security Force may be raised separately so that the NSG can perform the role for which it was created.

In a very similar suggestion N. Vittal, former CVC, said the huge force of Jawans who retire every year could form a parallel force to tackle the menace of terrorism. In his weekly column in *Mumbai Mirror* on February 11, 2008 Vittal wrote:

"What can the Central government do to tackle terrorism? There is a way out. There is an important source of disciplined manpower available in the country. This has not been effectively tapped so far. I refer to the enormous number of ex-servicemen and jawans who retire from the defence services every year."

"Would it not be worthwhile, especially in the context of terrorist threats, to use the disciplined force of ex-servicemen and create a parallel police force to specifically tackle the problems of terrorism and Naxalism? This is an idea, perhaps, whose time has come."

Apart from such security and police forces, the Think Tank suggestions also conclude on a proactive note:

"There is a need for examining the feasibility of proactive and more aggressive countermeasures to neutralise the ISI's activities. Such measures could include covert operations inside Pakistan, which would drive home to the ISI that India is more than capable of paying Pakistan back in the same coin."

Exactly the same sentiments were expressed by columnist Rajiv Shukla, who is a Congress MP, while concluding a piece titled *Dimensions of the biggest ever threat to the Indian nation-state* in the *Indian Express*. He wrote:

"With available evidence indicating that the hydra-headed agency (ISI) has penetrated deep into the western, central and southern parts of the country, it is believed that both the Union Government and its intelligence agencies are fighting a losing battle. In fact, so deep is the sense of dejection on this score that some responsible ministers were recently moved to suggest, in all seriousness, that there was only one sure way of nullifying the ISI – encouraging and actively supporting terrorism in Pakistan."

This astonishingly bold suggestion presupposed covert action, something that Brahma Chellany too bluntly recommended when he called for "hounding and smashing" ISI networks in India, saying, "against covert, unconventional aggression, counteraction must also employ clandestine, unconventional methods."

37

THREAT PERCEPTION

The Multiple Ummah

ISI is a threat to India. It poses a clear and present danger that keeps growing by the day as its tentacles spread virtually unchecked across India. Hence, a think tank of experts from the Army, Police and Intelligence devoting itself to identifying ways and means of meeting this menace is welcome.

But should India's threat perception stop at ISI? Does not India need a hard look at a deeper level? The answer lies in some harsh truths that must be faced.

The very first of them is that ISI is a tool of Pakistan, Pakistan is a terrorist state that swears by Islam, and as such it is part and parcel of international Islamic terrorism. In other words, ISI's Indian agenda is not a military agenda, nor a political agenda, it is an Islamic agenda. Today's Islamic terrorism in India has one, specific goal: To convert the *Dar-ul Harab* India of today into a *Dar-ul Islam* of tomorrow. Judging by the secret writings of Maulvis in circulation in Saudi Arabia, they consider as unacceptable the failure of 800 years of Islamic rule in this country to convert India into a 100 per cent Muslim nation, as they did in Afghanistan, Iraq, Iran, Egypt etc. This is the unfulfilled mission that is now sought to be accomplished.

First Threat Ummah

In his book *Islam* Anwar Shaikh calls it *The Arab Imperialism,* for the establishment of which the Quran even preaches divine politics, declaring that Believers are "Allah's Party" and non-believers Satan's Party. And as the end and aim of all party politics is dominance, so is that of Islam.

Elaborating this fundamental premise in an article in *Indian Express* of December 31, 2007 on Islam, in which he calls it one of "the Middle East traditions", Arun Shourie wrote:

"When a tradition has the following elements, as each of the three Middle Eastern traditions has, as do the secular traditions of the West – Nazism, Marxism-Leninism – it will invariably be exclusivist, intolerant and aggressive:

Intolerant Reality

- Reality is simple.
- It has been revealed to one man.
- He has put it in one Book.
- That Book is inerrant as well as exhaustive, so that whatever is in it is true, that it is true for all time, and that whatever is not in it or is contrary to what is in it, is false or useless or worse.
- But the Book is difficult to understand, hence you need a guide, an intermediary, a monitor, in a word, the Church, the Ulema, or the Party.
- There is only one Message. As the Message is the 'Truth, the whole Truth and nothing but the Truth,' those who do not accept the Message are cursed, worse, they are thwarting the Will of Allah, or its equivalent – the March of History in Marxism-Leninism.
- Hence, it is the duty of every believer to use all means to make them accept the Message, and if they refuse, to vanquish them altogether.

When these elements are present, the tradition will have one singular objective: dominance. It will become an ideology of power, a dogma that rationalizes everything in the pursuit of hegemony. The dogma will necessarily gravitate to, among other things, violence."

But violence for the sake of Islam is holy, it is Jihad, "holy war".

Rewards for Jihad

"That is why in the Hadis we find the Prophet repeatedly enumerating the boons that accrue to the martyr from Jihad, from killing and being killed in the Cause."

At the same time the definition of Jihad has been made so wide that every Muslim can enjoy the pious satisfaction of being a Jihadi and worthy of a reward for it.

Explaining this, Shourie writes:

"The pre-eminent rewards, of course, accrue to the one who joins in the fighting himself, the Prophet declares in scores of Hadis. But even the one who does not do so directly will be rewarded for every bit of assistance that he gives for the establishment, defence and spread of Islam, the Prophet declares. When a man keeps a horse for the purpose of Jihad, tying it with a long tether on a meadow or in a garden... whatever it eats from the area of the meadow or the garden where it is tied will be counted as good deeds for his benefit, and if it should break its rope and jump over one or two hillocks then all its dung and its footmarks will be written as good deeds for him."And again, even more generally, "If somebody keeps a horse in Allah's Cause motivated by his belief in His Promise, then he will be rewarded on the Day of Resurrection for what the horse has eaten or drunk and for its dung and urine." *Sahih al-Bukhari*, 52.44, 49,105, similarly, Muwatta' Imam Malik, 951, *Mishkat al-Masabih*, Book XVIII, Volume II, p. 822. The Hadis compilations as well as books on Shariah are filled with scores and scores of such exhortations and promises."

By contrast, "He who does not join the warlike expedition (Jihad) will be smitten by Allah with a sudden calamity." Hence, commands the Prophet, "Use your property, your persons and your tongues in striving against the polytheists." (*Sunan Abu Dawud*, 2496-98).

And there is a small something that, when added, would enhance Islamic piety — hatred. A book found in a mosque in the US called upon Muslims to "hate the infidels for their religion for Allah's sake." "In fact, the entire Islamic approach towards the non-Muslims is based on hatred, ill will and animosity", writes Anwar Sheikh in *Islam and Terrorism* (Principality Publishers, Cardiff, UK, 2004).

In short, being a Jihadi is that simple, so even those who neither kill nor get killed are ordained to engage in a Jihad against all infidels everywhere, and that includes the hateful Hindus.

On the societal level this ingrained animus towards the infidel, instilled in the Muslim mindset by strident Quranic teachings like those quoted above, reflects itself in various ways of discrimination against the Hindu. This has been described in various international reports. In recent times 10,000 Hindu temples were destroyed in Malaysia during an iconoclastic frenzy. In Pakistan there was a campaign to remove a judge because he was a Hindu.

This discrimination is even codified into laws and regulations. In Saudi Arabia, Hindus cannot worship even in the privacy of their homes. There is also a law there by which the worth of a Hindu life is half that of a Muslim. In Pakistan the testimony of a Hindu is worth half that of a Muslim. In Malaysia there have been bizarre cases in which a dead Hindu was declared by the court to have been a Muslim.

An unlikely factor that seems to strengthen the common Muslim's faith in his faith is ignorance. Describing the abysmal ignorance prevailing in the Ummah, the Muslim Brotherhood worldwide, Hussain Haqqani, Pakistani diplomat-columnist, wrote a revealing article that bears extensive reproduction:

"The contemporary Muslim fascination for conspiracy theories limits the capacity for rational discussion of international affairs".

Polio Conspiracy !

"The acceptance of rumours and the readiness to embrace the notion of a conspiracy does not apply exclusively to the realm of politics. Villagers in rural Nigeria are refusing to administer the polio vaccine to their infant children out of fear that the vaccine will make their offspring sterile."

"Some religious leaders in Pakistan's Pashtun tribal areas bordering Afghanistan have also voiced concerns about a "Western-Zionist conspiracy" to sterilise the next generation of Muslims as part of what they allege is an "ongoing war against Islam."

'Mobile' Conspiracy

"Mobile phones and internet, the pervasiveness of which is often cited as a measure of a society's progress and modernity, have become a means of spreading fear in the Muslim world. Text messages originating from the Pakistani city of Sialkot recently warned people of a virus if people answered phone calls from certain numbers. The virus would not hurt the phone, the messages said, but would kill the recipient".

"The panic caused by the rumours forced the Pakistan Telecommunication Authority to issue a denial. Phone companies sent out text messages urging people to be calm. A newspaper rejected the rumour but featured the headline "Killer Mobile Virus."

"A text message widely circulated in an Arab country claimed that trucks carrying a million melons had been smuggled across the country's northern border and the melons were contaminated with the HIV virus. No one paid attention to the fact that the HIV virus cannot be transmitted by eating melons".

Literate Illiterates

"The Muslim world has a high rate of illiteracy, but ignorance reflected by the readiness to believe unverified claims is not just a function of illiteracy. It is a function of bigotry and fear. Literate Muslims, such as those involved in the text message rumour-mongering, are as vulnerable to ignorant behaviour as illiterate ones".

"Conspiracy theories have been popular among Muslims since the twilight years of the Ottoman Empire as a way of explaining the powerlessness of a community that was at one time the world's economic, scientific, political and military leader. The erosion of the leadership position of Muslims coincided with the West's gradual technological ascendancy. Soon after the Ottomans took over Constantinople, Johann Gutenberg printed a Bible using metal plates".

Banned Printing

"Printing was introduced into the Ottoman Empire during the reign of Sultan Bayazid II (1481–1512) only to be virtually banned for use by Muslims in 1485. In Europe a full-grown book industry evolved, facilitating wide dissemination of ideas and knowledge. By 1501 more than a thousand printing presses had produced about 35,000 titles with ten million copies. But in the Ottoman Empire only Christians and Jews used printing technology".

"The Persian, Mughal and Ottoman empires controlled vast lands and resources, but many important scientific discoveries and inventions since the fifteenth century came about in Europe and not in the Muslim lands. Ignorance is an attitude, and the world's Muslims have to analyse, debate and face it before they can deal with it".

Muslim Universities

"The 57 member countries of the Organisation of Islamic Conference (OIC) have around 500 universities compared with more than five thousand universities in the United States and more than eight thousand in India. In 2004, Shanghai Jiao Tong University compiled an 'Academic Ranking of World Universities', and none of the universities from Muslim-majority states was included in the top 500. There is only one university for every 3 million Muslims".

Haqqani concludes with the observation – rather, admission – that the Muslims are obsessed with the tendency to accept rumours as fact and a readiness to believe anything that suggests a non-Muslim conspiracy to weaken or undermine the Muslims.

This is actually happening in Pakistan. According to recent press reports from the FATA region along the Afghan border the government's anti-polio campaign is opposed by Mullahs and Maulavis saying it is a foreign ploy to sterilise Pakistanis. A doctor conducting the vaccination drive in the Bajaur region was actually killed in a bomb blast.

And in India this ignorance is being exploited. For instance, the Mumbai Police had to file an affidavit with a tribunal justifying continuation of the ban on SIMI on the ground that it was trying to sabotage the pulse polio campaign in Muslim areas of Maharashtra by propagating that the polio dose was a dreadful way to cause impotency.

Doctrine of Dominance

The nonviolent aspect of Jehad was an artful device with which the Prophet ensured that in every Muslim mind there was an unalterable equation between Jehad and piety that pointed the way to paradise. Having achieved this, however, he bluntly declared, "Paradise lies under the shades of swords" (*Al-Bokhari*, vol. 4). That is, the Believer cannot attain Paradise except with the sword of Jehad in hand. This has been described at length by Anwar Shaikh, an acknowledged scholar of Islam, in his book *Islam: Sex and Violence* in the chapter *Jehad and Paradise*, which is peppered with quotes from a number of Hadiths.

A small selection:

1. "God has bought from the faithful their selves and their belongings against the gift of paradise, they fight in the way of Allah, they kill and get killed, that is a promise binding on Allah..." (*Repentance* 9:110)

2. Acting as Allah's soldier for one night in a battlefield is superior to saying prayers at home for 2000 years." (*Ibn-e-Majah*, vol. 2, p. 166)
3. The Prophet said: "If a man participates in a Jehad for only as long as it takes to milk a she-camel, he becomes entitled to paradise." (*Ibn-e-Majah*, vol. 2, p. 173).

To cap it all

The Prophet said, "He who murders another, property of the murdered becomes property of the murderer." (*Ibn-e-Majah*, vol. 2, p. 183)

And why murder? Because

"The worst of beasts in Allah's sight are the ungrateful who will not believe." (*Spoils of War*: 55).

Hence the cardinal point of Jehad which, says Anwar Shaikh, "must be noted carefully" is that "Jehad is all about massacre, mutilation and misery, and not about any moral, social or humanitarian service as the Muslim divines pretend." Again in *Islam and Terrorism* Shaikh writes, "It is said Jehad is of two types: One means controlling one's self through prayer and self-discipline. No matter how laudable that may sound, it is a misinterpretation of Jehad. The true Jehad is fighting with the sword (*Jehad-bis-saif*)." At another place in the book he says, "Jehad is a sacred name of terror", and so the true Believer is a "committed terrorist" by faith. In support of this assertion he gives quotes from the Quran, including *House of Imran* (3:142-45), which says, "We (Allah) will cast terror into the hearts of the unbelievers."

It was this terror-oriented Quranic definition of Jehad, preached 1500 years ago, that was refined by Mohammed bin Wahab in the 18th century, and in present times by many a Mullah, led by Mohammed Abdullah Azam, Osama bin Laden's mentor and al-Qaeda's ideologue. Wahab's preaching, known as Wahabism, was called "the most violent and fanatical version of Islam" by Bernard Lewis, leading Western scholar of Islam. Azam preached: "Jihad is holy fighting in Allah's cause with full force of numbers and weapons. By Jehad Islam is established."

The Infidel

The Infidel against whom Jehad is to be relentlessly waged is determined by Fatwas issued from time to time across the Muslim world, their common feature being that they are all ominously wide-ranging in their scope. According to one such Fatwa issued by Islamic scholars in recent years, all people living in infidel states, whether soldiers or civilians, are infidels, and hence deserve death in Jehad. This is said to be in imitation of the life and conduct of Prophet Mohammad in his policy of *ahl al-dhimma*, "retaliation of 'dhimmies'." In April 2002 Sheikh Hamid al-Ali, a lecturer on Islamic Culture in Kuwait and a leader of the radical Salafist sect, had issued a Fatwa laying down the circumstances in which it was permitted to kill civilians in the cause of Jehad. A few months later, on June 28, 2002, 28 scholars of the Al-Azhar University in Egypt declared that killing large numbers of Israeli civilians in Palestinian suicide bombing attacks was the "noblest act of Jehad". The Al-Azhar scholars argued that in conducting Jehad there is no need to make any distinction between soldiers and civilians, but between peace-seekers (Muslims) and war-mongers – "infidels" defined as "combatants, no matter what kind of clothes they wear."

Fanatical Wahabism

Since the 1970s the Saudi Arab Government has been aggressively promoting this fiercely fundamentalist Wahabi Islam across the globe. To date it is estimated to have spent more than 75 billion dollars to do so. This money has funded the construction of thousands of mosques and *madrasas* throughout the world and the printing of millions of religious books.

In modern times a Pakistani book shows that actually it is Indian Islam that is the fountainhead of Islamic terrorism. The book, *In the Abyss: Pakistan after the Coup*, is a compilation of the views of about a dozen Pakistani scholars who discuss this fear factor and its origin at Deoband in India.

According to one scholar, "A network of *madrasas* was established throughout the country... The children were taught to banish all doubts. The only truth was the divine truth ... written in the Quran and the Hadiths. These *madrasas* had a single function. They were nurseries designed to produce fanatics." "The dragon seeds sown in 2500 *madrasas* produced a crop of 2,25,000 fanatics ready to kill and die for their faith when ordered to do so by their religious leaders."

Another scholar says, "The *madrasas*... breed the Taliban mindset and feed the mills of lslamic fundamentalism and militancy." And a third adds, in the *madrasas* "children are indoctrinated in the military tactics of Jehad."

The syllabus for these *madrasas* originate at Deoband in Uttar Pradesh, the Indian centre of fanatic Islam. It would be no exaggeration to say that for the hardware of terrorism the software is from Deoband.

And if these scholars are to be believed, this Indian poison is spreading in Pakistan. For according to them the Deobandis have gained ascendancy over all other versions of Islam there (pages 25, 69-99), they want the Shias not only to be declared heretics but even to be physically exterminated. The Taliban movement is inspired by the Deobandi faith (p. 94), the Deobandi militias are waging war in Kashmir (p. 93), the Taliban jurisprudence based on Deobandi faith is becoming popular in Pakistan (p.96).

Another scholar who dwells on the Pakistani mindset is Dr. Anwar Shaikh, a self-exiled Pakistani Muslim. Writing about the genesis of Islamic separatism instilled in the general Pakistani society Anwar Shaikh writes in *Islam and Terrorism:*

"Radio Pakistan has been blaring Iqbal's fanatic poetry for the last 55 years, day and night. It has helped brainwash the people of Pakistan thoroughly."

"To him (Iqbal), Islam meant:

1. Total negation of national ties to be just a Muslim.
2. To fight for the glory of Islam with a view to creating *Hakoomat-e-Illahiya* (Government of Allah), which must be based on *Shariah* (the Islamic code of law).
3. Muslims cannot live under or with the non-Muslims. Therefore they must control the indigenous government by any means, including Jehad, or still better, partition the country on the basis of *Momin* and *Kafir* (Muslim and infidels).

Orthodox Islam requires a Muslim to be the enemy of non-Muslims for God's sake." (p. 206, 207.)

This is the virulent indoctrination that has built the Islamic terrorist mindset, even brutalizing small children. For instance, during the recent presidential election in the US a New York-based organisation called the Clarion Fund had sent copies of a movie about Islamist terrorism to more than 28 million households which included images of terror attacks around the world and scenes of Muslim children singing poems that celebrate suicide bombings.

Terrorist Ummah

That this mindset is wreaking havoc all over the world, from the Far West to the Far East, shows that the Ummah, the worldwide Islamic Brotherhood, now has a ferocious extension, namely the Islamic Terrorist Ummah.

This is the second dimension of the total threat to infidel Hindus, of which ISI is just the tip. In the Indian context ISI is aided and abetted by its global partner in terror al-Qaeda, not to speak of HUJI of Bangladesh as well as the Indian pack led by SIMI. This means even if ISI is effectively dealt with, the terror machine in India could go on functioning.

Next Dimension Pakistan

The next dimension of the terror threat is Pakistan – its people, its government, its Army, of which ISI is the sword arm, all latest assurances of civilian control notwithstanding.

It is a proven fact that the Pakistani society produces the greatest number of Jehadists. Why is that so? In an effort to find the basic answer to this question Sadanand Dhume, Indian columnist of the *Wall Street Journal* wrote in an article titled *Why Pakistan produces Jihadists* on May 5, 2010:

"Why do Pakistan and the Pakistani diaspora churn out such a high proportion of the world's terrorists?"

Indonesia has more Muslims than Pakistan. Turkey is geographically closer to the troubles of the Middle East. The governments of Iran and Syria are immeasurably more hostile to America and the West. Yet it is Pakistan, or its diaspora, that produced the CIA shooter Mir Ajmal Kasi, the 1993 World Trade Center bomber Ramzi Yousef (born in Kuwait to Pakistani parents), 9/11 mastermind Khalid Sheikh Mohammad, *Wall Street Journal* reporter Daniel Pearl's kidnapper, Omar Saeed Sheikh, and three of the four men behind the July 2005 train and bus bombings in London.

"The list of Jehadists not from Pakistan itself — but whose passage to Jehadism passes through that country — is even longer. Among them are Osama bin Laden and Ayman al-Zawahiri, Mohamed Atta, shoe bomber Richard Reid, and John Walker Lindh, the so-called American Taliban. Over the past decade, Pakistani fingerprints have shown up on terrorist plots in, among other places, Germany, Denmark, Spain and the Netherlands. And this partial catalogue doesn't include India, which tends to bear the brunt of its western neighbour's love affair with violence".

In Pakistan al-Qaeda not only rules a large swathe of territory but also the minds of men. Osama bin Laden, called the prime exponent of Jehad today, was a hero for the Pakistani people. In fact, this hero-worship is so firmly rooted in the Pakistani society that, to quote Haqqani, "only three per cent of Pakistanis believe that al-Qaeda was responsible for the 9/11 attacks in the US, notwithstanding the fact that bin Laden and his deputies had taken credit for the attacks on more than one occasion."A group of leading Pakistani Islamic scholars even awarded its highest honour – the title of "Saifullah" or "Sword of Allah" – to the al-Qaeda chief.

In concrete terms the Pakistani admiration for Osama bin Laden translated into Pakistan becoming the world's No. 1 stronghold for his global terrorist organization. A "Terrorism Index" jointly developed by the US "Centre for American Progress" in collaboration with the prestigious *Foreign Affairs* magazine rated Pakistan as the country most likely to become the next al-Qaeda stronghold after Somalia. Over 100 foreign policy experts were surveyed for the study.

At the same time the Pakistani psyche has also been "Talibanized". Arun Shourie had recently and extensively written about this phenomenon. To add a shocking illustration of what he wrote, there was public adulation of the assassin Qadri, who gunned down Punjab governor Taseer for expressing the need to amend Pakistan's blasphemy law. Qadri became such a hero in the people's eyes that when he was taken to court people thronged to congratulate him – including lawyers. One person placed a garland of roses round his neck, while another kissed him.

A really weird reflection of the fanaticism in the Pakistani mindset was the denigration of Pakistan founder Jinnah himself. For not long ago the biggest and most influential Islamic organisation of Pakistan, Jamiat-Ulema-e-Islamia, said "Jinnah did not really do anything extraordinary for Pakistan that he should be remembered". The chief of this organisation, Maulana Fazlur Rehman expressed this opinion about Jinnah, saying, "We cannot accept him as one of the Mujahidin-e-Azadi (freedom fighters)." It was "the discrimination against Muslims that led to partition, not anything that Jinnah did".

The double impact of the al-Qaeda-Taliban influence on the Pakistani society is clearly reflected in the Pakistani government. In 2006 the government declared that the concept of Jehad was an integral part of Islamic teachings and so would not be deleted from the school curriculum.

The result: All terror roads lead to Pakistan, noted author Salman Rushdie (of *Satanic Verses* fame) recently asserted.

Terming Pakistan as the centre of world terrorism, Rushdie said, "The fact is the world's terrorist organisations are all based in Pakistan. Taliban is there, al-Qaeda is there, LeT is there. They are all there with the active support of the Pakistani intelligence," he said while participating in a panel discussion at the Asia Society in New York.

Referring to the remarks of British Prime Minister Gordon Brown that three-fourths of terror plots had links to Pakistan and al-Qaeda, the India-born English novelist said "Islamabad can't go on pretending that there is no evidence. That's all garbage. When the President of Pakistan pretends that there is no evidence against somebody, he is also complicit in that. It is time to say to Pakistan this has to stop. You can't be a member of the free group of nations if you are among the world's sponsors of terrorism, which is what now they have been".

It is therefore not surprising that Osama bin Laden was and his deputy Ayman al-Zawahiri is hiding inside Pakistan. And ISI knew the whereabouts of Osama bin Laden but was keeping his location a secret and wanted to use the al-Qaeda chief as leverage over the United States. Noted military historian Stephen Tanner has said, as reported in March 2010, "We got to make a deal with Pakistan because I'm convinced that he (Osama bin Laden) is protected by the ISI. " Tanner, is the author of *Afghanistan: A Military History from Alexander the Great to the War against the Taliban.*

Further, denial after denial later, and barely weeks after it sacked its National Security Advisor for saying that the perpetrators of the Mumbai attacks could be from Pakistan, Islamabad took the first step towards admitting the fact. Under intense international pressure for a response to the Indian dossier, Pakistan's interior ministry acknowledged that the

26/11 terror attacks were launched from Pak shores and at least partly plotted on its soil. Even President Zardari admitted that "some of these terrorists might in fact have been born in Pakistan." But he added, "We believe that this operation was international, with significant support from within India itself."

Later, in the wake of the failure of the Foreign Secretary-level talks, a political commentator of *Indian Express* observed: "Pakistan has gone from Musharraf to Zardari and now to Gilani-Kayani (or Kayani-Gilani) in two to three years." The Indian establishment believes (or likes to believe) that Gilani, "as PM, has emerged far more empowered after the passage of the 18th amendment to Pakistan's constitution." But "it was Gilani himself who had first declared that Pakistan could not guarantee against another Mumbai-type attack." "Pakistan is itself facing Mumbai-type attacks almost every other day, and when we cannot protect our own citizens, how can we guarantee that there wouldn't be any more terrorist hits in India?" he said.

In much greater detail but with equal force Arun Shourie exposes the Pakistani government's complicity in terror when he says:

"Where do you think, and by who do you think, are the teachers instructed to ensure that students from class 1 onwards recognise the importance of Jihad, to ensure that they must be aware of the blessings of Jihad, to ensure that they 'create yearning for Jihad in his heart', to ensure that they develop 'love and aspiration for Jihad, *tabligh*, *shahadat*, sacrifice, ghazi, shaheed'?

"Where do you think, and by who, are teachers instructed to ensure that students from kindergarten onwards learn to make speeches on Jihad and *shahadat*, and are judged on their spirit while making speeches on Jihad? Do you think these are instructions issued by the Islamic fundamentalists to *maulvis* in *madrasas*? They are instructions given by the Government of Pakistan through official circulars to principals and teachers in government schools of Pakistan."

"You didn't know that? Exactly. That is a large part of the problem. You will find reams of these and other facts in the 2002 report edited by Pakistani academics, AH Nayyar and Ahmed Salim, and published by the Sustainable Development Institute, Islamabad. "The Subtle Subversion: The state of curricula and textbooks in Pakistan, Urdu, English, Social Studies and Civics". Get on to the Internet, download and read the report from www.sdpi.org"

Many specific instances of how Pakistani text books promote a culture of hatred of India in general and Hindus in particular can be quoted:

The class V book has this original discovery about Hindu help to bring British rule to India: "The British had the objective to take over India and to achieve this they made Hindus join them and Hindus were very glad to side with the British. After capturing the subcontinent, the British began on the one hand the loot of all things produced in this area, and on the other, in conjunction with Hindus, to greatly suppress the Muslims."

The VIII standard book says, "Their (Muslim saints) teachings dispelled many superstitions of the Hindus and reformed their bad practices. Thereby Hindu religion of the olden times came to an end."

On Indo-Pak wars the books openly eulogize `Jihad' and `shahadat' and urge students to become `mujahids' and martyrs.

According to a Class V book, "In 1965, the Pakistani army conquered several areas of India, and when India was on the point of being defeated she requested the United Nations to arrange a ceasefire. After 1965, India, with the help of Hindus living in East Pakistan, instigated the people living there against the people of West Pakistan, and finally invaded East Pakistan in December 1971. The conspiracy resulted in the separation of East Pakistan from us. All of us should receive military training and be prepared to fight the enemy."

The book prescribed for higher secondary students makes no mention of the uprising in East Pakistan in 1971 or the surrender by more than 90,000 Pakistani soldiers. Instead, it claims, "In the 1971 India-Pakistan war, the Pakistan armed forces created new records of bravery and the Indian forces were defeated everywhere."

And this great historic discovery is taught to V standard students: "Previously India was part of Pakistan!"

Commenting on this literature that spreads hate, leading Pakistani educationist Tariq Rahman wrote, "It is a fact that the textbooks cannot mention Hindus without calling them cunning, scheming, deceptive or something equally insulting. Students are taught and made to believe that Pakistan needs strong and aggressive policies against India or else Pakistan will be annihilated by it."

Yet another Pakistani educationist is much more specific. He shows evidence to prove the backing of state agencies for the Talibanisation of Pakistani society. The school curriculum is being tailored to reflect Taliban intolerance.

Teaching Jihad

According to the National Bureau of Curriculum and Textbooks, Class V children are expected to "acknowledge and identify the forces working against Pakistan, make speeches on Jihad and *shahadat*, understand Hindu-Muslim differences, India's evil designs, and demonstrate a belief in the fear of Allah".

A report early last year by Pervez Hoodbhoy of Islamabad's Quaid-e-Azam University and author of *Islam and Science: Religious Orthodoxy and the Battle for Rationality*, drew attention to thousands of Pakistani school-children who are taught that the Urdu equivalent of letter A stands for Allah, B for *Bandook* (gun) and J for Jehad. The books are being used in several schools and *madarsas* across Pakistan. In his article in the *Newsline*, Hoodbhoy pointed out that Allah, Bandook and Jehad were not the only examples that sound like a blueprint for a religious fascist state. "The Urdu letter T stands for *takrao* (collision), K for *khanjar* (dagger), H for *hyjab* (veil) and Z for *zunoob* (sins) such as watching television, playing musical instruments and flying kites".

"Saudi-isation" of Pakistan

In the article titled the *Saudi-isation of Pakistan*, the academic said Pakistan's self-inflicted suffering comes from an education system that, akin to Saudi Arabia, provides an ideological foundation for violence and future Jihadists. "It creates a sense of siege and embattlement in the minds of school-going children by stressing that Islam is under threat everywhere," Hoodbhoy said. He expressed shock that Class V students were expected to make speeches about Jihad. It was made mandatory for all government and private schools. It was prepared by the ministry of education and "sounds like a blueprint for a religious fascist state," he said. The academic said fear of taking on powerful religious forces prevented governments from correcting the curriculum and allowed young minds to be moulded by fanatics. "The education ministry estimate shows that 1.5 million students are receiving religious education in 13,000 *madarsas*. These figures appear to be way off the mark. The commonly-quoted figures range between 18,000 and 22,000. The number of students could be correspondingly larger," he said.

How these *madarsas* are playing havoc with little children was described by a Pakistani journalist Nasir Mirza in the *Daily Times* of Pakistan not long back. He wrote:

"Remote *madarsas* may be turning boys into drones, but then there are thousands of *madarsas* spread all over Pakistan's urban centres that are producing millions of neodrones who may not become suicide bombers but are totally unfit to live in this world".

"At full steam ahead in Pakistan, this is a monstrous experiment in brainwashing, and it is at par with, if not worse than, Nazi Germany's agencies. They did it in the name of science, here it is being done in the name of religion".

"Given our attitude towards birth control, an overabundance of young children is a natural outcome. In population growth we are not too far behind the six per cent population growth rate of our role model country, Saudi Arabia. There is an endless supply of young boys for *madrasas*. There are abducted, orphaned or abandoned young boys. Priestly abuse of children has been going on for as long as there have been priests and children. But never has this been done in such an organized manner as is the case here in Pakistan".

Social Situation

"Just step out of a large city, and all you would see around is hundreds and thousands of little children – from six to thirty-six months old. Until these kids are of an age to observe the ways of their elders, they lead a poor miserable social life. That's the real Pakistan. From Zia to Zardari, and all others in between, no one even acknowledged that we have an overpopulation problem. Such is the fear of backlash from religious conservatives. Here's the equation: a population that breeds like anything equals poverty equals despair equals cannon fodder for religious organizations and terrorist networks. In matters of religious beliefs, no one dare object. All kinds of evil, illegal or inhuman practices can be given sanction if a particular religion proves it is part of its belief. Our children face a frightening future because of the ultra-conservative wave of religion that has swept this country".

As for the young generation of Pakistanis, a recent and disturbing development in contemporary Pakistani society is that more and more young, educated and unemployed youths are swelling the ranks of Jehadists. Educated young men from the lower middle class are a substantial part of a new generation of Pakistani terrorists. As an illustration of this development, a news story by Waqar Gillani and Sabrina Tavernes in Lahore carried by *Indian Express* in March, 2010 described the case of Umar Kundi, a small-town boy who qualified as a doctor but went on to become one of Pakistan's most accomplished militants, working under a handler from al-Qaeda, till he was shot down by the police at the age of 29.

Describing the social situation that produced terrorist Kundi, the report said:

"In the 1980s, the US was financing Islamic radicals fighting the Soviets in Afghanistan, and General Zia-ul-Haq empowered hardline Mullahs and injected Islam into school textbooks. By the 1990s, recruiters for Jehad in Kashmir were holding rallies on public university campuses. After 2001, Lashkar was driven underground, but it continues to operate through a charity wing. American, Indian and Pakistani officials say it carried out the attacks in Mumbai in November 2008".

It is the lower middle class in Pakistan that is most vulnerable to radicalisation, according to Amir Rana, director of the Pakistan Institute for Peace Studies. They consume virulently anti-American media. They are recruited aggressively by Islamic student groups in public universities, which are attended almost exclusively by lower- and middle-class youth. Educated strivers who come from the lower middle class are part of a new generation that has made militant networks in Pakistan more sophisticated and deadly. The al-Qaeda has harnessed their aimless ambition and anger at Pakistan's alliance with the US, their generation's most electrifying enemy. "These are guys who use Google Maps to plan their attacks," said a senior Punjab Province police official. "Their training is better than our national police academy."

Like Kundi, many came of age in the 1990s when Jehad was state policy— aimed at challenging India in Kashmir — and Jehadi groups recruited openly in universities. Under the influence of al-Qaeda, their energies have been redirected and turned inward, against Pakistan's own government and people. "The situation now is quite confusing," said Tariq Parvez, director of the National Counterterrorism Authority in Islamabad. "In 2009, militant attacks killed 3,021 Pakistanis, three times as many as in 2006."

Gen. Ashfaq Kayani was due to retire in November 2010. Would he get an extension? *Indian Express* columnist Raja Mohan had asked on May 26, 2010: He wrote "The army's corps commanders who are the directors on the board of Pakistan's Army Inc. are supporting an extension to their chief ... Whoever wears the uniform will rule the nation." That is the truth, the whole truth, and nothing but the Pak truth. "For Pakistan remains a country that is controlled by the one institution that has controlled it for nearly all its decades of existence : the Army." So the columnist's question was pointless, Kayani continued.

And the Pakistan Army has its own Quran to abide by – a book titled *The Quranic Concept of War*. Written by Brig. SK Malik, it has a foreword written by Gen. Zia when he was President of Pakistan. The Pakistani Army brass treat it as their handbook.

Quoting convenient excerpts from the Quran, Brigadier Malik has attempted to prove that Quran ordains Jehad as mandatory for the pursuance of true Islam.

The book consists of ten volumes which dilate on rules of war, reasons of war, objects of war, strategies and tactics. It is emphasized again and again that victory is assured if one fights after embracing Islam. The theme of the entire book is that only Mussalmans are entitled to victory according to Divine Will. The book divides the world into two camps, *Dar-ul-Harb* and *Dar-ul-Islam*. *Dar-ul-Islam* are Islamic countries. The goal of Jihad, according to the book, is to convert *Dar-ul-Harb* into *Dar-ul-Islam* by war – Jehad – if not possible peacefully. The book dismisses peaceful conversion as a fiction.

Rushdie's assertion of Pakistan's status as a prime terrorist state also has a specific context, which is that Pakistan is a land of terrorist camps, where systematic terror training includes course modules in various types of arms and electronic devices, and where to get admission, reference letters are mandatory. These camps have a history of at least two decades.

Early accounts of Indians trained at terror camps in Pakistan date just prior to the Kashmir insurgency in the late 1980s, when a still missing SIMI leader from Kerala, Basheer, reportedly trained at a camp for Afghan *mujahideen* in the North West Frontier Province. Investigations into the Mumbai blasts of 1993 then threw up accounts of several of the accused undergoing a fortnight's training in the basics of handling of arms and explosives at camps in Pakistan in the run-up to the March 12 serial blasts. Subsequently, especially post 2002, investigations around the country have provided security agencies in India a fair idea of the nature of the terror training camps in Pakistan, their structure, content, location, and people involved.

Most people sent from India to camps in Pakistan have reported participating in a 21-day basic training module called the *Daura-e-Aam*. These *maaskars* or camps, specifically Lashkar ones, are a picture of rigorous set-ups where admissions "especially for advanced forms of training" need reference-letters, where data is maintained regarding all trainees and where advanced training facilities include an electronics laboratory. Apart from the *Daura-e-Aam* training modules available to most recruits, specially handpicked trainees undergo training under various modules like *Daura-e-Khaas*, an advanced commando training, the *Daura-e-Ribat*, an intelligence gathering module, and *Daura-e-Mutafajjirat* or exclusive training in explosives.

Daura-e-Aam: A compressed three-week training programme largely focused on motivating recruits for Jehad, where the basics of different types of arms, ammunition and explosives are provided. This camp is typically held at Baitul Mujahideen, near Muzaffarabad, the base of LeT's operations commander Zaki-ur-Rehman Lakhvi. Overall in-charge of all Lashkar training camps Abu Nasar Javed is also based here. He oversees admissions after perusing references and detailed profiles provided by trainees. When trainees arrive at this camp, they are thoroughly frisked for possession of cigarettes, tobacco, and opium before being given entrance. More than 100 trainees are reported to comprise every batch. A day begins at almost all the camps at 3 a.m. with prayers and physical exercise. This is followed by lessons on various types of weapons, discussions on Jehad and religious lessons.

Daura-e-Khaas: Admission to this advanced commando training course is under the scrutiny of a person called Abu Dawood, who also maintains records of all trainees undergoing the course. There are as many as 15 trainers at the course, who are called *ustaads*. The four-month course has a focus on survival in crisis situations and stresses on physical endurance with border crossing, river crossing, night marches and jungle survival being among the key elements in the programme. The course also gives detailed training in the handling of weapons introduced in the basic course. (The Mumbai attackers were all said to have undergone the *Daura-e-Khaas*.)

Daura-e-Ribat: This 15-20 day training programme in intelligence gathering functions under a man called Fahadullah. The lessons include surveillance and reconnaissance activities, maintenance of false identities, how to carry out personal meetings, how to do 'live drops' of consignments by using anonymous middlemen, how to do 'dead drops' of consignments without direct human contacts.

Daura-e-Mutafajjirat: This 20-day training in the manufacturing and planting of improvised explosive devices teaches trainees about various chemical combinations for explosives, different kinds of timer devices and how to carry out controlled explosions. A man called Abu Walid has been identified as one of the trainers at the course.

Electronics Lab: The electronics laboratory teaches trainees to use electronic equipment, including the manufacture of electronic switches for bombs. Some accounts describe the communications training as a short two-to-three day programme in the use of modern communication and navigation techniques including the use of satellite phones, Internet resources like Google Earth, chat and e-mail services. The training provides inputs on way to use different kinds of phones without coming on the radar of security agencies.

All this makes Pakistan such a full-equipped terrorist state that in 2007 the US Senate Committee on Foreign Relations called it the most dangerous country in the world. In 2008 Kissinger virtually called it a failed state and former US Secretary of State Madeline Albright an international migraine. In the Indian context, Pakistan can definitely be called the world's most dangerous neighbour.

ISI is the tangible form of this official Pakistani terror, and it continues unabated in the post-Musharraf chaos. CIA even presented a charge-sheet on ISI-terrorist links to Prime Minister Geelani on his first visit to Washington, and he was told to rein in the ISI. Obviously this was easier said than done. For the initial attempt by PPP chief Zardari to wrest control of ISI proved a rookie move that backfired, wrote the US journal *Newsweek*.

Now a coalition that refused to coalesce right from the start is trying to sit in the saddle. Of the two top leaders, Zardari, with a reputation as a playboy, is President, while the failed Prime Minister Nawaz Sharif is sulking in the wings. Consequently, Pakistan's present flirtation with democracy may well be as brief as before.

Maulana Amir Siddique, present head of the Taliban-controlled Lal Masjid, located in the heart of Pakistan's capital, has already declared that he is against democracy and would rather have the country governed by the rules of Islam. A few months later, hundreds of Islamist women gathered at this mosque and vowed to raise their children for Jehad. Chanting slogans of 'Jehad is our way', *burqa*-clad women, some with babies, listened to fiery speeches on the eve of the anniversary of the commando raid on the complex. "Our *mujahideen* laid down their lives for the enforcement of the Islamic system in Pakistan. We are left behind to carry forward their mission," the daughter of cleric Abdul Aziz told the rally in the mosque compound.

Several thousand men attended a similar rally to mark the anniversary of the raid. Shortly after the rally a suicide bomber attacked police guarding the gathering, killing 18 people, all but three of them policemen.

Pak Army

As for the Pakistan Army, a sizeable segment of it is highly indoctrinated in Islamic tenets. In fact fundamentalists have as much a stranglehold on the Army as on the civilian administration. It is this Army that will continue to call the shots even under its new chief, his talk of his army's apolitical mandate notwithstanding. No civilian government in Pakistan has ever had the ability to tell the military in Pakistan to rein in itself, and going by the way Kayani defies and countermands Zardari, the present government is not going to be an exception. In fact the Government led by President Zardari seems so manifestly incapable of taking any credible action in the face of opposition from the military that reporting the recent U-turns by the civilian establishment, the *Economic Times* asked in a heading 'Prez or Puppet'?

And Zardari is only the representative of the political establishment as a whole that promptly falls in line at the Army's command, witness the quick climbdown by Nawaz Sharif on Kasab's Pak origin and the December resolution of the Pakistan National Assembly. It said the country was with its armed forces to defend Pakistan's security interest at all costs, a sharp contrast to its October resolution after the Islamabad Marriott Hotel bombing, in which it referred to dictatorial regimes (that) pursued politics aimed at perpetuating power at the cost of national interest, and said Pak terrorism shall not be used for any kind of attacks on other countries.

Pakistani political analysts themselves are aware of this ground reality. For instance, writing in *Indian Express* in December 2009 Pakistani journalist Zahid Hussain speculated on what the future could hold for Pakistan's 14th Chief of Army Staff, Gen. Ashfaq Kayani, and concluded that it could "make General Kayani an important member of the power structure."

The same month Pakistani journal *Herald's* correspondent Massoud Ansari also wrote that the new Army Chief is the strongest player on the political scene.

Add to this the Pakistan Army's old expansionist ambitions. Following the Afghan involvement, which gave ISI a halo, from Gen. Jilani onwards all military chiefs of ISI were products of what Stephen Cohen calls the Paki generation. These generals from AkhtarAbdul Rehman to Hamid Gul and Asad Durrani "carried with them an Islamic Vision of crossing the Oxus".

As an initial step towards the fulfilment of this international vision, according to an old Intelligence report, even a decade and a half ago ISI had planned the creation of an Islamistan made up of the North-East, Bihar, and some districts of West Bengal.

Apropos the war hysteria that the Pakistan Army whipped up in the wake of the latest LeT assault on Mumbai *Organiser* columnist Nalapat asked, "Why did the Pakistan Army make its terrorist ancillaries go this far?" His answer: "Clearly the Generals were determined to punish Washington for continuously prodding the Pak Army to take action against its ally, the Taliban."

In fact, this unholy alliance was so deep-rooted that a top-level former Pakistani army officer had to forfeit his life for threatening to expose it, a British media report said in December 2008. Major-General Faisal Alavi, a former head of Pakistan's special forces, was murdered in Islamabad after he threatened to expose Pakistani Generals for deals with Taliban militants. In a letter to the Pakistani Army Chief Ashfaq Kayani he had named two Generals and said he would furnish all relevant proof. Alavi did not live to fulfil it. Aware that he was risking his life, Alavi gave a copy of the proof to a *Sunday Times* correspondent and asked him to publish it if he were killed. Four days later, he was driving through Islamabad when his car was ambushed. Two gunmen opened fire from either side, shooting him eight times, killing him and his driver on the spot.

Three years ago Alavi was mysteriously sacked as head of Pakistan's Special Services Group (SSG), for conduct unbecoming. The generals had cooked up a mischievous and deceitful plot to have him sacked because they knew he would expose them, Alavi wrote. Alavi believed he was forced out because he was critical of deals that senior generals had done with the Taliban. He had told the correspondent how one general had done an astonishing deal with Baitullah Mehsud, former Taliban leader, now seen by many analysts as an even greater terrorist threat than Osama bin Laden. According to Alavi, a senior Pakistani general came to an arrangement with Mehsud whereby in return for a large sum of money Mehsud's 3,000 armed fighters would not attack the army.

The Other Pakistan

In Bangladesh, now called the other Pakistan, Hindus are enemies. The law under which they were legally looted of their land is known as the Enemy (vested) Property Act. Under this law 12 lakh Hindus lost 24 lakh acres of land and other property valued at an estimated Taka (Bangladeshi Rupee) 3,50,412 crore, said a study sponsored by the Association for Land Reform and Development. The study report was published in the form of a book titled *Deprivation of Hindu Minority in Bangladesh: Living with Vested Property.*

During the last five years a massive campaign for ethnic cleansing of Hindus from border districts of Assam and West Bengal has been in progress. Thanks to the tremendous infiltration from Bangladesh as many as seven districts of Assam and four districts of West Bengal are now dominated by Muslims.

On the other hand Bangladesh has proved false the facile argument that economic deprivation incites Islamic fundamentalist mayhem. For two successive years before the change of government in 2001 the previous regime had brought about significant economic improvements in the state, once ridiculed by Henry Kissinger as a basket case. Even the rickshaw-pullers of Dhaka happily admitted they never had it so good.

And yet Begum Zia's fundamentalist rabble-rousers were able to capture power. And what was their winning card? It was the earlier mentioned slogan *Aamra Sabai Taliban, Bangladesh hobey Afghanistan* ("We are all Taliban, and Bangladesh will become Afghanistan"). An ally of Begum Zia's Bangladesh Nationalist Party, Islamic Okiya Jot, headed by fundamentalist Mullas, declared Jehad against the rule of law and constitutional governance. The Mullas not only challenged the Bangladesh High Court's right to outlaw Fatwa, they even conferred the death sentence on the two judges who committed the un-Islamic act of taking away the right of the Maulanas to issue edicts.

On the official level the close and active collusion between the Bangladesh government's Directorate General of Forces Intelligence (DGFI) and ISI in anti-India terrorism is an open secret. Bangladesh has become the major operational ground for waging proxy war on India. In 2000 a Bangladeshi institution called Muslim Research Institute had advocated the idea of an Islamic nation called Mughlistan made up of Bangladesh, Pakistan, Kashmir, West Bengal, Bihar, Uttar Pradesh, Punjab and Haryana. Going beyond this, ISI and al-Qaeda have a grand design to establish a Caliphate from Indonesia to Malaysia, Thailand, Bangladesh, *via* India and through Pakistan right into the Balkans. In this global design India is the only obstacle, populated by non-Muslims (read infidels).

This, then, is the fourth dimension of the threat to India in general and the Hindus in particular, the Pakistani Ummah, psychologically dominated by al-Qaeda-Taliban terrorists, governed by a rabid regime, and held in thrall by the Army-ISI combine.

The Americans

After the Islamic Ummah, the terrorist Ummah, and the Pakistani Ummah (comprising its people, its government, its army), an unlikely addition that needs to be made is the American administration, past and present. When the US vehemently declared global war on global Jehad, the Indian dispensation fondly believed that India's war on terror had a powerful, sincere ally on its side. But there is a decade-old report that put a question-mark on the honesty of American intentions, and could have disabused gullible Indian minds.

Prof. Michel Chossudousky of the University of Ottawa posted on the internet on Nov. 2, 2001 a revealing report on behalf of the Centre for Research on Globalisation (CRG), Montreal. Its title was *The Role of Pakistan's Military Intelligence (ISI)* in the September 11 attacks. Very significantly, the report's subtitle, placed above the main title, was *Cover-up or Complicity of the Bush Administration*?

The CRG summary preceding the full report is as follows:

"Pakistan's chief spy Lt. General Mahmoud Ahmad was in the US when the attacks occurred. He arrived in the US on the 4th of September, a full week before the attacks. He had meetings at the State Department after the attacks on the WTC. But he also had a regular visit of consultations with his US counterparts at the CIA and the Pentagon during the week prior to September 11. What was the nature of these routine pre-September 11 consultations? Were they in any way related to the subsequent post-September 11 consultations pertaining to Pakistan's decision to cooperate with Washington? Was the planning of war being discussed between Pakistani and US officials?"

On the 9th of September while General Ahmad was in the US, the leader of the Northern Alliance Commander Ahmad Shah Masood was assassinated. The Northern Alliance had informed the Bush Administration that the ISI was allegedly implicated in the assassination.

The Bush Administration consciously took the decision in the post-September 11 consultations with Lt. General Mahmoud Ahmad to directly cooperate with Pakistan's military intelligence (ISI) despite its links to Osama bin Laden and the Taliban and its alleged role in the assassination of Commander Masood, which coincidentally occurred two days before the terrorist attacks.

Meanwhile, senior Pentagon and State Department officials had been rushed to Islamabad to put the finishing touches on America's war plans. And on Sunday prior to the onslaught of the bombing of major cities in

Afghanistan (October 7th), Lt. General Mahmoud Ahmad was sacked from his position as head of the ISI in what was described as a routine reshuffling.

In the days following General Ahmad's dismissal, a report published in the *Times of India* revealed the links between Pakistan's chief spy Lt. General Mahmoud Ahmad and the presumed ring leader of the WTC attacks Mohamed Atta. The *Times of India* article was based on an official intelligence report of the Delhi government that had been transmitted through official channels to Washington. Quoting an Indian government source Agence France Press (AFP) confirms in this regard that: "The evidence we [the Government of India] have supplied to the US is of a much wider range and depth than just one piece of paper linking a rogue general to some misplaced act of terrorism."

The revelation of the *Times of India* article has several implications. The Indian intelligence report not only points to the links between ISI Chief General Ahmad and terrorist ringleader Mohamed Atta, it also indicates that other ISI officials might have had contacts with the terrorists. Moreover, it suggests that the September 11 attacks were not an act of individual terrorism organised by a separate al-Qaeda cell, but rather they were part of a coordinated military-intelligence operation emanating from Pakistan's ISI. The *Times of India* report also sheds light on the nature of General Ahmad's business activities in the US during the week prior to September 11, raising the distinct possibility of ISI contacts with Mohamed Atta in the US prior to the attacks on the WTC, precisely at the time when General Mahmoud and his delegation were on a so-called regular visit for consultations with US officials.

In assessing the alleged links between the terrorists and the ISI, it should be understood that Lt. General Ahmad as head of the ISI was the US-approved appointee. As head of the ISI since 1999, he was in liaison with his US counterparts in the CIA, the Defense Intelligence Agency (DIA) and the Pentagon. Also bear in mind that Pakistan's ISI remained throughout the entire post-Cold War era until the present, the launch-pad for CIA covert operations in the Caucasus, Central Asia and the Balkans.

The existence of an ISI-Osama-Taliban axis was a matter of public record. The links between the ISI and agencies of the US government including the CIA are also a matter of public record. The Bush Administration was fully cognizant of Lt. General Ahmad's role. In other words, rather than waging a campaign against international terrorism, the evidence would suggest that it is indirectly abetting international terrorism, using the Pakistani ISI as a go-between. The Bush Administration's links with Pakistan's ISI – including its consultations with General Ahmad in the week prior to September 11 – raise the issue of complicity. While Ahmad was talking to US officials at the CIA and the

Pentagon, ISI officials were allegedly also in contact with the September 11 terrorists.

In other words, according to the Indian government intelligence report, the perpetrators of the September 11 attacks had links to Pakistan's ISI, which in turn has links to agencies of the US government. What this suggests is that key individuals within the US military-intelligence establishment might have known about the ISI contacts with the September 11 terrorist "ring-leader" Mohamed Atta and failed to act.

Whether this amounts to the complicity of the Bush Administration remains to be firmly established. What is crystal clear, however, is that this war is not a "campaign against international terrorism". It is a war of conquest with devastating consequences for the future of humanity. And the American people have been consciously and deliberately misled by their government."

And since President Bush was succeeded by President Obama, things have gone from bad to worse for India. For starters, he clearly sided with the Islamic Ummah when, during his visit to Turkey, he spoke before Turkey's Parliament, assuring that the US is not and will never be at war with Islam. To Turkish lawmakers in Ankara, to whom he was introduced as Barack Husain Obama, he said: "America's relationship with the Muslim community, the Muslim world, cannot and will not just be based upon opposition to terrorism. We seek broader engagement based upon mutual interest and respect." "The US has been enriched by Muslim-Americans," he said. "Many other Americans have Muslims in their family, or have lived in a Muslim-majority country." "I know," the US President said, "because I am one of them." On another occasion Obama even went so far as to say, numbers-wise America was the biggest Muslim country. Such talk is dangerous, he had been publicly chided by an eminent American.

With the thinking reflected in such talk and translated into his policies, President Obama has shown that he is no friend of India. Rather, he has gone out of his way to show that he is a friend of India's two worst enemies, Pakistan and China. He keeps pumping money into Pakistan, and he publicly kowtowed to China, saying US and China could together lead the world in the twenty-first century.

Apropos Hillary Clinton's stern-sounding words on the Times Square incident, (and later after Osama bin Laden was found in a Pakistani hideout and killed) the 64000-dollar question is, do they presage a change in US thinking on Pakistan? The answer may well be: the more things change, the more they remain the same. C. Raja Mohan had written in his *Indian Express* column on 12 May 2010 that in view of the Obama administration's current dalliance with Islamabad Clinton's warning got much play in India. Scepties, however, would dismiss any suggestion of a fundamental change in Obama's Pakistan policy. They insist that the bigger the trouble with Pakistan, the larger will be the cheque that Washington will write for the Pakistan army headquarters in Rawalpindi. Fittingly enough, the column was titled "*Paying Pindi*", not paying Islamabad.

Organiser columnist Jai Dubashi was still more outspoken. Let's beware of Obama, he bluntly warned a couple of months earlier, and wrote: "America's principal partner in this part of the world is Pakistan, which is actually the epicenter of terrorism in the area. Straighten out Pakistan and you will break the back of terrorism in the region. But it does not look as if Barack Obama is at all keen to break the back of terrorism in Pakistan. He is, in fact, going all out to build up Pakistan, which also means ISI, as an American ally in South Asia, feeding it with billions of dollars worth of armaments year after year, and making it the kingpin of its defence strategy in this part of the world."

On the practical level the emergence of a former Guantanamo Bay prisoner as the deputy leader of al-Qaeda's Yemeni branch has underscored the potential complications in carrying out the executive order of President Obama that the detention centre be shut down within a year. The militant, Said Ali al-Shihri, is suspected of involvement in the deadly bombing of the United States Embassy in Yemen's capital Sana. He was released to Saudi Arabia in 2007 and passed through a Saudi rehabilitation programme for former jihadists before resurfacing with al-Qaeda in Yemen.

Almost half the camp's remaining prisoners are Yemenis. Al-Shihri returned from Guantanamo to his native Saudi Arabia and then travelled to Yemen 10 months ago. In fact Yemen is a nice safe haven for jihadists. When Guantanamo closes, many of its inmates will know where to go. In March 2008 al-Qaeda websites posted a message advising members to head for Yemen. The call, it seems, has been answered. The global terror franchise has released a video showing fugitive Saudi jihadists and their Yemeni hosts proclaiming a merger between their two branches, plus images of combat training in Yemen's rugged mountains. The Yemeni government says it expects most of the 100 odd Yemenis still held at Guantanamo, where they now make up the largest national group of inmates, to be home. With its rough terrain, weak central state and gun-slinging tribal culture, Yemen may prove a fairly secure redoubt for al-Qaeda.

Then in May 2009 a Pentagon report provided new details concluding that one in seven of the 534 prisoners already transferred abroad from Guantanamo has turned to terrorism.

Finally, self-confessed Indophile and one of the 'Republicans for Obama' former US Senator Larry Pressler feels let down by Barack Obama's policies regarding Afghanistan and Pakistan. But he is more saddened over New Delhi not speaking up against mistakes Washington is making in South Asia. "I have been disappointed in India not raising a voice about what's happening in Afghanistan, what a mistake we are probably making," Pressler, who was in India in February 2010 on a speaking tour, told the *Indian Express*. "We are creating a big problem for India, because at the end of the day India is going to have on its border a highly armed loose canon in Pakistan, a rogue state whose government is not what we espouse or support, a rogue Pakistan on steroids of US money".

Comity of Facilitators

And finally the danger from within – the comity of Indian facilitators of Islamic terror. This facilitation is mostly perceptible in the form of an acquiescent mindset in sections of three segments of the Indian society – the Indian Muslim, the Indian Secularist, and the Indian Communist.

Indian Muslims

Parthasarthy wrote in 2003: A few years ago a former Director General of ISI remarked to me that Pakistan would see to it that the Jehad in Kashmir would draw support from Muslims all across India, and that it would be made an issue of faith in the minds of the Muslims of India.

Towards this end, ISI has exploited the separatism fostered among Indian Muslim masses by their leaders, both religious and political. These leaders' misuse of numerical strength and political clout has become an integral part of Indian politics.

India's largest Muslim outfit, Jamaat-e-Islami Hind, has launched a Muslim party in which it seeks the participation of Jamiat-Ulema-e-Hind, Majlis-e-Mushawarat, All-India Milli Council, All Indian Majlis-e-Ittehad-ul-Muslimeen, Muslim League, and Muslim MPs in general. According to Jamaat leaders Muslims are in a majority in at least 8 Lok Sabha seats, while they are a deciding factor in around 80 constituencies. (According to another estimate the massive Bangladeshi infiltration into Assam has impacted as many as 24 Lok Sabha seats.) Now there is even a call for Mullahs in politics given by Maulana Kalbe Jawwad, former chairman of People's Democratic Front, because the "Muslims have been suffering from political slavery for the last 60 years".

What is still more bizarre, even terrorists have taken to politics. Some convicts and accused in the 1993 Mumbai serial blasts case have decided to form a political party. In an ad hoc committee formed in Arthur Road Jail in Mumbai, convict Mustafa Dossa *alias* Manjun was elected president.

Then in the wake of the serial bombing of Ahmedabad in July 2008, the Shahi Imam of Delhi's Jama Masjid referred to the arrest of Abdul

Bashir, the suspected kingpin, and threatened that if he was not set free there would be a fiercer agitation than that of 1947. He was also reported to be setting up a platform of Mullahs and Maulavis. He held a conference for this in the Masjid, which was attended by leaders of Jamiat Ulema-e-Hind and Jamiat-e-Islami, and openly supported by Samajwadi Party. SP leader Abu Azmi was present.

It is this background of repeated manifestation of a separatist psyche that gives a disquieting context to the fact that India is currently riddled with not only Pakistani terror teams, led by ISI, but also with made-in-India terrorists, with SIMI leading the pack. These are able to bomb Mumbai 7 times in 15 minutes, Hyderabad 9 times, Jaipur half a dozen times, and Ahmedabad as many as 16 times in half an hour. Such serial strikes need carefully worked out logistics which are impossible without a substantial local backup force. This force is apparently present and available to the terrorists whenever and wherever they choose to strike.

The religious indoctrination that nurtures separatism and eventually can lead to terrorism is unfortunately available to the Muslim masses of India, thanks to their leaders and institutions, both religious and political. On the religious level they have Dar-ul Uloom of Deoband where, a dozen Pakistani Islamic scholars assert, for the hardware for terrorism the software is manufactured.

It is the same with *madrasas*. Thousands of them are spread across so-called secular India, and the one thing they teach is separatism. According to reliable sources, 15 lakh students graduate from *madrasas* in the country every year.

The Task Force on Border Management, one of the four that the Government set up in the wake of the Kargil War, had reported with alarm about the way *madrasas* had mushroomed along India's borders. On the basis of information it received from intelligence agencies, it expressed grave concern at the amount of money these *madrasas* were receiving from foreign sources. It expressed the gravest concern at the way the *madrasas* were reinforcing separateness in those attending them. It pointed to the consequences that were certain to flow from the Talibanisation of the *madrasas*. (In spite of what the Task Forces themselves advised, namely that their reports be made public, the reports have been kept secret.)

This same separatism has spread in Indian Muslim politics. Muslim League's Banatwala had opposed the singing of Vande Mataram on the specious ground that it is against Islam. In fact the recent *fatwa* against singing the national song on the ground that it is un-Islamic and promotes idol worship is just the latest in a string that reaches back years.

Secessionism in Kashmir

In Jammu and Kashmir the clearly illegal autonomy resolution passed by the state assembly in the recent past was the thin end of the separatist wedge, for now the PDP leadership has come up with openly pro-Pak, anti-national demands, which the secular media euphemistically called "controversial" and Panther leader Bhim Singh bluntly dubbed "secessionist".

Former J&K chief minister and People's Democratic Party patron Mufti Mohammad Sayeed's daughter Mehbooba Mufti had, during her visit to Pugwash Conference in Pakistan, recommended dual power-sharing arrangement between India and Pakistan for Kashmir.

There is also a PDP 'self-rule' document listing the following demands:

- Jammu and Kashmir Governor to be elected by the state legislature.
- Phasing out Central Indian Services like IAS, IPS in Kashmir.
- Abolition of Article 356 in Kashmir.
- Separate regional assemblies for Jammu and Kashmir.

As if to underscore its anti-Indian separatism, the party even made a "vision on Kashmir" presentation recently in Srinagar in which it displayed a map of India showing Aksai Chin and the Karakoram region as parts of China.

PDP Terrorists: Providing a significant footnote to PDP's credentials Ghulam Nabi Azad had described in his last speech before resigning as Chief Minister the links between PDP and terrorist elements in the State. He had also clearly suggested the party's Pakistani, Talibani and Middle East links.

Not long ago, when stridently separatist leader Geelani was himself in a moderate phase, he had made a statement saying the Kashmir movement did not require guns, and called for a peaceful indigenous struggle to achieve the political goal, which was "to free Kashmir from Indian military occupation". Not long before that this same Geelani had been vociferously advocating the role of guns in Kashmir.

For the first time in history, the openly and increasingly separatist Hurriyat is going to open offices all over the Kashmir Valley. Hurriyat leader Shabbir Shah declared that the purpose of these offices was to get all sections of the people in the fold of on-going freedom struggle and take it to its logical political end. A conglomerate of 25 parties, the Hurriyat is currently undergoing an organisational revamp which is in the interest of the separatist movement, said another leader, Shahid-ul Islam.

In addition to covering the whole of the Kashmir Valley the Hurriyat also plans offices in hitherto uncovered regions like Ladakh and expand influence further in Jammu. It even wants to reopen its Delhi office.

On the issue of separatism the two top leaders of the Hurriyat, Geelani and Shabbir Shah have now joined hands. This was made clear in February 2008 by a tele-address to a Jamaat-ud-Dawa conference in Lahore by both of them. The Conference was presided over by Dawa chief and LeT founder Hafiz Muhammad Saeed.

The Muslim League factions have also reunited to back Hurriyat leader Geelani. Muslim League leader Mushtaq-ul-Islam announced at a press conference in Srinagar that the reunited factions of the League would back the Hurriyat hardline. The League leader said, "The leaders of the League, keeping in view their ideological goals, have decided to work for the freedom of Kashmir."

An ominous update on the separatism running rampant in Kashmir was a so-called seminar held in Srinagar on April 20, 2010, to which Pakistani terrorist leaders were cordially invited. Lashkar-e-Toiba founder Hafiz Saeed, Jaish-e-Muhammad chief Masood Azhar and Hizbul Mujahideen supremo Syed Salahuddin reportedly addressed the seminar organised by a little-known body called Human Rights Forum. The chairmen of both factions of the Hurriyat, Mirwaiz Umar Farooq and Syed Ali Shah Geelani, had also been invited to the seminar, titled Role of Pro-freedom Leaders vis-a-vis Kashmir issue. Saeed, Azhar and Salahuddin reportedly addressed the seminar by phone.

Another similar seminar, held in Delhi in October 2010, saw the height (or depth) of the Islamic pseudo-secularism of barren Indian intellectuals when Arundhati Roy openly called for Kashmir's *Azadi* – freedom from India. It was a crass example of sedition, and as it was clearly legally actionable it was initially reported that the Government would prosecute her. But, to no one's surprise, it got cold feet and backed out on the phoney pretext that such action would provide a handle for the separatists – as if they needed one.

Islamisation of Kashmir: All in all, with the forced departure of over three lakh Kashmiri Pundits from their homeland, Kashmir has, for all practical purposes, become a totally Islamic province.

Steps for removing Indian symbols in Kashmir are under implementation, such as renaming of towns and roads with Muslim names, "*assalam alekum*" replacing '*namaskar*' as greetings by Srinagar Doordarshan, burning of the Indian Constitution and the tricolour, and time zones synchronising with Pakistan time zones. In place of the Sanskritised Kashmiri language, Persianised Urdu has been made the official language.

So far as separatism is concerned, the National Conference does not lag behind Hurriyat. For instance, during Prime Minister Manmohan Singh's visit to Srinagar in June 2010 a National Conference delegation presented a memorandum to him demanding restoration of autonomy to

Jammu and Kashmir, claiming that it was the basic step towards the resolution of the Kashmir problem.

A bizarre expression of the psychological Islamisation of the situation was an official announcement in October 2008 by the Vice Chancellor of Kashmir University, Prof. Riyaz Punjabi, of the commissioning of the "first phase of the university's South Campus in Islamabad"! Actually the press release was not talking about the Pakistani capital but Anantnag, a town in south Kashmir, as, to quote the VC, "most people in the Valley call Anantnag Islamabad."

Against this background it was not surprising that Muslims in many towns in the Valley prayed for Osama bin Laden on learning of his death, and Muslim lawyers in Srinagar offered prayers in the courtroom. A still more disquieting show of alienation was seen during the over-hyped Mohali cricket match between India and Pakistan on March 30, 2011. To quote a press report of that day:

"Srinagar had shut down to watch the cricket match between India and Pakistan, but the team they cheered wasn't India. In hotels and in homes, at roadside stalls and in Srinagar's downtown sprawl, in villages, Kashmir was rooting for Pakistan. This support for Pakistan united mainstream politicians and separatists. Every Indian wicket prompted a flurry of fire crackers, and when Pakistan started batting, every run was cheered".

Elsewhere too small but significant pointers to the same alienation can be noticed. For instance, on learning of Osama's death Syed Ahmed Bukhari, Imam of Delhi's Jama Masjid asked, "Who said Osama bin Laden was a terrorist?" And Jamiat-e-Ulema Hind has offered legal aid for the defence of Indian Mujahideen terrorist Mansoor Peerbhoy. This body has been providing legal aid to terror suspects free of charge.

This, therefore, is the undeniable ground reality— that extreme separatism helps build a terrorist-friendly backup in a section (however small) of the Indian Muslim society without which terrorists cannot operate, much less succeed. In fact, in the opinion of Hamid Dalwai even today there is a formidable section among Indian Muslims whose ultimate demand is the Islamisation of the whole of India (*Muslim Dilemma in India*, p. 35).

The Pseudo-secularist

Another factor contributing to terrorism's unchecked spread through the length and breadth of India is the Indian edition of secularism, for which Advani was the first to coin the name pseudo-secularism.

This doctrine has generated some fashionable misconceptions and even some myths *apropos* terrorism that have vitiated India's threat perception.

Fashionable Misconceptions: Any response to Islamic terrorism, to be effective, needs the wisdom to assess the ground realities and the courage to look facts in the face. In the case of the Indian dispensation this is not possible unless some fashionable misconceptions are shed. *Organiser* columnist Ram Gopal has listed them thus:

- All terrorists, except a few, are foreign-sponsored.
- Terrorists have no religion.
- Because of the involvement of a few misguided Muslim youth, the entire Muslim community cannot be called in question.
- The aim of the terrorists is only to disrupt communal harmony and to stall India's economic progress.
- No special law, like TADA or POTA, is needed, as it is likely to be misinterpreted and misused against Muslims. (For that matter, all criminal laws should be scrapped, because they too are often misused.)
- Terrorism is a law and order problem that is mainly for the state government to tackle effectively.

Myths from Mumbai: In a similar vein Arvind Pangaria, an Indian professor at Columbia University, New York, examines some usual misconceptions from which the Indian mindset suffers *vis-a-vis* Pakistani terror. Writing in the wake of the Mumbai carnage in the *Indian Express,* he calls them Myths from Mumbai. To quote the major ones:

When it comes to terrorism, India and Pakistan are now victims of a common enemy. President Asif Ali Zardari of Pakistan has extensively promoted this myth and many in the West and some in India embrace it. In an interview on CNN, Zardari said: "The state of Pakistan is of course not involved. We're part of the victims." A week later he wrote in the *New York Times:* "Not only are the terrorists not linked to the government of Pakistan in any way, we are their targets and continue to be their victims." But this is a treacherous claim. True, Pakistan has been subject to terrorist attacks recently. But India and Pakistan are not victims of the same terror groups. Pakistan suffers at the hands of the Taliban and al-Qaeda. But Lashkar-e-Toiba (LeT) that sent terrorists to Mumbai recently and Jaish-e-Muhammad (JeM) that attacked the Parliament in 2001 do not terrorise Pakistani citizens. Instead, they have had a history of receiving patronage from Pakistan's intelligence agency, the ISI.

Pakistani government bears no responsibility for the recent Mumbai attacks. The statement is substantively false. For sometime now, there has existed an Army-ISI-Jehadi complex in Pakistan whereby retired officials of the army and ISI routinely participate in terrorist training camps that Jehadi outfits such as LeT and JeM run. In turn, these outfits actively assist the ISI. Therefore, even if there was no official contact between the government and LeT specifically on the Mumbai attacks, the army and ISI bear responsibility in an essential way. (In fact, in the first-ever confession of its kind, Pakistan's foreign secretary Shaharyar Khan acknowledged in interview to an Indian TV channel on May 28, 2011 that ISI may have been involved in the 26/11 attack on Mumbai.)

India itself is to be blamed for the terror attacks because of its ill-treatment of Muslims at home. In the aftermath of the attacks, commentators in the Western media disproportionately focussed on domestic ills as the principal source of terrorism facing India. Some among these observers continued to cling to the idea that discrimination at home had led local Muslims to carry out the attacks. Others naively believed that outfits such as the LeT would not send terrorists if India did not discriminate against Muslims. But these observers largely rest their case on association: If discrimination against Muslims exists, it must be responsible for Muslim terrorism. But this is wholly insufficient reasoning. For instance, listen to what LeT head Hafiz Saeed said at a rally in Karachi in 2000: "There can't be any peace while India remains intact. Cut them, cut them, cut them so much that they kneel before you and ask for mercy." Is this a man who will stop sending terrorists?

No amount of intelligence, training and equipment can prevent determined terrorists from striking. Taken literally, this is true, but in substance it is false. The US has successfully prevented attacks since 9/11. Given its more vulnerable borders, India's task is more difficult. Nevertheless, significant reduction in attacks and the damage from them is possible. Multiple checkpoints equipped with bulk-cargo scanners can make terrorist entry difficult. Intelligence, especially at local levels, can help catch some terrorists before they attack. And better weaponry, protection devices and training can improve the chances of the security personnel subduing terrorists in case the latter succeed in attacking. The best need not be the enemy of the good.

All in all, pseudo-secularism has so warped the mindset of Indian politicians on one hand and Indian intellectuals on the other that it has virtually destroyed the political will and national spirit that India needs to stand up to terror and overcome it.

Terrorists' Government

Addressing a rally in Jabalpur not long ago, LK Advani accused Prime Minister Manmohan Singh of turning India into a haven for terror and said, "Terrorists feel this is their government and are having a free run". He also questioned why the Government was dragging its feet on hanging Afzal Guru. "Dr. Manmohan Singh should answer why Afzal Guru is not being hanged despite court orders," he said, adding "don't duck under the clemency plea, you can decide on it in a day."

In a ridiculous effort to wish away terrorism by simply ignoring it the UPA Government's agenda for the National Integration Council (NIC) meeting had not even mentioned "terrorism" as a topic. Only after a strong protest by BJP Chief Ministers Narendra Modi and Vasundhara Raje was a one-word item included – "extremism".

On top of this the secular Government of India's Muslim Minister for Muslim (miscalled "Minority") Affairs AR Antulay "Turns Pak's Advocate", to quote the *Economic Times* heading for its report on his kite-flying on Karkare. Referring to the gunning down of ATS chief Hemant Karkare and two other top police officers during the latest terrorist assault on Mumbai Antulay said, "There is more than what meets the eye... Karkare was investigating some cases in which non-Muslims were involved." This was a clear endorsement of the theory floated by the political leaders as well as the media of Pakistan that the ATS chief was killed by Hindu outfits angry with his Malegaon investigation.

In her *Fifth Column* in *Indian Express* Tavleen Singh clubs Antulay with "enemies within India's borders that are more treacherous than those who come in boats from the sea", and adds: "If we had a real Prime Minister, instead of one by appointment to Her Majesty the Queen, not only would the minister for minority affairs be sacked, he would be tried for sedition."

Similar doubts were also raised about the genuineness of the shoot-out at Batla House in Delhi. Blatant lies that Atif *alias* Bashir and other suspected terrorists were dumped there the previous night to stage a "fake encounter" and that the firing was only one-sided were floated in the face of the stark reality that a valiant Delhi police officer, MC Sharma, lost his life in the encounter. Mushirul Hasan, Vice Chancellor of Jamia Millia Islamia, offered public funds to defend the suspected terrorists, justifying his action on the basis of faith and university. In other words he was helping his co-religionists. He relented only after public outcry against his pro-terrorist stance and persistent demands for his resignation. As if that was not enough, Muslim outfits formed a Coordination Committee of Indian Muslims against the "harassment of Muslims". The Committee launched a frontal attack on the police for its handling of the Jamia encounter and announced a mosque-driven countrywide campaign against the Government. In a spirited defence of members of the Indian Mujahideen (IM) and SIMI activists arrested for their involvement in Ahmedabad and Delhi serial blasts, the Committee demanded a judicial probe into the encounter and death of Inspector MC Sharma. A hurriedly compiled fact-finding report produced by a team of journalists and academicians (belonging to the secular-liberal brigade) that raised doubts about the genuineness of the encounter came handy for the Muslim community's campaign of vilification against the police to save the IM and SIMI activists involved in heinous crimes.

Political Secularists

Congress general secretary Digvijay Singh and Union Minister of State for Home Shakeel Ahmed publicly supported the pro-terrorist line of the Coordination Committee saying there was nothing wrong in asking for an independent inquiry into the incident, particularly because of certain doubts in the minds of the minority community. Several Muslim outfits took to the street condemning what they alleged was a fake encounter. Police investigation later brought to light the fact that Atif, who along with another terrorist killed in the encounter, was the one who had planned the serial bomb blasts in Delhi and Ahmedabad and was an activist of the Indian Mujahideen and SIMI.

Not for nothing has KPS Gill roundly condemned this obnoxious, so-called secularism as a "fraud" and "nonsense". On the government affidavit on the Ram Setu he had written:

"There is a new and escalating insensitivity in India secular thought, which not only insistently neglects the sensibilities of the majority community, but, worse, appears eager to cause injury to such sentiments. India's opportunistic political secularists feel that they cannot sufficiently proclaim their secularism without displaying at least a measure of contempt for Hindu beliefs and practices".

As if to provide an index of this Hindu-hating secularism of the Congress leadership, Digvijay Singh had some time back compared RSS with LeT, while Rahul Gandhi said in a speech in Bihar that he does not find any difference between RSS and SIMI. (RSS has sued both for defamation.)

How this distort secularism of those in power at the Centre can be exploited by separatist elements in Kashmir was shown by the fantastic idea of Hurriyat chairman Mirwaiz to ask Saudi Arabia to be a mediator in Kashmir, as reported by the media on May 16, 2010. During his visit to Riyadh, Prime Minister Manmohan Singh had sought the Saudi Arab king's help in "persuading Pakistan to stop abetting terrorism in India". Foreign Minister Krishna had also "indicated India's open mind about Saudi role in reconciliation between India and Pakistan", the report said. Thus we are now looking to the homeland of virulent Islam (and of the world's no. I Islamic terrorist) to help us against rabidly Islamic Pakistan!

No wonder level-headed analysts of the national scenario are too disgusted with India's pseudo-secular diaspora to mince words. KPS Gill has called them a fraud. George Fernandes said there are only two kinds of people in India — one secular, the other normal. MV Kamath calls them puerile, TVR Shenoy goes further and likens them to donkeys braying over lighted candles at the Wagah Indo-Pak border.

At the state level too wherever the devotees of secularism are in power it flourishes in wondrous ways. A noteworthy example of this was provided by the Mahdani case. When Abdul Nasser Mahdani, key accused in the 1998 Coimbatore serial blasts that targeted BJP leader L K Advani and killed 58 people, was in jail, the state governments of Tamil Nadu and Kerala were falling over each other in trying to woo him. As he, a Keralite, was in prison in Tamil Nadu, Kerala Chief Minister Achyuthanandan pleaded for Ayurvedic treatment for Mahdani languishing in prison for more than 8 years, having lost weight drastically from 104 kg to 54 kg. The plea apparently so moved Tamil Nadu Chief Minister Karunanidhi that on his orders a team of 10 masseurs and 4 senior Ayurvedic doctors gave Mahdani high quality treatment costing nearly Rs. 50,000.

In the pre-blast days the DMK, then ruling Tamil Nadu (1996-2001), was flirting with Muslim militancy and turning a blind eye to the activities of Jihadi groups like Al Ummah.

From Uttar Pradesh Maulana Mulayam, as this super-secularist is known, seems set to tie the knot with this Mahdani. Mahdani's People's Democratic Party a new name for his virulent Islamic Sevak Sangh was reportedly preparing to merge with Mulayam's Samajwadi Party which had given a clean chit to SIMI.

Another so-called secular UP politician is Mayawati, presently Chief Minister. In order to woo the Muslim vote bank she held a convention on the problems of the Muslim community, in which she announced several schemes-cum-sops for them.

In Delhi, ignoring the obvious fact that the flood of Bangladeshis into India has been a major factor in the growth of terrorism in the North-East, as also elsewhere in the country, Chief Minister Sheila Dixit said, "It has been our tradition to welcome all those who arrive in our country." About illegal immigrants being issued ration cards she said, "Nobody can be left without food." It was this very same unchecked, tremendous influx into India that BJP's LK Advani described as a huge risk to national security. And when, needled by Advani, the PMO asked Dixit in September 2008 for details on pending mercy pleas, she said a reply on convicted terrorist Afzal Guru would be sent at an "appropriate" time. She was in no hurry to do so. Not only in 2007 but even earlier, in October 2006 the Supreme Court had taken strong exception to the gross misuse of the power of clemency by the President of India and the Governors under Articles 72 and 161 of the Constitution.

In Maharashtra Hussein Dalwai, former minister and State Congress spokesman, has demanded 10% representation to Muslims in the Maharashtra cabinet. "Muslims should get appropriate representation in all decision-making positions," he said. Dalwai was addressing reporters in July 2007 on the implementation of the Sachar Committee recommendations in the state.

Intellectual Cowards

As for the intellectual secularists of India, they are cowards enough to stick to the safe limits of taking delight in injuring the sentiments of only Hindus. A shining example of their secular intellect is their defence of MF Husain. For them Husain's blasphemous painting of nude Hindu goddess Durga fornicating with an animal (with her name in the corner in bold Devnagari letters) was the expression of the freedom of art.

Two new recent additions to this secular-intellectual brigade are the authors of two books that blatantly give a clean chit to Pakistani terrorists. They are *Who Killed Karkare?* (English) by SM Mushriff, a retired police officer, and *RSS Ki Sazish – 26/11?* (Urdu) by Aziz Burney, editor of Urdu daily *Roznama Rashtrya Sahara*. Mushriff's book repeatedly denigrates the Intelligence Bureau, calling it "Brahmin-dominated" and claiming that it has been "taken over by the RSS...to implement the RSS agenda". Burney's book, released in the presence of Congress leader Digvijay Singh, is also full of lies, such as: RSS and BJP are responsible for the 26/11 terror attack on Mumbai, and one hundred Hindu organizations associated with RSS are involved in violent activities. When Burney was sued by a prominent RSS worker, he tendered a public apology for his falsehoods.

Secular Media

Secular India's mainstream media (that is, mostly the English-language press) wears its secularism on its sleeve. For its idea of secularism, anything to do with Hindus is a no-no. For instance, not long ago Islamic terrorists beheaded four Hindu priests, but this was ignored by the press as of no consequence. On the other hand India's biggest English-language daily, the *Indian Express*, ran a week-long series on how *madrasas* are pious institutions of religious teaching, and this in the face of their worldwide reputation as deadly training centres of Islamic terrorism.

Distinguished India-based French journalist Francoise Gautier once wrote: When for centuries being at the receiving end, a handful of Hindus dared to destroy a mosque, they were treated ruthlessly. The whole Indian media and political world went into a frenzy. Nazis, monsters, Hitlers, the end of secularism, the doom of democracy, the seed of India splitting, Hindu this, Hindu that. Yet the Hindu fundamentalists did not kill a single soul. In fact, during its long history, Hinduism has been one of the most peaceful creeds in the world... But what happened after Bombay blasts which were coldly and meticulously planned, killing more than 350 innocent souls, (Hindus), in one of the most horrifying terrorist bombings of this century?

Men (and women) of (English) letters are in the same secular boat as the English language media. A certain famous novelist is an example of virulent secularism. In the latest of her series of hysterical diatribes against India and all things Indian, she justified the attacks on Mumbai. There is a context to everything, she said, and so we must understand that the jihadis who want to destroy India have good reason to do so. The novelist is not alone in her hatred of all things Indian. Nearly every Indian writer who has written in the Western media since the attack on Mumbai has found reasons why the Jihad against India is justified. One British newspaper went so far as to say that India used 9/11 to treat its Muslims even worse than we did before. This editorial was used by a Pakistani journalist to explain what happened in Mumbai. It was appalling to read an editorial in the *Financial Times* while Mumbai was still under siege that said the terrorists could be Hindu because one of them (Kasab) wore sacred Hindu threads on his wrist! (It later came to light that these threads were deliberately bought and worn for deception.)

The Communist

Finally, the Islamic-terrorist friendly Communist. The Communist constituent of the United Progressive Alliance in power at the centre was actually a built-in opposition. An instance in point:

The CPM took the support of fundamentalist Islamic outfits in targetting the UPA government and provoking the Muslim community over anti-terror investigations. Left leaders Mohammad Salim and Atul Kumar Anjaan, aggressively flashed the Muslim sensitivity card at a meeting organised by the Jamaat-e-Islami Hind.

Indian Maoists have denied ties with Islamist extremists, but the then Home Minister Shivraj Patil had stated once that the Government possessed information to suggest coordination between the two. A report prepared by India's security agencies years ago suggested that the Maoists may be using other Indian separatist groups through whom to get arms and ammunition from ISI.

Nepali journalist Sanjay Upadhyaya has even written on an Islamist-Communist alliance on the international level. He says: "Patterns of a resurgence in cooperation between Islamic extremists and radical Communists, faint in some places, more pronounced in others, are emerging. While much of the current focus is on parts of Europe, South Asia could emerge as the principal arena for a Communist–Jehadist alliance."

38

EPILOGUE

The Core Truth

To return to the core truth of the ISI havoc in India, it is a means serving an Islamic agenda. The origin of this agenda lies embedded in the fanatical anti-Hinduism that is the *raison d'etre* of Pakistan. For Islam, by which Pakistan swears, "paradise lies in the shade of swords," as the Quran declares, and ISI is the sword-arm with which Pakistan wages Jehad, the holy war of terror, on India.

In this march of Islamisation the vivisection of India and the creation of Pakistan was the first step. The next step was the transformation of Bangladesh, which India liberated, into what is aptly called "the other (now equally rabidly Islamic) Pakistan". Now they not only want a "Muslim Pradesh" in Uttar Pradesh, they even want three Islamistans in the whole of secular India.

In Kashmir the Pandits were forced to flee their hearths and homes *en masse* as many as six times. Now the situation has reached such a critical point that the other day Farooq Abdullah warned that India may lose Kashmir.

This is not communal scare-mongering but a fact-based assessment, Parthsarathy said. In an online article in August 2001: "No action has been taken against Jehadi outfits in Punjab and NWFP, from where the bulk of ISI-supported Jehadis are drawn for action in Kashmir".

Under severe pressure from the Indian security forces the Jehadis are now hitting soft targets. The recent massacres of Hindus are a part of a concerted policy to follow up on the earlier one of Kashmiri Pandits. The aim of Pakistani Jehadis is to ethnically cleanse the Kashmir Valley and force the exodus of the entire Hindu population.

Exactly seven years later, in August 2008, the Research and Analysis Wing (RAW) warned that Hindus in the Valley are under threat from the Jehadis. A detailed report sent by RAW to the Prime Minister's Office (PMO) stated that Mushtaq Ahmed Zargar, one of the terrorists freed after the Indian Airlines plane hijack and now heading a terrorist outfit called Al-Umar Mujahideen, has issued directives to target Hindus. Similar directives have also been issued by the Harkat-ul Mujahideen (HuM) leadership, and Lashkar-e-Toiba (LeT) has even carried out reconnaissance operations to attack Hindu shrines.

And this Jehadi poison has spread across India. For instance, down South in Hyderabad, a city teeming with terrorists, Imams of mosques openly pray for Islam's victory in Kashmir. And Kashmir is just the thin end of the Jehadi wedge. For to repeat what Dr. Subramanian Swamy says in his book *Terrorism in India*, the target of terrorism in India is the Hindus. ISI has shown it, and al-Qaeda has said it.

At the same time there is another, much wider, dimension to Islamic terror in India. It is ISI's international Islamic vision, a Land of Islam stretching from the Muslim Middle East right up to the east end of South-East Asia, a region once replete with Hindu civilizational influence. The Hindu diaspora all over this region has dark days ahead. Today, a Hindu in a Muslim country is a second class citizen, if not still lower. In Saudi Arabia, a Hindu cannot perform Puja even in the privacy of his home. And in the medieval judicial system still prevailing in that country a Hindu's life is worth half that of a Muslim. In Pakistan a Hindu's testimony in court is by law worth half that of a Muslim. In Malaysia more than 10,000 Hindu temples have been destroyed in the recent past and the Hindu rights body Hindraf has been banned. Even in Indonesia, a country to which Hindus in India like to point as a still existing Hindu civilizational pocket, intolerant Islam is raising its head.

The Hindu American Foundation of USA brings out annual reports on the status of human rights of Hindus in various countries. The facts and figures in them make disturbing reading.

To conclude with the core truth of the situation: For the Ummah as a whole the Hindu is an infidel, and may be trampled upon with impunity. This is possible, and keeps happening, because in his own motherland the Hindu gets neither security nor honour. And this in turn happens because the Hindu today has forgotten to be a Hindu. He is a bemused Arjuna. "Arise, oh Arjuna !" the Lord commanded in the Gita. Once the Hindu heeds that celestial call, once he arises, awakes, he will prevail. For when Yogeshwar Krishna and Dhanurdhar Partha rise together, victory cannot be denied.

SOURCES CONSULTED

Books

1. *The Nefarious Activities of ISI* by Col. (retd.) Shyam Kumar. Online edition by Vishwa Hindu Parishad (VHP).
2. *Wikipedia,* Online encyclopedia.
3. *Islam and Terrorism,* by Anwar Sheikh. Published by Principality Publishers. Cardiff, UK, 2004.
4. *Al-Qaeda: Global Terror Incorporated,* by Sudhakar Raje. Published by Rambhau Mhalgi Prabodhini, Mumbai.
5. *Islam: The Arab Imperialism,* by Anwar Sheikh. Published by Principality Publishers, Cardiff, UK.
6. *Anti-Hindus,* by Prafull Goradia and KR Phanda. Published by Contemporary Targett, New Delhi.
7. *Islam: Sex and Violence,* by Anwar Sheikh. Published by Principality Publishers, Cardiff', UK.
8. *Facets of Proxy War,* Document prepared by the Government of India, 1993.
9. *Demography is Destiny,* by Sudhakar Raje. Published by Vishwa Samvad Kendra, Mumbai.
10. *Rashtra Jágar* (Marathi collection of articles including article titled *Dahshatvadachya Vilkhyat Tamil Nadu*). Published by Vishwa Samvad Kendra, Mumbai.
11. *Diplomatic Tales,* by Kiran Doshi.
12. *Fulcrum of Evil,* by MK Dhar.
13. *Insurgency Movements in North-East India.* by Phanjoubam Tarapot.
14. *Military Inc: Inside Pakistan's Military Economics.* by Ayesha Siddiqa.
15. *Bin Laden: The Man who Declared War on America,* by Youssef Bodansky.
16. *America and the Islamic Bomb,* by David Armstrong and Joe Trento.
17. *The Al-Qaeda Connection: International Terrorism, Organised Crime, and the Coming Apocalypse* by Paul Williams.
18. *The Tragedy of East Pakistan,* by Lawrence Zirling.
19. *Nuclear Black Market: Pakistan, Al-Qaeda, and the Rise of Proliferation Networks.* Dossier prepared by International Institute for Strategic Studies, London.

20. *Inside Al-Qaeda.* by Rohan Gunaratna.
21. *The Quran.*
22. *Military Studies in the Jihad against the Tyrants.* Prepared by al-Qaeda.
23. *Bikhra Peinda* ("Lost Path"), (Gurmukhi) by Sandeep Kaur.
24. *Will Pakistan Break Up?*, (Urdu) by Muneer Ahmed.
25. Original Sources
    (of reproduced published quotes)

Newspapers / Journals

26. Asian Age
27. Assam Tribune
28. Communalism Combat
29. Deccan Herald
30. Economic Times
31. Frontline
32. Hindu Resurgence
33. Hindu Vision
34. Hindustan Times
35. Indian Express
36. Mumbai Mirror
37. Observer
38. Organiser
39. Outlook
40. Pioneer
41. Sunday
42. Tehelka
43. Pánchjanya (Hindi)
44. Saamna (Marathi)
45. Loksatta (Marathi)

Pakistan

46. Daily Times
47. Dawn
48. Friday Times
49. Herald

USA

50. Nation
51. Forbes Magazine
52. Foreign Affairs

53. Newsweek
54. New York Times
55. New Yorker
56. Time
57. US News
58. Wall Street Journal
59. Washington Post

Britain

60. Jane's Intelligence Weekly
61. Guardian

Israel

62. Israel News

Russia

63. Komsomolskaya Pravda

Canada

64. Canadian National Post

Leaflets

65. Dr. KV Paliwal, Director, Hindu Writers' Forum, New Delhi.
66. Shri Anandshankar Pandya, Vice-President, Vishwa Hindu Parishad.

INDEX